BIBLIOTHECA HISTORICA LUNDENSIS 66

# Work, Family and the State

## Child Labour and the Organization of Production in the British Cotton Industry, 1780-1920

TO ROBERT LEE
FROM
Per Bol-Hout

Per Bolin-Hort

Lund
University
Press

Lund University Press
Box 141, S-221 00 Lund, Sweden

Art nr 20146
ISSN 0519-9700
ISBN 91-7966-094-0   Lund University Press
ISBN 0-86238-235-1   Chartwell-Bratt Ltd

Printed in Sweden
Studentlitteratur
Lund 1989

# Contents

# List of Tables

# Acknowledgements

The research on which this book is based started in earnest in the autumn of 1983 when I arrived in Edinburgh on a British Council scholarship. During these past years I have divided my time between Scotland and Sweden to such an extent that I feel almost equally at home in both places. That has given me the opportunity to take part in two different intellectual milieux, the British and the Swedish historical traditions. This book therefore has a rather mixed parentage, and I can only hope that it will make some kind of contribution at both ends.

Many people have helped me along the road. My supervisor, Dr. Lars Olsson, has patiently endured many of my rather wild suggestions and interpretations, while urging me to keep going. I have received much encouragement and assistance from my supervising Professors, Birgitta Odén, Ingemar Norrlid, and Eva Österberg. Dr. Lars Edgren and Professor Eva Österberg have scrutinized the manuscript, and indicated many inconsistencies that needed to be removed. Dr. Bengt Ankarloo has also read the manuscript in full.

At the British end, a great many people have provided me with advice. Professor John Butt, Strathclyde University, Glasgow, Professor D. A. Farnie, Manchester University, and Professor Michael Anderson, Edinburgh University, have given me guidance on material and research strategy, as well as introducing me to other scholars working in this field.

Dr. Eleanor Gordon, Glasgow University, Dr. Roger Davidson, Edinburgh University, Dr. Alan Fowler and Dr. Neville Kirk, Manchester Polytechnic, Dr. Trevor Griffiths, St Anthony's College, Oxford, Dr. Yutaka Taniguchi, Kurume University, Japan, and Dr. Michael Huberman, Trent University, Canada, have all taken part with me in long discussions on the cotton factory workforce or the problems of factory law enforcement. Without these interchanges of ideas and experiences this book would have been much poorer.

My friends at the Department of Social and Economic History at Edinburgh University, Dr. James J. Smyth, Dr. Donald J. Morse, and Dr. Ros Maclean, have provided both a social and an intellectual context. Without their comradeship the periods in exile would have been dreary indeed.

7

I am also grateful to the members of Eva Österberg's post-graduate seminar at the Department of History, Lund, for all the spirited and constructive discussions we have had over the past years.

The British Council and Svenska Institutet have provided me with generous financial support. Without these grants it would not have been possible to perform the necessary research.

I am also deeply indebted to my father-in-law, Patrick Hort, for reading the entire manuscipt and indicating where my English deviated too much from common usage.

Most of all I am grateful to my wife Katinka who has put up with me and my irregular working habits over these past years, and has patiently listened to my rambling monologues on work efficiency and factory inspection. I am also indebted to my daughter Elsa, who by her very arrival persuaded me that it was time to deliver and turn to more essential things.

# Chapter 1

# Previous Research, Theoretical Positions and Principal Questions

## Introduction

The purpose of this book is to study the use of child labour in the mechanized British cotton factories from the rise of industrial production in the late 18th century to the final abolition of child labour in 1920.

Especially regarding the early phase, this is a subject which has previously been treated with some animation. In the long debate between "optimists" and "pessimists" on the actual gains of the industrial revolution, child labour has often been used as an example of the inhuman effects of the rise of the factory system. This perspective has been brought forward by, for instance, the Hammonds, and more recently, by E. P. Thompson.[1] The image of poor children toiling in factories and mines has become a standard theme in the depiction of the human consequences of the industrial revolution.

While such reactions to early industrial child labour are very understandable, some qualifications are no doubt necessary. The use of children in industry was hardly a consequence of the industrial revolution; such practices were common in workshops, in proto-industrial trades, and in agriculture, well before the advent of the mechanized cotton factories. Apart from an early transitional period, it is also doubtful if factory child labour should be singled out as particularly deplorable. Conditions were scarcely better in smaller workshops and agricultural "gangs" than in the early cotton factories. Also, after the implementation of the 1833 and 1844 Factory Acts in Britain, working conditions were probably much better for children in the textile industry than for those employed in unregulated trades. Criticism of child labour practices should therefore not be reserved for the factories alone. Early wage labour was a fact of life for most working class children during this period.

---

1 Hammond, J L and Hammond, B [1917]: The Town Labourer, pp. 100-117; Thompson, E P (1980): The Making of the English Working Class, p. 384.

This book is comparatively silent on the sufferings of the factory children, partly because such histories have already been written. Another cogent reason is that the child worker has previously been seen solely as a victim. Middle-class reformers, philanthropists, and historians, have not been able to see how child labour was integrated in a more general context of working-class life and culture.

The purpose of this study is to ask questions and find explanations as to the rationale of industrial child labour rather than simply to condemn its existence. Why were children used in this type of factory work, and which processes in the spheres of production, family, and society were the cause? However, before going into the processes which were involved in the causation of factory child labour, it is necessary to summarize the research performed in this field.


# Previous Research

In British historiography there has long been a tendency to view industrial child labour as an evil which was gradually controlled by government interference in the form of factory and school legislation. The Hammonds early promoted this view, and it was predominant especially among Fabian historians. Hutchins and Harrison's work on the early factory legislation is another example.[2] Histories of English childhood are still written which are not much different in perspective.[3] Another scholarly tradition, undoubtedly more connected to a Tory interpretation of history, has seen the gradual decline of child labour in English industrial society as caused by the endeavours of certain upper-class humanitarians, especially the renowned Lord Ashley. While having few active proponents today, this view still lingers in textbooks and collective memory.[4]

However, very few serious works have been written in Britain on industrial child labour. Partly in reaction to the trends mentioned above, in their book on children in English society Ivy Pinchbeck and Margaret Hewitt have emphasized the employment in proto-industrial trades and agriculture, and have not contributed much to the study of child labour in the cotton mills.[5] Marjorie Cruickshank has in a more recent work pointed out

---

2 Hutchins, B L and Harrison, A (1911): A History of Factory Legislation.
3 See Walvin, J (1982): A Child's World. A Social History of English Childhood 1800-1914, pp. 62-78.
4 See the criticism of this conception in Cunningham, H (1987): Child Labour in the Industrial Revolution, passim.
5 Pinchbeck, I and Hewitt, M (1972-73): Children in English Society, Vols I and II. See especially Vol II, chapter 14.

that child labour in the early 19th century should be seen in a societal context where children and youths constituted a very large part of the population of the early factory towns.[6] But in other respects, Cruickshank does not say much about the processes behind the use of children in factories. Indeed, I have found no British historical work which has tried to make connections between child labour and the formation of the labour process.

Several such attempts are to be found in other countries. Jürgen Kuczynski, the doyen of G.D.R. labour historians, has suggested that industrial child labour was a part of a low-intensive phase of capitalist production, and was later abandoned as a part of the transition towards a high-intensive mode of production. Factory legislation did little more than hasten this process somewhat.[7] Similar approaches have been made by other researchers. In West Germany, K-H Ludwig has suggested a very firm technological explanation of the decline in child labour levels in the German cotton industry after 1850. Arguing against the opinion that this was occasioned by factory legislation, Ludwig instead connects the decline to the introduction of modern machinery from England. The new technology was too complicated to be operated by children, and as a consequence this form of labour was largely abandoned.[8]

Of perhaps even greater importance for this study is Clark Nardinelli's work on the decline of child labour levels in British textiles during the 19th century.[9] Nardinelli is an American economist who has tried to apply a strict neo-classical perspective to this field of study.[10] Like Ludwig, Nardinelli suggests a firm technological explanation of the decline of child employment in the British textile industry. He claims that the introduction of self-acting mules after 1835 very much reduced the need for child piecers. On the old hand-mules, children had been extensively employed in various assistant tasks, but on the new technology this work was much less required. Since it took more than fifty years before the self-actors had entirely replaced the older type of machines, the level of child labour decreased gradually during the 19th century.

Apart from the introduction of the self-actor, Nardinelli also suggests that other technological changes reduced the need for children. The transition from water-driven to steam-powered factories in the first half of the 19th century also had this effect. Nardinelli also maintains that the growth

---

6 Cruickshank, M (1981): Children and Industry, p. 51.

7 Kuczynski, J (1958): Geschichte der Kinderarbeit in Deutschland, pp. 118-213.

8 Ludwig, K-H (1965): Die Fabrikarbeit von Kindern im 19. Jahrhundert. Ein Problem der Technikgeschichte, passim.

9 Nardinelli, C (1980): Child Labor and the Factory Acts, passim.

10 See also Nardinelli, C (1982): Corporal Punishment and Children's wages in Nineteenth Century Britain, passim.

of the ring-spinning technology just before 1900 at the expense of the self-actor similarly reduced the employment of children in textiles.

However, Nardinelli also mentions other factors apart from technological change. The British Factory Acts of 1833 and 1844 made the use of child labour somewhat more costly, and can, according to Nardinelli, be treated as an extra tax on the employment of children. However, the effect of this factor was much less than that of technological change. Finally, Nardinelli suggests that the rise in income levels for British working-class adults in the second half of the 19th century was the most important reason behind the decline in child labour levels during this period. Nardinelli accordingly proposes two main causal factors behind the decrease in industrial child labour: technological change and rising standards of living among the working class.

In the Swedish context, the most important work has been done by Lars Olsson.[11] In his investigation of the Swedish match, tobacco, and glassware industries in the 19th century, Olsson concludes that the main process behind the decline in child labour was technological change, or a more thorough mechanization of production. Arguing against an emphasis among an older generation of historians on humanitarianism and early factory laws, Olsson shows that child labour levels declined drastically in match and tobacco factories well before restrictive legislation was implemented. Also, this decline took place at different times in the three industrial trades. Olsson therefore concludes that changes in the sphere of production constituted the most important causal process. In his empirical findings, Olsson also shows a convincing connection between the introduction of new technology, a change in the composition of the workforce, and a reduction in the number of very young operatives. Children were mainly used in simple manual tasks, and were made redundant when these operations were mechanized. The decline of industrial child labour is therefore seen in the context of a more complete mechanization of the factories, and a transition towards more intensive forms of production.

However, Olsson does not adhere to the same kind of technological determinism as Ludwig and Nardinelli. He explicitly states that the formation of the labour process is the result of power relations between operatives and management.[12] On the other hand, Olsson does not doubt that the

---

11 Olsson, L (1974): Barn- och ungdomsarbete i svensk industri 1860-1970; Olsson, L (1978): Barnarbete i de svenska tobaksindustrierna; Olsson, L (1980): Då barn var lönsamma. Om arbetsdelning, barnarbete och teknologiska förändringar i några svenska industrier under 1800- och början av 1900-talet.
12 See Olsson (1980), chapter 11.

manufacturers actually possessed the power to introduce new technology and to decide on the organization of work.[13]

Outside the sphere of production, Olsson lists two preconditions for industrial child labour. First, the poverty of working-class families served to provide the factories with very young operatives. The needs of the family made even the relatively small contributions of children much required. Second, the absence of ideological barriers to child labour in factories was an important precondition. However, Olsson notes that when political and humanitarian opposition to industrial child labour grew towards the end of the 19th century, these practices had already lost importance in most industrial trades. The factory laws which were passed in 1881 and 1900 merely codified this tendency. Moreover, trades where child labour was still important were either excluded from the scope of the law, or evaded it with considerable success in the absence of proper enforcement.

Lars Olsson's work has been commented on by several Swedish historians. Anita Göransson and Lennart Schön have questioned whether the early form of factory child labour differed much from that in proto-industrial trades or manufactories before mechanization. They also emphasize the reciprocity between factors such as labour supply, wage levels, productivity, technology change, and factory legislation.[14] The different kinds of technology used in various industrial trades would also give rise to considerable differences in the viability of child labour between branches.

Bengt Berglund has argued that it was the first generation of heavy and relatively unsophisticated machinery which was hard to handle for very young operatives. In the subsequent phase of technological development, child labour was again viable. Berglund therefore does not agree that the development towards more "intensive" forms of production would necessarily exclude children.[15]

Finally, Eva Österberg has argued that Olsson's emphasis on the labour process should be complemented with an analysis of trade cycles and labour markets. She also maintains that government initiatives and collective actions of the workers themselves on schooling and protective legislation

---

13 However, in his recent work on Swedish compositors, Olsson has described the formation of work more in terms of power and bargaining between the two parties rather than a result of a one-sided employer domination. See Olsson, L (1986): Gamla typer och nya produktionsförhållanden, passim.

14 Göransson, A and Schön, L (1976): Teknologi och barnarbete. However, in her recent investigation of the cotton spinning factory at Strömma, Sweden, in the mid-19th century, Anita Göransson links the decline of child labour to technological improvements in a way which is very similar to Olsson's. Göransson, A (1988): Från familj till fabrik. Teknik, arbetsdelning och skiktning i svenska fabriker, pp. 134-35.

15 Berglund, B (1982): Industriarbetarklassens formering. Arbete och teknisk förändring vid tre svenska fabriker under 1800-talet, p. 294.

are important for an understanding of the long-term decline of industrial child labour.[16]

Summing up the developments during the last two decades, there seems to be a rather distinct pattern. Attempts have been made by several researchers, like Ludwig, Nardinelli, and Olsson, to find causal links between the sphere of production and the level of factory child labour. In the case of Ludwig and Nardinelli, this link has taken the form of technological determinism. On the other hand, critics have emerged who want to see the inclusion of additional causal factors and a general broadening of the explanatory framework. However, few fully structured alternatives have actually been presented.

One important exception is the recently published work by Colin Heywood on child labour in 19th century France.[17] In a broad study of different forms of child labour in industry and agriculture, and the impact of factory legislation and compulsory schooling, Heywood concludes that the main force behind the decline of industrial child labour during the course of the 19th century was changes in the sphere of work. While technological change was undoubtedly very important, Heywood also stresses that children were made redundant when extensive, low-productive forms of work slowly gave way to an industrial organization striving to improve productivity through piece-rate structures and various incentive schemes. In the French setting, Heywood regards factory legislation as only a secondary force behind the decline of industrial child labour. Enforcement of the laws of 1841 and 1874 was never very stringent, partly because inspection resources long remained inadequate, and partly because the early factory inspectors often found themselves under pressure from political superiors to treat offending manufacturers leniently. Nevertheless, Heywood shows that enforcement was more forceful in some areas than in others, and also that many manufacturers dismissed child workers rather than being subjected to the factory laws. Compulsory schooling introduced in the 1880s finally forced the children below 13 in smaller workshops and the industrial trades which still employed them, as well as the children roaming the streets, to attend school. Consequently, while giving changes in the production process the pride of place, Heywood also sketches a more complicated picture of the processes involved.

---

16 Österberg, E (1982): Barnarbetet i Sverige, passim.
17 Heywood, C (1988): Childhood in nineteenth-century France. Work, health and education among the *classes populaires*.

Another important exception is the work of Anna Davin.[18] While mainly studying the lives and labour of working-class girls in London, Davin has also sketched the outlines of an investigation of industrial child labour. Such a study, she maintains, must comprise processes on several different levels: the place of the child in the labour process, the organization of the labour market, the role of protective legislation, the families' need for the children's wages, and the development of a "domestic ideology", or the conception of a male breadwinner earning the keep of a dependent wife and children. Davin maintains there was a complex interaction between these factors, but makes no further suggestions on how they relate to each other. Nevertheless, I agree with Davin that the problem of industrial child labour must be approached on several different levels. The analysis of the sphere of production must be complemented by a scrutiny of several other causal processes.

## Formulation of the Problem

The objective of this study is to investigate the use of child labour in the British and, to a lesser extent, the American cotton industry. It is primarily a study of child workers in mechanized factory production rather than an investigation of the transition from pre-industrial forms of production to the factory system. The general problem is how and why the use of children in cotton factories changed in extent and character from the early industrial capitalism in the late 1780s to the more developed and organized capitalism by 1920.

Where previous research has been mainly geared towards an explanation of the decline of child labour, generally in terms of one or two causal factors or processes, my perspective is somewhat different. A full understanding of the processes behind the decline of the level of industrial child labour requires a more thorough investigation of the different social contexts in which child labour constituted an important element. Above all, industrial child labour should be seen both in the sphere of the household and the sphere of production. How did the changes in the organization of production, labour recruitment patterns, and the wage-earning strategies of the working-class household influence the levels of industrial child labour?

---

18 Davin, A (1982): Child Labour, the Working-Class Family, and Domestic Ideology in 19th Century Britain, passim.

A third sphere which also has to be considered is the impact of factory and school legislation. What were the actual results of these forms of government initiatives on the use of children in factories?

Consequently, on one level the main task of this investigation is to recreate the causes and fluctuations of industrial child labour in one specific context, the British cotton industry. On a second level, the aim is to provide a more full theoretical understanding of the complicated processes and contexts which influenced the practice of industrial child labour. Finally, on a third level the task will be to explain how changes in these processes and contexts took place in the setting of a developing industrial capitalism.

This way of formulating the problem has its strengths as well as its weaknesses. Hopefully, it will result in a deeper understanding of the complex processes underlying the practice of factory child labour than has been reached in earlier research. In this way it will improve the current theoretical understanding of the phenomenon of industrial child labour. On the other hand, this investigation will not provide a new comprehensive theory for the general decline of child labour in the 19th century Western economies. This study is a depth analysis of one particular industrial trade, not an examination of the whole economy. The role of the present investigation is rather to provide complications and contrasts which will give some impetus towards new synthetical efforts.


## Theoretical Positions and Further Questions

My suggestion is that child labour should be studied in the triangle drawn up by the production process, the household or family, and the regulations imposed by the state. There were processes which had an impact on child labour practices within these formations as well as between them. Matters are further complicated by the fact that these processes took place in a specific historical and societal context which changed over time. The aim of this investigation is to chart the changes in processes and societal structures relating to child labour over a comparatively long time period.

One very important area of this study is the formation of the labour process. As I have shown previously, Nardinelli and Ludwig have tried to relate the decline of child labour in the British and German cotton industries to certain shifts in technology. However, this approach raises serious theoretical and empirical objections. Nardinelli and Ludwig do not take any account of the fact that work could be organized differently on the same technology in different countries or regions, and at different points in time.

The kind of technological determinism they advocate postulates that there was only one viable way of organizing industrial production.[19] Furthermore, Nardinelli and Ludwig have not considered the possibility that the relationship between technology and child labour was reciprocal rather than one-sided. It cannot be ruled out that the machinery in early factories was specifically constructed to be used by children.[20]

Also, the emphasis on technological change tends to neglect other forms of development of the labour process, like increases in work intensity and changes in the organization of work at the same type of machinery. Moreover, technological determinism does not consider the question of power relations in the formation of the labour process. My theoretical position on this issue is that the organization of production must be seen as a social construct, or the result of actions, strategies, and bargaining between management and operatives. This does not mean that all kinds of labour process formation are viable, but rather that differences in the organization of work must be open to empirical investigation. In the context of the present study, the connection between the labour process and the factory employment of children should be viewed in terms of work as a social construct, and with the potential of being organized in different ways.

The perspective of the process of production has to be complemented with that of the household. One area of interest is the long term changes in the ideology of work and family among the British working class. Especially among feminist historians, it has been suggested that there was a gradual shift during the 19th century from an ideology based on the employment of all family members to the conception of a male "breadwinner".[21] The question is to what extent this shift in family ideology actually took place among the cotton operatives, and what effect it had on work practices. How did the operatives themselves view the use of child labour, and what actions and strategies did they form on this issue?

Finally, the use of children in cotton mills also depended on the restrictive force of factory and school legislation. This involves not only the framing of certain legal measures, but also an estimation of actual enforcement and efficiency. The specific problems connected with a study of this kind will be treated in a later chapter. However, one important distinction is that the enforcement of factory laws could vary considerably between different areas. The process of enforcement is very complex and involves both the structures of the legal enactments and inspection resources as well

---

19 On the possibility of several routes of industrialisation, see Sabel, C and Zeitlin, J (1985): Historical Alternatives to Mass Production, passim.
20 See Elson, D (1982): The Differentiation of Children's Labour in the Capitalist Labour Market, passim.
21 See Davin (1982), passim; Seccombe, W (1986): Patriarchy stabilized: the construction of the male breadwinner wage norm in nineteenth century Britain, passim.

as the actions and strategies of factory inspectors, manufacturers, and operatives. These matters have to be considered in order to evaluate the true extent of child labour.

Similarly, the implications of educational requirements and compulsory schooling must also be taken into account. In the English context, it has often been noted that the decline of child labour levels in the cotton industry became pronounced when compulsory schooling was implemented. Was this a causal or merely a relatively unrelated process?

So far I have briefly described some fields and processes which are essential for the study of industrial child labour. In the subsequent sections, these themes will be discussed more closely in order to make some further analytical distinctions.

## Production Relations and the Formation of Work

During the last decade there has been a perceptible theoretical shift among labour historians and sociologists from structural and technological conceptions of labour process formation towards an emphasis on power and control. Harry Braverman's contribution on the deskilling of work in modern capitalism has been very influential, but has also led to the formulation of several strands of criticism.[22] David Montgomery and several other American researchers have emphasized the struggle of the workers themselves to influence the organization of production and the adoption of new technology. The operatives have been seen more as active agents pressing for certain aims than passive victims of the inexorable trends of modern capitalism. Historians and sociologists like David Montgomery, Richard Price, and Isaac Cohen, have seen the labour process as a contested terrain between workers and management. The concept of "workers' control" has become very central among these researchers.[23]

However, this concept is somewhat problematical. As Patrick Joyce has pointed out, the notion of workers' control seems to imply a simple dichotomy between control and absence of control. More subtle forms of compromise or bargaining do not fit in easily.[24] Richard Price has duly re-

---

22 Braverman, H (1974): Labor and Monopoly Capital. The Degradation of Work in the Twentieth Century.
23 See Montgomery, D (1980): Workers' Control in America. Studies in the History of Work, Technology, and Labor Struggles; Montgomery, D (1987): The fall of the house of labor: The workplace, the state, and American labor activism, 1865-1925; Price, R (1980): Masters, Unions and Men. Work Control in Building and the Rise of Labour 1830-1914; Price, R (1983): The labour process and labour history; Cohen, I (1985a): Workers' Control in the Cotton Industry. A Comparative Study of British and American Mule Spinning; Cohen, I (1985b): American Management and British Labor: Lancashire Immigrant Spinners in Industrial New England.
24 Joyce, P (1984a): Labour, capital and compromise: a response to Richard Price, passim.

sponded that notions of compromise are not incompatible with the concept of workers' control, but I believe the problem is not easily overcome.[25] The main connotation of "control" remains that of one-sided dominance. Furthermore, the group connected with "workplace control" has been criticized for not taking account of the importance of developed working-class organizations in the form of unions or political parties.[26]

Nevertheless, there has been a marked tendency among researchers in several countries to emphasize the importance of power and bargaining in the formation of the labour process. British sociologists like Craig Littler and S. Wood have argued that the actual organization of work must be seen as the result of the actions of both operatives and management, and that the power resources on both sides are of greatest importance.[27]

Similar developments have occurred in the Swedish context. Lars Ekdahl and Lars Magnusson have argued that the labour process is the result of initiatives and actions from both manufacturers and workers, and have also seen the power dimension in the relations of production as very important.[28] On a somewhat higher level of analysis, several Swedish researchers have seen the dimension of power relationships and power resources as crucial in the study of conflicts and bargaining between unions and employers.[29]

While supporting the notion that the dimension of power is crucial for the study of labour process formation, two qualifications should be made. First, this approach necessitates a full investigation of the strategies, aims, and options of both parties. For instance, it has to be recognized that there were several possible managerial strategies to enhance production. Second, there was also a terrain of possible compromises which could satisfy essential demands of both parties. The actual organization could reflect such a compromise rather than "control" by one of the parties.

In the context of the present study, this calls for more incisive questions about the relationship between child labour and changes in the labour process. If the formation of work is seen as a social construct which develops in a context of local relations of production, how did manufac-

---

25 Price, R (1984): Conflict and co-operation: a reply to Patrick Joyce, passim.
26 See Zeitlin, J (1987): From Labour History to the History of Industrial Relations, passim.
27 Littler, C R (1982): The Development of the Labour Process in Capitalist Societies. A Comparative Study of the Transformation of Work Organisation in Britain, Japan and the U.S.A.; Wood, S (1982): The Degradation of Work? Skill, Deskilling and the Labour Process. Introduction. See also Rueschmeyer, D (1986): Power and the Division of Labour.
28 Ekdahl, L (1983): Arbete mot kapital. Typografer och ny teknik - studier av Stockholms tryckeriindustri under det industriella genombrottet; Magnusson, L (1987): Arbetet vid en svensk verkstad: Munktells 1900-1920. See also Olsson (1986).
29 See especially Johansson, I (1982): Strejken som vapen. Fackföreningar och strejker i Norrköping 1870-1910; Åmark, K (1986): Facklig makt och fackligt medlemskap. De svenska fackförbundens medlemsutveckling 1890-1940; Sund, B (1987): Nattens vita slavar. Makt, politik och teknologi inom den svenska bagerinäringen 1896-1955.

19

turers and operatives act on the issue of employment of children? What kind of conflicts or compromises lay behind the formation of a labour process which was organized in such a way as to include children? Similarly, how did the parties act on the question of ceasing to utilize child labour?

There is also one further complication in the production relations in the British cotton industry which has to be discussed. There were two different ways of employing children in the mills: they were either directly employed by the manufacturers, or subcontracted by adult operatives. This distinction is very important. In the British cotton industry, subcontracting was the clearly dominant way of employing children at least from the 1820s, and remained so for the next hundred years. This raises several important considerations. Why was subcontracting so predominant in the cotton industry when such practices were relatively uncommon in other trades? If the children were subcontracted by adult operatives, who had the actual power over recruitment, the manufacturer or the subcontractor? In this sense, the power dimension at work was not only relevant for the organization of production, it was probably also relevant for the actual recruitment of child workers. The degree of authority among the adult operatives to hire children will be one important theme in the subsequent investigation.

The phenomenon of subcontracting of children also raises other questions. To what extent did it cause a split within the working class, with some operatives using the labour of others? Perhaps more importantly, it is also possible to see the subcontracting relationship as a link between the spheres of family and work, since this form of recruitment enabled the adult operative to utilize the labour of his or her own children. How did this influence the adult workers' perception of child labour?

Summing up this section, I view the labour process as the result of actions and strategies of both workers and management. In this context, the dimension of power, or the resources of power among the acting parties, is held to be essential. However, this does not exclude the possibility of compromises. In the case of the British cotton industry, the problem is further complicated by the fact that the child workers were often subcontracted by older operatives. Authority at work and over recruitment remain very important analytical concepts in my investigation. The next step is to look a bit more closely at the research on child labour in the context of household and family.

# Child Labour in the Perspective of the Household

Of the great amount of research done on the history of the household, what is mainly of interest here is the "family economy" approach.[30] Several historians and sociologists have treated child labour as a part of a family wage economy. Joan Scott and Louise Tilly have studied the familial ties and dependencies which still remained between children and the family even when the young ones had moved away to find work.[31] Michael Anderson has briefly touched on the employment of children in cotton factories in his work on family structure among the Preston working class, vieving it primarily in terms of family strategies to stay above the poverty line.[32] A similar approach has been made by Frances Early, who has studied the employment of children as a part of the family economy of French Canadian immigrants in the textile town of Lowell, Massachusetts.[33] Tamara Hareven has investigated family cohesiveness and employment strategies among textile workers at the great Amoskeag company in Manchester, New Hampshire.[34] In the Swedish context, Anita Göransson has analysed the child workers at the Strömma cotton spinning factory in terms of their economic contributions to impoverished households.[35] Anna Davin and Stephen Humphries have also emphasized that working-class children generally contributed to the family either by wage labour, by performing domestic tasks, running errands, or supplying the household with bits of coal and other useful commodities.[36]

All these initiatives have viewed child labour mainly in the perspective of family strategies for economic improvement. Naturally, this is an essential part of an analysis of industrial child labour.

However, a few qualifications should perhaps be made. In the first instance, the actual employment of children in factories must be seen as a decision taken primarily within the sphere of production. Working-class parents very often wanted to have their children employed in cotton factories, since such work was generally rather well-paid compared with other occupations for children. But these parents were clearly not in a position to

---

30 See Anderson, M (1980): Approaches to the History of the Western Family 1500-1914, chapter 4.
31 See Tilly, L A and Scott, J W (1975): Women's Work and the Family in Nineteenth Century Europe, passim.
32 Anderson, M (1971): Family Structure in Nineteenth Century Lancashire, pp. 26-32.
33 Early, F H: The French-Canadian Family Economy and Standard-of-Living in Lowell, Massachusetts, 1870, pp. 180-189.
34 Hareven, T K (1982): Family Time and Industrial Time. The Relationship beteen Family and Work in a New England Industrial Community.
35 Göransson (1988), pp. 252-61. See also Winberg, C (1989): Fabriksfolket. Textilindustrin i Mark och arbetarrörelsens genombrott, pp. 49-50, 59-63.
36 Davin (1982), passim; Humphries, S (1981): Hooligans or Rebels? An Oral History of Working-Class Childhood and Youth 1889-1939.

force the manufacturers to employ their children. My general impression is that all through the 19th century there was always a rich supply of working-class children whose parents tried to have them employed in factories.

This is also one reason why I have made very few connections between industrial child labour and demography. It could perhaps be argued that the demographical transition towards the end of the 19th century contributed to the decline in the level of child labour in factories. However, the relative surplus supply of working-class children seeking employment makes it less probable that a decline in family size actually influenced the level of factory child labour. Moreover, the argument could easily be reversed: the decline in the employment prospects for children was an important force behind the demographical transition towards smaller families.[37]

It is also questionable whether child labour should be exclusively connected with poverty. I do not doubt that this was very often the case, but to make this conclusion beforehand would be to miss the full complexity of the problem. My position is rather to see industrial child labour as a family strategy which could also be used by factory operatives who were in relative terms fairly well off. These practices should be analysed on the level of local working-class culture and stratification. Were the child workers in cotton the offspring of factory operatives, artisans, or casual labourers? Did the cultural acceptance of sending children to the mills only comprise the more impoverished part of the working class, or did it have a wider spread? In a historical perspective, which changes in this respect took place over time?

In conclusion, family strategies in connection with child labour must be considered as a part of the investigation. They were also relevant in the specific context of labour recruitment patterns, a field which was influenced by processes in the spheres of both work and the household.

### Child Labour and Labour Recruitment Patterns

The impact of different recruitment strategies and patterns on the composition of the workforce is a question which has previously been rather neglected. However, in recent years research into the early development of the cotton industry in different countries has found wide variations in recruitment patterns.

In the British context, Frances Collier and Mary Rose have investigated the shift from a recruitment pattern based on young parish apprentices to a

---

37 See Levine, D (1985): Industrialization and the Proletarian Family in England, passim.

family employment structure in the early 19th century.[38] The "apprentice" system appears to have been a British solution to early recruitment difficulties. Naturally, this meant that the composition of this early cotton workforce was heavily geared towards juveniles and children.

American researchers like Thomas Dublin have shown that the recruitment pattern in the early cotton mills in Lowell, Massachusetts, was much different. Young women from rural New England constituted the major part of the early factory workforce.[39] These girls were lodged in company boarding-houses. They worked only for a limited period, in the Massachusetts mills seldom more than ten years, and returned afterwards to their rural place of origin. The result of this recruitment strategy was a workforce which was very much dominated by females between 15 and 25 years of age.

Gary Saxonhouse and Gavin Wright have shown that a "boarding system" involving the recruitment of young females to the factories also dominated the Japanese cotton industry in the early 20th century.[40]

In contrast, several American researchers have pointed at the strong dominance of family employment structures in the American South around 1900.[41] The recruitment of poor white farmers with large families tended to create a workforce where child labour was a predominant feature.

A distinction can therefore be made between four different modes of workforce recruitment: the "apprentice" system, the "boarding" system, family employment, and "free" wage labour. Naturally, these categories are approximations. Several forms of recruitment often co-existed in the same industrial district, and even in the same factory. Nevertheless, the distinction between them is of clear analytical relevance.

In conclusion, the form of recruitment appears to have had a marked influence on the composition of the factory workforce, and therefore also on child labour levels. Seen in a longer historical perspective, how did the transition from one form of recruitment to another affect the employment of children?

38 Collier, F (1965): The Family Economy of the Working Classes in the Cotton Industry 1784-1833; Rose, M B (1986): The Gregs of Quarry Bank Mill. The Rise and Decline of a Family Firm, 1750-1914.

39 Dublin, T (1979): Women at Work. The Transformation of Work and Community in Lowell, Massachusetts, 1826-1860.

40 See Saxonhouse, G (1974): A Tale of Japanese Technological Diffusion in the Meiji Period; Saxonhouse, G and Wright, G (1984a): Two Forms of Cheap Labor in Textile History; Tsurumi, P (1984): Female Textile Workers and the Failure of Early Trade Unionism in Japan.

41 Saxonhouse and Wright (1984a); Hall, J D, Korstad, R, and Leloudis, J (1986): Cotton Mill People: Work, Community, and Protest in the Textile South.

# The Child and the State

Pinchbeck and Hewitt have noted several changes in the relationship between the state and the children. A more "caring" disposition during the Tudor period was replaced by a more general disregard during the 18th century, and after that a gradual growth of government regulations on various aspects of child life during the 19th and 20th centuries.[42] The general process could also be described as a breakdown of a mercantilist state with its legal and customary safeguards for the artisanal trades, a move towards a system of relatively free markets, and, in the light of blatant exploitation of child labour under these conditions, a gradual emergence of a more modern form of government interventionism.

The cotton trade only partly fits into this scheme. Since this trade did not have the position of a traditional craft, the early cotton operatives were not protected by statute. On the other hand, the large scale employment of children in the early cotton factories soon produced initiatives to invoke government regulation.

As I will show below, legislation on industrial child labour was one of the very few interferences in the sphere of production which 19th century governments were prepared to make. In many European countries, factory laws on the use of children in industry constituted the first step of government initiatives to ameliorate the conditions of industrial capitalism. The function of the state in early capitalist society was not merely to safeguard the existing power structures; it also had a wider responsibility and interest in societal cohesion and reproduction.

However, the actual strength of the early factory legislation, and its eventual enforcement, probably differed very much in various societal contexts. The political weight behind the initiatives towards government interference was probably very dissimilar in different European countries, and also, as I will indicate later, in different parts of the United States.

The other form of government regulation which has to be briefly considered is that of compulsory schooling for working-class children. State initiatives in this direction would naturally limit the scope for child labour, at least for the very young. But schooling was not merely a matter of imparting useful knowledge. In his work on the emergence of the Swedish educational system, Bengt Sandin has argued that a main concern among the authorities was to limit and control the vagrancy and begging of street children in the urban settings. The state also had a need of socializing the children of the poor and imparting necessary discipline and Christian morals. On the other hand, the schools cannot be seen entirely in a per-

---

42 Pinchbeck and Hewitt, passim.

spective from above. It is also necessary to see what working-class parents could gain from sending their children to school rather than letting them spend the days in the streets, sending them to work, or helping with domestic chores.[43]

In the British context, Richard Johnson has emphasized that the Victorian state used education as a vehicle of social control.[44] Researchers like Stephen Humphries and J. S. Hurt have also discussed the reactions of the working-class family to compulsory schooling.[45] Humpries and Hurt have stressed that there were considerable disadvantages for parents to send their children to school. Children in some instances earned regular wages, and were also very useful in many kinds of domestic work. In a similar way, working-class parents often reacted very negatively to the legal regulation of their children's employment. In the present study, one important aspect will be to see more specifically what strategies the parents employed when factory and school legislation was implemented.

Finally, Clive Griggs has pointed out that towards the end of the 19th century, improved schooling facilities for the working class became one very important objective for the English Trade Union Congress (T.U.C.), and later for the Labour Party.[46] The relationship between the working classes and the state was in no way simple or entirely one-sided.

The above discussions on the formation of the labour process, the household, and the state, illustrate the very complex nature of the study of child labour. But it is also necessary to make some comments on a more abstract level in order to make clear my conception of both causality and society.


# Structures and Agents

One major theoretical consideration in this study is an emphasis on the actions and strategies of agents rather than a description of structural factors. The development of child labour practices depended to a large extent on the actions of the several parties involved. By using this perspective I hope to avoid the teleological positions which are often the result of structural explanations.

---

43 See Sandin, B (1986): Hemmet, gatan, fabriken eller skolan. Folkundervisning och barnuppfostran i svenska städer 1600-1850; Sandin, B (1987): Om skolans nu svaga makt. Barnarbetslagstiftning och folkundervisning i Sverige under 1860- och 1870-talen; Sandin, B (1988a): Education, popular culture and the surveillance of the population in Stockholm between 1600 and the 1840s.
44 Johnson, R (1970): Educational Policy and Social Control in Early Victorian England.
45 Humphries, S (1981); Hurt, J S (1979): Elementary Schooling and the Working Classes 1860-1918.
46 See Griggs, C (1983): The Trades Union Congress & the Struggle for Education, 1868-1925.

Stressing the strategies and choices of agents also means that differences and contrasts become very interesting. Where technological determinists like Ludwig and Nardinelli have claimed that a certain type of machinery made child labour superfluous, the present investigation will instead ask whether child labour practices were the same in different regions using virtually the same technology. The perspective of technological determinism is replaced with one stressing the differences occasioned by variations in the social organization of work, households, and the general societal context.

The same approach will be made in the study of the formation of the labour process and the enforcement of the factory legislation, areas which constitute very important parts in this investigation. Differences in the organization of work and in the effect of factory regulations will be viewed in the light of the agents involved in these processes, their incentives and their relative strengths.

Naturally, this does not mean that I wholly disregard structures as a part of historical explanations. On the contrary, the result of the praxis of the agents must undoubtedly be viewed as a form of structures which, once established, in themselves have a decided causal impact. The organization of work, for instance, is viewed as a result of a struggle or bargaining between management and operatives. The actual organization which emerges can in turn be viewed as a structure which has a certain tangibility, inertia, and semi-independence. Similarly, the actual formulation of the legal text on factory regulation had a decided impact on enforcement viability. This was also the case with the organization of a factory inspectorate as a special bureaucracy to deal with these matters.

The important thing is to avoid viewing these structures as wholly independent and living a life on their own, and try to see that their relative permanence was the outcome of certain parties wanting their retainment. My perspective is therefore an attempt to bridge the dichotomy between agents and structures rather than a preference for one over the other.


### Gender, Age and Class

In this context it is necessary to discuss who constituted the agents. Generally speaking, I adhere to a Marxian definition of society in terms of classes defined according to their role in the production process. Manufacturers and workers are therefore the two basic analytical categories. But I will also make some further distinctions within these categories as well as some which are not really part of Marxist theory. The subcontracting relationship complicates matters by having one stratum of operatives employing another. The role of the subcontractor was that of an intermediate; exploited by the manufacturers but in turn exploiting the work of other operatives, primarily children and youths.

Some attempts have even been made to see child labour analytically in terms of a "seniority" system, a dimension of domination which parallells those of class and gender.[47] However, since age has a far more transitional quality than the other categories, it is perhaps not motivated to give it equal analytical status. Still, it has to be recognized that the position and interest of child workers were not identical to those of the adult operatives.

It is also necessary to define the concept "child", although such definitions must to some extent remain arbitrary. As a basic point of reference I have decided to use the age limits laid down by the British Factory Act of 1833. According to this law, persons below the age of 13 were designated as children, and those between 13 and 18 as "young persons". These limits regarding "factory age" remained in force in Britain until 1920, and formed the basic pattern in factory statistics all through the period. After the introduction of compulsory education in the 1870s, "child labour" has in a similar manner been seen as work performed by children who had not reached the minimum school-leaving age. However, such a definition of "child" cannot be applied in an absolutely strict manner. What may be described in official statistics as an ending of child labour practices may actually have been occasioned merely by a small movement over the age limit of 13.

The categories of age and class also have to be complemented with that of gender. Research during the past two decades, particularly by feminist historians, has shown the need for the dimension of gender as well as of class. The dimension of gender in fact cuts through all the three spheres mentioned above; production, household, and government restrictions on child labour.

Recent work by feminist historians has given an entirely new dimension to the study of labour process formation. Sonya Rose, Anita Göransson and Ulla Wikander have shown that work in 19th century industry in Britain and Sweden was very much segmented according to gender.[48] Moreover, women workers were practically always subordinated to male operatives. This was expressed in terms of both authority, command of technology, and wage levels. Complicated strategies between employers, male workers, and women, were always present in the process of assigning certain types of jobs to either the male or the female sphere.

47 Elson (1982), passim.
48 Rose, S O (1986): "Gender at Work": Sex, Class and Industrial Capitalism; Göransson (1988); Karlsson, L and Wikander, U (1987): Om teknik, arbetsdelning och ideologi som formare av kvinnors - och mäns - arbetsvillkor; Wikander. U (1988): Kvinnors och mäns arbeten: Gustavsberg 1880-1980.

The category of gender is also required for a full understanding of the processes behind the early factory legislation. Mariana Valverde and Christina Carlsson have argued that restrictive legislation on women's work must be seen in the context of patriarchal notions and strategies, both in the exclusively male political arena and among the male-dominated trade unions.[49]

Gender is also a specific part of the links between work and family. Jill Liddington, Jill Norris, Elizabeth Roberts and Mike Savage have shown that the work of women in the Lancashire cotton industry was closely linked to the needs and wage-earning strategies of the working-class household. The age of entry and the span of working lives were largely dictated by the gender patterns which ruled in the domestic sphere as well as in the factory.[50]

The gender dimension is therfore essential in several areas: in the formation of the labour process, the wage-earning strategies of the working-class household, and the development of factory legislation.


# Methods and Material

### The Comparative Approach

One effect of extending the scope of analysis to several causal processes rather than merely technological change or factory legislation is that the greater complexity makes it difficult to establish the degree of relevance of the causal relationships. In order to gain a better view on the importance of the different processes I have chosen a comparative approach; above all a comparison between the English and Scottish cotton industries, but in a more limited sense also with the United States.

This kind of approach leaves open the possibility that different processes relating to child labour were more important in some societal and historical contexts than in others. The comparative perspective is used mainly to show variations and unique developments, but also in order to qualify current theories on the use of child labour in industry. This approach will be used on three different levels: first, the organization of work and adoption of

49 Carlsson, C (1986): Kvinnosyn och kvinnopolitik. En studie av svensk socialdemokrati 1880-1910; Valverde, M (1988): "Giving the Female a Domestic Turn": The Social, Legal and Moral Regulation of Women's Work in the British Cotton Mills, 1820-1850.

50 Liddington, J and Norris, J (1978): One Hand Tied Behind Us. The Rise of the Women's Suffrage Movement; Roberts, E (1985): A Woman's Place. An oral history of working-class women 1890-1940; Savage, M (1985): Capitalist and Patriarchal Relations at Work: Preston Cotton Weaving, 1890-1940.

technology; second, the enforcement of factory legislation; and third, the societal context of recruitment and production.

Generally speaking, the use of comparative perspectives in historical research has become more widespread during the last decade.[51] This has also been the case in industrial sociology.[52] In economic and historical research on the 19th and early 20th century cotton industry, especially American scholars have used such an approach. William Lazonick, William Mass, Isaac Cohen, Margaret Freifeld, Gary Saxonhouse and Gavin Wright have all made very interesting comparisons between the cotton industries in, above all, the U.S.A., Britain, and Japan.[53] But it should perhaps also be pointed out that all these researchers have their main background in Economics and Sociology, fields where comparative perspectives have become more commonly used, rather than in History.

In contrast, there has been no similar tendency among the British researchers on the cotton industry. Comparisons between the English and Scottish industries, for instance, have been practically absent. In this respect, this investigation will break some new ground, and also qualify some of the American work by making a comparison which is primarily based on the British case.

Previous research on industrial child labour has not used a comparative approach. As far as I am aware, all such studies have been made in the context of a single country. Comparative perspectives, when used, have generally been confined to a study of different industrial trades within the same country. Consequently, this investigation offers a new approach to the study of industrial child labour, and will hopefully provide a fuller and more complex picture of the use of children in early industrial society.

However, this approach rests on certain preconditions; above all on that of comparability. In the specific case of the labour process, the comparative perspective has the advantage that the application of a certain kind of technology can be studied in very different societal settings. However, the precondition is that the technology in question was sufficiently identical as to be comparable. In the case of cotton textile machinery, I have concluded

51 For some recent discussions on the use of the comparative approach, see Grew, R (1980): The Case for Comparing Histories; Skocpol, T and Somers, M (1980): The Uses of Comparative History in Macrosocial Inquiry; Mörner, M (1981): Komparation: att vidga historiska perspektiv; Jonsson, U (1987): Komparation: en strategi för att fånga breda samhälleliga förändringsmönster och processer.
52 See Littler (1982).
53 Lazonick, W (1981a): Factor Costs and the Diffusion of Ring Spinning in Britain Prior to World War I; Lazonick, W (1981b): Competition, Specialization, and Industrial Decline; Lazonick, W (1981c): Production Relations, Labor Productivity, and Choice of Technique: British and U.S. Cotton Spinning; Mass, W (1984): Technological Change and Industrial Relations: The Diffusion of Automatic Weaving in the United States and Britain; Cohen (1985a); Cohen (1985b); Freifeld, M (1986): Technological Change and the "Self-acting" Mule: A Study of Skill and the Sexual Division of Labour; Saxonhouse and Wright (1984a); Saxonhouse, G and Wright, G (1984b): Rings and Mules Around the World: A Comparative Study of Technological Choice.

that this precondition is met. David Jeremy has shown that even during the early phase of industrialisation, British cotton machinery was well known and available on both sides of the Atlantic.[54] The British prohibition on the export of textile machinery was never very efficient, and was abolished already in 1842. The basic cotton textile technologies - mule-spinning, throstle-spinning, carding machinery, and powerlooms - spread to all parts of the world in the second half of the 19th century. Moreover, comparative studies on the adoption of textile technologies in different countries have not indicated any important differences between the machines belonging to the same basic category.[55] In other words, spinning-mules in Lancashire did not differ in any material way from those in Scotland or the United States. It is therefore possible to view the technology used as a relatively constant factor when comparing the formation of the labour process in the different locations.


## The Sources: Quantitative and Qualitative Material

Due to the nature of the questions asked, and the character of the British sources, this investigation relies rather heavily on qualitative material. Especially for the early period, figures on the cotton industry workforce are practically unavailable. More detailed statistics on machinery and the composition of the workforce hardly exist before the first Parliamentary factory returns in 1835. Moreover, the factory returns are only available on a very aggregated level, and contain very little information on the workforce in the different labour processes.

In addition, very few company records have survived, and those that have seldom provide information which is relevant for this study. One important exception is the records of the Quarry Bank Mill, Styal, north Cheshire, which have been used in the attempt to reconstruct the employment of children in the different labour processes.

Another important quantitative source has been the wage censuses collected in 1886 and 1906, which provide rather detailed information on the industrial labour force.[56]

However, the amount of reliable and detailed statistics remains small. In the comparison between Britain and the United States, the situation is fur-

---

54 Jeremy, J D (1981): Transatlantic Industrial Revolution: The Diffusion of Textile Technologies between Britain and America, 1790-1830s.

55 See, for instance, Saxonhouse and Wright (1984b), passim.

56 Parliamentary Papers (PP) 1889 LXX, Return of Rates of Wages in the Principal Textile Trades of the United Kingdom; PP 1909 LXXX, Report of an Inquiry by the Board of Trade into the Earnings and Hours of Labour of Workpeople of the United Kingdom. I. Textile Trades in 1906.

ther complicated by the fact that the available statistics on the age of the cotton industry workforce are aggregated in dissimilar age groups, which makes direct comparisons impossible.

The main weight of the argument is therefore supported by qualitative material like the reports and minutes of the factory inspectors, parliamentary investigations, newspapers, and the records of trade unions and employers' associations.

Naturally, I have approached these sources with some caution. In the parliamentary investigations, for instance, I have avoided the more contentious issues on the treatment of children, and instead used these sources for information on the labour process. Witnesses directly connected with manufacture, i.e. operatives and mill-owners, have been preferred to outside observers like clergymen. The reports of the factory inspectors have been used as a source for conditions in the industrial districts, but only with great circumspection in the estimation of the performance of the inspectors themselves.

One further problem with this material is that it emanates from the very male-dominated sphere of factory inspectors, cotton manufacturers, and trade unions. In an attempt to compensate this obvious gender bias I have tried to utilize the oral history material collected by Elizabeth Roberts on working women in the early 20th century.[57] In this way, the more "official" and male perspectives will be complemented with a more "female" one dealing with the basic experiences of everyday life.

However, it should perhaps also be pointed out that there is one type of material which I have chosen not to utilize. Primary census data remain which could be used to reconstruct household composition in the British industrial towns. This has been done, for instance, by Michael Anderson in his work on family structures in Preston, Lancashire.[58] There are several reasons why I have decided not to go in this direction. First, a study of this kind would necessarily be very local in character, at the very most comprising a few selected industrial towns. This would not fit very well with the comparative approach and the perspective of important differences between countries and regions. Second, this type of study would only make explicit some links between child labour and the family, while giving no information on the spheres of work and factory inspection. Third, primary census data are only available for the period between 1851 and 1881, which I find too short.

In the light of these difficulties, I have decided not to give priority to primary census data. This decision is also influenced by the fact that there is

---

57 Lancaster University Library. North-West Oral History Project (NWOHP). Transcripts of interviews.
58 Anderson, M (1971).

no major work on the use of children in the British cotton industry. In this book I will try to establish a general pattern of industrial child labour in British cotton factories up to 1920, and this picture can later be qualified on the basis of local studies.

## Design of the Investigation

The basic structure of this study is a comparison between the cotton industries of England, Scotland, and the U.S.A., primarily in respect of the use of children in the workforce. The choice of industrial branch should perhaps be given some further motivation. The British cotton industry constituted the forefront of mechanized production in the transition to industrial capitalism. From the very start it relied rather heavily on factory child labour. The mechanized textile trades in a sense pioneered the use of children in the new factories.

Moreover, children continued to be used to a considerable extent in the English cotton industry well into the 20th century. It has therefore been possible to study a relatively long time period; from the end of the 18th century to the 1920s.

In one sense, this study comprises the development of production and society in the transition from early industrial capitalism to the more organized type of capitalistic society after the First World War.[59] The aim of this study is to chart the important changes and variation in industrial child labour which took place during the development of this mode of production. The anatomy of industrial child labour will in this way be more clearly observable.

However, the comparative perspective, the emphasis on several causal processes, and the long time period which is studied, also impose certain limitations on the design of the investigation. The main focus will be on the English and Scottish cotton districts, while the American industry will be used mainly as a contrasting case and an illustration that other lines of development were possible.

The investigation will be even more assymetrical in the sense that a greater part will be devoted to the study of the English cotton district comprising Lancashire and small adjoining parts of Yorkshire, Cheshire, and Derbyshire.[60] This emphasis is motivated to some extent by the sheer

---

59 The concept of "organized capitalism" has been developed by the German group centering on Jürgen Kocka and Hans-Ulrich Wehler. On the relatively late development of organised capitalism in Great Britain, see Medick, H (1974): Anfänge und Voraussetzungen des Organisierten Kapitalismus in Grossbritannien 1873-1914.
60 For practical reasons, this district will henceforth be labelled "Lancashire" or the English cotton district.

size of the Lancashire industry, which dominated the world production of cotton goods all through the period, while the Scottish industry stagnated already in the mid-19th century. But a far more important reason for the emphasis on conditions in Lancashire is the fact that industrial child labour remained an important issue in the local cotton industry until it was finally abolished by law in 1917. In contrast, child labour in the Scottish cotton district in the vicinity of Glasgow became relatively unimportant already before 1850. My intention to provide explanations as to why child labour continued to be extensively used in the Lancashire district also during the period of "mature" industrial production has led me to concentrate my empirical research to the English industry.

Guided by the theoretical considerations dealt with in a previous section, I have chosen to gear the empirical study primarily towards the formation of the labour process, the changes accompanying new technology, and the actual effects of factory legislation and inspection. Problems connected with these areas will be studied rather closely.

However, this should not overshadow the fact that I see industrial child labour as a phenomenon dependent on processes in the sphere of the household as well as in those of work and government regulations. But as I will argue later, I have the impression that the strategies of employment among working-class families remained relatively permanent during the whole period of investigation. The study of changes in the sphere of production and the effects of restrictive legislation have therefore been given priority in terms of space.


## Disposition

When writing this book I have tried to combine a chronological sequence with occasional comparative sections and chapters. This approach has led to some repetition, which is unfortunate but probably unavoidable.

The first empirical chapter deals with the early period, from around 1780 to 1840. The organization of production in the early British cotton mills, differences in labour recruitment methods, and the wage-earning strategies of working-class households are discussed. There is also a brief comparison with American conditions.

The subsequent part contains an examination of the British factory inspection, a governmental body created by the 1833 Factory Act. The actual impact of the factory legislation on child labour practices has to be established, and this necessitates an assessment of true enforcement levels.

This is followed by a chapter on technology change and the formation of work in the period between 1840 and 1890. The comparative perspective is used to illustrate vital differences in these respects between England, Scotland, and Massachusetts, U.S.A., and the implications of these differences for child labour practices are discussed.

The Lancashire industry is the object of analysis in the subsequent chapters. A reconstruction is made of the relations of production, the structure of industrial bargaining, and the authority patterns regarding the employment of children. This is followed by an investigation of the changes in the organization of production, and the spread of a new generation of textile technology after 1890. In the final chapter on Lancashire, the attitudes and actions of the cotton operatives on the child labour issue are dealt with. These attitudes are seen in a context of employment practices, gender patterns, and persistent notions of a "family wage".

In the final two empirical chapters, I will contrast the developments in Lancashire with those in Scotland, Massachusetts, and the Southern U.S. states. The comparative perspective will be used in order to gain more knowledge on the processes behind the use of children in factories during this period.

# Chapter 2

# Child Labour in the Cotton Mills: the Early Phase, ca. 1780-1840

It is well known that the British cotton factories in the late 18th century were to a very large extent operated by children. Large country mills like New Lanark in Scotland, Holywell in Flintshire, Wales, and Samuel Oldknow's factory at Marple, relied heavily on the work of young pauper apprentices. Other early manufacturers, like Richard Arkwright at Cromford and Jedediah Strutt at Belper, hired the children of the local miners and nailmakers.[1] Sir John Sinclair's Statistical Account of Scotland noted in the late 18th century that at New Lanark, there were 275 pauper children who received "maintenance, education and cloathing for their work".[2] Robert Owen later estimated that the number of parish apprentices at New Lanark in 1799 was closer to five hundred, constituting about a third of the total workforce.[3] However, there are few exact figures on the age structure of the early cotton operatives. From the Statistical Account, we know that children below 13 constituted 40 per cent of the total workforce at New Lanark, while not more than 31 per cent of the operatives were above 18 years of age.[4] But in most instances the descriptions are rather vague.

However, there can be no doubt that the proportion of child workers lessened perceptibly during this early period. Already by 1816, Arkwright's mill at Crompton contained a workforce where only seven per cent were children below 13, and 37 per cent were operatives below 18.[5] In the same year G. A. Lee, a Manchester manufacturer, claimed that the operations in

---

1 Unwin, G, Hulme, A and Taylor, G (1924): Samuel Oldknow and the Arkwrights. The Industrial Revolution at Stockport and Marple, pp. 95, 170; Fitton, R S and Wadsworth, A P (1958): The Strutts and the Arkwrights 1758-1830, pp. 80, 103-4, 225; Chapman, S D (1967): The Early Factory Masters. The Transition to the Factory System in the Midlands Textile Industry, chapter 9; PP 1816 III, Minutes of Evidence taken before the Select Committee on the State of the Children employed in the Manufactories of the United Kingdom, evidence of Robert Owen, New Lanark, pp. 20-22.
2 The Statistical Account of Scotland 1791-1799 [1800], Vol VII, p. 462.
3 PP 1816 III, Minutes of Evidence taken before the Select Committee..., evidence of Owen, p. 20.
4 The Statistical Account of Scotland 1791-1799, Vol VII, p. 463.
5 PP 1816 III, Minutes of Evidence taken before the Select Committee..., evidence of Richard Arkwright, p. 281. Similarly, 43 per cent of the operatives in the Holywell mill in Flintshire were below 18 years in 1816. See ibid., pp. 374-75.

the 1780s had required five times the current proportion of children below ten years of age.[6]

To a considerable extent, this decline can be explained as a result of technological change, above all the mechanisation of the preparatory processes of picking and carding which were initially performed by hand. However, this was not the only relevant causal process involved. There was also a marked shift in recruitment patterns, from parish apprentices and family employment to a predominance of "free" wage labour. The rise in the age structure was to some extent caused by a process of "maturation" of the workforce, or the creation of a specific class of textile operatives. Furthermore, developments hardly moved consistently in one direction. There were several trends and tendencies involved, some of which counteracted each other. There was also ample scope for different policies among the manufacturers on the recruitment and the composition of a workforce.

## Changes in the Pattern of Recruitment

The recruitment of parish apprentices was a common strategy among the early British cotton manufacturers to get a sufficient number of young workers to their mills. Describing the origin of the trade, John Fielden, a manufacturer and adherent of the factory reform movement, wrote in 1836:

> Thousands of hands were suddenly required in these places, remote from towns; and Lancashire...being till then but comparatively thinly populated and barren, a population was all she now wanted. The small and nimble fingers of little children being by very far the most in request, the custom instantly sprang up of procuring "apprentices" from different parish work-houses of London, Birmingham, and elsewhere... [7]

Another contemporary observer confirmed that the demand of the cotton manufacturers for young children exceeded the local supply, and they chose to look for them in "London, Bristol and other great towns".[8] To some extent, therefore, the apprentice system was caused by a lack of young workers in the neighbourhood of the factories.[9] But the use of parish apprentices was also the outcome of certain societal and cultural developments. The processes of proletarisation and urbanisation, and the emer-

---

6 Ibid., evidence of Lee, p. 365.
7 Fielden, J (1836): The Curse of the Factory System, p. 5.
8 Farey, J: Agriculture in Derbyshire, Vol III, cited in Chapman, S D (1967), p. 168.
9 See 1816 III, Minutes of Evidence taken before the Select Committee..., evidence of Sir Robert Peel, pp. 134-35.

gence of specific poor law measures to deal with this situation, were important preconditions for the rise of the apprentice system. The practice of sending pauper children as apprentices had been established in Britain well before the rise of the cotton industry, and this seems to have formed a cultural precedent for their recruitment to the early mills.[10]

Still, what has to be explained is the eventual dissolution of the apprentice system in the early 19th century. The investigations of factory child labour by the 1816 Select Committee shows that apprentices were by then very seldom used. The reasons for this should probably be sought both in the obvious disadvantages of the system, and in the general process of urbanisation during this period. The disadvantages for the manufacturer when relying on apprentice labour must have been substantial. The mill-owner had to pay the full cost of the housing, feeding and clothing of the apprentices. They also had to be kept when they were ill or disabled. The manufacturer was not able to dismiss them during periods of bad trade, strikes among the other operatives, or when production was stopped due to damaged machinery. Moreover, work discipline was a constant problem when using parish apprentices. Since they did not receive any wages, and could not be threatened with dismissal, it was very difficult for the manufacturer to turn them into an efficient workforce. This is evident in a statement by Henry McConnel, a substantial Manchester mill-owner, in 1833. When asked if he would not consider hiring parish apprentices, he answered that he was not prepared to use this kind of labour. The housing and maintenance of these children, he claimed, would alone be more costly than their labour was worth. Moreover, the apprentices would not have any inducement to do their work properly.[11]

After 1815 the use of parish apprentices only survived in isolated mills on the outskirts of the cotton district, where the recruitment of labour remained difficult. One example of this kind is Quarry Bank Mill, Styal, where apprentices continued to be used until the late 1840s.[12] The children were mainly recruited from the Liverpool poor-house.[13] But even at Quarry Bank the system was in obvious decline after 1838, when the mill employed 100 apprentices. In the beginning of the 1840s it seems as if the owners, the

---

10 See Cage, R A (1981): The Scottish Por Law 1745-1845, p. 59; Hutchins, B L and Harrison, A (1911): A History of Factory Legislation, p. 13.

11 PP 1833 XX, First Report from... Commissioners...[on] the Employment of Children in Factories, evidence of Henry McConnel, p. E9.

12 On Quarry Bank Mill, see Collier, F (1930): An Early Factory Community; Collier, F (1943): Samuel Greg and Styal Mill; Lazenby, W (1949): The Social and Economic History of Styal; Rose, M B (1977): The Gregs of Styal 1750-1914: - The Emergence and Development of a Family Business; Rose (1986). On the persistence of the apprentice system in a remote Derbyshire mill, see Smelser, N (1959): Social Change in the Industrial Revolution, p. 187.

13 PP 1833 VI, Report from the Select Committee on Manufactures, Commerce and Shipping, evidence of William Rathbone Greg, cotton manufacturer, p. 680.

Greg family, simply let the indentures expire. By 1847 there were only six apprentices left.[14] It was probably the case that the apprentice system became more expensive when run on a smaller scale, since the cost of housing and supervision was relatively inflexible.[15] The Gregs also experienced problems with apprentices running away and with general work discipline.[16] Their eventual solution was to abandon the apprentice system and build a factory village to house a more stable workforce.[17]

This development was more or less the same in most older cotton mills situated in country locations. The use of parish apprentices was gradually abandoned, and instead the manufacturers built more permanent factory settlements. As a part of this process, child labour levels fell substantially. Generally speaking, the composition of the workforce became above all dependent on the demographic profile of the village population. As far as possible, the manufacturers seem to have avoided the employment of adult men.[18] These were preferably employed in agriculture or handloom weaving. But the result of the transition to regular factory villages was still a general rise in the age structure of the cotton mill workforce.

Still, different manufacturer strategies were possible in the context of recruitment. Some Lancashire mill-owners decided not to build up a permanent workforce, and instead utilized the cheap labour of the children of the rural poor. One contemporary observer claimed that manufacturers were abandoning the use of apprentices in favour of "the children of the poor in the immediate neighbourhood...thus continuing or augmenting their profits".[19] However, the major impression is still that the building of mill villages was the more dominant tendency in the country locations.

Simultaneously, other processes of change were going on in the British cotton industry. The shift from water-power to steam as the main source of energy after 1800 created a possibility for the localisation of new factories to the towns. Already by 1825 the urban factories dominated the Lancashire industry, and by 1838 the steam-driven cotton mills consumed more than eight times the power of those driven by water.[20] In general terms, the result

---

14 Manchester Central Library. Greg Collection. C5/1/7/1-2, Weekly Accounts, Quarry Bank Mill.
15 According to the weekly accounts, the mere maintenance cost per apprentice more than doubled between 1838 and 1846. See ibid., and also Rose (1977), pp. 99-100.
16 See Greg Collection C5/8/22, Account of the Circumstances Connected with the Punishment of Esther Price and Lucy Garner, 1836; Lazenby (1949), p. 151.
17 Rose (1986), pp. 54-55.
18 Unwin, Hulme and Taylor (1924), pp. 167-68.
19 Brown, H (1840): The Cotton Fields and Cotton Factories, p. 114. In the Swedish context, Anita Göransson has found proof of this mill-owner strategy at the Strömma cotton-spinning mill. See Göransson (1988), pp. 252-61.
20 Taylor, A J (1949): Concentration and Specialization in the Lancashire Cotton Industry 1825-1850, pp. 114-15.

was an urbanisation of the cotton industry. In Scotland, practically all new factories were sited not more than 25 miles from Glasgow.[21]

The urbanisation process was also connected with a transition from apprentice or family labour to a predominance of "free" wage labour. The labour market in the early industrial towns was much more flexible than in the country locations. This, I would argue, created scope for widely differing employer strategies on recruitment. Many manufacturers in urban settings geared their hiring practices to the children of the local poor. A high birth-rate and the migration of young persons and families to the Lancashire towns ensured that there was a very large supply of child and juvenile labour. As I will argue more fully below, this took predominantly the form of "free" wage labour, not family employment.

The manufacturers were no doubt able to draw on the cultural accept-ance of child labour which was predominant in the households of casual labourers, handloom weavers, proto-industrial workers, and agricultural labourers. Among large sections of the working class, the employment of children in factories was primarily seen as a welcome additional contribu-tion to the family economy. For these reasons, it was possible for the town manufacturers to employ a workforce with an age profile which was con-siderably lower than that of the country factories.

This is evident in the figures presented to the 1816 Select Committee. While the proportion of workers below 18 at Arkwright's country mill at Cromford was 37 per cent, the corresponding figure in the Preston cotton mills was 68 per cent. Indeed, the Preston manufacturers seem to have aimed specifically at recruiting the children of the urban poor, many of them Irish.[22] But the figures also indicate that there were great differences in child labour levels between geographical areas. Cotton manufacturers in some districts, particularly Scotland, did not utilize child labour to the same extent as those in Preston:

---

21 Bremner, D [1869]: The industries of Scotland. Their Rise, Progress and Present Condition, pp. 277-79; Hamilton, H (1932): The Industrial Revolution in Scotland, p. 136.
22 PP 1816 III, Minutes of Evidence taken before the Select Committee..., evidence of John Moss, Preston, p. 184.

Table 1.  Cotton mill workforce according to age in different locations, 1816.
per cent.

| Location | 8-9 | Age 10-17 | 18- | N |
|---|---|---|---|---|
| Preston | 11.2 | 56.8 | 32.0 | 1,651 |
| Manchester & dist. | 5.8 | 42.4 | 51.8 | 12,890 |
| Scotland* | 4.1 | 40.9 | 55.0 | 10,000 |

* The Scottish figures do not comprise New Lanark and specialized weaving factories.

Sources:  PP 1816 III, Minutes of Evidence taken before the Select Committee on the State of the Children Employed in the Manufactories of the United Kingdom, pp. 240-41, 261, 274-75.

One tentative interpretation is that the Preston manufacturers tried to utilize younger and cheaper labour than mill-owners in other areas. Generally speaking, it is evident that the urbanisation of the cotton industry did not lower the levels of child labour. In fact, it rather seems to have been the reverse.

However, there can be no doubt that there was a general decline in child labour levels between the 1780s and 1816. This change was to a large extent caused by the mechanisation of the preparatory processes of picking and carding, and the abandoning of the apprentice system. But another process which has to be considered is the general "maturation" of the cotton factory workforce. Research by Saxonhouse and Wright on the Japanese and Southern U.S. cotton industry indicates that the first generation of operatives tended to be considerably younger than those following. After the industry had become established, the manufacturers actually had the option to hire older and more experienced workers. This alternative had not existed when starting up the operations. The result was a rise in the age profile of the workforce, occasioned by the mill-owners' retaining some of the operatives when they reached a more mature age.[23] There is no reason to believe that the development was much different in the British industry. One part of the decline in child labour levels could therefore be explained by the manufacturers having access to a supply of older operatives who had been trained in the mills since they were young.

Perhaps more importantly, there are also some suggestions that there was a marked change in mill-owner perception of the optimal workforce. The first generation of cotton manufacturers seems to have held a rather

---

23 Saxonhouse and Wright (1984a), passim.

simplistic view of work efficiency and productivity. They seem to have believed that the machinery would run on its own accord, and would only have to be tended by the cheapest labour possible, namely that of children. Witness, for instance, that kind of naivety in the Statistical Account of Scotland in the 1790s when describing the effect of power-driven jennies at New Lanark:

> [It] reduces very considerably the number of men that formerly were necessary in working the common jennies. Such being the case, widows with large families are much wanted here, as children can manage the patent jennies with great ease, while their mothers are employed in other branches. [24]

In the next statistical survey of Scotland a few decades later, the outlook had changed considerably:

> A great object expected to be obtained by this improvement was, that, instead of employing men as spinners, which was indispensable when the machine was to be worked by hand, children would be able to perform every office required. /.../ But after a short trial of this mode of spinning it was discovered that a greater amount of produce might be obtained, and at a cheaper rate, by taking back the men as spinners... [25]

This suggests that the mill-owners' initial preference for children was perhaps not always rational. A part of the subsequent decline in the proportion of children must therefore be ascribed to their finding out that older operatives could very well be a better choice in some parts of the labour process. Adult males were increasingly to be found in the mills as jenny-spinners and cardroom hands, a change which cannot wholly be ascribed to the development of more complicated machinery.

Generally speaking, the decline in child labour levels during this early period should perhaps not be too strongly tied to changes in technology, but rather be seen in the context of a shift in the methods of production from a low-wage, low-intensive organsation of work, which to a large extent involved children, to a more high-intensive, high-paying method, where factory children were less wanted.[26] But before going further in this direction, a brief look at the American example will provide some interesting contrasts to the British development.

---

24 The Statistical Account of Scotland 1791-1799 [1800], Vol VII, p. 464.
25 The New Statistical Account of Scotland (1845), Vol VI, p. 142.
26 Heywood (1988), pp. 320-23; Hobsbawm, E (1968): Custom, Wages and Work-load in Nineteenth Century Industry, passim.

# A Contrasting Case: Recruitment Strategies in the Early U.S. Cotton Industry

The American case shows that there were several possible solutions to the early recruitment problem. The cotton mills in southern Massachusetts and Rhode Island in the first decade of the 19th century relied very much on the labour of children brought in from the neighbourhood farms. This system gradually gave way to a family employment structure where adult males, juveniles and children were employed in the mill, while the married women largely remained at home.[27] Even as late as 1820, children constituted two-thirds of the textile workforce in Pawtucket, Rhode Island.[28] In contrast, a very different system developed in the northern part of Massachusetts and in New Hampshire. Here recruitment was geared almost completely towards the hiring of young women, generally farmers' daughters recruited from a wide area of New England. They were lodged in company boarding-houses, and were under close supervision even during their spare time. The moral and paternalist attitude assumed by these firms towards the young women workers was at least partly a consequence of their intention to have mill-work designated as a "respectable" occupation, and to calm parental worries about their daughter's honour when away from the family sphere. This practice of employment is known as the Waltham system, and it very much dominated the rapidly expanding cotton towns of Lowell and Lawrence.[29]

The emergence of the Waltham system should at least partly be seen as the result of conscious manufacturer strategy. The early mill-owners wanted to avoid the responsibilities connected with the building up of a permanent factory village. The cotton trade was prone to great fluctuations, and a permanent workforce would have to be kept also during the bad periods. One great advantage with the Waltham system was therefore that the young women could be sent home to their families during periods of depressed trade.[30] But it should perhaps also be seen as a solution which fitted in with the general economic context of New England. The relative absence of urban poverty compared to Britain, and differences in the regulation of the poor, were main reasons why solutions like parish apprentices could not be used. The Waltham system was more compatible with a society very much dominated by independent farmers, where the labour of young daughters could well be utilized outside the household in exchange for board and a

---

27 Ware, C F (1966): The Early New England Cotton Manufacture, pp. 22-37; Dublin (1979), pp. 15-17; Tucker, B M (1980): The Family and Industrial Discipline in Ante-Bellum New England, pp. 56-60.
28 Dublin (1979), p. 16.
29 Ware (1966), pp. 198-200.
30 Ibid., pp. 64-65.

monetary contribution.[31] In the perspective of the young women themselves, mill-work gave them an opportunity to save towards a dowry before going back to their own community to get married. For most of them, factory work was just a short period of their lives, generally between the ages of fifteen and twenty-five.

Naturally, the manufacturers' adoption of the Waltham system also meant that the composition of the cotton workforce became very different from that in Britain or Rhode Island. The mills were dominated by juvenile girls and young women, while child labour in the British or Rhode Island form was relatively unimportant. In his investigation of the records of a Lowell firm, Thomas Dublin concludes that the proportion of children below fifteen was approximately 3 per cent in 1836, while women above that age constituted 85 per cent.[32] At the same time, Caroline Ware has estimated that the proportion of children in the Rhode Island cotton industry was 41 per cent in 1832.

Admittedly, it could be argued that the Rhode Island industry was more geared towards mule-spinning, and the Lowell industry towards throstle-spinning. But there is no real reason to assume that the former method required more child workers than the latter. Children could be used equally well as doffers at the throstle as piecers in mule-spinning. Moreover, the argument could easily be reversed. Mule-spinning was not used to a large extent in Lowell because the manufacturers wanted to have a workforce primarily composed of young females, and males were often preferred in that process due to its greater requirement of physical strength. The main difference between the two areas was that of recruitment systems. In northern mills organized according to the Waltham system, adult men and children were generally not wanted. This example shows that recruitment policies could have a very marked influence on child labour levels in the early cotton industry.


# Changes in the Labour Process and Child Labour in the British Cotton Industry, 1816-1833

The perspective will now be moved back to the British context for an evaluation of developments after 1816. Child labour in the textile factories

---

31 A boarding system for young women was also the main form of employment in the Japanese cotton industry towards the end of the 19th century, where in similar manner the daughters of small farmers were recruited to the mills. See Saxonhouse (1974), p. 164; Saxonhouse and Wright (1984a), passim.
32 Dublin (1979), pp. 26-27.

was investigated by a Parliamentary commission in 1833, and it is therefore possible to make some estimations of the changes which took place between those two dates. The overall impression is that there was a slight decline in child labour levels, at least in Manchester:

Table 2.  Workforce composition according to age in British cotton factories, 1816 and 1833. per cent.

| Location | 8-9 | Age 10-17 | 18- | N |
|---|---|---|---|---|
| Manchester & district 1816 | 5.8 | 42.4 | 51.8 | 12,890 |
| Manchester 1833 * | 4.6 | 38.1 | 57.3 | 17,235 |
| Scotland 1816 ** | 4.1 | 40.9 | 55.0 | 10,000 |
| Scotland 1833 | 0.8 | 45.5 | 53.7 | 12,188 |

\* Sample of 43 mills.
\*\* See table 1.

Sources: PP 1816 III, Minutes of Evidence taken before the Select Committee, pp. 240-41, 274-75; PP 1833 XX, First Report of...Commissioners...[on] the Employment of Children in Factories, p. D2 107; PP 1834 XX, Factories Enquiry Commission. Supplementary Report Part I, pp. 21-22.

In the Scottish context, the most obvious tendency seems to have been a decline in the number of very young child workers, and a rise in the group between ten and seventeen years of age. But it is also possible to make a rather more detailed comparison between city and country mills in 1833:

Table 3.  Workforce composition according to age in different locations, 1833. per cent.

| Location | 8-9 | 10-11 | 12-13 | Age 14-15 | 16-17 | 18- | N |
|---|---|---|---|---|---|---|---|
| Manchester * | 4.6 | 7.9 | 10.3 | 9.6 | 10.3 | 57.3 | 17,235 |
| Glasgow ** | 4.3 | 14.8 | 16.5 | 12.7 | 13.6 | 38.2 | 5,273 |
| 2 country mills, Lanc.*** | 1.2 | 7.0 | 10.1 | 9.6 | 10.7 | 61.5 | 2,044 |

\* Sample of 43 mills.
\*\* Sample of 29 mills collected by Kirkman Finlay, Glasgow.
\*\*\* Ashton's mill, Hyde, and Compstall Mills, near Stockport.

Sources: PP 1833 XX, First Report of...Commissioners, pp. D2 29, 83, 107; Kirkman, F (1833): Letter to the Right Hon. Lord Ashley, on the Cotton Factory System and the Ten Hours' Factory Bill, Appendix.

Just as in 1816, child labour was more prevalent in the cities than in the country mills. But what also stands out in this comparison is that the Glasgow industry relied on a considerably younger workforce than was the case in Manchester. According to the survey presented by Kirkman Finlay, a substantial Glasgow manufacturer, children below 14 constituted 35.6 per cent of the workforce in the Glasgow mills as compared to 22.8 per cent in Manchester.

Naturally, there may have been several reasons for this difference. Since the Manchester industry constituted a vanguard in textile technology, it is probable that the Glasgow machinery was slightly older. Another possibility is that the Glasgow industry competed by using cheaper labour than the Manchester mill-owners. But before going into the managerial strategies in the Glasgow industry, it is essential to describe more fully the changes in the labour process which were taking place during these decades, and how this affected the employment of children.

Generally speaking, there seem to have been two counteracting tendencies. While the rate of child labour declined in the preparatory and carding processes, it simultaneously increased in the mule-spinning department.[33] In 1816 the manager of Horrocks, Miller and Co, a very large Preston firm, presented a sketch of the production process where the description of the carding-room shows a workforce consisting of 14-17 children and two adult operatives.[34] Seventeen years later a carding overlooker from Manchester claimed that the need for child labour in his department had lessened due to the more complete mechanisation of the carding process.[35]

In the same investigation, a picking-room operative stated that there were no longer any workers below 16 years of age in the picking department.[36]

The general impression is that the child workers became increasingly concentrated to the mule-spinning process during the period from 1816 to 1833. In the three Manchester firms investigated by the factory commissioners in 1833, 91 per cent of the children were found to be working as piecers in the mule-spinning process.[37] Similarly, the large Manchester firm of McConnel and Kennedy employed 89.5 per cent of its child workers below 15 as piecers in 1836, and in the fine-spinning mill investigated by

33 Neil Smelser has only observed the changes in the mule-spinning process, and concludes that child labour levels were increasing during this period. See Smelser (1959), pp. 197-202.
34 PP 1816 III, Minutes taken before the Select Committee.., evidence of William Taylor, p. 258. However, it should be remembered that Preston probably had a distinctly higher proportion of children in the workforce than was the case in Manchester.
35 PP 1833 XX, First Report of...Commissioners, evidence of John Rowbotham, p. A1 127.
36 Ibid., evidence of James Young, p. A1 70.
37 PP 1834 XIX, Factories Enquiry Commission. Supplementary Report Part II, pp. 119j-119k.

Andrew Ure in the same year the corresponding proportion was 90 per cent.[38] Consequently, the impression is that by the early 1830s a great majority of the factory children in cotton were employed as piecers in mule-spinning. But this picture has to be qualified in several ways.

All the mills in the 1833 investigation were geared towards the production of fine yarn. Fine-spinning mills were not only considered to require more child labour in the form of piecers, they were also wholly dominated by the mule-spinning technology. The rival technology, throstle-spinning, was much more prevalent in the production of coarser yarn. It is therefore very probable that the evidence presented above does not take account of the children employed in throstle-spinning.

Unfortunately, there is very little material which provides any indication of how work was organized in that labour process. Historians have also tended to neglect throstle-spinning in favour of the rival process of mule-spinning. This is probably not unconnected to the fact that throstle-spinners were invariably young, low-paid females, while mule-spinners were predominantly men. According to Andrew Ure, throstle-spinners were generally young women from 17 years of age and upwards.[39] However, it is not altogether clear if children were employed as "doffers", removing the full bobbins from the throstle-frames, a practice which was common towards the end of the century. One Manchester manufacturer specifically stated to the 1833 commissioners that he did not employ any children in the throstle-spinning process.[40] Some isolated evidence from a Preston mill in 1834 also indicates that special doffers were rarely used. 96 young throstle-spinners were listed, but only 10 doffers.[41] On the other hand, a Glasgow mule-spinner testified in 1832 that "very young" children were employed in throstle-spinning.[42] The factory commissioners of 1833 also reported that in a Manchester mill, the throstle-spinning department was staffed by 18 older operatives and 8 young doffers.[43] The indications are, then, that different practices existed in the organization of work in throstle-spinning in the early 1830s, and the real extent of child labour in this process is therefore difficult to estimate.

Andrew Ure also indicated that a small number of children were still employed in the cardrooms as spreaders, card-tenters, and back-tenters at the roving frames. The same observation was made by Sub-commissioner

38 See Lee, C H (1972): A Cotton Enterprise 1795-1840. A History of M'Connel and Kennedy, fine Cotton Spinners, p. 173; Ure, A (1836): The Cotton Manufacture of Great Britain, Vol II, p. 449.
39 Ure (1836), Vol II, p. 131.
40 PP 1833 XX, First Report of...Commissioners, evidence of J. Bell Clarke, p. D2 18.
41 PP 1834 XLIII, Reports of the Inspectors of Factories (RIF), p. 56.
42 PP 1832 XV, Report from the Committee on the Bill to Regulate the Labour of Children in the Mills and Factories of the United Kingdom, evidence of William Smith, p. 237.
43 PP 1833 XX, First Report of...Commissioners, p. D1 34.

Cowell in 1833.[44] Indeed, there is some scattered evidence which suggests that factory children were not altogether to be found in the mule-gates. An analysis of the young workers at Swainson, Birley & Co's mill at Fishwick, Preston, by the newly appointed Factory Inspector Rickards in 1834 shows that the children below 13 were evenly spread between the carding, mule-spinning and throstle-spinning processes.[45] Approximately the same result is reached by a close examination of the workforce at Quarry Bank Mill, Styal, north Cheshire, in 1846. Factory records show that children below 13 constituted 8 per cent of the workforce in both carding, self-actor mule-spinning, and throstle-spinning.[46]

However, in spite of these examples there was probably a predominant trend in the 1820s and 1830s towards the concentration of factory children to the mule-spinning process. The retention of children in the carding process may well have been the result of the latest machinery having not yet been introduced. The Manchester evidence cited above should be given some extra weight in the knowledge that this city tended to be in the vanguard of technological change. It is also clear that mule-spinning increasingly dominated the cotton trade at the expense of the throstle. Recent estimates indicate that mule spindles constituted only 8 per cent of the total spindleage in 1788, but in the period between 1811 and 1841 this proportion lay consistently around 90 per cent.[47] The position of the throstle was possibly weakened even more during the subsequent decades.[48] Taken together, these considerations motivate a closer look at the changes in the mule-spinning process during this early period, and an examination of the relations of production in this sector of the trade.

## Mule-spinning in Lancashire, ca. 1790-1835

According to Andrew Ure, children performed several different tasks in the mule-spinning process. The organization of work was built around one adult spinner, who was assisted by:

---

44 Ure (1836), Vol II, p. 449; PP 1834 XX, Factories Inquiry Commission. Supplementary Report Part I, pp. 119i-119k.
45 PP 1834 XLIII, RIF, p. 56.
46 Greg Collection. A combination of C5/8/28 Statement of number of hands at Quarry Bank Mill and C5/1/15/2-3 Wage Books.
47 See von Tunzelmann, G N (1978): Steam Power and British Industrialization to 1860; Farnie, D A (1979): The English Cotton Industry and the World Market 1815-1896, p. 180; The Barefoot Aristocrats. A History of the Amalgamated Association of Operative Cotton Spinners (1987), Appendix VIII.
48 See Chapman, S J (1904): The Lancashire Cotton Industry, pp. 70-71.

...one or more "piecers" to join the threads which break during the spinning, and to remove the cops, when formed, from the spindles; a "creel filler" to place the "rovings" from which the yarn is to be spun...and a cleaner or "scavenger" to remove the waste cotton...and to clean the machine generally. [49]

The mule-spinner, most often a man between 20 and 40 years of age, worked two mules placed opposite each other. His work consisted in walking between the two machines, pushing the head-stock with manual power while at the same time guiding the winding motion in order to form good cops of yarn. This work required both skill and physical strength. Especially the latter requirement grew in importance during this early period. The main technological change between 1790 and 1830 was that the mules were built ever longer and made to carry an increasing number of spindles. While most mules immediately after 1800 carried less than 300 spindles, the Manchester manufacturers introduced machines carrying 400-500 spindles during the 1820s, and even up to 600 in the early 1830s.[50]

As a consequence, the number of young piecers and scavengers per spinner increased considerably. While in 1790 a mule-spinner was normally assisted by one piecer, by 1830 this number had probably more than trebled.[51] As Andrew Ure commented in 1836, "factories which have mules containing most spindles employ the largest proportion of juvenile piecers and scavengers".[52] G. A. Murray, a large Manchester manufacturer, testified in 1833 that recent improvements in mule technology had increased the number of young piecers per spinner.[53]

Naturally, this means that there were great variations in the ratio between spinners and piecers. Some Glasgow mule-spinners giving evidence in 1832 stated that one spinner normally had three piecers.[54] On the other hand, the material gathered by the 1833 factory commissioners in Manchester indicates that each mule-spinner in that city had between three and five young piecers.[55] Being the main centre of technological development in the cotton industry, it is probable that the mules were longer in Manchester than in other places. In the whole Lancashire sample of 151 mills collected by the commissioners the ratio was only 2.2 piecers per

---

49 Ure (1836), Vol II, pp. 194-95.
50 Mason, J (1987a): Cotton Spinning in the Industrial Revolution, pp. 4-5.
51 For the earlier date, see Catling, H (1970): The Spinning Mule, pp. 45-54.
52 Ure (1836), Vol II, p. 446.
53 PP 1834 XIX, Supplementary Report of...Commissioners...[on] the Employment of Children in Factories, p. D1 232.
54 PP 1832 XV, Report from the Committee..., evidence of William Smith, p. 236; Ibid., evidence of James McNish, p. 251.
55 PP 1833 XX, First Report from...Commissioners, evidence of Mary F., piecer, p. D1 33; Ibid., evidence of Jane A. B., reeler, p. D1 36; Ibid., evidence of Jane H., jack-frame tenter, p. D1 39.

mule-spinner, which indicates that there was still a substantial number of rather short mules in the district.[56]

However, for the present purpose it is enough to conclude that there had been a substantial rise in child labour levels in the mule-spinning process between 1790 and 1833. The development of longer mules had been accompanied by an increase in the number of young piecers to each adult spinner.

This development was not altogether straightforward. The male mule-spinners early became the most unionized section of the cotton factory workforce, and many manufacturers were keen to find solutions which would end their reliance on this group of skilled operatives. One such solution was the employment of female mule-spinners on smaller machines. Accordingly, striking spinners in Salford in 1807 were replaced with female operatives.[57]

The male workers tried to counteract this by mobbing the female mule-spinners, striking the mills where they were employed, and by refusing them entry to their trade unions. But in the end, it is probable that the development of longer mules was a more forceful barrier to the employment of female spinners.[58] Women were disadvantaged on these machines, which required considerable physical strength. At the same time, the greater productivity of the longer mules also made the work of female spinners on short machines less economically viable. As I will discuss in more detail in a later chapter, the manufacturers instead tried to displace the male mule-spinners by making the machine "self-acting", or driven entirely by power. But in the present context, it is enough to conclude that the male Lancashire mule-spinners managed to keep their trade under control in the late 1820s.

However, industrial relations remained far from peaceful. Before the Combination Acts were repealed in 1824, active trade unionists risked being prosecuted on charges of conspiracy. In the Stockport strike of 1818, the manufacturers took this opportunity to have some leading strikers imprisoned.[59] Nevertheless, the mule-spinners built up local unions in most important Lancashire cotton centres, with their strongest organizations in Manchester and Bolton. Their main aim was to establish equal piece-rates for spinning in the whole district, which would restrain some manufacturers from undercutting others by paying on a lower scale. Mills who paid too low were struck, and the operatives supported by those still at work in other

56 The commissioners reported in total 3,797 mule-spinners, 7,157 piecers, and 1,247 scavengers. See PP 1834 XX, Factories Inquiry Commission, p. 125.
57 Mason, J (1987b): Mule Spinner Societies and the Early Federations, p. 17.
58 See PP 1834 XX, Factories Inquiry Commission. Supplementary Report Part I, p. 119aa; Lazonick, W (1979): Industrial Relations and Technical Change: The Case of the Self-acting Mule, pp. 234-35; Freifeld (1986), pp. 333-36.
59 Glen, R (1984): Urban Workers in the Early Industrial Revolution, p. 75; Mason (1987b), pp. 21-22.

areas. This method of "rolling strikes" was the main strategy of the Lancashire mule-spinners.

Even if they were relatively successful, it has to be said that their union strength has sometimes been wildly exaggerated. Isaac Cohen has recently claimed that in the Lancashire cotton towns, the mule-spinners were close to 100 per cent organized during the 1820s and 1830s.[60] This is clearly an overstatement. Even at the high point of union power in 1829, when the perceived threat from female spinners had been much reduced, a delegate of the Bolton spinners complained at a conference that less than 500 of the 700-800 mule-spinners in that town were members of the local union.[61] Another participant at the meeting claimed that the manufacturers outside the large towns, like in "that degraded hole in England, Hyde", more or less disregarded the unions.[62]

After the defeat in the strikes of 1829 and 1831, the reconstructed union in Manchester only contained a third of the local mule-spinners by 1834.[63] Similarly, the Preston union contained considerably less than half of the local spinners when an attempt was made in 1836 to raise their piece-rates to the Bolton level. The Preston manufacturers refused to accept the union, hired strike-breakers, and the mule-spinners were eventually defeated.[64] Manchester, and to some extent Bolton, remained the strong centres of spinners' unionism during this period. Nevertheless, the manufacturers managed to impose wage cuts after strikes in both 1829 and 1831. While the mule-spinners no doubt constituted the most unionized part of the cotton factory workforce, their strength should not be exaggerated.

It is also necessary to make some connections between the spinners' union strategies and the organization of work. The construction of longer mules and the increase in the number of piecers per spinner could potentially have created a situation where a far greater number of operatives aquired the skills needed in mule-spinning than could actually find jobs in this position. The mule-spinners perceived that one of the most potent threats to their organizations and their current wage levels was if the trade were to be "swamped" by a multitude of piecers who had learned the tricks of mule-spinning, and who could be used by the manufacturers to replace the older segment of spinners. Their main strategy to forestall this development was to impose restrictions on the piecers by not allowing them

---

60 Cohen (1985a), p. 71.

61 A Report of a Delegate Meeting of the Operative Spinners of England, Ireland and Scotland, Assembled at Ramsey, Isle of Man (1829), p. 37.

62 Ibid., p. 31.

63 Mason (1987b), p. 32.

64 See Ashworth, H (1838): An Inquiry into the Origin, Progress, and Result of the Strike of the Operative Cotton Spinners of Preston, from October, 1836, to February, 1837..., passim; Lowe, J (1860): An Account of the Strike in the Cotton Trade at Preston in 1853, p. 209.

to perform the actual spinning operations. John Doherty, secretary of the Manchester mule-spinners, complained in 1829 that "the baneful practice... of allowing piecers to spin" had resulted in a situation where there were two skilled spinners to every job. Doherty demanded that the mule-spinners' unions should not allow any piecer to learn to spin who was not a son or a brother of a mule-spinner.[65]

The mule-spinners obviously feared that a surplus of skilled operatives would make it much easier for the manufacturers to reduce wage levels. A Bolton delegate to the 1829 meeting complained that the mill-owners in that town had formed a practice to set young piecers to spin at a much lower rate than that of the adult men.[66] This was a development which could not be accepted.

In this context, it has to be considered that the adult mule-spinner generally subcontracted his young piecers and scavengers. Within the sphere of the mule-gate, the spinner had a very high degree of authority in the workplace. He was paid on a piece-rate scale, and in turn paid set time wages to his young assistants. As a part of the subcontracting relationship, the mule-spinner recruited, trained, and fired his own piecers and scavengers. While this arrangement was undoubtably to some extent caused by union strength and strategy, it also had certain advantages for the mill-owners. The manufacturers were relieved from the trouble of finding, training, and disciplining this very substantial number of young workers.[67]

However, for the present discussion the important thing is that the sub-contracting relationship allowed the mule-spinners to regulate the employment of piecers according to their union interest. As I have stated above, the spinners had to employ a considerable number of young assistants, but on the other hand they wanted to restrict the recruitment of new spinners to their own sons or relatives. The solution was to employ children from other working-class families as piecers, but only for a very limited period of time. After a couple of years, they were dismissed and replaced by a younger child. In this way, recruitment to the profession could be kept under control.

This meant that the piecer group was really divided into two distinct parts; the sons of the spinners who were expected to stay on and in time take over a couple of "wheels" of their own, and the children from other working-class backgrounds who were simply used as "free" wage labour for a limited period. According to Shuttleworth's investigation of 19 fine-

---

65 A Report of A Delegate Meeting...(1829), pp. 17, 36. Doherty's motion was passed by the meeting, but a delegate from Oldham stated that his union was not happy about it since it was a custom that an older piecer took charge of the mules while the spinner was taking his meal-breaks. Ibid., pp. 39-40.
66 Ibid., p. 18.
67 See Anderson, M (1976): Sociological history and the working class family: Smelser revisited, p. 320.

spinning mills in Manchester in 1843, only 15 per cent of the young piecers were related to the adult mule-spinners.[68]

The recruitment structure in mule-spinning can therefore be seen as a combination of family employment and free wage labour; a combination which was devised to meet certain trade union objectives. Naturally, this was not the only reason for the mule-spinner when hiring his piecers. Since the adult spinners actually paid the wages of their assistants, they also had a certain interest in reducing their expenses by hiring relatively young piecers. Moreover, since their union power clearly fluctuated within the Lancashire district, it is not clear to what extent the spinners were actually allowed to carry out their recruitment strategies. Very much depended on the power resources in the local relations of production. But in the context of the present investigation, one important conclusion must be that the composition of the workforce in mule-spinning was influenced by union strategies and goals. The desire to use only rather young piecers, apart from those allowed to learn the trade, must have been an important force behind the very general use of child labour in mule-spinning in the 1820s and 1830s.

The subcontracting relationship also formed a link between work and family, in the sense that the spinner was free to employ his own children. This was held to be an important right, since it saved him the expenses and troubles involved in finding other children to perform the piecing and scavenging. It was also a way to provide his sons, if not his daughters, with an entrance to a skilled trade. The right to hire their own children therefore remained an important objective for the Lancashire mule-spinners during the decades to come. But as I have shown previously, only a minority of the piecers were a part of this family recruitment structure. The whole system rested very much on the employment of children from other segments of the working class, often from families of casual labourers or handloom weavers. For these families, the wages of their children were an important contribution, even if they did not amount to more than a couple of shillings a week. Generally, the wages of the children were paid to their parents. This is the picture rendered by a Manchester observer in 1833:

> It is almost universally the case, that the children are placed as piecers by their parents, and the custom in Manchester is, that on a Saturday morning the mothers, or some other member of the family, bring their children's breakfast to the mills, at which the children are employed, and receive the wages due to their children from the spinner; and at the close of the Saturday, when the machinery is cleaned, the spinners gives his piecers 2d. each, which is called "the child's twopence", and is all the child really receives for itself." [69]

---

68 Shuttleworth, J (1843): On the Vital Statistics of the Spinners and Piecers Employed in the fine Cotton-Mills of Manchester, p. 93.
69 PP 1833 XX, Report of...Commissioners, evidence of John Redman, Manchester, p. D1 42.

These findings perhaps also throw some new light on the discussion on family employment in the Lancashire cotton industry. Neil Smelser has argued that the adult operatives employed their own children as assistants, and that the trade was dominated by family employment up to the 1830s.[70] However, this is most probably an exaggeration. Edwards and Lloyd-Jones have argued that Smelser has overstated the prevalence of family employment structures in the early water-powered mills.[71] Also, Michael Anderson has shown that a clear minority of the young workers in Lancashire mule-spinning were part of a family employment structure.[72]

The important thing is perhaps not the supposed decline in family employment practices, but rather the recognition that in the form of subcontracting in the mule-spinning process, a link between family and work remained in the Lancashire cotton industry for the rest of the century. Instead of family employment proper, the emerging structure was a combination of "free" wage labour and subcontracting practices.

In conclusion, the level of child labour in Lancashire mule-spinning was the result of several complex processes. The development of longer mules, spinners' strategies to limit recruitment to the trade, and their use of the subcontracting relationship to attain this objective, were very important processes in this respect. It should also be emphasized that subcontracting formed a link between the spheres of family and work, and that the spinner was dependent on the recruitment of children from other segments of the working class, not just his own family. Child labour should therefore be seen in the context of both work and family.


## Mule-spinning and Industrial Relations in Scotland, 1800-1837

Developments in the Scottish district differed in several respects from those in Lancashire. I have previously indicated that child labour levels were higher in Glasgow than in Manchester. If the perspective is changed from age to gender, the same kind of pattern appears. Girls and women were used in the Scottish cotton industry to a greater extent than in Lancashire.

---

70 Smelser (1959), p. 189. This opinion has been adopted by many historians. See, for instance, Mathias, P (1980): The First Industrial Nation. An Economic History of Britain 1700-1914, p. 203; Cruickshank (1981), p. 47.

71 Edwards, M M and Lloyd-Jones, R (1973): N. J. Smelser and the Cotton Factory Family: A Reassessment, pp. 309-10.

72 See Anderson, M (1976), passim.

Table 4.    Workforce composition according to gender and age in the Lancashire
and Scottish cotton industries, 1833. per cent.

| Location | 8-13 | | Age 14-17 | | 18- | | N |
|----------|------|------|------|------|------|------|------|
|          | M    | F    | M    | F    | M    | F    |   |
| Manchester * | 13.6 | 9.2  | 9.1  | 10.8 | 25.5 | 31.9 | 17,235 |
| Lancashire   | 12.1 | 10.9 | 11.0 | 12.5 | 26.4 | 27.1 | 7,610 |
| Scotland     | 9.9  | 12.0 | 8.3  | 16.1 | 20.7 | 33.0 | 12,188 |

* Sample of 43 mills.

Sources: PP 1833 XX, First Report of...Commissioners, p. D2 107; PP 1834 XX, Factories Inquiry
Commission, Supplementary Report Part I, pp. 21-22.

Women and girls constituted 61 per cent of the workforce in the Scottish
cotton industry, as compared to approximately 50 per cent in Lancashire.
But these figures really obscure the fact that the Scottish district was
actually composed of two very different areas, namely the mills in Glasgow
and those in the surrounding countryside. Outside the city of Glasgow, the
cotton factories seem to have been strongly dominated by female labour. In
the large country mills of Ballindalloch, Catrine, Deanston and New
Lanark, most of the spinning was performed by women on throstles and
short mules.[73] This was also the case with the mills in the vicinity of Paisley.[74]

The preference for female labour seems to have been part of a managerial strategy to compete with the Lancashire industry by paying wages on a
lower scale. This was probably the one field where the Scottish manufac-
tureres felt they had a clear advantage over their competitors south of the
Border. In other respects, they suffered the disadvantage of lagging behind
the Manchester industry in terms of technology. The machinery in Scottish
mills was generally several years behind the standard set by Lancashire.[75]

From the very beginning, the Scottish cotton manufacturers relied on the
relatively cheap labour of dislocated Highlanders and immigrant Irish.[76] The
main managerial strategy in the country mills after 1800 was to employ

73 The New Statistical Account of Scotland, Vol VI, p. 143; PP 1833 XX, First Report of...Commissioners,
evidence of James Smith, manager of Deanston works, p. A1 66; Ibid., evidence of John Alexander, manager
of New Lanark, p. A1 96; Ibid., evidence of Andrew Gordon, warehouse man, Glasgow, pp. A1 93-94.
74 PP 1833 XX, Report of...Commissioners, evidence of Arthur Craig, managing partner of Broadley cotton
mill, near Paisley, p. A1 115; Ibid., evidence of Adam Calderwood of James Dunlop & Sons, near Paisley,
A1 116.
75 See, for instance, PP 1824 V, Artizans and Machinery, evidence of Henry Houldsworth, Glasgow cotton
manufacturer, p. 378; PP 1833 VI, Report from the Select Committee on Manufactures, Commerce and
Shipping, evidence of Henry Houldsworth, Glasgow, p. 310.
76 PP 1833 VI, Report from the Select Committee on Manufactures..., evidence of Henry Houldsworth,
Glasgow mill-owner, pp. 311-14; Butt (1987): Labour and Industrial Relations in the Scottish Cotton
Industry during the Industrial Revolution, pp. 142-43.

female spinners in order to keep wage levels down and to prevent the emergence of unions. The male mule-spinners who were eventually employed in some mills were paid on a lower scale than in Glasgow, and their attempts to build up a union position were effectively countered by the manufacturers.[77]

In contrast, the Glasgow mule-spinners managed to form the strongest union in the whole trade, Lancashire included. The Glasgow union was founded around 1800, and was influenced both by artisan forms of organization and the new kind of trade unionism developed by the Manchester mule-spinners.[78] From the start their main objective was to gain control over recruitment, and to hinder the Glasgow mill-owners from employing female spinners or operatives from the country district outside the city. The manufacturers tried to break the union by a lockout in 1810, but only managed to force the mule-spinners' organization underground. In the same way as in Lancashire, the Glasgow mule-spinners preferred to strike one mill at a time, a method which made it possible for the members in work to support those who were out.

In 1818 a factory belonging to James Dunlop & Co was struck over the introduction of female spinners. The firm had decided to use women operatives on short mules in a newly built mill. According to the testimony of the manufacturer, the women were mobbed on their way to and from work, and some of them were also "dreadfully beaten". Dunlop stated that he had introduced the female spinners specifically to counteract the union, and that in a country factory in his posession, women operatives were more generally employed. As an outcome of the disturbances in 1818, Dunlop had to give up the attempt to use female spinners in the Glasgow mill.[79] When another Glasgow manufacturer tried to employ female spinners at a lower rate in 1833, the actions of the union, and the mobbing of the young women in question, forced the employer to pay the female spinners according to the same piece-rate as that of the men.[80] The union obviously reckoned that this would make the use of female labour unprofitable.

In spite of concerted employer lockouts in 1823, 1824, and 1825, the Glasgow spinners remained firmly in control well into the 1830s. But this was only achieved by sealing off the city's industry from that of the surrounding countryside. It is well established that mule-spinners from the

77 A Report of a Delegate Meeting..(1829), pp. 28-29; Butt (1987), pp. 144, 148-49.
78 Butt (1987), p. 150.
79 PP 1824 V, Artizans and Machinery, evidence of James Dunlop, cotton manufacturer, pp. 551-52.
80 PP 1833 XX, First Report of...Commissioners, evidence of David Sloan, manager of J Dennistoun & Co, Glasgow, pp. A1 84-85; Ibid., evidence of George Milne, Glasgow mule-spinner, p. A1 85; Ibid., evidence of Agnes Robertson, Glasgow mule-spinner, p. A1 86; Brassay, Z G (1974): The Cotton Spinners in Glasgow and the West of Scotland c. 1790-1840: A Study in Early Industrial Relations, pp. 144-45.

country districts were not allowed to seek employment in Glasgow.[81] The higher piece-rates and the degree of workplace control which existed in Glasgow could really only be maintained by a very firm grip over recruitment. At the same time, Glasgow was surrounded by a manufacturing district where female spinners were very common, and where both unionization and wage levels were relatively low. This sharp contrast between city and country also explains why industrial relations in Glasgow were so hostile during the whole period. The manufacturers obviously wanted to break the union's grip over recruitment, lower the piece-rates to the level of the surrounding area, and have the option to employ female spinners. For the mule-spinners it was a matter of having full control or none at all.

As a part of their control over recruitment, the Glasgow mule-spinners used a slightly different strategy than the one employed in Lancashire. Their main objective was naturally to limit as much as possible the number of piecers who were allowed to become spinners in order to ensure that there was no great surplus of skilled mule-spinners. At the 1829 delegate meeting of mule-spinners, a Glasgow spinner claimed that piecers in his city were not allowed to spin on any account. This was regarded as a "most ruinous practice".[82] Only sons and brothers were allowed to enter the trade, and they were also the only boys who were permitted to work as piecers. Probably as a special safeguard, the Glasgow mule-spinners very generally employed young girls in this position.[83] One operative spinner testified in 1832 that two-thirds of the piecers in the Glasgow mills were girls.[84] But in the same way as in Lancashire, it is very probable that the Glasgow mule-spinners also kept the ages of their piecers down in order to avoid their picking up the skills of the trade.

However, the firm control of the Glasgow union really rested on very precarious foundations. In the early 1830s, the manufacturers were becoming increasingly restless to break the spinners' position of power. In Lancashire the mill-owners had managed to reduce the piece-rates on the longer mules after major strikes in 1829 and 1831, but in Glasgow the mule-spinners refused to allow any cuts in the local rate. As profit margins melted away, industrial relations in Glasgow became increasingly strained. This is essentially the background to the strike of 1837, which proved to be a watershed in the industrial relations of the Glasgow cotton trade. The

---

81 A Report of a Delegate Meeting...(1829), pp. 27-28. John Doherty regretted the "exclusive sort of spirit" among the Glasgow spinners. Ibid., p. 29. See also PP 1837-38 VIII, First Report from the Select Committee on Combinations of Workmen, evidence of Henry Houldsworth, Glasgow mill-owner, p. 2 Q. 22-27.
82 A Report of a Delegate Meeting...(1829), p. 17.
83 Fraser, W H (1976): The Glasgow Cotton Spinners, 1837 p. 32.
84 PP 1832 XV, Report from the Committee..., evidence of William Smith, Glasgow mule-spinner, p. 236.

mule-spinners were finally defeated, and were never again able to assume their former position. That strike has been extensively studied by other historians, and I will not go into any details here.[85] I will only say that the outcome of the strike was that Glasgow was more or less put on a par with the conditions in the country districts. Attempts to re-establish the union were counteracted, and female operatives were introduced wherever it was deemed possible. In terms of managerial policy, the Scottish industry turned more or less completely towards the utilisation of low-paid female labour. However, as I will show in later chapters, the hiring of children below 13 years of age was largely abandoned in connection with the implementation of the 1833 Factory Act.

# Conclusions

In this introductory chapter I have outlined the existence of several different processes which were relevant for the changes in child labour levels, some of which worked in opposite directions. In the British country mills there was a general shift from apprentice labour to family employment and "free" wage labour, most often coupled with the creation of factory villages. As a result of these changes, the proportion of children in the workforce was reduced considerably. On the other hand, cotton factories located in the towns and cities relied to a great extent on the recruitment of the children of the urban poor. By 1816 child labour levels were higher in the town factories than in the country, in spite of the fact that the town mills generally used more modern technology. One key point in this process was the richer supply of young workers available to the urban manufacturers. These labour market conditions left room for managerial strategies to utilise relatively young and cheap labour, a policy which seems to have been very pronounced in the Preston industry.

In contrast, the American cotton industry in northern Massachusetts and New Hampshire was to a very large extent operated by young females, while the level of child labour remained very low. There clearly existed several possible managerial strategies when creating the early cotton workforce. Similarly, female operatives were also more common in the Scottish industry than in Lancashire.

There were also important changes in the labour process during this period. The full mechanization of the preparatory processes, and improvements in the carding machinery, are important explanations for the decline

---

85 See Brassay (1974); Fraser (1976); Butt (1987).

in the use of children. Apart from changes in technology, there was also a shift in production methods away from a low-intensive, low-paying structure involving the labour of children, and towards a high-intensive, high-paying method involving a larger degree of adult operatives.

However, it is evident that child labour increased considerably in the mule-spinning process between 1790 and 1833. The construction of longer mules, and the unwillingness of the adult spinners to hire older piecers, were processes which both tended in this direction. The subcontracting relationship in mule-spinning provided the operatives with a possibility to keep down the ages of piecers hired from other families, while at the same time it provided a link between work and family for the mule-spinner himself. Child labour practices were therefore connected both with the local relations of production, and with the family wage strategies of working-class parents.

Chapter 3

# Correcting Great Moral Evils: Child Labour and the British Factory Inspection, 1834-1914

In the context of the present study, it is necessary to evaluate the impact of the early British factory legislation on child labour practices. However, it is not sufficient to merely note the emergence and structure of such legislation. The efficiency of inspection, and the level of true enforcement of the legal provisions, must be assessed. It is also important to see the societal and political context in which the early British Factory Acts were established.

## The Making of the British Factory Legislation

The question of child labour in textile factories was a recurrent issue in British politics during the early decades of the 19th century. Partly as a reaction against the social consequences of industrialisation, some land-owners, clergy, and middle-class professionals actively worked to achieve some legislation which would abolish or at least regulate the use of children in factories.[1] Demands for legislation were often accompanied by claims that factory child labour was on the increase. However, as I have shown in the previous chapter, child labour levels in textile factories had in fact declined gradually since the late 18th century. Early factory legislation can therefore hardly be seen as the response to a growing social problem, or as a "logical" development of early industrial capitalism, but rather as a result of the concerted efforts of several political actors.

However, the first attempts to legislate on factory child labour were not successful. Initiatives by, among others, Robert Owen, Sir Robert Peel, and

---

1 Pinchbeck and Hewitt have argued that it was mainly the concentration of children in the textile factories which aroused the sentiments of the reformers, not that children were in any sense better treated in agriculture or in small workshops. However, I believe they have underestimated the new and threatening quality of the social relations in the factory setting as perceived by the "outside" critics. See Pinchbeck and Hewitt (1972-73), pp. 390-413, but esp. p. 403.

John Cam Hobhouse did result in legal enactments in 1819, 1825, 1829, and 1831, but these laws were generally disregarded.[2] Initiatives by the Manchester mule-spinners' union and by individual mill-owners to prosecute offending manufacturers were in most instances unsuccessful, and these attempts soon ceased.[3] In the terminology of W. G. Carson, factory offences constituted a "conventionalized" crime during this period.[4] Mill-owners did not regard the factory laws as binding, and overstepped the prescribed time limits as a part of everyday activity. There was no effective stigmatisation of offenders.

The obvious inefficiency of the early factory legislation was one reason behind the substantial increase in popular support in the textile districts in the late 1820s for more forceful measures, above all the legal enactment of the Ten Hour Day. The history of the Factory Movement is well known, and I will not go into any details here.[5] Still, it has to be said that the established historians of the Factory Movement have probably overstated the importance of upper-class figureheads like Lord Ashley and Richard Oastler at the expense of the popular following among the textile workers.[6] The mule-spinners' unions constituted the hard core of the local Short Time Committees which emerged during this period of agitation. The aim of the spinners was clearly not merely to limit the working day of the young operatives but to obtain a Ten Hour Day for all, well knowing that the factory workforce was not easily separated.[7]

Popular pressure and discontent with existing provisions were absolute social prerequisites for the enactment of more adequate factory laws. One part of the strategy of the reformers was to achieve an effective criminalization of the offending mill-owners. Richard Oastler maintained in 1832 that the law would only be effective if convictions resulted in imprisonment, flogging, and pillory.[8] He also designated the manufacturers

2 See MacDonagh, O (1977): Early Victorian Government 1830-1870, pp. 22-32; Ward J T (1971): Owen as Factory Reformer, passim.

3 PP 1833 XX, First Report of Commissioners..., evidence of Henry McConnel, a Manchester manufacturer, p. E8; Ibid., evidence of Thomas Worsley, a Stockport shopkeeper, p. D1 4. See also Kirby, R G and Musson, A E (1975): The Voice of the People. John Doherty, 1798-1854. Trade Unionist, Radical and Factory Reformer, pp. 357-64.

4 See Carson, W G (1970): White Collar Crime and the Enforcement of Factory Legislation, passim; Carson W G (1979): The Conventionalization of Early Factory Crime, passim.

5 See Ward, J T (1962a): The Factory Movement 1830-1855; Ward J T (1962b): The Factory Reform Movement in Scotland; Driver, C (1949): Tory Radical. The Life of Richard Oastler.

6 See Kirby and Musson (1975), pp. 347-50. For a recent criticism of the conception of Lord Ashley as the saviour of the factory children, see Cunningham (1987), passim.

7 See Chapman, S J (1904): The Lancashire Cotton Industry, p. 98.

8 PP 1832 XV, Report from the Committee..., evidence of Oastler, p. 460.

who disregarded the factory legislation as lawbreakers who were "as honourable as thieves".[9]

As Robert Gray has recently shown, the battle over factory reform was fought in languages belonging to many different discourses.[10] Since the reform movement comprised landed gentlemen and clergy as well as operatives, it is not surprising that the official discourse contained notions of "moral economy" and the mutuality between master and man as well as more radical assertions of factory workers' right to independence and respect. In one sense it is perhaps not strange that these very disparate social forces could unite in the defence of the hapless factory children. As one factory inspector claimed in a pamphlet a few years later, the protection of children should be recognized even by the "most cold and severe principles of political economy".[11]

However, one unifying tendency which ran through all the discourses of reform was the expression of patriarchy. The emphasis on the protection of children shifted gradually towards demands for the regulation of women's work, coupled with efforts to define the women's sphere as the home rather than the workplace.[12] The reformers alleged that the long working hours made the women operatives useless in domestic matters, being unable to cook, sew, or to fulfil basic familial duties. Such was the view of James Turner, a cotton yarn dresser, in 1832:

> ...when [the factory girls] come to get married, they are quite ignorant of the domestic duties they have to discharge, so much that many of them don't know how to repair their own linen, or cook their own victuals; and this renders the condition of the working classes in the manufacturing districts the most miserable of any we have to deal with, the ignorance of our females. [13]

There were also sexual allusions that the heat of the spinning-mills caused "scantily dressed" males and females to work in close proximity. Factory work was described as an inroad to vice and prostitution. One Glasgow mule-spinner giving evidence in 1833 claimed that several former girl piecers in his workroom were now prostitutes in the city.[14] It is clear that exclusion strategies on the part of the male operatives were combined with the domestic ideology embraced by the middle and upper-class adherents of

---

9 Infant Slavery. Report of a Speech delivered in favour of the Ten Hours' Bill by Richard Oastler, Esq, at a numerous meeting held at Preston, on the 22nd of March, 1833..., p. 6.

10 Gray, R (1987): The languages of factory reform in Britain, c. 1830-1860, pp. 145-79.

11 Horner, L (1840): On the Employment of Children, in Factories and other Works in the United Kingdom and in some Foreign Countries, p. 15.

12 Gray, R (1987), pp. 150-52; Valverde (1988), pp. 625-30.

13 PP 1832 XV, Report from the Committee..., evidence of James Turner, p. 308.

14 PP 1833 XX, First Report of...Commissioners.. [on] the Employment of Children in Factories, evidence of James McNish, a Glasgow mule-spinner, p. A1 77.

the factory movement. One gentry observer claimed that factory work induced young women to live "unchaste", frequent the galleries of theatres, and indulge in drink.[15] Lord Ashley, the prime Parliamentary spokesman of the reform movement, saw the "domestic system" as "one of the first ordinances of God", which had to be revived by factory legislation.[16] These upper-class sentiments on family and society constituted a considerable political force behind the regulation of work of adult women in the 1842 Mines Act and the 1844 Factory Act.

It was also a position which was readily embraced by the mule-spinners' unions, already under the threat of the newly constructed self-acting mule. The notion of a male breadwinner supporting his wife and children remained an important ideological theme within the British working class for more than a century. This aim very often led the male operatives to formulate demands for the exclusion of women workers in a language clearly adapted to upper-class sentiments.

Patriarchy, I would argue, was not only a common theme within the reform coalition. It was probably a unifying factor which made the movement cohesive and, eventually, successful. Naturally, there were also certain areas in common in the discourses on the plight of the factory children. The image of the suffering factory child cut across social divides and provided important support for factory reform among middle-class professionals, clergy, and landowning gentry.

Naturally, it is very difficult to get a clear impression of how factory children were actually treated. The reformers claimed that instances of brutality, of overlookers beating and maltreating small children, were frequent occurrences. Not surprisingly, the manufacturers generally denied these charges. Edward Baines, a contemporary historian of the cotton trade connected to the manufacturing interest, admitted that instances of cruelty had occurred in some factories, but these were exceptions rather than the rule.[17] Indeed, it is probable that changes in production, recruitment, and supervision practices had made physical assaults on child workers less common. The transition from a factory system built on parish apprentices and hired children supervised by a few overlookers to the urban setting where the younger workers were all "free" wage earners probably tended to make beatings both less frequent and less severe. The concentration of child workers to the mule-spinning process where they were constantly under the eye of an adult spinner probably worked in the same direction. This lends some credibility to the conclusion of the 1833 Factory

15 Sir Charles Shaw (1843): Replies of Sir Charles Shaw to Lord Ashley, M.P. Regarding the Education and Moral and Physical Condition of the Labouring Classes, p. 28. See also Humphries, J (1981), pp. 23-25.
16 Glasgow Sentinel 25/10/51, report from a public meeting with Lord Ashley in Manchester.
17 Baines, E (1835): History of the Cotton Manufacture in Great Britain, pp. 453-54.

Commissioners that the maltreatment of children had lessened compared with previous times.[18]

Nevertheless, the beating and overworking of small children in textile factories was an important part of the public discourse of the reform movement. Early in 1832, an alliance between Tories and Radicals secured the appointment of a select committee on the question of child labour in factories, and also made sure that the committee was dominated by reformers. Starting the proceedings by taking evidence from witnesses in favour of legislation, the committee presented a sequence of enfeebled, stunted, and deformed operatives, whose injuries were allegedly caused by overwork and maltreatment.[19] The intention of the reformers was to use the arousal of public opinion which this evidence occasioned to press for a legal enactment of the Ten Hour Day.

However, these matters were overshadowed by the Parliamentary reform of 1832, and the return of a Whig majority later in that year. The new government did not support the legislation of a Ten Hour Day, mainly because the regulation of work or wages of adult operatives was an absolute anathema in current political economy. On the other hand, the popular reform movement in the textile districts as well as the public opinion incensed by the revelations of the 1832 Select Committee demanded a solution of the child labour issue. Choosing to disregard the evidence of the previous committee, the government instead decided to appoint a special commission of inquiry to re-examine the question and suggest remedies.

The commissioners performed their task with great speed in spite of the resistance and partial boycott of the reformers. Demonstrations met the commissioners in the worsted district of Yorkshire, accompanied with allegations of their being "engaged in the work of Murder".[20] In Scotland, the commissioners took part in a heated argument with the Glasgow Short-Time Committee over the purpose of their appointment.[21] John Doherty, the spokesman of the Manchester mule-spinners, was clearly of the opinion that the investigators were instruments of the mill-owners.[22] The reformers suspected that the Whig government planned to introduce some superficial measure and thereby bury the question of the Ten Hour Day. But it is clear from later events that the manufacturers were not especially happy with the proposals put forward by the commissioners.

---

18 PP 1833 XX, First Report of...Commissioners, p. 24. See also ibid., evidence of Humphrey Dyson, an operative cotton twiner, p. D1 101.
19 PP 1832 XV, Report from the Committee...
20 Statement of the Leeds Short-Time Committee, cited in Ward (1962a), p. 97.
21 PP 1833 XX, First Report of...Commissioners, p. A1 69.
22 See Kirby and Musson (1975), p. 381.

In this context, the political and ideological composition of the 1833 commissioners has to be taken into account. The investigation was led and dominated by persons connected to the "philosophical radical" wing of the Whig grouping. Being much influenced by the philosopher Jeremy Bentham and his ideas on effective legislation, many of the commissioners leaned towards an early form of social engineering.[23] Edwin Chadwick, the co-ordinator of the investigation, later assumed the same pivotal role in poor law and sanitary reforms.

The concept of "inspectability" had been very important to Bentham, as is also evidenced by his construction of the panopticon.[24] The commissioners argued that due to the concentration of factory children in distinct buildings, and their work being regulated by "military discipline", inspection was indeed possible.[25] They also suggested a bureaucratic solution to the problem of factory law enforcement, where the reformers had merely striven to strengthen the criminalization process by making the penalties more severe. The commissioners proposed the appointment of special factory inspectors, salaried by the Home Office and invested with powers to fine and to prosecute offenders:

> The necessity of the appointment of Inspectors has been most urgently stated by those manufacturers who have had chiefly in view the restriction of the hours of labour in other factories to the level of their own. The greatest necessity of the appointment of some special agency for the enforcement of the measures we have recommended must be admitted, when it is recollected that they relate solely to the children, and are not directly conducive to the immediate interests either of the master manufacturers, or of the operatives, or of any powerful class, and are not therefore likely to receive continuous voluntary support. [26]

The commissioners concluded that it was consistent with the principles of political economy for the state to interfere on the behalf of children, since these could not be regarded as free agents capable of securing their own interests. Exploited by manufacturers, older operatives, and even their own parents, the only likely guardian of the factory children was the state. Legislation was required since the very long hours worked by children led to "permanent deterioration of the physical constitution" or various kinds of disease, and also because it excluded the children from the possibility of obtaining elementary and moral education.[27] The legal working day for

---

23 See Henriques, U R Q (1974): Jeremy Bentham and the Machinery of Social Reform, passim; Finer, S E (1952): The Life and Times of Sir Edwin Chadwick, pp. 51-52.
24 Henriques (1974), p. 182.
25 PP 1833 XX, First Report of...Commissioners, p. 51.
26 Ibid., p. 68.
27 Ibid., p. 52. Even Edward Baines admitted that state intervention to check the overworking of children was justified, but argued that the work was very light. See Baines (1835), pp. 455-56.

children below 13 years of age in the textile trades should therefore be limited to eight hours, and the minimum age set to 9. The commissioners further suggested that the children should be used in relays, and their working day thus separated from that of the adult operatives. In this way the work of the factory children would be regulated, and their hours reduced more than had been demanded by the reformers, while at the same time the law avoided the interference with the conditions of older workers.

Against the recommendations of the commissioners, Parliament chose to include young persons below 18 in the category of protected workers in the 1833 Factory Act, setting their working day to twelve hours, and also proceeded to include adult women workers in this regulation in the 1844 Amendment. Only the work of adult men in textile factories remained unregulated.[28]

Besides the proposals on government inspectors and the above age limits, the commissioners made some further suggestions which were duly included in the 1833 Factory Act. The factory children had to produce medical certificates, issued by a surgeon, stating that they had attained the legal age to be eligible for employment. They also had to attend school for two hours per day, and certificates of school attendance were to be kept by the employer. The manufacturers were not formally held responsible for educational facilities, but since in most instances the number of schools was insufficient, they were in practice very often forced to organize factory schools for their young workers below 13.

In the absence of compulsory education, the schooling provided by the early Factory Acts was the only form of elementary education which the state could force working-class children to attend. There can be no doubt that the education clauses of the early Factory Acts met with substantial support in Parliament, and they should really be seen as one important reason why the 1833 Act was actually passed. The fear of an uneducated and inflammable factory proletariat was widely felt among the classes represented in Parliament, and a measure of Christian and moral education was seen as a vehicle of societal cohesion.[29] As a consequence, after 1833 the politics of factory and school legislation became very much intertwined. One of the recurrent arguments when factory legislation was to be extended

28 The very substantial political obstacles in Parliament on the issue of regulating the labour of adult men is illustrated by the case of the handloom weavers, who remained unprotected in spite of severe distress and several Parliamentary investigations. See Richards, P (1979): The State and Early Industrial Capitalism: The Case of the Handloom Weavers, pp. 94-114.

29 In the Swedish context, the work of Bengt Sandin on this issue has been very influential. See especially Sandin (1986), passim.

to comprise new branches of industry was that the children employed in those works would be given the benefit of education.[30]

The making of the 1833 Factory Act was a very complex process which involved popular pressure, a political alliance which centered on the protection of children and patriarchal notions on women's work, and also a final draft much influenced by benthamite social engineering. In the political process on factory legislation, the manufacturer interest was isolated and marginalized by a compound of radicals, landowners, and liberals in favour of limited state interference.[31]

In conclusion, the public and political pressure generated by the Factory Reform Movement is a major explanatory factor behind the genesis of the 1833 Factory Act. But it has to be emphasized that the reform movement was welded together by common patriarchal notions of domestic ideology and the dependency of women and children on the male breadwinner. The agrarian interest, middle-class professionals, and the male mule-spinners' unions, could all share in this discourse. But the actual solution of the problem, the framing of the legislative measures and the appointment of a special factory inspectorate to enforce them, was mainly the work of the benthamite commissioners.

This is not to say that other solutions or lines of development were wholly impossible. W. G. Carson has argued that the harsher penalties suggested by the reformers would have criminalized factory offences more effectively than the mere fines imposed by the 1833 Act.[32] It is undeniable that offending manufacturers did not risk imprisonment even after gross or repeated transgressions, and this demonstrates the essential class character of the early factory laws. Still, the 1833 Factory Act should perhaps not be judged primarily against alternatives which were politically impossible to realize, but rather in the light of the effects it actually had. Those effects will be investigated in the next two sections.

---

30 Leonard Horner, one of the first factory inspectors, argued along this line when proposing the extension of the 1833 Act to comprise industrial trades outside textiles. See Horner (1840), pp. 16-18.

31 However, it has to be pointed out that some researchers have taken an entirely different view, claiming that the manufacturers played a decisive role in the making of the 1833 Factory Act. W. G. Carson has maintained that the report of the commissioners shows the substantial influence of the manufacturers in the drafting of the proposals. See Carson, W G (1974): Symbolic and Instrumental Dimensions of Early Factory Legislation: A Case Study in the Social Origins of Criminal Law, pp. 133-35. Similarly, H. Marvel and C. Nardinelli have argued that the large Manchester cotton manufacturers were the most important social force behind the legislation. See Marvel, H (1977): Factory Regulation: A Reinterpretation of Early English Experience, passim, Nardinelli, C (1985): A Successful Prosecution of the Factory Acts: A Suggested Explanation, passim. However, their case rests very much on biassed evidence from the Factory Reform Movement, whose adherents tended to discredit the 1833 Act in order to reopen the issue of the Ten Hour Day.

32 Carson (1974), p. 138.

# The Enforcement of the Early Factory Legislation in England, 1834-1914

The question which will dominate this chapter is the actual effects or level of enforcement of the early Factory Acts. This is a problem which still causes a considerable amount of controversy among researchers. To some extent, this situation may be seen as the legacy of a historical tradition which has viewed the early British factory inspection as a great achievement. The work of Hutchins and Harrison and M. W. Thomas was concentrated on the gradual increase of governmental initiatives to ameliorate social conditions during the industrial revolution, and stressed the important roles of the factory inspectors in the enforcement of the law in spite of the resistance from mill-owners, operatives and magistrates.[33] The prime object of study was the expansion of the inspectorate and the gradual "improvement" in factory legislation, while the more difficult issue of the true level of enforcement was largely avoided. This perspective dominated historical writing up to 1970.[34]

During the last two decades, researchers have developed a variety of revisionist stances. The earlier emphasis on the emergence of various kinds of government inspectorates in Victorian Britain has been criticized by P. W. J. Bartrip, who rightly claims that it is not sufficient merely to chart the emergence of certain inspectorates; it is also necessary to evaluate the actual effects of their performance.[35] However, being intent to show that the achievements of the early inspectors have been overstated, Bartrip tends to portray all types of inspectorates as equally inefficient. This is clearly not a satisfactory approach. It has to be recognized that some forms of government inspection were more successful than others.

In general terms, the dominating tendency among researchers during recent years has been to emphasize the enforcement problems and relatively poor efficiency of the early factory legislation. This contention is evident in the work of Ursula Henriques, W. G. Carson, P. W. J. Bartrip, and P. T. Fenn.[36]

---

33 Hutchins and Harrison (1911); Thomas, M W (1948): The Early Factory Legislation.

34 See Martin, B (1969): Leonard Horner: A Portrait of an Inspector of Factories. Naturally, there were also some dissenting voices, above all in the discussion on "the Revolution in Government". Historians like Oliver MacDonagh argued that the growth of the Victorian inspectorates was more a response to changing societal conditions than an experiment in social engineering. However, the value of that perspective is rather doubtful. See MacDonagh, O (1958): The Nineteenth-Century Revolution in Government: A Reappraisal; and the subsequent criticism in Parris, H (1960): The Nineteenth-Century Revolution in Government: A Reappraisal reappraised; Hart, J (1965): Nineteenth Century Social Reform: A Tory Interpretation of History.

35 Bartrip, P W J (1982): British Government Inspection, 1832-75: Some observations, passim.

36 See Henriques, U R Q (1971a): An Early Factory Inspector: James Stuart of Dunearn; Henriques (1971b): The Early Factory Acts and their Enforcement; Henriques (1979): Before the Welfare State.

In this section I will scrutinize the achievement of this historical tradition. Re-examining the empirical evidence, I will argue that the researchers mentioned above have underestimated the real efficiency of the early Factory Acts. Moreover, they have not succeeded in developing a satisfactory theoretical framework for the estimation of true enforcement. In the following text I will concentrate mainly on the work of P. W. J. Bartrip and P. T. Fenn, who have provided the most recent and also the most theoretically innovative framework for the contention that the early British factory legislation was relatively inefficient. Ursula Henriques's contribution on the early Scottish factory inspection will be specifically dealt with in a later section of this chapter.

Space does not allow me to go into a full theoretical discussion on factory law enforcement. I will therefore only refer to those parts of Bartrip and Fenn's work which are most relevant for this study.

Bartrip and Fenn argue that there were three major reasons why the early Factory Acts were relatively poorly enforced: first, lack of manpower resources within the inspectorate; second, the low level of fines meted out by the local magistrates, and third, the complexity and shortcomings of the law itself. The relative level of prosecutions under the Factory Act is shown to have fallen after an initial hectic period in 1837-38, and this is explained by Bartrip and Fenn as a case of the inspectors having lost their appetite for prosecutions when faced with severe enforcement problems.[37]

However, Bartrip and Fenn do not take any account of the fact that the early factory legislation contained several different clauses, and that some of these were more easily enforced than others. This is quite remarkable, since they have overtly stated their opinion that "the nature of the law and the legal system conditioned enforcement practice".[38] As I will show below, it was definitely the case that enforcement possibilities varied considerably according to the type of offence which was committed. Above all, a distinction should be made between offences which could be detected at each inspection, like the absence of time-books or the insufficient fencing of machinery, and illegal practices which could only be detected when actually being performed, for instance overworking or the cleaning of machinery in motion. Strangely enough, previous research on the implementation of the early Factory Acts has not made this vital distinction.

---

Social Administration in Early Industrial Britain; Carson (1970); Carson (1974); Carson (1979); Carson (1980): Early Factory Inspectors and the Viable Class Society - A Rejoinder; Bartrip (1982); Bartrip, P W J and Fenn, P T (1980a): The Administration of Safety: The Enforcement of the Early Factory Inspectorate, 1844-1864; Bartrip and Fenn (1980b): The Conventionalization of Factory Crime - A Re-assessment; Bartrip and Fenn (1983): The Evolution of Regulatory Style in the Nineteenth Century British Factory Inspectorate.
37 See Bartrip and Fenn (1980a); Bartrip and Fenn (1980b) and Bartrip and Fenn (1983).
38 Bartrip and Fenn (1980b), p. 182.

Bartrip and Fenn also tend to have a rather primitive view of the policy making process. Their main explanation of the allegedly poor enforcement results - strained resources - does not take account of the fact that the means at the inspectors' disposal was the result of political and administrative actions. Their notion of a "community" making rational decisions as to how much resources should be apportioned to factory inspection is a simplification which cannot be accepted.[39] Many of the workers who desired improvements in factory and workshop inspection were not allowed to take part in the political process. This was especially the case with women employed in factories or working in the "sweated trades". The resources at the disposal of the inspectors must therefore be seen as created by political actors, and also in a context of gender and class.

Before turning to the empirical material, it should be recognized that the question of true enforcement raises some rather thorny methodological issues. An evaluation of the performance of the early inspectors necessarily rests on qualitative evidence in the form of inspectors' reports, the minutes of their meetings in London, and the testimony of contemporary observers.[40] But to use the inspectors' printed reports, by far the most extensive source, in an evaluation of their own enforcement practices is definitely connected with some problems. On the one hand, it is very probable that some inspectors tended to exaggerate the difficulties they encountered in order to elicit some action from the Home Office or Parliament. Leonard Horner, the best known factory inspector during the early period, clearly used his reports to propagate his views on remaining deficiences in the Acts which he believed impeded the possibility of true enforcement.[41] Consequently, inspectors' reports which concentrate on evasions of the law may have been factually correct, but it is also possible that they mainly expressed the inspectors' desire to have the regulations amended.

On the other hand, reports which stated that few transgressions of the Act had been committed are not easy to interpret either. The inspectors who wrote them may have been lenient and uncommitted, and not too much bothered about evasion practices. But it also possible that these rather blank reports really reflected a situation of relatively stringent and uncomplicated enforcement. The methodological key to this situation must be to judge the reports in connection with an appreciation of the goals and intentions of the inspector who wrote them. With this in mind, it is now

39 See Bartrip and Fenn (1980b), p. 178. For a criticism of Bartrip and Fenn on this point, see Carson (1980), p. 190.
40 See Bartrip (1985), p. 425; Peacock (1985), pp. 433, 436.
41 See Martin (1969), pp. 430-31.

time to turn from the theoretical and methodological discussion and confront the empirical material.

### Factory Inspection in Lancashire, 1834-44:
### Times of Strife and Evasions

When Robert Rickards, newly appointed Factory Inspector for the district of Lancashire and some adjoining areas of Yorkshire and Cheshire, commenced his duties in 1834, the problems which faced him seemed insuperable:

> From the commencement, to the end of my circuit, there was no variation in the language held out to me, both by masters and operatives, on the present Factory Act; the former declaring certain parts of it to be impracticable, and the latter apprehensive that it would materially affect the future earnings of themselves and [their] families. That the only way to remedy this inconvenience was to have two sets of children to attend the machinery for 12 hours, or to discharge their younger hands, and to procure others of an age that should not subject them to the annoyance of the objectionable clauses. Regarding the first of these alternatives, one and all declared [with three exceptions], that it would be quite impossible to procure a sufficient number of young hands to work by relays; or if it could be done, it must be by means of fresh emigrations from Ireland... It was also observed to me, in many of the towns through which I passed, that the country abounded with mills, situated in, or near, small villages, or on streams of water in still more obscure parts, where all the working hands procurable were just the establishment now employed in such mills, and where additional hands, whether of the younger or older age, were not to be had. [42]

One hardly gets the impression that the 1833 Factory Act was popular among the manufacturers. The "objectionable clauses" connected with child labour which Rickards mentions were probably on the requirement of educational certificates, which in many instances forced the employers to organize factory schools. Still, it has to be remembered that Parliament had decided to extend the implementation of the 1833 Act over a span of two years, thus giving the manufacturers some time to adjust to the new conditions. Only in 1836 would the regulations encompass the 12 year old workers. However, disillusioned by the seemingly small prospects of enforcement, Rickards proposed that the scope of the legislation should be restricted to the factory children of nine and ten years of age. To introduce

---

42 PP 1834 XLIII, Reports of the Inspectors of Factories (RIF), pp. 24-25.

the final stage of the Act, he declared, would be "impracticable", "unadvisable", and "likely to prove fatal to manufacturing prosperity".[43]

A Parliamentary Bill proposing the lowering of the age limit for young workers to 12 was duly introduced by Poulett Thomson, an M.P. closely allied to the manufacturer interest, and it was generally expected to pass.[44] Leonard Horner, who replaced Rickards as Factory Inspector in the Lancashire district in 1836, found that the manufacturers acted as if Poulett Thomson's bill had already passed, in spite of the fact that Horner had publicly advertised his intention to enforce the law as it stood. Horner reported that the Lancashire manufacturers had taken advantage of the lapse of inspection caused by Rickards's illness and had employed children of 12 years of age, and many even younger, during the whole working day.[45]

There seems to have been a great measure of uncertainty among both manufacturers and inspectors on the enforcement issue during the initial two years. But when Poulett Thomson's bill was withdrawn after its first reading due to insufficient support, the government clearly indicated that the 1833 Act was to be enforced in all its provisions. The inspectors duly responded by taking offenders to court in substantial numbers. In the English cotton district, the inspectors secured 466 convictions between May and December 1836, 498 in 1837, 403 in 1838, 183 in 1839, and 86 in 1840.[46]

Naturally, this drop in the level of both prosecutions and convictions could be explained in several ways. According to Bartrip and Fenn, it was caused by an attitude of resignation among the inspectors after only having obtained minimal fines against offenders. "...this development must have disheartened the inspectors, as the practice [of laying several informations against an offender] did not continue, and the levels of both prosecutions and informations declined after 1838".[47] However, it must be said that Bartrip and Fenn do not produce any real evidence indicating that the inspectors stopped prosecuting out of resignation. They merely point to instances of inspectors complaining to Home Office about the insufficient level of fines.[48] Also, they do not recognize that the tone of voice in these reports was influenced by Leonard Horner's intention to stir the Home Secretary into action.

---

43 PP 1834 XLIII, RIF, p. 38. Rickards also reported that 10,470 children of 12 years of age were employed in the cotton mills in his district. See PP 1836 XLV, A Return of the Number of Children of the Ages of 12, 13 and 14 Years, who are now Employed in the Mills and Factories of the United Kingdom..., p. 3.
44 See the passage in Baines (1835), p. 479.
45 PP 1837 XXXI, RIF, p. 4.
46 PP 1837 L, A Return of the Number and Names of Persons Summoned for Offences against the Factory Act..., pp. 4-55; PP 1837-38 XLV, A Return of the Number and Names..., pp. 2-57; PP 1839 XLII, A Return of the Number and Names..., pp. 2-68; PP 1840 XXXVIII, A Return of the Number and Names..., pp. 2-34; PP 1841 XVIII, A Return of the Number and Names..., pp. 2-22.
47 Bartrip and Fenn (1980b), p. 180.
48 Bartrip and Fenn (1983), pp. 208-9.

Similarly, Bartrip and Fenn's argument on the insufficient manpower resources of the inspectorate contains some essential weaknesses. They have claimed that the inspectors were "supported by seven grossly underpaid Superintendents whose powers did not even include the right of entry to mills".[49] Since the Superintendents lacked this right, "virtually the whole burden of enforcement...fell upon just four officials".[50] This is hardly in accordance with the empirical evidence. The records of the factory inspectorate show that already in 1837 the number of Superintendents had been increased to 15.[51]

Furthermore, even if the Superintendents did not have the actual legal right to enter the workrooms in the factories, in practice very few mill-owners denied them access. Leonard Horner estimated in 1840 that not more than 15 manufacturers in his district refused to let Superintendents enter their factories.[52] In the final report of the 1840 Select Committee on the Act for the Regulation of Mills and Factories, it was maintained that the mill-owners had "very generally admitted the Sub-inspectors to all parts of their mills".[53] The point of interest when estimating the level of enforcement must surely be the actual practice which was established, not the legal text in itself. In the case of the access of the Superintendents, the inspecors had managed to establish a praxis which exceeded the letter of the law.

Bartrip and Fenn have therefore seriously underestimated the prospects of enforcement. This also means that they have probably misinterpreted the reasons for the observed decline in prosecution rates after 1838. An alternative explanation, which is never overtly discussed in their work, is naturally that there was a real drop in the level of detected offences.

This interpretation is supported by a substantial amount of qualitative evidence. When taking up his duties as factory inspector in Lancashire and Yorkshire in 1836, Leonard Horner found "a very imperfect observance of the law". He reported that there had been a great many flagrant violations

---

49 Bartrip and Fenn (1980b), p. 181.
50 Bartrip (1982), p. 613.
51 Public Record Office, Kew, London. LAB 15/1. Minutes of the Meetings of the Inspectors of Factories, 24/7/37.
52 PP 1840 X, First Report from the Select Committee on the Act for the Regulation of Mills and Factories, pp. 27-28 Q. 942-3, 957. This number included Robert Hyde Greg and Henry Ashworth, who probably excluded the Superintendants from the workrooms out of political principle. On R. H. Greg's position in this matter, see his 1837 pamphlet "The Factory Question", pp. 130-31.
53 PP 1841 IX, Report from the Select Committee on the Act for the Regulation of Mills and Factories, p. 10. The issue of the Superintendents' right of entry to all rooms in the factory also questions the notion that the inspectors lacked support from their political superiors. Already in 1837, Horner was instructed by Maule, secretary of state in the Home Office, to outline a new bill which would "improve the machinery of the present Act". Horner was specifically instructed to "propose to extend the powers of the Superintendents". Letter from Maule to Horner, 27/1/37. LAB 15/1, Minutes of the Meetings of the Inspectors of Factories. The right of entry was supported by the 1840 select committee, and it was finally included in the 1844 Factory Amendment Act.

of the most important clauses of the Act, and that children had very often been employed without the required certificates.[54] But already in the summer of 1838, the inspectors reported to Lord John Russell that the Act was "on the whole better observed than at any former period".[55]

The lower number of detected offences could have been the result of four different processes: first, a lessening of mill-owner resistance to the new Act which lowered the actual number of transgressions; second, a movement away from easily detected offences to others more difficult to find out; third, improved evasion strategies on the part of the mill-owners; and fourth, a change in the organization of the labour process, above all a tendency among employers to stop using child workers below 13 years of age, and in this way avoid being subjected to the main clauses of the Factory Act.

It is evident that the first of these possibilities has a solid backing in the available qualitative sources. Leonard Horner's reports from the 1830s serves as an indication that the initial employer resistance towards the introduction of the Act lessened after a few years.[56] Early in 1837, Horner reported that employer resistance to the Act was still substantial:

> I regret to have to report that it has been necessary to institute many prosecutions in the last quarter. My Superintendents, in a large proportion of instances, where they found things wrong, were satisfied with assurances that there was no intention to break the law, and by promises that it should be strictly attended to in future; but there were unfortunately too many cases where this disobedience went greatly beyond mere acts of omission, and where there was evidently a wilful disregard of the statute. [57]

However, already in June 1837 Horner stated that the Factory Act was "viewed with less dislike than formerly" by the mill-owners, who had found that it was less onerous to observe the Act than they had previously believed. Horner claimed that this was one major reason why the number of prosecutions had been reduced by more than half.[58] By 1839 Horner estimated that the main provisions of the law were "very commonly observed", and in 1840 he stated that "the chief evils that formerly existed have been remedied to a great extent".[59]

54 PP 1837 XXXI, RIF, p. 4.
55 LAB 15/1, Minutes of the Meetings of the Inspectors of Factories, joint report to Lord John Russell, 6/7/38.
56 See PP 1837 XXXI, RIF, pp. 5-7; PP 1837-38 XXVIII, RIF, 1st Quart. Rep. 1837, p. 4; Ibid., 2nd Quart. Rep. 1837, p. 15; Ibid., 4th Quart. Rep. 1837, p. 26; PP 1839 XIX, RIF, 4th Quart. Rep. 1838, p. 3; Ibid., 2nd Quart. Rep. 1839, p. 12; PP 1840 X, First Report from the Select Committee..., evidence of Leonard Horner, p. 32 Q. 511.
57 PP 1837-38 XXVIII, RIF, 1st Quart. Rep 1837, p. 4.
58 Ibid., 2nd Quart. Rep. 1837, p. 15.
59 PP 1839 XIX, RIF, 2nd Quart. Rep. 1839, p. 12; PP 1840 XXIII, RIF, 4th Quart. Rep. 1839, p. 11.

This does not mean that the manufacturers fully accepted the Factory Act; rather that they gave up their overt resistance and instead developed various strategies to minimize the actual impact of the legislation on the operation of their mills. Some indication of this shift in strategy can be found in the factory prosecution statistics for the years 1836 to 1840. The great majority of the convictions obtained during these years were on the formal clauses of the factory regulations, which prescribed that time-books, registers of workers, and medical and school certificates should be kept.[60] From 1 May 1836 to 31 December 1837, of the 964 convictions under the factory law in the cotton district, 656 or 68 per cent were on the formal clauses. Approximately 200 of these convictions were on the complete absence of time-books and registers.[61] After that, the level of convictions fell and the cases of complete neglect of time-books and registers became rare. In the early 1840s, no more than a couple of such cases were recorded each year.[62]

This proof is not conclusive on its own, but combined with the available qualitative evidence I would argue in favour of the following interpretation: in 1836-38 resistance to the implementation of the Factory Act was widespread among the mill-owners in the cotton district. Many manufacturers simply refused to adjust to the new regulations. In this situation, the main strategy employed by the inspectors was to force the employers to adhere to the formal requirements of the Act. Absence of registers or certificates was taken as an indication of wilful neglect, and prosecution immediately followed. In 1837, multiple convictions were used against employers who had obviously ignored the Act completely. They were prosecuted separately for each offense: missing time-book, register of workers, school certificates, medical certificates, not hanging a sign of rules in the mill, not having a sign indicating meal times, and so on.[63] This strategy proved successful, for basically three reasons: first, because these offences were easily detected. It was mainly a question of checking the book-keeping and the signs displayed in the factory. Second, because the undertaking of the required book-keeping did not cost very much, and third, because the clauses in the

---

60 Horner had introduced a system of registers and time-books in the period 1835-36, and it was soon adopted by the other inspectors. See LAB 15/1, Minutes of the Meetings of the Inspectors of Factories, 8/9/36; Thomas (1948), pp. 142-45.

61 PP 1837 L, A Return of the Number and Names of Persons Summoned for Offences against the Factory Act, pp. 4-55; PP 1837-38 XLV, A Return of the Number and Names..., pp. 2-57.

62 PP 1843 XLII, A Return of the Number and Names..., pp. 2-16; PP 1844 XXXIX, A Return..., pp. 2-18; PP 1845 XXXVII, A Return..., pp. 2-22.

63 The strategy of using multiple convictions on the formal clauses is very clear in PP 1837-38 XLV, A Return of the Number of Names..., pp. 2-57. See also Horner's report in PP 1837 XXXI, RIF, p. 6.

Factory Act on the formal requirements were unequivocal and not open to interpretation by the local magistrates.[64]

A major point is that in the case of the prosecutions for neglecting the formal requirements of the Act, even a low level of fines seems to have been sufficient. Since compliance with these clauses was so easily checked, and subject to multiple fines, the mill-owners had in the long run to abandon this kind of obstruction. It has to be noted that when the inspectors complained loudly of the insufficient level of fines meted out by the magistrates, this mainly concerned cases of children or juveniles working beyond the legal day. In such cases, the inspectors complained that the gain from the illegal work exceeded the cost of the fine.[65] In contrast, there was no immediate gain for the manufacturer when refusing to keep the required books. It is therefore plausible that after a few years, this kind of open resistance to the factory legislation was largely abandoned.

This does not mean that all kinds of evasions of the law disappeared. But it is important to note that efficient inspection presupposed the existence of certificates and registers. The observance of these clauses was necessary in order to go further and enforce the length of the legal working day, and the ages and schooling of children.

Theoretically, what the inspectors did in the late 1830s was to break up a consensus among mill-owners as to the nature of factory crime. Returning to the concept introduced by W. G. Carson, what the inspectors strove to do was to turn a "conventionalized crime" into a socially recognized crime.[66] Prior to 1833, several factory acts had existed but, due to the essential class character of the judicial process and the absence of any independent machinery of enforcement, they had not been generally observed. During this early period, factory offences were "conventionalized", that is, the dominating opinion among mill-owners was that these regulations could be broken without stigmatization and as a part of everyday life. The initial resistance among the Lancashire manufacturers can thus be seen as a struggle over the societal conception of factory offences. This is also one reason why the inspectors largely resorted to prosecutions in the period between 1836 and 1838. By convicting the offending mill-owners in court,

---

64 Not surprisingly, A. E. Peacock has found a high conviction rate for factory offences during this period. See Peacock (1984), passim. However, the very low level of fines meted out by most magistrates serves as an indication that these officials hardly enforced the law in a zealous manner. See Bartrip (1985), passim; Henriques (1979), p 103. See also Horner's complaints of lenient magistrates in PP 1837 XXXI, RIF, p. 6; PP 1837-38 XXVIII, RIF, 1st Quart. Rep. 1837, p. 4.

65 PP 1837-38 XLV, RIF, p. 3; PP 1844 XXVIII, RIF, 4th Quart. Rep. 1843, p. 12; PP 1852-53 XL, RIF, 2nd Half-yearly Rep. 1852, p. 16.

66 Carson (1979). Carson, however, working on the question of white collar crime, uses the term to signify factory offences after the Act of 1844.

the symbolic message was brought home that breaches of the Factory Act were no longer socially acceptable and were to be regarded as crimes.

Prosecutions were used both as a symbolical measure to designate crime, and also because the inspectors estimated that the offences had been wilfully committed. The choice of enforcement measures was therefore dependent on the strategies of the manufacturers. It should also be noted that the lukewarm support from the local magistrates did not constitute a major obstacle in this process. Since prosecutions were mainly brought on neglect of required book-keeping and the over-working on children, clauses which were stringently formulated in the regulations, the magistrates were in most instances forced to convict. The court-room was clearly the public arena where the re-definition of the nature of factory crime took place. This was probably one reason why the inspectors hardly ever fined "on the spot", a power which was given them in the 1833 Act. The designation of crime was a public affair.

In this process, the consensus among mill-owners broke down. While some, according to Leonard Horner, were "insensitive to the discredit of a prosecution", others reacted more strongly.[67] Robert Hyde Greg wrote very emotionally about the inspectors being "spies" of the government, and in similar terms about the prospect of being "dragged into a court of justice" and convicted.[68] Henry Ashworth, another substantial Lancashire mill-owner, was convicted for a trivial factory offence in 1837, and reacted by dismissing nearly all of his child workers. Three years afterwards he still employed only half the previous number of children.[69]

Naturally, the potency of the legislation rested to some extent on the cultural notions of honesty and respectability among the class of manufacturers. Employers who aspired to some standing in bourgeois society were naturally rather sensitive to the prospect of being prosecuted in public. The inspectors successfully used these notions of respectability to split the mill-owners into an "honest" and a "dishonest" fraction. The policy of prosecuting offenders publicly was the wedge, and the high rate of convictions was the hammer. Once the evaders had dwindled to a small minority, the inspectors could claim they had the support of the "honest" mill-owners and were combatting unfair competition. One crucial factor, therefore, was the inspectors' ability to break up the consensus among the manufacturers on factory offences. In the struggle over the implementation of the Factory Act in the late 1830s, this objective was achieved.

---

67 See Horner's report in PP 1837 XXXI, p. 7.
68 Greg R H (1837): The Factory Question, Considered in Relation to its Effects on the Health and Morals of those Employed in Factories..., pp. 134-5, 161.
69 PP 1840 X, Third Report from the Select Committee..., evidence of H. Ashworth, pp. 1-2 Q. 4,013-23; Boyson, R (1970): The Ashworth Cotton Enterprise, pp. 164-71.

Several objections may be raised against this interpretation. Previous research has, for instance, emphasized that the local magistrates constituted the "ultimate" obstacle to the implementation of the Act, not only by imposing minimum fines but also by frequently mitigating even these.[70] It is true that the inspectors regarded this as a very serious problem.[71] Mitigation of the penalties not only lowered their deterrant effect; it was also a symbolic gesture which obscured the impact of the conviction as a designation of crime. But two things have to be borne in mind regarding this question: first, that the inspectors used their reports to put pressure on the Home Secretary to intervene in cases where magistrates did not conform to the spirit of the Act. Second, from a close reading of these reports it is possible to distinguish a geographical pattern in the complaints on recalcitrant magistrates. In 1837 Horner specifically pointed out the magistrates in Bury, Rochdale, and Huddersfield for only imposing minimal fines in factory cases.[72] In the following year the Rochdale and Oldham area had become the main centre of magistrate opposition.[73] Horner stated that 7/8 of all prosecutions were made in that district, and he was convinced that this was connected with the practice of the Rochdale magistrates to mitigate penalties. The official return of prosecutions confirms that a substantial number of fines imposed in this court were mitigated.[74]

However, these findings do not suggest that magistrate resistance was a general problem. Even if the actions of the Rochdale magistrates made the enforcement process difficult in that district, this was clearly not the case in other areas. Mitigation of penalties was obviously not a problem in other parts of the cotton district.[75]

Furthermore, the inspectors employed several counteracting strategies. Besides putting pressure on the Home Office to intervene, Horner increased the possibilities of surveillance by placing one of his Superintendents permanently at Rochdale, while at the same time using himself

---

70 See Henriques (1979), pp. 103-4.

71 See, for instance, Horner's report in PP 1837 XXXI, RIF, pp. 6, 48-49.

72 PP 1837 XXXI, RIF, p. 6.

73 PP 1837-38 XLV, RIF, p. 3.

74 PP 1839 XIX, 4th Quarterly Report 1838, RIF, p. 4; PP 1839 XLII, A Return of the Number and Names..., pp. 14-44. Horner's criticism of the Rochdale magistrates was sustained by the 1840 select committee. See PP 1841 IX, Report from the Select Committee..., p. 18.

75 PP 1839 XLII, RIF, pp. 2-68. As to the question why the resistance was stronger in the Oldham-Rochdale district than in other parts of Lancashire, I can only make a suggestion. The area was probably dominated by smaller mill-owners, and it is possible that they formed a sub-culture which persisted in regarding factory offences as inconsequential and which had a different notion of respectability from the areas dominated by larger mill-owners. On the structure of the manufacturer class in Oldham, see Gadian (1978): Class Consciousness in Oldham and the other North-West Industrial Towns, pp. 168-70.

and other Superintendents as a more mobile force.[76] Far from being discouraged by the enforcement difficulties, the evidence suggests that the inspectors' response to resistance was to increase the levels of both surveillence and prosecutions. By the time of the 1840 Select Committee on the operation of the Factory Act, the instances of open resistance to the Act seem to have all but vanished.[77]

This does not mean that the enforcement of the 1833 Factory Act was entirely successful. The question remains if the manufacturers changed their evasion strategies away from easily detectable offences to others more difficult for the inspectors to control. But in this context it should also be recognized that there were wholly legal ways for the mill-owners to reduce the impact of the factory regulations; above all their ceasing to hire children below the age of 13. Indeed, I would argue that yet another reason why the mill-owners split over the implementation of the 1833 Factory Act was that for many the most feasible strategy to minimize the impact of this legislation was to stop employing child workers altogether.[78] It has to be remembered that the main provisions of the 1833 Act dealt with the use of children below 13 years of age in textile factories.[79] Especially in larger cities like Glasgow and Manchester with large supplies of unskilled juvenile workers, children could with comparable ease be replaced with 13 and 14 year-olds.

This is an important reason why the factory statistics at the time showed a substantial reduction in the level of child labour. The proportion of the work performed by children below 13 in the cotton district decreased from 13.4 per cent in 1835 to 3.3 per cent in 1838.[80]

Naturally, this was not the only reason for the fall in child labour statistics. The manufacturers' second option was to evade the Act by using children below 13 who could produce medical certificates of having attained that age. This seems to have been one of the most difficult enforcement

---

76 PP 1837-38 XLV, RIF, p. 3. However, these tactics were initially impeded because the resident Superintendent proved unsatisfactory. Superintendent Webster borrowed considerable sums of money from the local mill-owners, and was finally dismissed in 1839. See HO 87/1, Letter from Maule, Home Office, to Superintendent Webster, 2/7/39. But even this measure did not stop enforcement problems from reappearing in the Rochdale district in 1841. See PP 1842 XXII, RIF, 3d Quarterly Report 1841, p. 4.
77 PP 1840 X, First Report from the Select Committee..., evidence of Horner, p. 32 Q. 511.
78 Cf Thomas: The Early Factory Legislation, p. 83.
79 Bartrip and Fenn's main empirical work has been on the safety regulations of the 1844 Act, and they do not seem to be aware that the strategies which the manufacturers employed in connection with the child labour clauses were very different from those which were used on the safety measures. Above all, they have not seen that in the former case there were wholly legal ways of escaping the impact of the legislation, while such was not the case on the safety regulations - apart from the option to observe them.
80 PP 1836 XLV; PP 1839 XLII, Factory Returns. Consideration has been taken to the fact that the working day for children in 1838 had been reduced to 8 hours.

problems which faced the early inspectors. The objective of this strategy was to be able to keep these young workers for the full twelve hours, and also to avoid being held responsible for the children's schooling. Consequently, in the late 1830s the inspectors found themselves confronted with a great many child workers clearly younger than 13, but who had all obtained certificates stating that age.[81] In 1836 Horner wrote that "fully one half" of the children certified to be 13 were in fact below that age.[82] During the course of inspection, Horner often reacted on the prevalence of certified young workers who were clearly below the legal age of 13:

> In my visits to the mills of Stalybridge, I found no less than one hundred and twelve children certified by one surgeon as being thirteen years of age, not one of whom had, in my judgement, the ordinary appearance of children of that time of life in that part of the country; and seventy-five of them were either indisputably younger, or palpably defective in growth and strength for that age. [83]

Horner tried to establish reliable indications of age, such as height or the development of second teeth, but these attempts were not successful.[84] In the absence of such indicators, the inspectors very soon realized that in order to enforce the age limits prescribed by the 1833 Act they would need to exercise some control over the issuing of medical certificates. Rickards found that such documents had been issued by a "drunken ale-house keeper" and a "druggist's apprentice", and declared already in 1835 that he would accept medical certificates only from surgeons of his own appointment.[85]

Horner immediately adopted this practice when he took over from Rickards the year after.[86] But it is interesting to note that they had very little backing in the legal text for this measure. The 1833 Act did not give the inspector the right to dismiss certificates he believed were manifestly wrong; this measure was only included in the 1844 Amendment. Initial attempts by Horner to make the appointment of surgeons a part of the regulations issued by the inspectors received a setback in 1837, when legal opinion ruled that any person acting as surgeon was entitled to grant certificates.[87] Moreover, the safeguard prescribed by the 1833 Act, that the certificates

---

81 See Horner's reports, PP 1837 XXXI, RIF, pp. 4-5, 43-45; PP 1837-38 XXVIII, RIF, 3d Quart. Rep 1837, p. 26; Ibid., 1st Quart. Rep. 1838, p. 4; PP 1839 XIX, RIF, 4th Quart. Rep. 1838, p. 3; PP 1844 XXVIII, RIF, 1st Quart. Rep. 1844, pp. 13-15.
82 Senior, N (1837): Letters on the Factory Act, p. 34.
83 PP 1839 XIX, RIF, 4th Quart. Rep. 1838, p. 3.
84 PP 1837 XXXI, RIF, p. 42; Memoir of Leonard Horner (1890), Vol I, p. 352, letter from Horner to his wife, 30/10/37; HO 45/61, Letter from Howell to Graham, Home Office, 2/11/41.
85 PP 1834 XLIII, RIF, p. 28; PP 1835 XL, RIF, pp. 6-8.
86 LAB 15/1, Minutes of the Meetings of the Inspectors of Factories, 8/9/36.
87 HO 87/1, Letter from Secretary of State Phillipps to Horner, 11/8 1837. See also LAB 15/1, Minutes of Meetings of the Inspectors of Factories, joint report 22/7/37, minutes 5/7/38.

should be countersigned by a local magistrate, was never effective. Magistrates simply signed the documents without seeing the children in question.[88]

Nevertheless, the inspectors seem to have achieved some measure of control over the appointment of surgeons in spite of the very limited backing of the law. The evidence of Leonard Horner indicates that at least by 1840 his right of appointing surgeons was no longer challenged by the manufacturers.[89] In the same way as with the Superintendents' right of access to the workrooms, the inspectors managed to establish a praxis which exceeded their actual legal position. Consequently, while the actual level of evasions by means of incorrect medical certificates remains very difficult to estimate, we do know that control over the issuing surgeons tightened after a few years, and also that the inspectors' complaints of this type of evasion became more rare. We also know that Horner did not hesitate to dismiss surgeons he found to be incompetent or unreliable.[90] It therefore seems reasonable to infer that this problem was coming increasingly under control.

However, one type of offence continued to be difficult to counter: the working of children beyond the legal hours. One especially weak point of the 1833 Factory Act was that it limited the legal working day of children and juveniles, but allowed the manufacturer to use them within a time span of fifteen hours. The correct keeping of time books and registers was therefore absolutely necessary for enforcement, but the inspectors still found it very difficult to ensure that protected persons were not worked beyond the legal time. Rickards found this task almost impossible:

> I believe too that the limitation of one class of children to a certain number of hours, and another class to another, in the same mill, can never be put in force by legal or official means. Evasion is so easy in the interior of mills, and detection so difficult, that when private interests combine, the vigilance of public officers, if not always on the spot, may and will be continually defeated. [91]

As long as a child was allowed to work for eight hours at any time during a working day of fifteen hours, it was very difficult for the inspectors to know

---

88 PP 1837 XXXI, RIF, p. 43; PP 1837-38 XXVIII, p. 26; LAB 15/1, Minutes of Meetings of the Inspectors of Factories, 19/7/37.
89 PP 1840 X, First Report from the Select Committee..., evidence of Leonard Horner, pp. 52-54 Q. 743-46, 777-78. In their final report, the committee acknowledged that the inspectors had managed to gain control over the appointment of surgeons, but still demanded that this should be formalized in law. See PP 1841 IX, Report from the Select Committee..., pp. 8, 10. See also Henriques (1979), p. 100.
90 Horner dismissed at least three surgeons between 1836 and 1838. See PP 1837 XXXI, RIF, p. 5; PP 1839 XIX, RIF, 4th Quarterly Report 1838, p. 3.
91 PP 1834 XLIII, p. 39.

if the regulations were really obeyed. Also, the very low level of fines was hardly a deterrent against this type of offence. In 1840 Horner pointed specifically to these problems in a pamphlet, claiming that the eight hour clause was "frequently evaded with impunity".[92] His attempts to promote the working of children in relay systems remained only a very modest success, as is evidenced in one of his reports from 1843:

> In two-thirds of the mills where children are employed (522, with 4113 children), they work them eight hours, and do without them the other four hours. In a great many cases, this I am confident amounts to no more than *they say* they do without the children; there is no doubt that the liberty given by the Act to employ children at any period of the day between half past five in the morning and half past eight in the night, opens the door wide open to fraud very difficult of detection. [93]

However, it should not be forgotten that Horner's writings were probably somewhat influenced by his intention to have the 1833 Act amended in certain respects. It should also be remembered that by 1839 only 48 per cent of the Lancashire mills employed children below 13 at all.[94] The main manufacturer policy in connection with the 1833 Factory Act was obviously to avoid hiring children altogether. Still, overworking was difficult to check in those mills where they were employed. This problem remained until the passing of the 1844 Act, which prescribed a regular half-time system for children below 13.

### Changes in the Nature of Inspection, 1845-1914: Overworking and Safety Regulations

After 1845 the work of the inspectors changed dramatically. According to the new Act, children were only allowed to work for 6½ hours per day, and only before or after the mid-day meal hour. The prospects of enforcement of the legal time limits for children therefore increased considerably. In his first report after the implementation of the 1844 Amendment, Horner stated:

> The objects of the legislature, in restricting and regulating the labour of children and young persons in factories, have unquestionably been more generally and effectively attained during the last seven months, than they have ever been since Parliament first

---

92 Horner (1840), p. 7. This pamphlet was written to promote suggestions for changes in the law which he was not free to publish in his official reports.
93 PP 1844 XXVIII, 4th Quarterly Report 1843, p. 15. See also PP 1840 XXIII, 2nd Quarterly Report 1840, p. 12; PP 1840 X, First Report from the Select Committee..., evidence of Horner, p. 31 Q. 511.
94 PP 1840 XXIII, RIF, 4th Quarterly Report 1839, p. 14. 689 out of 1,442 factories employed children below 13.

began to correct the great moral evils that had taken root and extensively spread in these branches of industry. [95]

Prosecutions on the child labour clauses soon became very rare. The main reasons behind this development were the improvement in the legal structure, and the organization of child labour in an easily inspected half-time system. Instead, the main task of the inspectors after 1845 was to enforce the new clauses on safety regulations and the limited working day for women operatives.

However, these clauses were never as well enforced as those regulating child labour. In the case of the safety regulations, the inspectors met with strong resistance from the manufacturers. The 1844 Act prescribed that machinery should be "securely fenced", which the inspectors interpreted to mean the entire system of revolving shafts within seven feet from the floor. Such fencing requirements would have been relatively costly for the manufacturers, who generally refused to comply with these demands. The inspectors soon found that the magistrates very often tended to support the view of the mill-owners in this matter.[96] The conviction rate in safety measure cases deteriorated from over 80 per cent in the mid-1840s to less than 40 per cent one decade later.[97] After a substantial amount of lobbying from the manufacturers, the safety regulations were finally watered down in a special enactment in 1856.

The overworking of women and juveniles in the Lancashire cotton industry also proved to be a persistent issue. Overworking was both profitable and difficult to detect. In contrast to the formal requirements of certificates and time-books, this type of offence had to be detected while it was actually being committed in order to secure a conviction. It was impossible for the inspector to know if overworking had been committed since his last visit: these offences left no permanent traces.

The only way for the inspectors to counter overworking offences was to increase surveillance levels and to use repeated prosecutions. When overworking became prevalent in certain areas, Horner concentrated his force of Superintendents to that district in order to obtain a larger number of convictions.[98]

These measures probably limited the extent of severe overworking. Still, minor offences of this kind, locally known as "time cribbing", continued to

---

95 PP 1845 XXV, RIF, 1st Half-yearly Report 1845, p. 13.
96 LAB 15/2, Minutes of the Meetings of the Inspectors of Factories, 2/6/46; 26/6/46; LAB 15/3, Minutes..., 25/5/55.
97 Bartrip and Fenn (1980a), p. 96.
98 HO 45/5221, Letter from Horner to Waddington, Home Office, 29/7/54; HO 45/4074, Letter from Horner to Walpole, Home Office, 14/7/52.

prevail in the Lancashire cotton industry well into the 20th century. One important reason why it remained so difficult for the inspectors to eradicate "time cribbing" was that these offences very often had the support of both workers and managemant. Both mule-spinners and weavers were paid on piece-rate, and overworking would tend to increase the weekly wage packet somewhat. Inspectors frequently complained that the operatives obstructed their efforts to bring "time cribbing" under control.[99]

Another type of offence which remained difficult to control was that of cleaning machinery in motion. As in the case of overworking, these offences had to be detected while actually being committed in order to be prosecuted. The repeated complaints of the inspectors during the second half of the 19th century illustrate that this practice proved very difficult to eradicate.[100]

### Factory Law Enforcement in Lancashire: Some Conclusions

The question of true enforcement of the early Factory Acts has proved to be much more complicated than has been claimed in recent research. Above all, some parts of the legislation were better enforced than others. While the safety regulations and the clauses on overworking women and juveniles remained difficult to enforce, the regulations on the ages and working hours of children below 13 were relatively well observed already by 1845.

Previous research, instead of investigating enforcement prospects and results on the separate clauses, has tended to make generalizations from one type of regulations to the others. The work of Bartrip and Fenn is clearly marked by their tendency to apply the patterns found on the enforcement of the safety regulations to all parts of the legislation. The consequence is that they have seriously underestimated the enforcement of the child labour clauses.

Also, I find no support for Bartrip and Fenn's general thesis that the drop in prosecution levels in the late 1830s was the outcome of resignation among the inspectors in the face of enforcement difficulties. In the early phase, mill-owner resistance to the Act in the form of open refusal to adopt

99 See PP 1892 XXXV, Royal Commission on Labour, evidence of Henderson, Supervising Inspector, pp. 292-93 Q. 7,265-70; PP 1902 XII, Report of the Chief Inspector of Factories and Workshops, (RCIFW), pp. 100-101; PP 1906 XV, RCIFW, p. 173.
100 See PP 1849 XXII, RIF, 1st Half-yearly Report 1849, p. 9; PP 1850 XXII, RIF, 2nd Half-yearly Report 1849, pp. 14-16; PP 1852 XXI, RIF, 1st Half-yearly Rep. 1852, p. 10; PP 1867 XVI, RIF, 2nd Half-yearly Rep. 1866, p. 15, 63-64; PP 1884-85 XV, RCIFW, pp. 3-4; PP 1901 X, RCIFW, p. 312; PP 1906 XV, RCIFW, p. 174.

the required book-keeping measures was effectively countered by prosecutions. The Act was "successful" in the sense that it turned a conventionalized crime into a recognized crime.

Indeed, the evidence indicates that the employers' main evasion strategy after 1838 was the use of incorrect medical certificates. One implication is that since the enforcement process at this point was not primarily staged in the courts, the activities of the local magistrates were no longer of prime importance. These findings undermine the notion that the low fines and the partiality of magistrates constituted a decisive obstacle to the implementation of the Factory Acts in the late 1830s. Moreover, it should be recognized that more than half of the mill-owners avoided the more onerous parts of the Factory Act simply by hiring juvenile workers instead of children.

Finally, in an international perspective, it is obvious that the early British factory inspection was comparatively "successful". The legal measures were weaker and inspector resources considerably less in, for instance, France, the Nordic countries, and the U.S.A.[101]

# Factory Inspection in Scotland, 1834-1870: The Disappearance of the Factory Children of Glasgow

The next step in this investigation is to study the implementation of the 1833 Factory Act in the Scottish context. Did the same pattern and sequence of evasions emerge? Even a rapid glance at the picture rendered by the inspectors' reports reveals a situation which was very different from that in Lancashire. The available statistics show a dramatic decline in the labour force participation of children below 13, above all in the Glasgow cotton industry:

---

101 See Reid, D (1986): Putting Social Reform into Practice: Labor Inspectors in France, 1892-1914; Hordern, F (1983): Les Industriels Alsaciens et la Loi de 1841 sur le Travail des Enfants; Olsson (1980), pp. 114-16; Heywood (1988), pp. 237-319; Bull, E (1958): Arbeidermiljö under det industrielle genombrudd, pp. 145-48; Massachusetts Bureau of the Statistics of Labor, Annual Report 1870, pp. 134-39; Ibid., 1871, pp. 256-57, 264, 466-67; Ibid., 1872, pp. 162-63; Ibid., 1873, p. 281; Ibid., 1882, pp. 202, 209; 61st Congress 2nd Session. Senate Document No 645. Report on the Condition of Woman and Child Wage-Earners, pp. 157-69.

Table 5.      Child labour in the Glasgow cotton industry 1833-1840, as a proportion of the performed work.[102]

| Year | Age 9-12 | 13-17 |
|------|------|-------|
| 1833* | 15.4 | 30.1 |
| 1837 | 0.4 | 34.1 |
| 1838 | 0.5 | 38.9 |
| 1840 | 0.3 | 39.2 |

\* The figures for 1833 are taken from a sample of 12,188 cotton operatives in Glasgow and district collected by the factory commissioners of 1833.

Sources: PP 1834 XX, Factories Enquiry Commission.Supplementary Report Part I, pp. 21-22; PP 1837-38 XXVIII, RIF, p. 11; PP 1839 XLII, Factory Returns, pp. 304-5; PP 1840 X, Fourth Report from the Select Committee on the Act for the Regulation of Mills and Factories, evidence of Daniel Walker, Superintendent, Glasgow, p. 3 Q. 4,923-27.

The proportion of children in 1833 in the mills situated in Glasgow proper was probably even higher than these figures indicate. A survey published in 1833 by Kirkman Finlay, a substantial Glasgow cotton manufacturer, showed that children below 12 constituted 19.1 per cent of the workforce in 29 Glasgow spinning factories.[103]

According to these figures and estimates, the factory children of Glasgow vanished almost completely within a few years after the implementation of the 1833 Act. Naturally, this steep decline may have been partly illusory. The low number of cotton operatives below 13 may have been a result of wide-spread evasions of the age clauses. It is therefore necessary to estimate the level of enforcement in the Glasgow district.

In equally stark contrast to the situation in Lancashire, it is clear that very few factory cases were taken to court in Scotland. During the four years between 1836 and 1840, only eleven convictions were made in Scottish courts for breaches of the 1833 Act. The corresponding figure for convictions in the Lancashire cotton district during the same period was 1,550.[104] At the same time, James Stuart, the Scottish factory inspector, repeatedly claimed that the law was stringently enforced in his district. For instance, early in 1837 he reported:

---

102 The figures have been adjusted to the shorter working hours of children below 13 after 1836. However, it should be emphasized that these are the official figures on child labour, which means that they do not reflect the impact of evasions.

103 Finlay, K (1833): Letter to the Right Hon. Lord Ashley, on the Cotton Factory System and the Ten Hours' Factory Bill, Appendix. N = 5,273.

104 PP 1840 X, Second Report from the Select Committee..., evidence of James Stuart, appendix 8; PP 1837 L, A Return of the Number and Names..., pp. 4-55; PP 1837-38 XLV, A Return of the Number and Names..., pp. 2-57; PP 1839 XLII, A Return of the Number and Names..., pp. 2-68; PP 1840 XXXVIII, A Return of the Number and Names..., pp. 2-34.

I have now the pleasure to state that the result of my inspection of the factories I have enumerated, which comprehend...Glasgow and Dundee, the two chief seats of manufacture in my district, is most satisfactory; and that, with one very trifling exception, the provisions of the Factory Act, and the regulations of the Inspectors for carrying them into effect, are duly and *strictly* adhered to. [105]

Naturally, the assertions of the factory inspector are by no means a guarantee of strict enforcement. Most historians dealing with the subject have focussed on the character and policies of James Stuart, factory inspector in the Scottish district between 1836 and 1849. It has been implied that he neglected his duties and was in close colloboration with the Glasgow mill-owners. J. T. Ward has claimed that Stuart applied the law lightly, and only punished the most extreme transgressions.[106] Bernice Martin has described Stuart as "lax and possibly corrupt".[107] Ursula Henriques maintains that his appointment was a clear case of jobbery, and that he was jealous, irascible, tactless, biassed, and even shady.[108] The 1833 Act was not enforced in Scotland, and Stuart's optimistic reports should be seen as an attempt to cover up his failure.[109] Henriques's work on Stuart and the contention that the 1833 Act was very poorly enforced in Scotland are now part of received historical opinion.[110]

In this section I will state an entirely different case. I will argue that previous research has rested too much on an evaluation of the character and policies of James Stuart, and has not perceived the full complexity of the enforcement process. This does not mean that I will try to redraw the portrait of James Stuart.[111] What I will try to establish is that his performance was made in a social context which was very different from that of Lancashire. Above all, the Glasgow manufacturers adopted strategies connected with the implementation of the 1833 Act which were somewhat different from those of the Lancashire mill-owners. This important contrast between the two regions has not been perceived in previous research.

Before proceeding any further in this direction, I will first examine the evidence on which Henriques and other historians rest their case. The obvious starting point is the speech in Parliament in 1838 by the Irish

---

105 PP 1837-38 XXVIII, RIF, p. 12. For similar assertions of Stuart, see also PP 1837 XXXI, RIF, p. 63; PP 1837-38 XLV, RIF, p. 10; PP 1839 XIX, RIF, p. 57; PP 1840 XXIII, RIF, 1st Quarterly Report 1840, p. 10.
106 Ward (1962b), p. 111. It must be said, though, that Ward's evidence for this opinion is very thin.
107 Martin (1969), p. 429.
108 Henriques (1971a), p. 27.
109 Henriques (1979), p. 105.
110 See, for instance, Smout, T C (1986): A Century of the Scottish People 1830-1950, p. 95; Butt (1987), p. 148.
111 Stuart's rather shady past included the killing of another man in a duel, and an alleged fraud followed by a hasty trip to America. See The Trial of James Stuart, Esq., younger of Dunearn, before the High Court of Justiciary, 10 June 1822 (1822), passim.

member Daniel O'Connel, in which he declared that the 1833 Act was not enforced in Scotland:

> It appears that in Glasgow the Factories Act is totally neglected; it is observed by nobody, and violated by everybody. They there find it too inconvenient to work with, and have in practice repealed it. [112]

O'Connel had received his information as a member of the Select Committee on the Combinations of Workmen in 1838, where he had questioned three Glasgow mule-spinners called Campbell, McCaffer, and McNish, on the enforcement of the 1833 Act. The spinners testified that in Glasgow, factory children were worked longer than the legal eight hours per day. The 1833 Act was not observed.[113]

While O'Connel seems to have accepted this evidence without hesitation, it is difficult for a critically minded historian to do the same. During the late 1830s the spinners' unions and the short-time committees tried hard to disparage the working of the 1833 Act. John Doherty, former secretary of the Manchester mule-spinners, stated before the same committee on combinations that the Factory Act was not and could not be enforced in Lancashire.[114] It is therefore hardly satisfactory to let the notion of poor enforcement levels in Glasgow rest on the evidence of the operative spinners.

It should perhaps also be mentioned that Stuart immediately contested their testimony and the notion that the 1833 Act was not enforced in Glasgow. He questioned 186 witnesses under oath, all but one stating that the law was in full operation in Glasgow.[115] Naturally, this evidence cannot be accepted either. Stuart was obviously intent on defending his performance as factory inspector, and there is no knowing to what extent he picked or intimidated witnessess, or suppressed evidence which deviated from his own position.

Indeed, in order to assess the enforcement level in Glasgow one has to understand that the structure of industrial relations in the local cotton industry differed much from those prevailing in Lancashire. In chapter 2 I indicated that the relations between the Glasgow manufacturers and the mule-spinners were very strained. After 1825 the operatives had a firm

---

112 Cited in Thomas (1948), p. 258.
113 PP 1837-38 VIII, First Report from the Select Committee on the Combinations of Workmen, evidence of Angus Campbell, p. 50 Q. 991-92. Ibid., evidence of James McNish, p. 64 Q. 1,292-94, 1,297. Moreover, when asked to confirm the statements of the Glasgow spinners, Archibald Alison, Sheriff of Lanarkshire, answered he did not know anything about it, but did not doubt that the spinners' evidence was correct. Ibid., p. 113 Q. 1,993-94.
114 Ibid., evidence of John Doherty, p. 256 Q. 3,464-67, p. 261 Q. 3,580-83.
115 PP 1839 XIX, RIF, pp. 32-57, 76-87.

control over piece-rate structures and recruitment in the mills within the city, while wage levels were considerably lower in the country factories where the unions were much weaker. Wage reductions in the Lancashire industry in 1829 and 1831 also lessened the profitability of the Glasgow firms, and put considerable pressure on the manufacturers to find ways to erode the powerful position of the mule-spinners. It was in this context of very tense production relations that the 1833 Act was implemented. When the government declared in 1836 that the law as it stood should be stringently enforced, the Glasgow manufacturers responded by prohibiting the employment of children who could not show certificates of their being 13 years of age. If we return for a moment to the evidence of James McNish, the rationale and repercussions of this strategy become more clear:

> Were you rightly understood to have said, that the law is violated with respect to the age of the piecers, and that they are brought in younger than the law allows? - Yes, the law is violated.
> And generally violated? - Yes; and our employers are throwing all the responsibility of that violation of the law upon the operative. The operative is obliged to violate it, or allow his machinery to stand.
> In what way is that accomplished by the Masters? - I cannot tell; they have put up placards in through the factories, that they will not be accountable for the spinners employing piecers under a certain age; and we have instances of spinners having been summoned before the Justices of the Peace, and fined for employing children under the age; not the employer but the spinner. [116]

The objective of the manufacturers' strategy was to transfer all the extra trouble connected with the 1833 Act to the operative spinners. Since the great majority of factory children were piecers subcontracted by the adult spinners, the latter were made legally responsible for children found working without the required certificates. This conclusion is also supported by the reports of James Stuart. He clearly stated that the Glasgow manufacturers had hung placards in their mills prohibiting the employment of children below 13, and that they held the operative spinners responsible for any transgression of these rules. Stuart therefore dismissed the complaints of McNish, claiming that the 1833 Act ruled that the operative was legally responsible "when the offence had been committed without the personal consent or concurrence of the Master".[117]

It is probably wrong to see Stuart's actions merely as an expression of partiality in favour of the Glasgow manufacturers. Leonard Horner, who was factory inspector in Scotland for two years before being transferred to

---

116 PP 1837-38 VIII, First Report from the Select Committee..., evidence of James McNish, p. 64 Q. 1,278-80. See also ibid., p. 65 Q. 1319, p. 66 Q 1,326-29.
117 PP 1839 XIX, RIF, p. 57.

the Lancashire district, also held that the operative spinners were the legally responsible party. Early in 1836 he reported that he had recently made four prosecutions in Glasgow, all against mule-spinners who had disregarded the orders of their employers and taken in children without certificates of age.[118] Horner maintained in 1840 that a mill-owner who had ordered his overlookers and operatives to obey the law and had taken "reasonable pains" to ensure that his orders were followed, could not be held legally responsible for the offences committed.[119] It is probably more correct to see Stuart's actions against the operatives in the context of certain manufacturer strategies directed against the Glasgow mule-spinners. This, in turn, must be seen in the general context of the very strained industrial relations in the Glasgow cotton trade in the 1830s. It should also be pointed out that the mule-spinners' ability to find counter-measures was seriously weakened by their defeat in the 1837 strike, in which their union was virtually destroyed.

There can be no doubt that the strategies employed by the manufacturers imposed considerable disadvantages on the operative spinners. The prohibition of the employment of piecers below 13 years of age meant that the mule-spinners were not free to employ their own children if they were below that age. Indeed, the recruitment of young piecers generally became much more difficult. The spinners had to exert themselves to find young workers who were able to pass for being 13 years of age. At least after 1837 there are some indications that the Glasgow manufacturers threatened the operative spinners with dismissal if they could not find the required piecers. This is evident in the testimony of Henry Dunn, a Glasgow mule-spinner, before the 1840 committee on the operation of the 1833 Act:

> Is it the practice of the Masters in your neighbourhood to require that the spinners should find piecers who have certificates that they are 13? - Yes, they must find them, they insist upon that, but they get the certificates quite handy; they get them forwarded, and they come in, and perhaps in Glasgow there may be half a dozen pairs of wheels [hand-mules] standing in the course of a forenoon, and the spinners are away in the streets looking for piecers, and cannot get them; if a spinner does not get a piecer, he runs the chance of losing his work; the first that comes with a piecer gets the job, so that they make every sacrifice to get children. [120]

According to Henry Dunn there was in 1840 a constant pool of 250 to 300 redundant mule-spinners in Glasgow, all eager to get employment.[121] The

---

118 PP 1836 XLV, RIF, p. 12. Horner's only prosecution of a Glasgow manufacturer was the case of Dixon & Co for working children and young persons during the night. See PP 1836 XLV, A Return of the Names of all Persons Fined under the Factory Acts, p. 20.
119 PP 1840 X, First Report from the Select Committee..., evidence of Horner, p. 51 Q. 735.
120 Ibid., Sixth Report, evidence of Henry Dunn, p. 29 Q. 8,724.
121 Ibid., p. 27 Q. 8,691.

prevailing unemployment among the Glasgow spinners, and the defeat of their union in 1837, must have made the threat of dismissal very forceful. It is in this light, therefore, that the evidence of the Glasgow spinners before the 1838 committee on combinations has to seen. Since they were themselves very much oppressed by the specific way the 1833 Act was implemented in Glasgow, it is very probable that their main aim was to have it repealed and replaced with the Ten Hour Act.

Perhaps more importantly in the context of the present investigation, the unemployment and weak bargaining position of the Glasgow mule-spinners also sharpened the enforcement strategy of James Stuart. His initial policy of prosecuting the operative spinners who hired children in an illegal way increasingly gave way to his demanding the dismissal of both the adult and the child. Not surprisingly, the Glasgow manufacturers readily granted every such application.[122] In terms of inspector policy, the demand for the dismissal of the operative spinner was easier to effectuate than prosecutions. It was also much more effective. Permanent unemployment was a more threatening prospect for the spinner than that of being convicted and fined. See, for instance, one of Stuart's reports from 1840:

> Whenever...after a full investigation of facts, I have found that an operative spinner has wilfully committed a serious offence against the Act, in relation to the employing of children or young persons, by knowingly giving false information, I have notified to his employer my intention to prosecute, unless he immediately dismissed the spinner in fault; and my intimations to this purpose have been attended to in almost every case, and have, I am quite certain, led to infinitely greater caution on the part of the spinners. /.../ The spinners were warned by the regulations, put on the walls of every factory, of the provisions of the law, and yet they were truly the only persons whom I found fraudulently violating it. The number of dismissals of operative spinners on my suggestion, or with my knowledge and concurrence, does not amount in all to a dozen; but the effect of the dismissals, since they have become known, has been most beneficial, and has had a most salutary influence in putting an end to the system of evasion and fraud as to certificates of age, which formerly prevailed, especially at Glasgow. [123]

Stuart did not have any backing in the 1833 Act for his policy of having offending operatives dismissed, and his course of action may well be seen as an expression of partiality.[124] But in the context of enforcement, I have no doubts that these measures were uncommonly efficient. Indeed, I would argue that the 1833 Act was probably much better enforced in the Glasgow district than in Lancashire. Through the active co-operation between Stuart

---

122 See Stuart's reports in PP 1837-38 XXVIII, RIF, p. 12; PP 1839 XIX, RIF, p. 58.
123 PP 1841 X, RIF, 4th Quarterly Report 1840, p. 31. See also PP 1839 XIX, RIF, p. 58; PP 1840 XXIII, RIF, 1st Quarterly Report 1840, p. 10.
124 See Henriques (1971a), p. 30; Henriques (1971b), p. 13.

and the Glasgow manufacturers, the mule-spinners were designated as the perpetrators of the detected offences. Without the support of the mill-owners, and without control over registers and book-keeping, the mule-spinners were in a very vulnerable position. Their ability to aviod detection under these circumstances must have been very limited, while at the same time the consequences of detection were very serious. In contrast, the Lancashire manufacturers did not in the same way transfer the legal responsibility for offences to the operatives.[125]

It is therefore misleading to see Scottish factory inspection merely as a result of the character and policies of James Stuart. The strategies of the mill-owners and the alliances between the acting parties in the enforcement process were very different in Scotland and in Lancashire.

However, contemporaries involved in factory reform were somewhat suspicious of Stuart's close collaboration with the Glasgow manufacturers. He was forcefully criticized by the 1840 Select Committee on the operation of the 1833 Factory Act for his policy of demanding the dismissal of mule-spinners found to have offended against the Act, instead of prosecuting the manufacturers.[126] Stuart was also made to admit that he relatively seldom inspected the workrooms in the factories, often being content with an examination of the registers and the recently employed young workers.[127]

The surviving picture of Stuart has been largely formed by the bad impression he made before the 1840 committee.[128] However, the evidence given before this committee is much more ambiguous than has previously been understood. The committee members clearly used the situation in Lancashire as a point of reference and did not perceive the very material differences which prevailed in the Scottish district. Leonard Horner had through his reports, and as the first witness before the committee, more or less defined the problems of enforcement connected with the 1833 Act. The committee was therefore very suspicious of Stuart's avoidance of prose-cutions and his close collaboration with the Glasgow manufacturers. Being much influenced by the Lancashire situation of considerable evasions on the part of the employers, the committee found it especially remarkable that Stuart seldom inspected the workrooms of the mills. Stuart was put under hard pressure as to how he could assert that the law was observed if he did not check the factories thoroughly. His main answer, that the Glasgow manufacturers were more sensitive to prosecutions than those in

125 Apart from the more general evidence on industrial relations and evasion patterns in Lancashire, this is also suggested in the evidence of John Doherty before the 1838 committee on combinations. See PP 1837-38, VIII, First Report..., p. 261 Q. 3,587.
126 PP 1840 X, Second Report from the Select Committee..., evidence of James Stuart, pp. 85-86 Q. 3,516-17, 3,534-35.
127 Ibid., p. 76 Q. 3,392-94.
128 See, for instance, Henriques (1979), p. 105.

Lancashire, hardly convinced his questioners.[129] The impression of partiality and general mismanagement was probably increased by Stuart's haughty, un-cooperative, and sometimes dishonest answers. However, a closer reading of the evidence shows that the committee was to some extent mistaken.

Indeed, the questioning of Stuart illustrates one of the typical difficulties when interpreting sources based on interrogation.[130] The questioners were eager to receive answers which fitted their specific conception of the problem, while the respondent, finding that his answers were not accepted, was forced on the defensive. The discourse and the resulting protocol therefore contain a heavy imprint of the anticipations of the questioners, which tend to overshadow and deform the evidence given by the witness.[131]

A closer reading of the testimony of the operative spinners actually provides a radically different estimation of enforcement levels in Glasgow than was formed by the 1840 committee. Henry Dunn had stated that there were many children working in the Glasgow cotton mills with incorrect certificates of age, but when asked to be more specific he claimed that there was "one or two, more or less, to be found in almost every factory".[132] When compared to the sometimes chaotic situation which prevailed in Lancashire in the late 1830s, this actually seems to have been a very modest level of evasion. Similarly, when the mule-spinner James McNish was pressed for particulars on factory offences, he stated that younger children tended to work in the mills until the surgeon came by on his round, refused them a certificate and had them turned away.[133] This hardly gives the impression of systematic evasions.

Indeed, the silence in the testimony of the operative spinners actually provides some important clues on enforcement levels. The members of the 1840 committee were much disturbed by the fact that Stuart seldom inspected the workrooms in the factories, and seem to have concluded that

---

129 PP 1840 X, Second Report from the Select Committee..., evidence of Stuart, pp. 76-78 Q. 3,392-94, 3,418, 3,420. In their final report, the committee specifically stated that the inspectors should be instructed to go through all parts of the factories. PP 1841 IX, Report..., p. 23.

130 On this problem, see Ginzburg, C (1981): The Cheese and the Worms. The Cosmos of a Sixteenth Century Miller; Ginzburg, C (1983): The Night Battles. Witchcraft and Agrarian Cults in the Sixteenth and Seventeenth Centuries; Portelli, A (1985): Oral Testimony, the Law, and the Making of History: the April 7 Murder Trial, passim.

131 In great exasperation after the questioning by the committee, Stuart wrote a letter to Lord Ashley, who acted as chairman. But before sending it, he forwarded a copy to the Home Secretary, Lord Normanby, for approval. The Home Secretary answered that "this letter is written in a tone of great disrespect to that Committee, and...would be most reprehensible". He also found the letter "highly indecorous and improper", and told Stuart to control his public communications "within the bounds of decorum" if he wanted to retain his position as factory inspector. HO 87/1, Letter Book on Factories, Letter from Maule to Stuart, 14/7/40.

132 PP 1840 X, Sixth Report from the Select Committee..., evidence of Henry Dunn, mule-spinner, Glasgow, p. 24 Q. 8,637.

133 PP 1839 XIX, RIF, p. 53.

extensive evasions may have taken place unknown to the inspector. However, Henry Dunn, James McNish, and the other Glasgow spinners giving evidence hardly give any indication at all that such evasions were practiced in the Glasgow mills.[134] It is inconceivable that such transgressions could have taken place without the knowledge of the operative spinners, or that they would not have mentioned it when giving evidence, since it would materially have strengthened their case. But the testimony of the mule-spinners is conspicuously silent on this matter. All their criticism of the operation of the 1833 Act was concentrated on the issue of medical certificates, and their contention that these documents did not reflect the true age of the children. But as Henry Dunn's evidence indicates, this type of evasion seems to have been much more prevalent in the Lancashire district than in Glasgow. The overall conclusion must be that the 1833 Act was much more stringently enforced in the Glasgow cotton district than in Lancashire.

On the question of age certificates, there is also some further evidence which indicates that these were more reliable in the Glasgow district than in Lancashire. Stuart adopted Horner's policy of appointing the certifying surgeons, and reinforced it by regulating that the children were to be examined and certified at the factories. The surgeons were no longer allowed to perform this work in their homes. Instead, they went regularly round to the mills in their respective district, examined the young workers who had been employed recently, granting certificates to some while turning others away. The certificates were then kept in the factories, generally pasted in a book in the counting-house. Stuart claimed that these tightening measures had put an end to the local trade in medical certificates.[135] Even if this assertion may have been somewhat of an overstatement, there is no denying that the measures regulating the issuing of certificates in Glasgow were more strict than those applied in Lancashire. It is also clear that Stuart had no real backing from the legal text when requiring that surgeons had to perform their duties at the factories, and that this solution rested on the cordial co-operation between Stuart and the mill-owners.[136]

Admittedly, Stuart seems to have entertained a very high opinion of the quality and discrimination of the appointed surgeons, regarding them as the

---

134 The only exception is one case of concealment of children evidenced by Henry Dunn in 1840. See PP 1840 X, Sixth Report from the Select Committee..., evidence by Dunn, p. 26 Q. 8,665.
135 See, for instance, PP 1837-38 XXVIII, RIF, pp. 12, 22, 47.
136 HO 87/1, Letter from Phillipps, Home Office, to Stuart, 28/3/37.

best judges of childrens' ages.[137] There is also some evidence that he disagreed with the other inspectors in this matter, claiming that the inspector had no legal right to disqualify certificates which had been properly granted by surgeons.[138] On the other hand, Stuart's enforcement practices were never really dependent on the right to disqualify certificates. His general practice was to examine all children and young persons employed since his last visit, and compare their appearances with the medical certificates. When he occasionally objected to the employment of some young workers, Stuart simply asked the manufacturer to dismiss them. This demand, he claimed, was always complied with.[139]

The co-operativeness of the manufacturers in this matter may appear strange, but it has to be remembered that the recruitment of the young piecers was handled entirely by the mule-spinners. The extra exertions required to replace those dismissed by the surgeon or by Stuart was simply not a concern of the mill-owners. The compliance of the Glasgow manufacturers with Stuart's occasional demands for dismissals was easily obtained since it cost them practically nothing. It is no wonder that Stuart could confidently claim that "the fault, wherever an erroneous certificate appears, is seldom, if ever, with the factory owner, who takes no interest in the matter".[140]

On the question of enforcement in the Glasgow district, it should also be pointed out that Stuart's depiction of the situation was corroborated by the resident Superintendent, Daniel Walker. In a letter to Stuart in 1838, Walker wrote:

I cannot conceive where Mr. O'Connel got his information, that the Factory Act is here a dead letter. So far from this being the case, I do not think there is a single town in the whole Kingdom where the Act is more strictly attended to in all its provisions than in Glasgow. The mill-owners evince every disposition to carry the Act into full and complete effect. [141]

Walker also claimed that he was always given free access to all parts of the factories, and that the mill-owners readily dismissed all the children whose age certificates he objected to.[142] In 1840 Walker reasserted his opinions before the Select Committee:

137 See, for instance, PP 1837 XXXI, RIF, p. 66; PP 1840 X, Second Report from the Select Committee..., evidence of James Stuart, pp. 77-78 Q. 3,420; PP 1840 XXIII, RIF, 1st Quarterly Report 1840, p. 10; PP 1841 X, RIF, 4th Quarterly Report 1840, pp. 26-27.
138 LAB 15/1, Minutes of the Meetings of the Inspectors of Factories, 6/7/38; PP 1837 XXXI, RIF, p. 66.
139 See PP 1837-38 XXVIII, RIF, p. 22, 47-48; PP 1837-38 XLV, RIF, p. 10; PP 1840 XXIII, RIF, 1st Quarterly Report 1840, p. 10; PP 1841 X, RIF, 4th Quarterly Report 1840, pp. 24, 33.
140 PP 1837-38 XXVIII, RIF, p. 47. See also ibid., p. 12.
141 Letter from Walker to Stuart, 30/6/38. Printed in PP 1837-38 XLV, RIF, p. 12.
142 Ibid.

Is it your opinion, after the experience you have had now above two years, that the law is generally observed at Glasgow? - Yes, I think so; and that is the opinion of mostly all the people connected with factories in Glasgow. [143]

When asked by the committee to explain the diminished rate of child labour in the Glasgow factories, Walker stated that he could not induce the managers to employ children below the age of 13, "because of the great trouble they say it gives them".[144] As I will describe more fully in a later chapter, a reason often put forward by the Glasgow manufacturers for not employing children below 13 was that they did not want to be legally responsible for the schooling of the factory children. Walker's evidence also indicates that surveillance levels were much higher in Glasgow than in the Lancashire district. Each Glasgow mill was visited six times per year, which was approximately twice as frequent as the normal inspection practice in Lancashire.[145] These findings substantiate the notion that enforcement levels were relatively high in the Glasgow district.

The evidence of Daniel Walker has been entirely overlooked by those historians who have focussed their attention on the person and policies of James Stuart.[146] However, what stands out in this investigation is the distinct "otherness" of the Glasgow industry, an impression which is substantiated by a brief look outside Stuart's term of office. Already in 1833, Leonard Horner reported after his first meeting with the Glasgow mill-owners that "a very general disposition was evinced on the part of the mill-owners to give effect to the Act as far as it is in their power".[147] Apart from the prevalence of incorrect age certificates, Horner claimed in his subsequent reports that the law was duly observed in its main provisions.[148] But Horner also regretted the fact that the Glasgow manufacturers had decided to dismiss all children coming under the Act:

I regret...to say, that in the greater number of factories in my district, the owners have shown an unwillingness to take even that moderate degree of trouble which would

---

143 PP 1840 X, Fourth Report from the Select Committee..., evidence of Daniel Walker, p 3. Q. 4,928.

144 Ibid., p. 20 Q. 5,333. The Glasgow manufacturers' great dislike for the educational clauses of the 1833 Act was commented on already by Horner in 1835. See PP 1835 XL, RIF, p. 2.

145 PP 1840 X, Fourth Report from the Select Committee..., evidence of Walker, p. 11 Q. 5,116; Ibid, First Report, evidence of Leonard Horner, p 3. Q. 56. See also PP 1840 XXIII, RIF, 1st Quarterly Report 1840, p. 3. According to the figures in PP 1839 XLII, Return of the Number of Mills visited by each Inspector, p. 9, Daniel Walker's visiting rate in 1838 was 6.7 inspections per factory and year.

146 Walker is conspicuously absent in the work of Henriques on factory law enforcement in Scotland. It might also be added that Daniel Walker remained with the inspectorate and was eventually promoted to the second highest position in the organization.

147 PP 1834 XLIII, RIF, p. 2. See also the letter from Horner to his daughters, 14/4/34, in Memoir of Leonard Horner (1890), Vol I, p. 290.

148 PP 1835 XL, RIF, pp. 1-2; PP 1836 XLV, RIF, pp. 4, 12-13.

have been sufficient to insure [sic] an improvement in the moral condition of the children by attendance at school, and have followed the easier course to themselves of dismissing all under 12 years of age. [149]

Similarly, Horner stated before the 1840 committee that practically all children had been excluded from the Scottish factories.[150]

During the early 1840s, Stuart continued to report that the law was strictly enforced in his district.[151] But it seems that the strictures he had received from the 1840 committee had made him somewhat more cautious. On the matter of the dismissal of mule-spinners found responsible for transgressions, Stuart wrote in his last report for 1840:

My interference is now seldom or ever required; for the mill-owners, of their own accord, without any suggestion from me or the Superintendents, dismiss every spinner whom they or their overseers find guilty of any fraudulent attempt to impose on them or their managers, or the certifying surgeon... [152]

The same deterrant remained, but now possibly without the active involvement of the inspector. But it should perhaps also be pointed out that there was a slight increase in prosecutions during brisk periods of trade.[153] The return of summoned persons shows that there was a sudden increase in prosecutions after the passing of the 1844 Act also in Stuart's district. Twenty-two convictions were obtained against Glasgow manufacturers for overworking women and juveniles, and ten were convicted on the child labour clauses.[154]

There is also some evidence which indicates that Stuart was not inclined to show leniency when he was convinced that manufacturers had committed a clear offence. When Dunlop & Sons, Glasgow, were convicted in 1848 for employing five young persons to clean the machinery during the meal hour, Stuart positively refused to have the penalties mitigated.[155] He also involved

---

149 PP 1836 XLV, RIF, p. 4. At the time of the report, the 1833 Act did not yet encompass children of 12 years of age.

150 PP 1840 X, First Report from the Select Committee..., evidence of Leonard Horner, p. 61 Q. 875-77. See also Horner's report in PP 1857 2nd Session XVI, RIF, 1st Half-yearly Report 1857, p. 26.

151 PP 1841 X, RIF, 4th Quarterly Report 1840, p. 24; PP 1847 XV, RIF, 2nd Half-yearly Report 1846, p. 36; PP 1847-48 XXVI, RIF, 2nd Half-yearly Report 1847, p. 37; PP 1849 XII, RIF, 1st Half-yearly Report 1849, p. 46.

152 PP 1841 X, RIF, 4th Quarterly Report 1840, p. 31.

153 See PP 1844 XXVIII, RIF, 4th Quarterly Report 1843, p. 29; PP 1845 XXV, RIF, 1st Half-yearly Report 1845, p. 54.

154 PP 1846 XXXIV, A Return of the Number and Names..., pp. 52-58.

155 HO 45/2274 Letter from Stuart to Cornewall Lewis, Home Office, 30/10/48. Stuart also reacted sharply when magistrates refused to convict in cases which he though were very clear. See LAB 15/2, Minutes of the Meetings of the Inspectors of Factories, 10/12/45, 12/12/45, on a case of a Glasgow operative seriously injured due to unfenced machinery, where the magistrates had convicted the employers but had not inflicted

himself in a case of a young operative, who had been dismissed for giving evidence against his employer, to such an extent that he was censored by the Home Secretary and told to assume a more neutral position.[156] The recurring conflicts which were such an predominant feature of Stuart's life really suggests that he could become vindictive when opposed. But from the present investigation it seems clear that his policies were practically never resisted by the Glasgow manufacturers.

Stuart's last years in office were marked by sharp conflicts with the other factory inspectors, above all over the contested legality of the working of women and juveniles in relays.[157] Matters did not change until Stuart's death in November 1849. It is very probable that this dispute largely discredited Stuart's performance as inspector within the organization. A Swedish investigator of the British factory legislation who visited the inspectorate in the late 1880s, was told that the early Scottish factory inspector, presumably James Stuart, had been dishonest in the execution of his duties.[158]

However, if there had been a great deal of mismanagement in the Scottish district one would anticipate that such evidence would have been brought forward when Stuart was replaced by Kincaid as factory inspector. Yet, the only case of irregularity which Kincaid reported to the other inspectors was that Stuart had exempted handloom weavers who worked within a mill from the regulation of the Factory Acts.[159]

Moreover, Stuart's successors continued to point out that the Scottish district differed in very material aspects from that of Lancashire. Kincaid, who was responsible for the Scottish district between 1849 and 1862, continued to report that the Factory Acts were well observed. In 1857, for instance, he reported:

---

any penalty. See also HO 87/2, Letter from Manners Sutton to Stuart, 8/4/46, on Stuart's complaints on the Kilmarnock magistrates.

156 LAB 15/2, Minutes of the Meetings of the Inspectors of Factories. Letter from Manners Sutton, Home Office, to Stuart, 25/11/44. Stuart had acted together with the secretary of the local short-time committee to have the boy re-employed. Stuart duly promised not to co-operate with officials of short-time committees or any other form of organized interest. HO 45/658, Letter from Stuart to Manners Sutton, Home Office, 30/11/44.

157 HO 45/1117, Confidential letter from Saunders to Somerville, Home Office, 5/1/47; LAB 15/2, Minutes of the Meetings..., 7/1/47, 6/12/48, 21/12/48, 27/12/48, 2/1/49, 9/1/49, 13/1/49; HO 45/2272, Letter from Stuart to le Marechant, Home Office, 22/4/48; HO 45/1851, Letter from Stuart to Cornewall Lewis, Home Office, 14/8/48. See also Stuart's lengthy argumentation in PP 1849 XXII, RIF, 2nd Half-yearly Report 1848, pp. 130-46.

158 Fredholm, J H G (1890): Arbetarelagstiftningen och fabriksinspektionen i utlandet, p. 131.

159 LAB 15/3, Minutes of the Meetings of the Inspectors of Factories. Letter from the inspectors to Sir George Grey, 30/6/51. This was contrary to the practice of the other inspectors, and was not previously known by them.

It is a great satisfaction to me to be able to report so generally that the laws which regulate the employment of women, young persons, and children in factories, continue to be so strictly observed by the mill-owners of Scotland... [160]

Kincaid repeated this central theme many times during his period of office.[161] The main problem of inspection still seems to have been the reliability of medical cerificates and the surgeons' estimations of true age. Kincaid hoped that these problems would be lessened by the passing of a Registration of Births Act for Scotland in 1854.[162] In other respects, there are no indications of any problems encountered in the course of factory inspection. Kincaid's appreciation of the Glasgow manufacturers closely resembled that of his predecessor. In 1857, for instance, Kincaid reported that the mill-owners manifested an "anxious desire" to observe the Act.[163] It is also clear that the few prosecutions which eventually took place in his district were mainly in Dundee and Aberdeen, not in Glasgow.[164] In one of his reports in 1860, Kincaid summed up his experiences in the Glasgow district:

I feel it due to the mill-owners in the Western division of the district of Scotland to state, that I have not had occasion to take proceedings in a single case in that district, for many years, although it includes the extensive manufacturing counties of Renfrew and Lanark. [165]

Fortunately, we do not have to rely exclusively on the evidence of the inspectors for an estimation of enforcement levels in Glasgow during Kincaid's term of office. A local Radical paper, the Glasgow Sentinel, reported extensively during the 1850s on the struggle of the Lancashire inspectors to control illegal overworking. Commenting on Kincaid's report in 1858 that no prosecutions had been staged in Scotland, the editors asked their readers to communicate to them any cases of violation of the Factory Act in the Glasgow district. However, there is no trace of such information

---

160 PP 1857-58 XXIV, RIF, 2nd Half-yearly Report 1857, p. 29.
161 See PP 1851 XXIII, RIF, 2nd Half-yearly Report 1850, p. 39; Ibid., 1st Half-yearly Report 1851, p. 35; PP 1852 XXI, RIF, 2nd Half-yearly Report 1851, p. 20; PP 1856 XVIII, RIF, 2nd Half-yearly Report 1855, p. 42; PP 1857 1st Session III, RIF, 2nd Half-yearly Report 1856, p. 64; PP 1859 XII, RIF, 2nd Half-yearly Report 1858, p. 20; PP 1859 2nd Session XIV, RIF, 1st Half-yearly Report 1859, p. 18.
162 PP 1854 XIX, RIF, 2nd Half-yearly Report 1853, pp. 36-37; PP 1854-55 XV, RIF, 2nd Half-yearly Report 1854, p. 56.
163 PP 1856 XVIII, RIF, 2nd Half-yearly Report 1855, p. 42.
164 For Dundee, see PP 1857 2nd Session XVI, RIF, 1st Half-yearly Report 1857, p 30, on a case of the overworking of women in a flax factory. For Aberdeen, see PP 1854 XIX, RIF, 2nd Half-yearly Report 1853, pp. 34-35, where two textile manufacturers were prosecuted for the overworking of young persons and women, and high penalties inflicted.
165 PP 1861 XXII, RIF, 2nd Half-yearly Report 1860, p. 7.

in later issues of the Glasgow Sentinel.[166] The conclusion must be that factory offences were relatively unusual in that district also in the 1850s.

After the resignation of Kincaid in 1861, the Scottish district was taken over by Alexander Redgrave. He made very much the the same estimation of enforcement and the actions of the local manufacturers as the prevoius inspectors. One year after taking over responsibility in Scotland, Redgrave reported that he had made no prosecutions in that district, and that he had been "struck by the earnest desire" for the observation of the Factory Acts among the mill-owners.[167] According to the testimony of the Glasgow Sub-inspectors, the factory regulations were still generally observed in 1876.[168] Stuart was, after all, perhaps not such a strange case as has been claimed by some historians.

# Conclusions

Previous research on the British factory inspection has seriously under-estimated the enforcement of the child labour clauses of the early Factory Acts. The present investigation shows that the formal requirements of the 1833 Act on the keeping of age certificates, time-books, and registers of workers, were well enforced already by 1840. The overworking of children beyond the legal time was much reduced after the passing of the 1844 Act, when the work of children below 13 was organized in a regular half-time system. In the second half of the 19th century, overworking of women and juvenile operatives, and breaches of the safety regulations, constituted the main factory offences in the Lancashire cotton industry.

In the Scottish context, I have challenged the predominant notion that the early factory legislation was not enforced in the Glasgow cotton district due to the partiality and incompetence of the early factory inspector James Stuart. The enforcement level in Glasgow has to be seen in the context of the specific strategies of the mill-owners in the implementation of the 1833 Act. The very hostile industrial relations which prevailed in the Glasgow industry induced the manufacturers to make the operatives responsible for the hiring of child workers below 13. The enforcement policies employed by James Stuart were designed to fit this particular context.

Stuart's own innovation of having operatives dismissed for breaches of the Factory Acts no doubt lacked legal backing, but in the context of

---

166 Glasgow Sentinel 13/2/58.
167 PP 1863 XVIII, RIF, 2nd Half-yearly Rep. 1862, p. 7.
168 PP 1876 XXX, Factory Commissioners, evidence of W. E. Stokes and H. W. Kindersley, Sub-inspectors, Glasgow, p. 696 Q. 14,541-43.

enforcement these measures were very effective. The main type of evasion which remained in the Glasgow district was the issuing of unreliable medical certificates, but even here there are some indications that these problems were somewhat less serious than in Lancashire. Contrary to received historical opinion, the child labour clauses of the early Factory Acts were on the whole much better enforced in Glasgow than in the Lancashire cotton district.

One important implication of these findings is that child labour in the Glasgow cotton industry virtually ceased in the late 1830s. Obviously,the main reason behind this was the strategies employed by the Glasgow manufacturers when the 1833 Act was implemented. However, development in the Lancashire district was very different. This will be evident in the examination of the processes and relations in the Lancashire industry in subsequent chapters.

# Chapter 4

# Child Labour, Technology, and the Composition of the Cotton Factory Workforce

In this and the subsequent chapters I will try to describe and explain the changes in the use of child labour in cotton factories over time and between different regions. One obvious starting point is an examination of the factory returns, which were collected by the inspectors approximately every five years. These statistics show that child labour levels were considerably lower after 1845 than had been the case before the 1833 Act was implemented. But there were also several important variations in this pattern:

Table 6. The work of children below 13 as a proportion of the total working time in the Lancashire and Scottish cotton industries.[1] per cent.

| Year | Lancashire | Scotland |
|------|------------|----------|
| 1835 | 13.4 | 12.5 |
| 1838 | 3.3 | 2.4 |
| 1845 | 4.4 | ? |
| 1847 | 3.3 | 1.2 |
| 1850 | 2.3 | 1.0 |
| 1857 | 4.0 | 1.3 |
| 1862 | 6.0 | 1.0 |
| 1867 | 7.3 | 0.8 |
| 1870 | 6.4 | 1.0 |
| 1874 | 9.4 | 1.3 |
| 1878 | 8.4 | 2.5 |
| 1885 | 6.7 | 1.6 |
| 1890 | 6.1 | 1.5 |

Sources: British Parliamentary Papers, Factory Returns 1835-1890; PP 1846 XX, RIF, p 14; HO 45/455, Factories in the United Kingdom, 1839.

---

1 The figures have been adjusted for the fact that the legal working day for children below 13 was reduced in 1836 and 1845.

By the time of the first factory return in 1835, children of 12 years of age were still allowed to work the full 12 hours per day. They were not included under the Factory Act until 1836. Consequently, the reason for the comparatively high figure in 1835 was probably that 12 year olds were still employed to a considerable extent. It should also be pointed out that the figures from 1838 should not be taken at face value due to the substantial number of evasions of the age clauses before 1840.

Still, it is obvious that child labour levels in Lancashire did by no means decrease evenly in the wake of the 1844 Act. After 1850 there was a clear rise in the labour force participation of children, followed by a peak in the mid-1870s, and a decline during the subsequent decade. The Scottish pattern was very different. The level of child labour remained very low after 1845, with only a small peak in 1878.

However, these are aggregated statistics which should be seen as the final outcome of several different processes. But the very unevenness of the pattern is in a sense illuminating, since it implies a sharp contrast between the Lancashire district and Scotland.

Returning to the comparative perspective, one major task in this chapter is to examine the effects of technological change on workforce composition and child labour levels in Britain and the U.S.A.. This investigation is particularly required since one of the few recent attempts to explain the changes in the use of factory children in the English cotton industry postulates a firm technological link. Clark Nardinelli has asserted that the decline in child labour levels in the textile trades after the passing of the 1833 Factory Act was mainly caused by the transition in spinning technology from hand-mules to "self-actors".[2] Nardinelli's thesis will now be tried empirically.


### Technological Change and the Decline of Child Labour: the Case of the Self-acting Mule

I have previously shown that by the early 1830s the major form of employment of children in the British cotton mills was as piecers in mule-spinning.[3] At that point in time, the machine-maker Richard Roberts finally managed to construct a commercially viable self-acting mule.[4]

Nardinelli has suggested that the long-term decline in the level of child labour over the period 1836-1890 was caused by the gradual introduction of the self-actor. This machine could at first only be used commercially on the

---

2 Nardinelli (1980), passim.
3 See chapter 2.
4 Catling (1970), pp. 63-67.

coarser counts of yarn, but during the above time period it was gradually improved, making it increasingly viable on the finer counts. Towards the end of the century the self-actor had replaced the hand-mule on all qualities of cotton spinning.

While the gradual transition to the self-actor technology is a rather well-known fact, it remains to explain the link with child labour. The main reason why children were dismissed at the introduction of the self-actor was, according to Nardinelli, that the new machine required a lesser amount of piecing than the old hand-mule, and this operation was mainly performed by children. However, it must be said that Nardinelli's line of argument is not altogether clear. He goes on to state that the child workers were replaced with women, which does not really make sense if the operations performed by children were no longer required. Nardinelli also states that the long-term increase of operatives' earnings was the major factor behind the decline of child labour. Again, this simply does not fit with his insistence that the introduction of the self-actor made child workers redundant.

Leaving aside the question of logical consistency in Nardinelli's article, there is the question of the empirical support he has produced. He does not provide any evidence on factory level to show that children were not employed on the new self-actors. Nor does he refer to any qualitative sources claiming that this was the case. His argument rests entirely on an interpretation of the aggregated factory statistics, figures which on closer scrutiny hardly support his case. The changes in child labour levels after 1833 hardly correlate with the gradual introduction of the self-actor. The sharp contrast between the Lancashire and the Scottish patterns also makes this technological link very dubious.

More importantly, there is some additional empirical evidence which points in the opposite direction. One of the most extensive sets of factory records from this period which has survived is the Greg Collection in Manchester, covering wage and production books of Quarry Bank Mill, Styal. When self-acting mules were introduced at this factory in the late 1830s, it is evident from the wage book material that the workforce at the self-actors comprised a considerable proportion of children. Indeed, the use of children below 13 actually seems to have increased substantially in the process of self-actor spinning between 1840 and 1867.[5] This indicates that children were not made redundant by any specific requirements of the new technology.

---

5 Greg Collection. Wage and Production books; Statement of number of hands at Quarry Bank Mill. That the new mules were really self-actors is confirmed in Rose (1986), p. 70.

Similarly, the 1833 commissioners found that in Birley's mill, Manchester, the hand-mule spinners employed on average 1.8 young assistants each, while the self-actors in the same mill were staffed by 4.6 piecers to each pair.[6] The large difference is to some extent explained by the fact that the hand-mules were old and relatively short, on average carrying 221 spindles each. But this evidence still refutes the claim that the self-actor removed the need for child labour.

Indeed, Nardinelli does not seem to have perceived that the self-actors were initially staffed entirely with young workers. The manufacturers were above all interested in getting rid of the skilled mule-spinners, and initially tried to run the self-actors entirely with child and juvenile piecers. This is evident from the testimony of several manufacturers who adopted self-actors in the 1830s.[7] The immediate result of the adoption of this new spinning technology was therefore a marked increase in the proportion of young workers in this part of the labour process. Only after a while did the manufacturers accept the employment of adult men as self-actor minders.

For the later period, Nardinelli's thesis is strongly questioned by the evidence of the 1886 Wage Census. This investigation was based on a sample of 28 per cent of the English cotton operatives[8], and from the tables it is possible to reconstruct the composition of the workforce at the separate processes.

If Nardinelli were correct, one would expect to find a considerably higher child labour level on the hand-mules than on the self-actors. However, the outcome is rather the opposite. In hand-mule spinning, the proportion of child workers below 13 was only 2.5 per cent of the workforce, which was less than half of the proportion found in self-actor spinning. In a sample covering 121 pairs of hand-mules in fine-spinning Bolton, not a single child worker was found. At the same time, the proportion of half-timers in Bolton self-actor spinning was 3.6 per cent of the workforce.[9]

---

6 PP 1833 XX, First Report of...Commissioners, evidence of Samuel Holt, head overlooker, Birley's mill, Manchester, p. D1 66.

7 PP 1833 VI, Report from the Select Committee on Manufactures..., evidence of William Graham, Glasgow mill-owner, p. 323; PP 1833 XX, First Report of... Commissioners, evidence of Thomas Ralphs, James Hall, Daniel Connelly, mule-spinners, and John Rushton, overlooker, Manchester, p. D2 117; PP 1833 XXI, Second Report of... Commissioners, evidence of Peter Ewart, cotton manufacturer, Manchester, p. D2 37; Ibid., evidence of Benjamin Kirk, cotton manufacturer, Manchester, p. D2 54; PP 1837-38 VIII, First Report from the Select Committee on Combinations of Workmen, evidence of Charles Todd, cotton manufacturer, Glasgow, p. 24 Q. 522-23. See also Rose, H (1825): Manual Labour versus Brass and Iron: Reflections in Defence of the Body of Cotton Spinners, Occasioned by a Perusal of the Description of Mr. Roberts's Self-Acting Mule, passim.

8 PP 1889 LXX, Return of Rates of Wages..., p. vi.

9 Ibid., pp. 11-13, 21-24, 55-58. N for the hand-mule workforce = 715; N for the Bolton self-actor workforce = 2,413. The proportion of children below 13 in Lancashire self-actor spinning was 5.5 per cent, N = 19,351.

The conclusion must be that the hand-mule did not in itself require more child labour than the self-actor, and that the decline in the use of children in the mule-spinning process over the period 1840-1890 seems to have occurred in both hand-mule and self-actor spinning.[10] Consequently, this development must have been caused by other processes than the technology shift.

Moreover, an examination of the wage census material questions Nardinelli's notion that child piecers were replaced by women at the self-actors. Of all the big piecers in the sample of self-acting mule spinning operatives, only 6.8 per cent were women, and of these a majority came from the Manchester district.[11] In the rest of Lancashire women piecers were very unusual. These findings really illustrate the hazards of basing historical interpretations solely on aggregated statistics.

However, there were some minor changes in the organization of work in spinning which tended to reduce the need for piecers. The task of fetching the roving from the carding-room had previously been performed by the young assistants, but it was now increasingly done by adult male "bobbin-carriers". They were initially paid out of the spinners' wages, but that custom was dropped after a few decades. This meant that the work-team at the mules did less of the carrying tasks.[12] There is also some justification in the position that the piecing requirements were less on the self-actor, since on this machine the spinner was liberated from the task of pushing the headstock and was therefore free to take part in the piecing operations.[13]

But there were also tendencies in the opposite direction. The actual need for piecing was determined by several different factors; above all the speed of the machinery, the length of the mules, and the quality of the roving. Running the self-acting mules at higher speed, or using a lower quality of raw cotton in the roving, or introducing longer machines with more spindles; all these changes would increase the number of breakages and necessitate more piecing operations. As I will show in later chapters, such changes did take place during the second half of the 19th century. Self-actors in Lancashire were built longer, run at higher speeds and using inferior cotton. Three piecers per spinner became the norm for mules above 1,200 spindles. Contrary to Nardinelli's assertion, I would therefore

---

10 There are some indications that the proportion of piecers to spinners was higher in the 1830s and 40s than later became the norm. Shuttleworth's inquiry in 1843 into the large Manchester fine-spinning mills shows that each adult hand-mule spinner was on average assisted by almost four piecers, or 3,233 piecers to 837 spinners. However, this material does not state whether some piecers were below 13 years of age and used in relays. See Shuttleworth (1843), p. 93.

11 PP 1889 LXX, Return of Rates of Wages..., pp. 7-58.

12 Cotton Factory Times 11/4/90; 20/10/99; Banks, T (1888): A Short Sketch of the Cotton Trade in Preston..., p. 1; Harris Library, Preston. Preston Spinners' Minutes, 28/1/92; 11/2/92.

13 Mason (1987a), p. 9.

suggest that the piecing requirements increased substantially during this later period.

These findings make it highly debatable if there was any direct causal link between piecing requirements and child labour. Instead, I would argue that the labour force participation of children was mainly determined by the actual organization of work at the self-actor, or a part of the more general formation of the labour process. This, in turn, must be seen as a social construct, and a result of the relations and negotiations between operatives and management. Child labour practices have to be seen in the context of a specific organization of work.

Here the comparative perspective becomes useful. In Lancashire, the work at the self-actor crystallized in the form of one adult male "minder" assisted by one "big piecer" and one "little piecer" or "creeler". In contrast, in the American cotton industry, the self-actor spinner generally did all the piecing himself, and was only assisted by a "back-boy" supplying him with rovings. The wider issue of differences in work organization and their origins will be treated more fully in the subsequent section.

### Authority, Gender, and the Organization of Work in British and U.S. Self-acting Mule Spinning, 1835-1890

19th century cotton spinning in Lancashire has received a great deal of attention in historical, sociological and economic research. One of the "classic" questions has been why the skilled male hand-mule spinners were not replaced with cheap female labour when the "automatic" self-actor was introduced in the early 1830s.

This invention was commissioned by a group of manufacturers with the express intention of relieving them from their dependence on skilled male operatives.[14] Contemporary adherents of political economy like Andrew Ure predicted the immediate end of the mule-spinners' unions as a result of the new invention. According to Ure, the self-actor dispensed wholly with the adult spinner and could be staffed entirely by children.[15] From a very different point of view, Karl Marx saw the self-actor as a capitalist weapon directed against the spinners.[16] Nevertheless, it is clear that these predictions did not come true. The organization of work on the new self-actors in Lancashire remained practically the same as on the old hand-mule. The adult male spinner or "minder" worked a pair of self-actors on a

---

14 Catling (1970), pp. 63-64. But attempts to construct a self-acting mule had been going on in Britain and in the U.S. all through the 1820s. See Jeremy (1981), p. 213.
15 Ure (1836), Vol II, p. 199.
16 Marx, K (1979) [1867]: Capital, Vol I, p. 563.

piece-rate basis, and subcontracted two piecers to assist him. Why, then, was the traditional organization of work not abandoned and the male operatives replaced with cheaper female workers?

Several different explanations have been put forward. The retention of the traditional organization of work and the right of the spinner to subcontract his piecers has been seen as an outcome of union strength. This opinion has been expressed by, among others, H. A. Turner, Roger Penn, and Isaac Cohen.[17] From a feminist point of view, Mariana Valverde has recently argued that the exclusionist practices of the male mule-spinners' unions served to bar women workers from this occupation.[18]

Other contributors to this debate have pointed out that spinning on the self-actor was by no means so devoid of skill as has previously been maintained. Harold Catling argued along these lines already in 1970, and more recently Margaret Freifeld has convincingly shown that the self-actor was not fully "automatic" before the 1880s.[19] During the first fifty years, the winding motion on the self-actor was anything but perfect and still needed skilful attention.

Freifeld sees the persistence of the skill requirement as one part of the reason why female operatives were not used in Lancashire self-actor spinning. She argues that the development of longer hand-mules in the late 1820s effectively barred the employment of female spinners, since the operation of the larger machines required considerable physical strength. As a result, there were very few skilled female spinners left when the self-actor was introduced in the mid-1830s. The physical requirements were removed on the new technology, but the machine still needed skilful handling. Freifeld therefore sees the absence of women operatives on the new technology as occasioned by a gap in the transition of skill between women. This was the main reason why self-actor spinning remained a male preserve and the old structures survived.[20]

A rather different line of argument has been developed by William Lazonick, who has suggested that the fierce competition and low profit margins in the late 1830s and the 1840s effectively hindered the manufacturers from experimenting with alternative ways of staffing the self-actors. Mistaken experiments could, he argues, have meant the complete ruin of

17 Chapman (1904), p. 257;  Turner, H A (1962): Trade Union Growth, Structure and Policy. A Comparative Study of the Cotton Unions, p. 194; Thorpe, E (1969): Industrial Relations and the Social Structure: A Case Study of the Bolton Cotton Mule-Spinners 1884-1910, p. 118; White, J L (1982): Lancashire Cotton Textiles, pp. 213-14; Penn, R (1983): Trade Union Organization and Skill in the Cotton and Engineering Industries in Britain, 1850-1960, passim; Penn R (1985): Skilled Workers in the Class Structure, pp. 45-46; Cohen (1985a).
18 Valverde (1988), pp. 621-25.
19 Catling (1970), pp. 82-113 149; Freifeld (1986), passim.
20 Freifeld (1986), passim.

the firm. Moreover, Lazonick states that adult males were preferred because the work was potentially very arduous, and also because men commanded more respect in the supervisory functions.[21]

While space does not allow me to comment on all the contributions to this debate, some criticism is no doubt required. First, Lazonick's and Freifeld's perspectives both postulate that the transition to the minder-piecer system, as I shall call it subsequently, on the new self-actors was uniform and with few variations. Severe competition between fragmented manufacturers or, alternatively, a lack of skilled female spinners, would leave little room for alternative ways of organizing the labour process. However, very recent research has claimed that the degree of variation in the staffing of the self-actors has previously been underestimated.[22] Experiments with multi-pair systems were staged, and there were also attempts to employ female and juvenile spinners. In Lancashire several mills, including Holland Hoole's outside Manchester, tried to use female minders.[23] These findings make Lazonick's main argument less plausible.

Freifeld, however, makes a double error which to some extent cancels out. She has underestimated both the survival of female spinners and the extent to which women operatives were employed on the new self-actors. This is most clearly spelled out in her treatment of the Scottish case. Claiming that female spinners did not exist in Scotland, she has overlooked the fact that women spinners on short mules were fairly common in the country factories. In Glasgow, women had been largely prevented from staffing the mules by male exclusionist practices, but on the other hand, girl piecers were much used.[24] There was in Scotland certainly no lack of young women with experience of cotton spinning.

There is only very scanty evidence on what happened when self-actors were introduced in Glasgow. As I will show in a later chapter, it can at least be established that young women were employed as minders after the strike of 1837. Paradoxically, what Freifeld cannot explain is why women spinners did not completely replace the men in the Glasgow industry. By 1860 there were still as many male as female spinners in Glasgow.[25] Only when the skill requirements were lowered on technically improved self-actors in the 1880s did female spinners finally take over the Glasgow trade.

Freifeld's theory is problematic also in the Lancashire context. If the transition to the self-actor was very piecemeal, why did not the remaining nucleus of women spinners form the core of the new generation of

---

21 Lazonick (1979), passim.
22 Mason, J (1987c): Spinners and Minders, pp. 52-3.
23 Kirby and Musson (1975), pp. 13-14, and also PP 1842 XXII, RIF, 3d Quarterly Report 1841, p. 85.
24 See chapter 2.
25 London School of Economics. Webb Trade Union Collection, Vol 34 folio 413.

minders? To give one concrete illustration on factory level, when self-actors were adopted at the Quarry Bank Mill, Styal, in the late 1830s, the only operatives with any experience of the handling of yarn were the female throstle-spinners. Nevertheless, young male operatives were chosen as minders.[26] Union resistance to the employment of woman minders can hardly have been the cause, since the mill in question had a wholly non-unionized workforce.

All this suggests that the employers had some material reasons for preferring male minders to female. Michael Holbrook-Jones has argued that the male spinners were retained because of the capitalist's need to mediate authority. However, the weakness of this perspective is that it cannot explain why authority was mediated by the spinners and not by overlookers.[27] Instead, I would argue that the reasons were twofold: first, because the self-actor still needed considerable skill when used commercially. This made female labour less suitable, simply because women had a much shorter expected working life than male operatives. Women generally left factory work at marriage or at their first confinement. This meant that female minders would be expected to have a relatively short working life as fully trained operatives.[28] The women's responsibility for childcare and housework must be taken into account. This also means that the ideological conception of women, especially married women, as belonging in the context of the home rather than the factory, may have influenced the composition of the workforce.

Secondly, female minders were disadvantaged because the relatively high capital and running costs of the self-actor as compared to the hand-mule necessitated a high rate of work productivity. Tentatively, I would suggest that males had some physical advantage in the area of work intensity, and more importantly, that male operatives were more susceptible to various incentive schemes like bounty systems.[29] All these factors would tend to make male minders a more economical choice. Indeed, previous research

---

26 Greg Collection. Quarry Bank Mill Wage Books.

27 Holbrook-Jones, M (1982): Supremacy and Subordination of Labour. The Hierarchy of Work in the Early Labour Movement, pp. 13-14, 159-60. Holbrook-Jones is also too simplistic in his assertions that the minding of self-actors did not require skill.

28 PP 1833 XX, First Report..., evidence of John Stephen, manager of the Old Adelphi Mill, Glasgow, p. A2 50. One of the 1833 sub-commissioners, Dr Mitchell, concluded that few Scottish women worked in factories after marriage. PP 1834 XX, Factory Inquiry Commission, Supplementary Report Part I, p. 38. Margaret Irwin estimated in 1893 that a woman operative in the Glasgow cotton industry had a working life (in the factory) of nine years, usually entering at the age of 14. PP 1893-94 XXXVII Pt I, Royal Commission on Labour, p. 173.

29 The strategy of the Glasgow spinners to demand equal piece-rate for the female spinners seems to have been formed in the assurance that under such conditions the use of women operatives would not be profitable. See PP 1833 XX, First Report..., evidence of David Sloan, manager of Dennistoun and Co, Glasgow, p. A1 85.

may have been misled by the fallacy that cheap labour has to be the most economical. I would argue that the main strength of the minder-piecer system was its high level of work productivity, and that this compensated for the higher wage costs of the male spinners.

Moreover, it is interesting to note that female minders seem to have been used mainly for reasons of principle and as an expression of hostility towards the mule spinners' unions. As I have shown previously, the Glasgow mill-owners had been opposed in a powerful way by the local spinners' association before the disastrous strike in 1837, and they seem to have been determined to remove the "troublesome spinners" by introducing the self-actor. The evidence of several Glasgow manufacturers in the 1830s points clearly in this direction.[30]

As I have argued previously, the initial strategy of the manufacturers was to run the self-actors entirely with young workers. But it is probable that those who tried such cheap labour solutions soon found them to be unsuccessful. When self-actors were introduced in Quarry Bank Mill, Styal, in northern Cheshire, they were initially staffed with juveniles and children. But already in 1842 the work was reorganized, with two of the young male operatives put on a piece-rate scheme and supplied with several younger time-paid piecers.[31] Generally speaking, the managerial strategy of staffing the self-actors entirely with cheap female or juvenile labour was soon abandoned in Lancashire, but not in Scotland.

Before this important difference can be more fully treated, account has to be taken of the remaining major hypothesis on the retention of the traditional organization of work in Lancashire spinning, namely, that this was occasioned by union strength. In this passage I will concentrate on the work of Isaac Cohen, which provides the fullest, the most recent, and, for my purposes, the most relevant version.

Cohen is less concerned with the question of female minders, stating that they were mainly excluded by the sheer arduousness of the work.[32] His main perspective is on the degree of spinners' authority at the workplace as expressed in the subcontracting of piecers and the very relaxed supervisory functions of the Lancashire overlookers. By contrast, in the American cotton mills subcontracting and the use of piecers were largely discontinued by the manufacturers at the adoption of the self-actors. Foreman supervision was also much more harassing in the U.S.

---

30 PP 1833 VI, Report from the Select Committee on Manufactures..., evidence of W. Graham, pp. 322-24; Ibid., evidence of Kirkman Finlay, p. 40; PP 1837-38 VIII, First Report from the Select Committee on Combinations..., evidence of Charles Todd, pp. 20-24 Q. 452, 454, 521-23.
31 Greg Collection. Quarry Bank Mill Wage Books, 1840-44.
32 Cohen (1985a), p. 67.

Cohen's emphasis on authority and the survival of the subcontracting system in Lancashire mule-spinning is a very central issue also for my study of child labour practices in that part of the labour process. As I have indicated previously, I view the creation and support of subcontracting forms of employment as a very important part in the complex issue of industrial child labour. But in this specific context, I disagree with Cohen over the reasons for the retention of subcontracting practices in Lancashire.

In his comparative perspective, Cohen tends to see the permanence of the Lancashire minder-piecer system mainly in terms of union strength. He argues that if the employers had tried to change the organization of work at the self-actors, they would have encountered a "formidable union resistance".[33] However, this supposition fits badly with recent historical findings. It is becoming recognized that union strength among the Lancashire mule-spinners was probably at its lowest in the period 1831 to 1860, which was the most crucial period of transition to the new self-actor technology.[34] After major defeats in the strikes of 1829 and 1831, and threatened by the prospect of the new self-actors, the spinners' unions were seriously weakened and only revived fully a few decades later. This runs counter to Cohen's postulation of firm union power in Lancashire at the time of the adoption of self-actors.

On the contrary, it could well be argued that the relative weakness of spinners' unions after 1830 was one important reason why the employers were prepared to allow the traditional organization of work to remain.[35] The manufacturers' victory in the strikes of 1829 and 1831 had lessened their fear of spinners' unionism, and they seem to have been content to man the self-actors with male juveniles according to the usual pattern.[36]

Furthermore, Cohen has an altogether one-sided view of the character of the subcontracting relationship. He claims that it was a way for the minders to control the entry to the trade and to gain a "complete shop floor control of piecers", and that union power alone can explain the survival of the subcontracting system.[37] However, there is one alternative possibility. The subcontracting system should be seen as having advantages for both the operative spinners and the employers. The workers naturally wanted to keep the system in order to retain a certain control over recruitment and also in order to employ their own children or kin. But subcontracting was

---

33 Ibid., p. 70.
34 Lazonick (1979), pp. 239-40; Freifeld (1986), pp. 338-39.
35 Lazonick (1979), p. 240. For an account of the weakness of the spinners' union in Preston during these decades, see Banks (1888), pp. 3-8.
36 Mason (1987c), passim.
37 Cohen (1985a), pp. 72, 85.

also in several ways advantageous for the manufacturers, above all in matters of work discipline and the recruitment of young operatives.

Subcontracting was also useful for the employers in the sense that the piecers' demands for increased wages were shifted over to the operative spinners.[38] Moreover, as Michael Anderson has pointed out, the manufacturers were also liberated from the task of finding, training and supervising the young workers.[39] However, the most potent advantage for the manufacturers was that subcontracting was an easy way to solve the recruitment problems of young workers in the wake of the 1833 Factory Act. As I have described in the previous chapter, the manufacturers' main strategy when faced with the requirements of the factory legislation was to replace their child workers with those who could show certificates of being 13 years of age. This meant that the competition for youngsters who could pass for thirteen increased considerably.

It is therefore not surprising that the manufacturers found it very convenient to have the recruitment task performed by the operative spinners. The subcontracting agreement was simply used by the manufacturers as a way to force the spinners to exert themselves to find 13-year-old piecers. The repressive side of the subcontracting relationship is shown most clearly in the Glasgow industry, where spinners who could not manage to find suitable piecers risked immediate dismissal.[40]

The strategic value of the subcontracting system in the context of the recruitment problems connected with the specific manufacturer responses to the implementation of the Factory Acts is an aspect which has been entirely overlooked by previous research on the workforce composition in the British cotton industry.

This perspective is also supported by the case of the Glasgow spinners. After the 1837 strike, the spinners' union collapsed and the mill-owners were more or less free to reorganize production as they pleased. The piece-rate was broken, shorter mules were joined together, and girls were set to mind self-actors. But the manufacturers did not touch the subcontracting system. Instead, it was used to make sure that the trouble and extra cost of hiring 13 year old piecers had to be met by the spinners. This, and not union power, was probably the main reason why subcontracting was allowed to remain at the self-actors in Lancashire as well as in Scotland. In a similar

---

38 For instance, the Oldham strike of 1875 was partly occasioned by the minders' unwillingness to be responsible for the wage advances of the piecers. See Wood, G H (1910): The History of Wages in the Cotton Trade during the Past Hundred Years, pp. 52-53.

39 Anderson, M (1976), p. 320. See also Lazonick (1979), p. 244.

40 See PP 1837-38 VIII, First report..., evidence of James McNish, Glasgow operative spinner, p. 64 Q. 1,278-80; PP 1840 X, Sixth Report from the Select Committee..., evidence of Henry Dunn, Glasgow mule-spinner, p. 29 Q. 8,724; PP 1839 XIX, RIF, p. 57. See also chapter 3 above.

way, subcontracting of young "back-boys" seems to have occurred in the cotton mills of Fall River, U.S.A., when recruitment proved difficult.[41]

However, the American case shows some interesting deviations from the British pattern.[42] When self-actors were introduced in the 1840s the work was thoroughly reorganized. The spinner was no longer allowed to have any subcontracted assistants, and was set to do all the piecing himself, assisted only by a "back-boy" who did the creeling. Both the back-boy and the spinner were under the supervision and authority of a foreman. Teams of "doffers" removed the full bobbins on all the mules.

As I will explain more fully in a later chapter, the main reason for this reorganization was the determination of the American manufacturers to reduce the spinners' shopfloor position and turn to them into mere labourers. The American minder was given less power over the adjustment of the mules than his Lancashire colleague, and was subjected to much more harassment and driving from the foreman. The decision to reorganize the work at the self-actor must be seen in the specific context of American industrial relations, and also points at the necessity of investigating employer strategies and objectives as well as estimating union strength. The main difference which stands out in the American-Lancashire comparision is indeed that while the American manufacturers were determined to re-organize the work at the new self-actors, the Lancashire employers were not.

The best way to capture the essence of this difference is to describe it as two different strategies to enhance work productivity. The American way was to increase the managerial control over the labour process and the division of work, and also to use close supervision and a high degree of overlooker authority in the workplace in order to make the operatives exert themselves. These strategies later became formalised in "scientific management" or Taylorism. The systematic "driving" or "grinding" of the American mule-spinners by their foremen has been described by Cohen, who concludes that they were much harder worked than the Lancashire spinners.[43]

But this method had two important drawbacks: first, it necessitated close supervision and a high proportion of overlookers to a given number of

---

41 Lazonick (1981c), p. 507.
42 Freifeld's perspective seems to be somewhat more fruitful in the New England context. The fact that girls had not been used as piecers on hand-mules seems to have made the employers less interested in having female minders on self-actors. See Montgomery, J (1840): The Cotton Manufacture of the United States of America Contrasted and Compared with that of Great Britain, p. 76.
43 Cohen (1985a), pp. 67, 73; Cohen, I (1985b): American Management and British Labor: Lancashire Immigrant Spinners in Industrial New England, pp. 637-38. See also Silva, P T (1975): The Position of Workers in a Textile Community: Fall River in the Early 1880's, pp. 233-34.

minders. From Cohen's own calculations it emerges that the proportion of supervisory staff used in the U.S. mills was approximately ten times higher than in Lancashire mule-spinning.[44] However, this may be an exaggeration. Thomas Ashton of the Oldham Spinners' Association reported from a visit to Fall River, Massachusetts, in 1902 that five supervisory staff were used in American mills where two had sufficed in Lancashire.[45] Still, the differences in supervision practices between Lancashire and Massachusetts were remarkable.

Secondly, it is questionable if "grinding" and increasing the division of labour really was the best managerial strategy to enhance work productivity in mule-spinning. William Lazonick has recently suggested that the commercial use of the self-actor technology was still very dependent on high levels of work intensity. Introducing the concept of "effort-wage bargaining", Lazonick has argued that the actual input of work effort was the result of a complicated bargaining process between operatives and management.[46] One crucial precondition for the operatives' acceptance of increased workloads was that they had to feel reasonably certain that additional efforts would be balanced by a permanent raise of wages. On the other hand, a social context of relatively hostile industrial relations and unstable piece-rates did not provide the spinners with any incentive to increase actual work effort. The response to the management strategy of "grinding" was therefore a variety of restrictive practices or "go slow" tactics in order to resist any increases in workloads.

In contrast, the system used in Lancashire tended to enhance productivity by creating an "inner incentive" to accept higher workloads. The minder-piecer system in combination with relatively stable piece-rates proved to be a most efficient formula. When spinners felt sure that piece-rates would not be slashed if they increased their efforts, "go slow" strategies could be avoided.

A very important part of this process was the development of stable regional price-lists in Lancashire after 1850. The piece-rate structures were defended by both the trade union organizations and the employers' associations, which made it very difficult for individual manufacturers to pay below the list. The relative stability of the piece-rates and the comparatively large power resources on the part of the unions were important

---

44 Cohen (1985a), p. 75.

45 Mosely Industrial Commission (1903), p. 129.

46 See Lazonick, W (1982): Production, Productivity, and Development. Theoretical Implications of some Historical Research, passim; Lazonick, W and Mass, W (1983): The Performance of the British Cotton Industry, 1870-1913, passim; Lazonick, W (1986): The Cotton Industry, passim. I rely rather heavily on Lazonick's contribution on the connections between work intensity and the structures of industrial relations, but, as will be evident in a later chapter, I strongly disagree with him over the reasons for the lack of technological and organizational change in the Lancashire industry after 1900.

preconditions for an industrial climate where the operatives were willing to work harder and mind ever longer and faster self-acting mules. The Spinners' Amalgamation was therefore an ardent supporter of the piece-rate structure, seeing it as a major precondition for work efficiency and prosperity.[47]

In terms of supervision requirements, the Lancashire piece-rate systems provided an inner incentive which made the control of overlookeers almost unnecessary. The stable piece-rates induced the minders to serve as pace-makers for their time-paid piecers, and this particular form of close super-vision therefore became institutionalised in the minder-piecer system. There can be no doubt that the result was an industrial organization which was very conducive to increases in productivity. Contemporary observers agree that Lancashire mule-spinning was uncommonly work-intensive. An investigator of industrial efficiency was clearly impressed by the work intensity which was displayed by the minders in a Bolton mill in 1905:

> The self-actor minders worked stripped to the waist and with bare feet. Theirs is the most skilled and hardest work, and they address themselves to it with an intentness and an absorption which is not surpassed by any workman anywhere. [48]

Some of the lists were particularly successful ingredients in the forming of an industrial context of greater work efforts, while at the same time providing the manufacturers with an incentive to invest in more modern machinery. Above all, this was the case with the Oldham list which came to dominate the coarse end of the Lancashire mule-spinning industry. According to this price list, productivity gains were split equally between the operative spinners and the employers.[49]

Also, if the competitiveness of the Lancashire industry in foreign markets is taken into account, it cannot be doubted that the English way of increasing productivity in mule-spinning was very successful. Lancashire continued to dominate the world market in cotton goods during the second half of the 19th century, while the American industry had to rely to a large

47 See, for instance, PP 1886 XXI, Royal Commission on the Depression of Trade and Industry, evidence of J. Mawdsley, General Secretary of the Spinners' Amalgamation, p. 174 Q. 5,080-81, where he argued that the piece-rate system in Lancashire cotton spinning had a beneficial effect on productivity. See also Webb, S and Webb, B (1897): Industrial Democracy, p. 289.
48 Shadwell, A (1906): Industrial Efficiency. A Comparative Study of Industrial Life in England, Germany and America, Vol I, p. 75. For other contemporary observations on the high work intensity of the Lancashire industry, see von Schulze-Gaevernitz, G (1895): The Cotton Trade in England and on the Continent, passim but esp pp. 102-4, 109-11; Merttens, F (1893-94): The Hours and Cost of Labour in the Cotton Industry at Home and Abroad, passim; Merttens, F (1903-4): Productivity, Protection, and Integration of Industry, p. 13.
49 Jewkes, J and Gray, E M (1935): Wages and Labour in the Lancashire Cotton Spinning Industry, pp. 37, 41-42. The structure of the Oldham list especially created an incentive towards longer mules. Ibid., pp. 58-59, 110.

degree on tariffs in order to keep their domestic market. In 1886 several Lancashire manufacturers gave evidence to a parliamentary committee which indicated that they met with very little competition in neutral markets.[50]

The above conclusions are vital for an understanding of the long-term permanence of the minder-piecer system in Lancashire mule-spinning. It is true that the increasing strength of the spinners' unions after 1870 probably served to discourage the manufacturers from making further experiments with alternative ways of staffing the mules.[51] It should also be pointed out that the minder-piecer system became in a sense institutionalised by the gradual building up of regional price-lists which presupposed the existence of a minder-led work-team, and which also specified the number of piecers for different lengths of mules.[52] The minder-piecer system therefore became buttressed by the structure of industrial bargaining which completely dominated the Lancashire district after 1870. But the main asset of the Lancashire minders was still the efficiency and competitiveness of the traditional organization of work. The employers had no viable alternatives to the existing system, and were therefore not prone to co-operate in order to break the power of the Spinners' Amalgamation.

### Child Labour Outside the Mule-spinning Process

While this study has so far been mainly focussed on production relations and the formation of the labour process in mule-spinning, this is not the full story. In the second half of the 19th century, children were used in several other processes, most notably in weaving, throstle-spinning, looming, and as assistants on the roving frames. Above all, there was a marked increase in the labour force participation of children in the weaving factories. Factory returns show that while children in powerloom weaving were relatively scarce in 1850, towards the end of the century their proportion of the workforce was considerably higher than was the case in mule-spinning mills.

---

50 PP 1886 XXI, Second Report of the Royal Commission..., evidence of S. Hinrichsen, Manchester merchant, pp. 215-17 Q. 6,055-56, 6,061-63, 6,068-71, 6,093-94. Apart from some competition from the Bombay mills on very coarse counts, most employers did not expect any threat from foreign manufacturers. See ibid., evidence of S. Andrew and S. Taylor, Oldham employers, p. 153 Q. 4,511-12; Ibid., evidence of A. Simpson, a Preston mill-owner, p. 196 Q. 5,546-49; Ibid., evidence of G. Lord, Manchester Chamber of Commerce, p. 183 Q. 5,279. It is apparent that no competition was expected from the American cotton industry. See also the Textile Recorder, Oct. 1904, p. 162. For the earlier period, see Bils, M (1984): Tariff Protection and Production in the Early U.S. Cotton Textile Industry, passim.
51 Farnie (1979), pp. 264-65.
52 See Thorpe (1969), pp. 51-52, on the structure of the Bolton list, and also Lazonick (1979), p. 247.

By 1890, children below 13 years of age constituted 11.4 per cent of the workforce in the Lancashire weaving industry, as opposed to 6.5 per cent in the spinning mills.[53] On factory level, the Quarry Bank Mill wage books also indicate that child labour levels increased very much in the weaving process towards the end of the century.[54]

Child workers were also to be found in other positions in the cotton mills. In the looming process, the operative twisters and drawers hired child "reachers-in" to help them prepare the warp beams for weaving. The 1886 wage census, which recorded the different parts of the labour process separately, shows that half-time children constituted 18.4 per cent of the workforce in looming.[55]

Children were also used as "doffers" in throstle- and ring-spinning. Unfortunately, very little attention has been given to the throstle-spinners and their doffers, who were almost invariably women and young girls. An investigation in 1873 stated that a "large number" of girls between 8 and 14 years of age were employed as doffers in this process.[56] The 1886 wage census indicates that 16.9 per cent of the operatives in throstle-spinning were half-time doffers.[57]

Finally, a comparatively small number of half-time girls were used by operative slubbers and rovers to clean the machinery and do some sweeping. But the wage census figures indicate that in absolute numbers, the use of factory children in the mid-1880s was by far the most prevalent in weaving and self-actor spinning:

---

53 PP 1850 XLV, Factory Returns; PP 1890 LXVII, Factory Returns.
54  Greg Collection. Quarry Bank Mill Wage Books, 1840-1899.
55 PP 1889 LXX, Return of Rates of Wages..., pp. 9-58. N = 2,256.
56 PP 1873 LV, Report...on Proposed Changes in Hours and Ages of Employment in Textile Factories, p. 14.
57 PP 1889 LXX, Return of Rates of Wages..., pp. 9-58. N = 4,370.

Table 7. Distribution of Lancashire half-timers in different processes of cotton manufacturing. 1886 sample.

| Labour process | % | N |
|---|---|---|
| Weaving | 75.5 | 8,151 |
| Self-actor spinning | 10.8 | 1,172 |
| Throstle/ring spinning | 6.4 | 695 |
| Looming | 3.8 | 407 |
| Slubbing/roving | 2.0 | 219 |
| Reeling/winding | 1.1 | 115 |
| Carding | 0.2 | 20 |
| Hand-mule spinning | 0.2 | 18 |
| | 100.0 | 10,797 |

Source: PP 1889 LXX, Return of Rates of Wages in the Principal Textile Trades of the U.K., pp. 9-58.

Naturally, it has to be remembered that this sample may have been somewhat slanted towards weaving factories. It is nevertheless striking that such a clear majority of the child workers were now employed in the weaving process.

This is an indication of a second major shift in the employment of factory children in the Lancashire cotton industry. While in the period after 1800 most children had been used in the preparatory processes of picking and carding, mule-spinning probably took over this role in the 1820s and 1830s. However, by the 1880s there can be no doubt that the majority of the half-timers were to be found in the weaving process.

Even if the nature of children's employment had changed dramatically, it is still important to emphasize that subcontracting relationships continued to dominate. Children employed in weaving, mule-spinning, and looming were all subcontracted by adult operatives. Back-tenters at the roving frames were at least to some extent hired by the operative slubbers and rovers. The major exception to this rule was the child doffers in throstle- and ring-spinning, who were directly employed by management. The strong domination of the subcontracting form of employment can be illustrated by the sample of the 1886 wage census, which shows that well over 90 per cent of the half-timers in identifiable processes were subcontracted.

However, it remains to be explained how child labour practices could develop in the weaving factories in the second half of the 19th century.

## Factory Weaving and the Rise of the "Tenter-system"

The workforce composition in Lancashire weaving differed quite markedly from that in mule-spinning. From the very beginning, powerloom weaving was a mixed occupation employing both men and women, even though young females probably constituted a majority.

In the 1830s, each powerloom weaver usually minded one or two machines. In a Manchester weaving factory, the 1833 commissioners found that 29 of the operatives worked on two looms each, while 5 workers were in charge of four looms each. Similarly, the 372 weaving operatives at Birley and Kirk's mill, Manchester, were said to mind two looms each.[58] But there is also some evidence of cases where male powerloom weavers operated three or four machines with the help of a child assistant.[59] Where powerloom weaving was a mixed occupation, it is possible that the use of child "tenters" was more widely spread.

In the Lancashire context, there seems to have been a link between the increase in the ratio of looms per weaver and the spread of the "tenter-system". In order to be able to mind more looms, the weaver subcontracted a young tenter to help with re-threading the shuttles, cleaning the machinery, and a number of other tasks. But the question is, why did the Lancashire weavers accept minding a greater number of looms? This necessitates a brief look into the structure of industrial relations and the methods of pay.

The general wage system in Lancashire weaving was a flat piece-rate. According to Lazonick's theory on work-effort bargaining, the weavers would be encouraged to accept minding more machines if they could feel sufficiently secure that the price list would not be slashed arbitrarily. A higher rate of work intensity was achieved through permanent rises in real earnings and, at the same time, in cultural wage expectations.[60]

In Lancashire the increase in the number of looms per weaver was paralleled by the establishment of relatively stable piece-rate lists. The recognition of the Blackburn List for weaving in 1853 was an important first step. During the following decades, district lists in other areas were acknowledged by the local employers. The importance of the district list lay in the fact that it hindered or severely limited the individual employer's option of reducing the piece-rate. The list could only be changed through

---

58 PP 1833 XX, First Report..., evidence of Jane L., powerloom weaver, Manchester, p. D1 34; Ibid, pp. D2 127-28.

59 PP 1832 XV, Report from the Committee..., evidence of James Turner, cotton-yarn dresser, Manchester, p. 323.

60 See Clark, G (1987): Why Isn't the Whole World Developed? Lessons from the Cotton Mills, passim, for a discussion on the links between work efficiency and customary wage levels.

negotiations between the local weavers' union and the employers' association. A manufacturer could choose to stand outside the organization in order to retain his "right" to lower the piece-rate, but in doing so he risked being a target of strikes, and without any right to obtain financial assistance from the employers' associations.

The establishment of district lists was the main objective of the weavers' unions. Being "open" organizations with both male and female membership, they were not by any means as highly unionised as the spinners. Yet, by the 1890s practically the whole Lancashire weaving trade was governed by list systems. This development can partly be explained by the fact that the system emerged during a period of "paternalist" industrial relations, a phenomenon which I will return to in the next chapter. However, it should also be remembered that stable district lists found favour with manufacturers who wanted to obtain calm industrial relations, no stoppages of production, and at the same time hinder competitors from cutting costs by reducing wages.

Mainly as a result of the specific industrial relations which were embedded in the list systems, the normal complement of looms for a trained weaver rose to four. The 1886 wage census indicates that in the Blackburn/Burnley/Colne district in north Lancashire, the mean number of looms per weaver was 3.7.[61] The absence of restrictive practices and strategies actually meant that the ability to mind more looms enhanced the weaver's standing within the working-class community. For example, one observer remarked in 1873 that "the admiration of their companions, and the approbation of the overlooker, appear to be at least as powerful inducements as the increase of their wages", with the result that "weavers gladly accepted more looms".[62]

In order to manage the additional number of machines, the weaver subcontracted a child "tenter" as an assistant. This is the origin of what I have called the "tenter-system" in Lancashire weaving. The tenter assisted the weaver by changing shuttles, filling the weft, carrying cloth to the warehouse and cleaning and sweeping the looms. He or she was paid a set weekly wage out of the weaver's gross earnings. The tenter-system should be seen as a way for the weaver to operate more looms and increase his or her income. Consequently, it should be seen as a change in the organization of work devised to enhance productivity. As the secretary of the Burnley manufacturers expressed it in 1909, "as a result of the half-time

---

61 PP 1889 LXX, Return of Rates of Wages..., pp. 33-38. N = 12,049. Young learners were included in this sample, which lowers the mean figure.
62 PP 1873 LV, Report...on Proposed Changes..., pp. 20-21.

[system] in weaving, we have a number of six-loom weavers, but if we had not these half-timers, we should have only three- or four-loom weavers".[63]

The stability of the list system in weaving, the difficulty for employers to pay below the set rates, and the character of the subcontracting relationship, all served as disincentives to the manufacturers to reorganize the operations which were performed by the child tenters. If ancillary tasks like carrying and cleaning were performed by special adult operatives, the employers would still have to pay the operative weavers according to the list. The structure of the list system had tended to increase work intensity, but at the same time it limited the manufacturer's choice of alternatives in the formation of the labour process.

The "tenter-system" became the dominant form of organization in the Lancashire weaving industry, and the level of child labour in the weaving process increased substantially during the second half of the 19th century. At the same time, the situation in Scotland and the U.S.A. was very much different. In both these countries, child labour in the weaving process remained marginal. I shall treat these matters more fully in later chapters, but I will give a short summary here in order to make a comparison with the development in Lancashire.

In the Scottish case there was no movement towards a tenter-system. The number of looms per weaver remained at a very low level compared to Lancashire. From the sample taken in the 1886 wage census, it emerges that of the 3,772 recorded Scottish powerloom weavers, 18.0 per cent worked on 3 looms, 80.7 per cent tended 2 looms, and the remaining 1.3 per cent minded one loom each.[64] Four-loom weavers simply did not exist.

To some extent, this could be explained by the fact that Lancashire competition in the production of plain cloth had forced the Scottish factories to concentrate on fancy weaving. But this was not the main reason. Margaret Irwin, who investigated the employment of women in Scotland for the 1892 Royal Commission on Labour, found that the Glasgow weavers stubbornly defended the traditional work organization of two looms per weaver. Although these weavers were all non-unionised young women, an attempt in 1890 to make them tend three looms each had immediately produced a strike. They refused even to allow a single experiment on a three-loom system. Irwin made the interesting conclusion that the real reason behind the inflexibility of the operatives was to be found in the absence of recognized price-lists for weaving.[65] She was probably right. In a

---

63 PP 1909 XVII, Vol II, Report of the Inter-Departmental Committee on Partial Exemption from School Attendance, evidence of F. A. Hargreaves, p. 119 Q. 3,379.
64 PP 1889 LXX, Return of Rates of Wages..., pp. 60-62.
65 PP 1893-94 XXXVII, Royal Commission on Labour, Pt I, pp. 173-175.

context of production relations where the piece-rate was arbitrarily set by the individual employer and the workers were not backed by any union, the defending of traditional workloads became the dominant strategy among the Glasgow weavers. The tenter-system never emerged in Scotland because the existing production relations were not conducive to progress in the wage-effort bargain.[66]

The American case was completely different. In Massachusetts weaving rooms the labour process was much more divided than was the custom in Lancashire. The ancillary tasks of sweeping, cleaning, and weft and cloth carrying were not performed by the weavers, but by special operatives. As a result, the American powerloom weavers were set to work a larger number of looms each than was the case in Lancashire. This organization of work was known in England after 1900 as the "American system" in weaving. The division of work probably increased management's control over production and the prospects of increasing the number of looms per weaver.

The application of the American methods in weaving seems to have had direct implications for the question of child labour. There were simply no child "tenters" in the Massachusetts weaving departments. A wage census conducted by the Bureau of Statistics of Labor in 1884 shows that there were no children below 14 years of age, and only 12 below 18, in a total sample of 3,256 operatives.[67] By that time, the weaving process in Lancashire was by far the most important employer of child labour. This clear contrast supports an explanation based on differences in production relations and the actual organization of work.


# Child Labour, Technology and the Formation of Work: Some Conclusions

There was no major connection between technological change and child labour levels in the Lancashire cotton industry after 1830. Children

66 The differences found between Scotland and Lancashire also have some relevance for the German case. K-H Ludwig's assertion that child labour in German weaving factories was discontinued after 1850 because of the increased demands on the operatives which were posed by the modern powerlooms, is a notion which is clearly challenged by the Lancashire example, where child labour levels *increased* substantially after 1850 on the most modern types of looms. However, von Schulze-Gaevernitz indicated in the 1890s that German weavers customarily minded only two powerlooms each, in contrast to the normal four in Lancashire. The absence of child workers in German weaving factories could therefore more plausibly be ascribed to the fact that an organization of work similar to the tenter-system did not develop. See Ludwig (1965), pp. 75-76, 81, 83; von Schulze-Gaevernitz (1895), p. 109.
67 Massachusetts Bureau of Statistics of Labor, 15th Annual Report, 1884, pp. 189-96.

continued to be employed as piecers and scavengers on the new self-actors in virtually the same way as they had previously been employed on the hand-mules. The subcontracting of young workers was a part of the minder-piecer system in mule-spinning which continued to dominate the Lancashire industry until the 1930s.

Similarly, subcontracted children became increasingly common in the weaving and looming processes after mid-century. The powerloom weavers in Lancashire employed young "tenters" to help with ancillary tasks and to enable the adult operatives to mind more looms. By the 1880s, child "tenting" in weaving was by far the most common form of child labour in the Lancashire cotton industry.

Both weaving and mule-spinning became increasingly regulated by intricate piece-rate lists during the second half of the 19th century, which formed the core of a highly developed structure of industrial bargaining. The specific work structures of the minder-piecer and tenter systems became more or less embedded in the established form of industrial bargaining. It is true that these organizations of work were defended by the operatives and their unions. But what has not been generally recognized is that the manufacturers also had substantial reasons for retaining these structures. The outcome of the Lancashire model of production was a high level of work intensity, few stoppages, and a check on "dishonest" competition. The continuation of subcontracting in mule-spinning should also be seen in the specific context of recruitment problems regarding juvenile workers in the wake of the 1833 Factory Act.

In contrast, the development in Scotland and Massachusetts was very different. In New England mule-spinning, subcontracting was ended by the manufacturers when the self-actors were introduced, and the minders were set to perform all the pieceing operations. Child labour levels were therefore lower in the Massachusetts mills than in Lancashire.

An even clearer contrast has been found in powerloom weaving. Child labour was virtually unknown in this part of the labour process in both Scotland and Massachusetts. Equivalents of the Lancashire tenter-system simply did not develop.

So far I have attempted to reconstruct the actual organization of the labour process in spinning and weaving. A comparative perspective has been used in order to indicate the existence of varying systems of organization, and to suggest the most important reasons which lay behind these differences. The actual structure of the labour process, and the presence of subcontracting forms of employment, are seen as important determinants of the level of child labour. But these structures have in turn to be explained, and seen as the result of the actions of single and collective agents. The conclusion to be drawn from the comparative study is that differences in the formation of the labour process must be seen in a context of industrial relations. In the next chapter, the perspective will be shifted from the labour process to the field of industrial relations in the Lancashire cotton industry during the second half of the 19th century.

## Chapter 5

# Industrial Relations and the Paternalistic Compromise in Lancashire, 1850-1900

One general theme in this book is the centrality of power and authority in the relations of production. In this chapter I will investigate two long-term changes in the nature of industrial relations in the Lancashire cotton industry which took place in the second half of the 19th century.

After 1850 there was a marked shift towards a more amicable and co-operative interaction between mill-owners and operatives. Industrial relations had previously been dominated by "political economy" notions of labour as a commodity which had to find its own price, and the employers had strongly defended their "right" of full control over the process of production. After mid-century this approach slowly gave way to one expressing the importance of social ties and interdependence between employers and operatives. This new set of industrial relations has been described as a "paternalistic" system or culture.[1] However, towards the end of the 19th century the system of industrial relations changed once again towards an "economic" designation of the bond between worker and employer.

A closer study of paternalism in the Lancashire setting is required for at least two reasons. First, the specific organization of work which developed in the Lancashire cotton industry after 1850 must be seen in the context of the prevailing structure of industrial relations. Second, I will argue that one part of the paternalistic formula was that the manufacturers accepted the employment of half-timers and the operatives' authority over recruitment.

During the last decade, the phenomenon of paternalism has been much discussed among labour historians.[2] In the Lancashire context it has been most elaborately studied by Patrick Joyce, whose depiction of the paternalistic system has been exceedingly influential. But even though he has received a substantial amount of critical attention, I believe that the critics

---

1 Joyce, P (1982): Work, Society and Politics. The Culture of the Factory in later Victorian England.
2 In the Swedish context, see Svensson, T (1986): Japansk företagsledning och svenska bruk - en felande länk?; Magnusson, L (1986): Patriarkalism och social kontroll. See also Reid, D (1985): Industrial Paternalism: Discourse and Practice in Nineteenth-Century French Mining and Metallurgy.

have not really managed to strike at the core of Joyce's argument.[3] Above all, there have been few alternative explanations of the emergence of paternalism. For this reason, this chapter is very much a discussion with Patrick Joyce.

Joyce explains the origin of the paternalist system in terms of rising social and political ambitions among the more substantial manufacturers, and also as a part of the general development of capitalist enterprise. The emergence of large firms, the full mechanisation of production, and the rise of a group of large mill-owners eager to win recognition in political society were all parts in this process.

Paternalism was essentially a system in which the operatives were subordinated and dominated by the employers. Since skill was no longer required in fully mechanised production, the operatives were not in possession of trade union strength. Their main objective under the new conditions, Joyce asserts, was to gain continuous employment in order to avoid periodical poverty. Following Gareth Stedman Jones' reading of Marx, Joyce claims that paternalism was the result of a transition from formal to real subsumption in fully developed factory production.[4] The large manufacturers established a "social hegemony" where the part played by the operatives was that of dependence and deference.

The paternalistic relationship was expressed in terms of personal responsibilities and attachments between employers and employed. The manufacturer showed concern and responsibility for "his" operatives, who reciprocated with expressions of deference. Employer benevolence took the shape of great tea-parties, festivities, and excursions to Blackpool by the sea. The operatives responded by showing proper gratitude and deference, and by expressing their loyalty to the manufacturer and his family. The factory brass band would serenade the employer below his bedroom window, and at festive occasions in the owner family, like weddings and comings of age, the factory and the machines would be festooned with flags, garlands and flowers.[5]

Indeed, Joyce sees the institution of the family as a very important symbolic link between the operatives and the owners. Sons of manufacturers were often sent "through the mill" as a part of their education to

3 See Dutton, H I and King, J E (1982): The Limits of Paternalism: The Cotton Tyrants of North Lancashire, 1836-1870; Price (1984); Kirk, N (1985): The Growth of Working Class Reformism in Mid-Victorian England; Price, R (1986): Labour in British Society. An interpretative history, chapter 4; Huberman, M (1987): The Economic Origins of Paternalism: Lancashire Cotton Spinning in the first half of the Nineteenth Century.
4 Joyce (1982), p. xix; Jones, G S (1975): Class Struggle and the Industrial Revolution, passim. For an interesting criticism of Marx' postulations on the effects of mechanisation, see Lazonick, W (1986): Klasserna i det kapitalistiska företaget, passim.
5 Joyce (1982), chapter 5.

managerial positions. Also, in large concerns, the sons of the owner generally took charge of individual mills on their own, thus reinforcing the quasi-personal relationship between management and workers. But the institution of the family also served as a means of identification across the class divide, which in turn tended to reinforce the movement towards paternalist relations. Joyce also claims that wider social interaction in the working-class families and local community buttressed the paternalist relationship. Social bonds in the factory were both reflected and outlined more sharply in the schools, churches, and political contexts of the local community. The employer's hegemony in the workplace was carried over to the political and denominational divisions of society. Moreover, the ties between the working-class family and paternalism were strengthened by the fact that family members often worked in the same factory. The relations of the workplace, the local community, and the family together constituted the framework of the paternalistic culture.

Joyce clearly puts the main emphasis of this culture in the sphere of personal relations and identification with the owner family. This is shown by his depiction of the eventual decline of the paternalistic system towards the end of the century. His main explanation is that the old type of family owned firms slowly gave way to large limited liability companies. In these new firms, he claims, the possibilities of mutual personal relations and identification were lost. The limiteds were run by professional managers on a contractual basis. In such contexts, the personal dependencies which were the backbone of paternalism could not develop. Industrial relations again turned more "economical" and impersonal. Attitudes of social responsibility for the well-being of the operatives were discarded in favour of demands for wage cuts and increased work productivity. The old family firms could not in the long run resist this kind of competition, and were forced to resort to the same methods or withdraw from business. The paternalist culture was broken.

While I agree with Joyce that there were marked shifts in the quality of industrial relations during this period, I differ from him when it comes to the social foundations of the paternalistic system, and also on the question of its essence and generality. In the following passage, I will voice some criticism of Joyce's work on several levels: method, interpretation, validity, and the explanatory framework. First, his reconstruction of the operatives' participation in the paternalist relation has to be questioned. One methodological problem with Joyce's approach is that he uses gleanings from newspapers, pamphlets, and memoirs as evidence for paternalist relations. He does not discuss the fact that publications of this kind were generally intended for a wide audience and not without connections to mill-owner or middle-class perspectives.[6] This must be crucial in the case of the large Lancashire manufacturers, since Joyce holds that political ambitions were a main force behind their venture into paternalism. Newspaper reports on the great achievements and generosity of a certain manufacturer should be seen in this context. Another weakness is that Joyce does not deal with the problem that the deference expressed by the operatives could have been of an essentially ceremonial nature. Speeches by selected operatives, generally overlookers, at festive occasions do not constitute the best measure of real workplace relations, yet these figure prominently in the newspaper reports on which Joyce bases his argument.

Another question which Joyce has not really answered is how general the paternalistic system actually was in the factory district of Lancashire. This is a point where Joyce has met with strong criticism. Dutton and King have shown that industrial relations remained antagonistic in Preston, north-west Lancashire, during the 1850s.[7] Neville Kirk has shown that industrial disputes in the cotton industry continued in substantial numbers during the 1850s and 60s in the Ashton district in the South.[8] However, Kirk concentrates on areas where there was still a considerable degree of hostility among the manufacturers towards union initiatives, and he therefore does not acknowledge the important shift in the character of industrial relations which occurred after mid-century in other areas, for instance in Bolton and Blackburn.[9] The problem of estimating the generality of the "paternalistic" culture remains.

Another point where Joyce has encountered strong criticism is his depiction of a weak, deskilled, and subordinated factory proletariat. Richard Price and Neville Kirk have argued that this is to underestimate the reciprocity which was expressed in the paternalist relation, and also the degree of influence and unionization on the part of the operatives.[10] Moreover, his notion that the skill requirements had more or less vanished as an effect of complete mechanisation is simply not correct.[11] This criticism seems to have had some effect. In the matter of subordination, Joyce has in a recent article moved away from his initial position, conceding that he has over-

---

6 See Beatty, B (1984): Textile Labor in the North Carolina Piedmont: Mill Owner Images and Mill Worker Response, 1830-1900, for a similar criticism of historians of paternalistic systems in Southern U.S. cotton mills.

7 Dutton and King (1982), passim.

8 Kirk (1985), pp. 243-68.

9 Kirk also uses the stalwart adherent to political economy, Henry Ashworth, and the non-paternalist Burnley manufacturers, as typical examples of employer attitudes in industrial relations. See Kirk (1985), pp. 267-68. On Ashworth, see Boyson (1970), p. 134.

10 Price (1984), passim; Kirk (1985), pp. 16-18, 283-84.

11 See Freifeld (1986), passim, and the discussion in the previous chapter.

emphasized the degree of the operatives' internalisation of the "paternalist ethos". Instead, paternalism should be seen more in the perspective of interdependence or compromise than as a system of one-sided employer dominance.[12]

While Joyce's new theoretical position is considerably more constructive than the old, it still has to be pointed out that he has not indicated which were the elements of the compromise.[13] Abandoning a vital part of his explanatory framework, he actually leaves open the question of the causes behind the paternalistic system.

Michael Huberman is a Canadian historian who has recently tried to fill that explanatory void. He sees the origin of the paternalistic compromise in the specific labour market conditions of the first half of the 19th century. The employers faced a labour supply which varied much in quality, and one of their main objectives was to recruit the most productive operatives and to reduce labour turnover. The low profit margins made the mill-owners dependent on the skill and efficiency of their labour force. In return, they were willing to grant the workers' demands of stable piece-rates and more secure conditions of employment.[14] Another important objective of the operatives was that depressions of the trade should be met with short-time working, not with cuts in the piece-rate. Huberman sees the acceptance of these demands as an "invisible handshake" which constituted a precondition for the paternalistic system.[15]

His contribution is no doubt very constructive. I have myself in a recent article characterised the paternalistic compromise as an "informal contract".[16] However, Huberman has mainly studied the period up to 1850, which to some extent leads him to place the origin of paternalism well before it actually emerged.[17] Also, Huberman only provides a part of the tacit agreements which constituted the paternalistic "contract". An attempt will now be made to reconstruct the other clauses.

My suggestion is that the most important demand on the part of the operatives in the paternalistic relationship was the recognition of the district piece-rate lists. After 1850, this was the main objective of the local unions.

---

12 Joyce, P (1984a): Labour, capital and compromise: a response to Richard Price, pp. 74-76.
13 Naturally, one persistent problem is that Joyce is never able to make any links between paternalism and the social organization of work, authority structures, and industrial bargaining. In his later work, Joyce tends to view the problem entirely on the level of language, culture, and discourse. See Joyce, P (1984b): Languages of reciprocity and conflict: a further response to Richard Price, passim; Joyce, P (1987): The historical meanings of work: an introduction, passim.
14 Huberman (1987), pp. 178-9.
15 Ibid., pp. 183-88.
16 Bolin, P (1987): Paternalism och underkastelse, pp. 61-64.
17 See Rose, M B, Taylor, P and Winstanley, M J (1989): The economic origins of paternalism: some objections, passim.

During the following three decades, both spinning and weaving became increasingly regulated by district lists. The Bolton and Oldham lists for spinning, and the Blackburn list for weaving soon became the most important ones.[18]

The acceptance of the regional lists was to some extent a result of union pressure, but the manufacturers also had tangible reasons of their own to support this development. Employers who wanted to improve their relations with the workpeople, reduce turnover, and attract the best operatives, seems to have accepted that adherence to the regional list was the price they had to pay. But, as Joyce has shown, it was also a way to gain political prestige. Not surprisingly, it was the Conservative manufacturer Hornby who led the way on the part of the employers in the acceptance of the important Blackburn List for weaving in 1858.[19]

This development clearly ran counter to earlier notions among the manufacturers that standard lists were impossible constructions, and that the only thing which could be allowed to regulate wages was the state of supply and demand.[20] On the part of the workers, symbolic expressions of paternal relations became a way to separate good employers from the bad. The good mill-owner accepted the local price-list, and was rewarded by being met with gestures of deference and subordination.

The piece-rate list was not the only component of the informal agreement. Other parts of the "contract" dealt with the conditions of work. In mule-spinning factories, I would suggest that one employer concession was to respect some degree of worker autonomy on shopfloor level and not to attempt any alternative ways of staffing the machines. This element was probably present much more strongly in spinning than in weaving. As I have indicated above in the section on the formation of the labour process, the decades after 1850 constituted the period when the minder-piecer system became virtually unchallenged in Lancashire. The spinners were granted a very large degree of authority over piecers and the right to adjust the machinery, while the role of the overlookers in mule-spinning was kept very limited. Paternalism was to some extent combined with a tacit acceptance of spinners' authority in the workplace. Indeed, part of its popularity was due to the fact that the spinners could appeal to the owner when an overlooker interfered too much in their business.

---

18 See British Association for the Advancement of Science (1887): On the Regulation of Wages by Means of Lists in the Cotton Spinning Industry, passim; Wood (1910), p. 1.
19 Dutton and King (1982), p. 71.
20 See Ashworth, H (1854): The Preston Strike. An Inquiry into its Causes and Consequences, pp. 7, 10-12, 95; Robinson, S (1854): Friendly Letters on the Recent Strike from a Manufacturer to his own Workpeople, passim.

Another part of the "contract" was on the promotion of piecers to minder positions. While being nominally in the hands of the overlookers, it is clear that the operatives wanted to have promotion granted on the basis of seniority in order to avoid favouritism. In the Bolton mule-spinning mills, where paternalist relations grew relatively strong, the general principle on promotion was that of strict seniority.[21]

On the other hand, the resulting organization of work in spinning proved to be very successful. As I have shown previously, stable piece-rates helped to create an inner incentive to increase work effort and productivity while reducing the need for close supervision. The result was an efficient organization of work with very little friction with management. The last point is very important. The autonomy of the minder-piecer system caused very little everyday conflicts with management. As long as the general clauses of the agreement were adhered to, paternalism was allowed to flourish. During the second half of the 19th century, fine-spinning Bolton developed as a prototype for the new kind of industrial relations.[22]

It should also be noted that there were some areas of co-operation between operatives and management which lay outside the immediate context of the workplace. The spinners' unions and the employers shared interests in combatting speculation in raw cotton, in supporting the activities of the Cotton Growing Association to promote more cotton cultivation within the British Empire, and also on the question of imposing factory legislation on the Indian cotton industry.[23]

The arguments above give some indication as to why paternalism was much stronger, and also different in character, in the spinning sector of the industry compared to weaving. There was, for instance, a clear difference in authority structures. In weaving factories, supervision was much more onerous and everyday friction much greater. Overlookers were generally paid by poundage and were often accused of driving the operatives too hard in order to increase their own earnings. Generally speaking, the overlookers in weaving had the main authority in the workplace. They recruited, promoted, and fired operatives in their workroom. Most adjustments and repairs of the machinery were performed by the overlookers, and they often used this position as an indirect way to discipline the weavers. Operatives who were not favoured would find themselves waiting to have their looms

---

21 See Thorpe (1969), p. 252.
22 Ibid., pp. 179-87. Joyce's notions of the importance of family for the paternalistic culture and the "destructive" effect of the public limited companies have both been taken over from Thorpe.
23 Ibid, pp. 48-49, 56. As for Joyce's emphasis on the importance of the relations within the working-class family and community for the development of the paternalist culture, I am of the opinion that they were a mediating rather than a causal structure. They can only explain how paternalist relations were reinforced, not why they were created.

put in order, which seriously lowered their earnings.[24] It is therefore not surprising to find that the paternalist culture in northern weaving towns like Blackburn seems to have rested mainly on the good relations between employers and the overlookers, not the operative weavers.[25]

In this context, it is very important to recognize that there was not one single form of paternalism, but rather several varieties. The Bolton type of paternalism rested on a completely different set of social relations and compromises to that in Blackburn. Above all, the Bolton formula involved a very high degree of union presence and workers' authority on the shop floor. Joyce's conception of paternalism as the "social hegemony" of large employers over a relatively weak factory proletariat does to some extent capture the essence of Blackburn, which was dominated by weaving factories and comparatively large employers. But his perspective has practically no relevance for the expressions of paternalism in mule-spinning factories in central Lancashire.

Moreover, paternal relations were much more unusual in the weaving sector of the industry, and where they emerged, they had a more authoritarian character than in mule-spinning.[26] This probably made the operative weavers more prone than the spinners to react sharply when the paternalist did not deliver the goods. For instance, it is notable that during the bitter strike of 1878, the home of the Blackburn paternalist Sir Harry Hornby was stoned by a crowd of operatives.[27]

Also, paternalism of the Bolton kind had very little in common with employer dominance in large country factories. The inability to identify different kinds of social foundations and preconditions for paternalism in different contexts is one of the most serious shortcomings of Joyce's analysis.

The suggested connection between the emergent list systems and paternalism is further strengthened by the fact that in the districts where the employers resisted the establishment of price lists, paternalistic relations

---

24 See Savage (1985), passim; Roberts (1985), pp. 47-49.

25 Joyce makes this point in an earlier article, but surprisingly not in his book. See Joyce, P (1975): The Factory Politics of Lancashire, pp. 541-2. The fact that the overlookers were the social foundation for paternal relations in Blackburn is convincingly shown by Trodd, G (1978): Political Change and the Working Class in Blackburn and Burnley, 1880-1914, p. 150. Indeed, Trodd argues that the transition of the overlookers from being a "tool" of the manufacturers to being close to the other textile unions, a shift which took place between 1890 and 1910, lessened the fragmentation within the working class and was an important part of the political transition from paternalism to labourism. Ibid., pp. 302-3.

26 One of the major problems when studying paternalist relations is that they could contain very different degrees of authoritarian structures. As Alice Russell has concluded in her study of paternalistic expressions in Ashton and Accrington, Lancashire, they did not preclude the occasional use of "draconian strategies" on the part of the employer in order to "recreate an organic unity founded on the spurious symbiosis of unequals which characterized the paternalist's world view". Russell, A (1987): Local Elites and the Working-Class Response in the North-West, 1870-1895: Paternalism and Deference Reconsidered, p. 162.

27 Trodd (1978), p. 146.

132

did not develop. This was the case in Preston in the 1850s and in Burnley during the entire period.[28] The latter town was dominated by smaller employers, parvenu capitalists who were aggressively competitive and unwilling to submit their independence to the greater structures of industrial relations which were being built up to enforce the list systems. An official of the local weavers' associaton described the Burnley manufacturers in 1892 as "mushroom men" who were very difficult to come to terms with.[29]

However, Burnley constituted an exception to the rule. In the other parts of Lancashire, the district lists developed in the 1870s and 1880s to form an elaborate system of industrial relations.[30] As a counterpart to the growing unions, the employers organized in federations of their own. The question of changes in list prices was soon negotiable only at top level between officials of the two parties. On the mule-spinning side of the industry, this development culminated in the Brooklands Agreement of 1892.

Somewhat paradoxically, it is possible that the rationale of the paternalist compromise was weakened by the development of a more rigid structure of industrial bargaining. For instance, the institutionalised system of industrial relations left practically no room at all for the individual employer to interfere in the matter of piece-rates. The system of industrial relations was devised to take care of complaints of "under-paying", or not keeping to list prices. An investigation was made by the secretaries of the two organizations, and the employer had to abide by their decision. If he did not comply he risked having a dispute without receiving any assistance from the employers' association. The Lancashire cotton trade and the industrial bargaining structure were thus regulated in a joint effort by the unions and the employers' associations.

Typically, union officials found their counterparts in the employers' association much easier to deal with than individual or unaffiliated manufacturers.[31] One official of the Weavers' Amalgamation stated in 1892 that out of 23 recent strikes, 20 had been directed against unaffiliated manufacturers.[32] His conclusion was that an even higher degree of industrial organization would lessen the number of disputes. "We want every employer to

---

28 Dutton and King (1982), passim; Trodd (1978), chap. 2-3.

29 PP 1892 XXXV, Royal Commission on Labour, evidence of David Holmes, p. 44 Q. 1,078. On the absence of paternalist relations in the Burnley weaving industry, see also Russell (1987), pp. 168-69.

30 For a positive appraisal of the Lancashire list systems and the machinery of industrial conciliation in the cotton trade, see Webb and Webb (1897), pp. 195-204; Webb, S and Webb, B [1894]: The History of Trade Unionism, pp. 207-8.

31 See PP 1892 XXXV, Royal Commission on Labour, evidence of T. Birtwistle, Weavers' Amalgamation, pp. 55, 57, Q. 1,341, 1,411; Ibid., evidence of W. H. Wilkinson, Weavers' Amalgamation, p. 66 Q. 1,665-71; Ibid., evidence of D. Holmes, Burnley Weavers', and W. Booth, Ashton Weavers', p. 34 Q. 896.

32 Ibid., evidence of W. H. Wilkinson, Weavers' Amalgamation, p. 67 Q. 1,708.

become a member of the employers' association, and then we think that the biggest part of the strikes will be averted".[33] This description was corroborated by the secretary of the employers' association.[34] The joint committee which had been formed to negotiate over wage issues had created a better understanding between the two top organizations, but not between the individual manufacturer and the operatives.[35]

The formalised structure of industrial relations, and the increasing strenght of the unions, probably served to reduce the operatives' interest in taking part in the paternalistic relationship. But the final decline of this system towards the end of the 19th century should perhaps be explained in somewhat different terms. The suggestion of an informal contract as the basis of the paternalistic system does imply a somewhat different explanation of its decline than that provided by Joyce. He probably has a point, though, when stressing the importance of the emergence of the new public limited companies from the 1880s. But it was not only a matter of severing the mediating ties of identification which had been supplied by the owner family. The managers of the new limited companies seem to have been markedly negative towards customary rights and authority on the part of the operative spinners. The public limiteds were also more hesitant to take part in the existing structure of industrial bargaining, and more keen to speed up work.[36] They were also more prone to resort to illegal overworking. In Oldham, which was the major centre of the public limited firms, the spinners' union claimed that the managers of these companies "never cared what they did to human beings so long as they secured a dividend".[37]

The final demise of the paternalist system should also be seen as breaches against some clauses of the "contract" in the broader context of generally deteriorating industrial conditions. Competition had hardened perceptibly by 1890. The main causes were the expansion of limited companies in spinning, the growth of the Burnley district in weaving, and by the development of the Bombay cotton industry and the partial loss of the Indian market.[38] Owners of small family firms found it difficult to compete

---

33 Ibid., p. 67 Q. 1,712.

34 Ibid., evidence of J. Rawlinson, p. 95 Q. 2,428-29, p. 118 Q. 2,950-52.

35 Ibid., evidence of J. Rawlinson, p. 97 Q. 2,482.

36 Smith, R (1954): A History of the Lancashire Cotton Industry between the years 1873 and 1896, p. 384.

37 Cited in Smith (1954), p. 399.

38 James Mawdsley of the Spinners' Amalgamation complained in 1886 that the speculation in limited liability companies had increased competition, overstocked markets, and lowered the profit margin. PP 1886 XXI, Second Report of the Royal Commission..., Part I, pp. 172-73 Q. 5,039-45. Albert Simpson, a Preston mill-owner, agreed that the limited companies had exacerbated competition, and asked for a change in the legislation to make it compulsory to have 3/4 of the shares subscribed. Ibid., pp. 196-97 Q. 5,556, 5,598-5,603. J. Rawlinson, secretary of the North & North-East Lancashire Cotton Spinners' and Manufacturers' Association, concurred in that demand. Ibid., p. 205 Q. 5,813. The Textile Recorder, a manufacturer perodical, also advocated a legal alteration as to control the floating of public limited companies. See the

with the large limited companies.[39] As a result of the increased pressure, many employers started to cut costs by using inferior qualities of raw cotton and yarn.[40] This made the work of the operatives more arduous, since the bad cotton caused more frequent breakages of the yarn. Furthermore, since both spinners and weavers were paid by piece-rate, the use of inferior cotton also lowered their actual earnings. The deteriorating conditions of work very much increased friction between operatives and management. In 1892 James Mawdsley, the general secretary of the Spinners' Amalgamation, claimed that 9/10 of all disputes were over the use of bad cotton.[41] There was also an increasing number of conflicts caused by overlooker "tyranny" and "driving".[42] The paternalist "contract" was clearly breaking up.

Similar developments also occurred in the Lancashire weaving factories. The managerial strategy of cutting costs by using inferior qualities of yarn was accompanied by practices of "heavy sizing" and "steaming". The former meant that a mixture of china clay was added to the yarn to make it stronger, while steaming meant an artificial dampening of the air in the weaving rooms. Both methods had a decidedly detrimental impact on working conditions. Also, the structure of industrial relations had been devised to handle wage questions and interpretation of the price lists, and it proved to be inadequate when dealing with complaints of bad material and steaming. Consequently, the union officials found that it was very difficult to get the conditions improved.[43] The special feature of these strategies was that they circumvented the existing structure of industrial bargaining, and again increased the room of manuever for the individual mill-owner. The result was a growing tendency of friction and disputes over bad cotton, steaming, and driving. In this context, the paternalist formula, which had always been comparatively superficial in weaving, finally proved inadequate.

Still, it was doubtless the case that paternalist relations survived longest in old family firms, and especially so in the fine-spinning mills of Bolton which were much less threatened by competition from India or the new public limited companies than was the case in the coarse-spinning sector of the trade.[44] It is therefore no wonder that even a trade unionist like A. H. Gill of the Bolton spinners saw the rise of the public limited companies as a

---

Textile Recorder, August 1894, p. 130. On the effects of the competition from Burnley weaving firms, see PP 1892 XXXV, Royal Commission on Labour, evidence of W. Booth, Ashton Weavers', p. 34 Q. 895. On the competition from the Bombay mills on coarse counts of yarn, see Farnie (1979), p. 110.
39 PP 1892 XX, RCIFW, pp. 22-23.
40 See Smith (1954), pp. 46-47, 457-58, 627-28.
41 PP 1892 XXXV, Royal Commission on Labour, p. 25 Q. 736.
42 Bullen, A (1987c): The Making of Brooklands, p. 100.
43 Bullen (1984), pp. 20, 28.
44 Thorpe (1969), pp. 184-87; Smith (1954), p. 382 note 6.

force which would sever the bonds between the mill-owners and the operatives.[45]


# Conclusions

What I have tried to illustrate in this chapter is two major changes in the nature of workplace relations: first, from the "economic" and relatively antagonistic type of industrial relations in the period from the 1820s to the 1840s, to the more consensus-dominated system after 1850. Paternalism should be seen as a part of that latter system of industrial relations, emphasizing stable piece-rates and secure working conditions. Later in the century, the structure of industrial relations was eroded by increasing competition, the spread of cost-cutting practices, and the emergence of limited companies which disregarded customary agreements between operatives and employers.

While the work position and unions of the skilled male operatives had been under constant threat during the first "antagonistic" period, these attitudes lessened perceptibly after mid-century. The consensus or paternalist period was marked by a larger degree of worker autonomy and union recognition. Attempts to find ways to replace the skilled men largely stopped. In this way, the general structure of work organization was stabilized. Here is part of the reason for the marked permanence in the organization of the labour process in Lancashire cotton after mid-century.

Another important implication of the first shift in industrial relations was on the matter of subcontracting and recruitment of children. Previously, the manufacturers had largely used the subcontracting system to make the spinners recruit piecers who could pass for being 13 years old. After 1850, however, there are indications that the operatives were given a freer hand in matters of recruitment. My suggestion is this can be seen as a part of the paternalistic "contract". As a consequence, the employment of children below 13 years of age increased considerably. While in weaving this was undoubtedly caused by the emergence of the "tenter-system", in mule-spinning the reason was simply that a larger proportion of piecers below 13 was recruited. This will later be analysed in terms of shortage of juvenile labour, but it is important to emphasize the change of attitude among the manufacturers in favour of the half-time system after 1850. In the spinning sector, I would suggest that the main reason behind this process was the operatives' increased authority over recruitment as a part of the consensus

---

45 Gill, A H (1904-5): The Organisation of Labour as a Political Force, passim.

formula. In times of labour scarcity, this meant that the spinners had the option to recruit half-timers. The subtle shift in authority over the recruitment of children was therefore a major reason behind the expansion of the half-time system after 1850.

# Chapter 6

# Legal Restrictions on Child Labour and the Working-Class Family

In the two previous chapters, I have studied child labour practices in the context of the labour process and the relations of production. This perspective will now be extended to comprise developments in the legal framework which regulated the work and schooling of children, and also the response of working-class parents to those regulations. I will also indicate that labour market constraints had at least some relevance for the continuation of child labour practices. But the main emphasis will be on the actions of manufacturers, operatives, and parents within the institutional framework in the creation of the half-time system for factory child labour.

The legal framework of the half-time system was set by the 1844 Factory Act, which ruled that children below 13 years of age could only be employed for 6½ hours per day. This solution proved to be more practical for managers and operative spinners when organizing work than the previous practice of allowing children to work for eight hours per day. It also made it much easier for the factory inspectors to ensure that children were not worked beyond the legal hours. The previous system had never been popular either among operatives or employers. Most of the factory children in the 1840s were piecers subcontracted by mule-spinners, who needed their assistance for the full twelve hours of the working day. After 1844 two half-timers in succession proved to be a much more convenient formula. The fact that the half-time system was comparatively practical and easily organized must be seen as one reason for its relative success.

## The Making of the Half-time System in Lancashire, 1840-1870

During the decades after 1844, there was a marked increase in the use of child labour in the Lancashire cotton district. The factory inspectors saw this mainly as a result of the simplifying legislation of 1844 and a growing scarcity of juvenile operatives. Leonard Horner commented in 1846 on the increase of factory children:

They are now employed in many mills where they were excluded on the passing of the Act of 1833, and I ascribe the change mainly to two causes; in the first place, the restriction of the working of children to half a-day, and the consequent simplifying of the regulations affecting them, has made their employment more easy, and greatly diminished the risk of the work-people whom they assist employing them illegally; and in the second place, the masters have found out by the scarcity of piecers of 13 years of age, and the high price they are obliged to pay for them, that in formerly excluding those under 13 years of age, they were cutting off the springs of their supply... [1]

The same kind of observation was to recur several times during the 1850s and 60s. The rapid expansion of the Lancashire cotton industry during these decades created a scarcity of juvenile workers, which in turn induced employers and operative spinners to employ half-timers in larger numbers.[2] The manufacturers were now allowing the recruitment of half-timers to a greater extent than previously. As I have indicated in the previous chapter, this should be seen in the context of a shift in industrial relations towards co-operation and paternalism.

However, it is also possible that a part of the increase in child labour statistics actually reflected the fact that enforcement of the Factory Act had become more stringent. As I have argued previously, the working of children in the half-time system was much easier for the inspectors to check than previous practices. The 1844 Act also gave the inspectors full formal powers to appoint surgeons and to annul medical certificates which they believed to be incorrect. This made evasions of the child labour clauses of the Act much more difficult. Consequently, part of the increase in the "official" figures on child labour could reflect the fact that some illegal, and therefore unregistered, practices had ended.

The observable result was a more general spread of the half-time system in the Lancashire cotton district. The major exception to this rule was the Manchester manufacturers, who largely did not employ half-timers. But it has to be pointed out that the disinclination of the Manchester manufacturers to hire children below 13 was never as strong or as concerted as in Glasgow. Large employers like Birley, McConnel, and Kennedy, organized the work of children in relays already in the 1830s.[3]

---

1 PP 1846 XX, RIF, 1st Half-yearly Rep. 1846, p. 4.

2 PP 1852-53 XL, RIF, 1st Half-yearly Rep. 1853, pp. 19-20; PP 1856 XVIII, RIF, 2nd Half-yearly Rep. 1855, p. 17; PP 1860 XXX, RIF, 2nd Half-yearly Rep. 1859, p. 8; Ibid., 1st Half-yearly Rep. 1860, pp. 24-25; PP 1871 XIV, RIF, 1st Half-yearly Rep. 1871, p. 58.

3 PP 1840 X, Third Report from the Select Committee..., evidence of Richard Birley, p. 25 Q. 4,345-50; Memoir of Leonard Horner (1890), Vol I, p. 329, Letter from Horner to his daughter Katharine, 7/8/36. In HO 45/423, Letter from Horner to Graham, Home Office, 6/4/43, a part of the Manchester Superintendent's report is enclosed. This shows that a majority of the mills did not employ children, but there was also a considerable number of exceptions.

Still, the Manchester case perhaps throws some light on why half-timers were more readily accepted by the manufacturers in other parts of Lancashire. The city of Manchester had a relatively large unskilled juvenile labour market, which meant that it was comparatively easy to find a full complement of young workers above 13 years of age. But during the brisk activity of the cotton trade in 1860, even the Manchester mill-owners had to counter the scarcity of juvenile operatives with a more general employment of half-timers.[4] However, the change proved to be short-lived. The half-time system never became as established in Manchester as in the other parts of Lancashire.

If the perspective is shifted to Britain as a whole, it is clear that in the districts of factory inspector Stuart in Scotland and the northern part of Ireland, and inspector Howell in southern England and Ireland, the general response from the textile manufacturers on the implementation of the 1833 Factory Act was to stop employing children below 13. In contrast, Lancashire and the West Riding of Yorkshire developed as the main centres of the half-time system.[5]

One effect of the restrictions on the use of child workers was to turn them into a kind of labour reserve. The required extra book-keeping, the responsibility for the children's education, and the risk of being prosecuted for irregularities, were the perceived disadvantages for the manufacturers when using child labour. Many employers preferred to employ full-timers over 13 if they were available. Half-timers were therefore mainly used during periods of brisk trade, expansion, and labour shortage. There was never a real lack of child workers themselves.

This does not mean that the level of child labour was directly determined by industrial expansion and a scarcity of young operatives. Rather, the labour market constraints served as one part in the complex process of workforce formation, and mainly as an additional inducement for the manufacturers to allow the employment of children. Nevertheless, one perceptible result of this reserve labour function was that the official statistics over the proportion of child workers in the cotton industry can be said to correlate with the economic fluctuations. The proportion of child labour was higher in boom periods than in slumps. However, it should be emphasized that these changes were spurious in the sense that they were in practice occasioned by very small movements of the age composition across the "magic" line of 13 years of age.

---

4 PP 1860 XXXIV, RIF, 1st Half-yearly Rep. 1860, pp. 24-25; PP 1861 XXII, RIF, 2nd Half-yearly Rep. 1860, p. 20.
5 See PP 1844 XXVIII, RIF, 4th Quart. Rep. 1843, pp. 14-15, and also the section on Scotland in chapter 3.

Furthermore, the use of half-timers as a reserve probably varied greatly depending on the composition of the local working class, the building of new cotton mills, and the labour requirements of other industries in the area. However, local studies of this kind lie outside the scope of this investigation.

Another important fact is that there was at this point no major political force advocating the abolition of the half-time system in textiles. The Lancashire cotton industry especially was regarded as very well-regulated compared to other industrial trades.[6] Potteries and match factories were not included under the Factory Acts until 1864, and the metal trades not until 1868.[7]

Indeed, during this period the use of half-timers in textile factories was rather encouraged by middle-class interest groups outside the sphere of manufacturing. Since there was no enactment on compulsory schooling before 1870, the educational requirements of the Factory Acts were really the only guaranteed measure of schooling which was imposed on working-class children. Half-time education for labouring children was regarded as ideal by contemporary observers belonging to as different camps as Edwin Chadwick and Karl Marx.[8] Furthermore, the extension of factory regulation to other trades was regularly motivated with the argument that this would provide more working-class children with the benefit of education. The half-time system was also strongly defended by the factory inspectors, which can be examplified by a report from Leonard Horner in 1853:

> This scarcity of hands has lead to a considerable increase in the number of children employed in my district, which indeed has been going on, happily, for a long time; I say "happily" without hesitation, for now that children are restricted to half a day's work, and are required to attend school, I know no description of work so advantageous for them as that in a factory. [9]

The Scottish factory inspector, Sir John Kincaid, found that the refusal of the Glasgow cotton manufacturers to adopt the half-time system had led to a deplorable increase in the street-selling and loitering of children:

---

6 Even Marx declared that after 1850 the Lancashire cotton trade was "England's model industry". Marx [1867], p. 380 footnote 78.
7 PP 1865 XX, RIF, 1st Half-yearly Rep. 1865, passim; PP 1867-68 XVIII, RIF, 2nd Half-yearly Rep. 1867, p. 36.
8 Silver, H (1977): Ideology and the Factory Child: Attitudes to Half-time Education, passim.
9 PP 1852-53 XL, RIF, 1st Half-yearly Rep. 1853, pp. 19-20. See also Horner's report in PP 1851 XXIII, RIF 2nd Half-yearly Rep. 1850, pp. 15-16, where he states that the main benefit of half-time employment was that it provided the child with some education.

...the majority of that class not employed, instead of being at school, was generally to be seen idling about the streets at the every age when poverty and idleness are most likely to lead to evil habits and associations that can never be shaken off.. [10]

The point I am trying to make is that there was a wide-spread support for regulated child labour practices even among factory inspectors and social reformers. According to this middle-class perspective, factory work hindered children from loitering in the streets, gave them some degree of work discipline, and also provided them with some elementary schooling. Education was seen as a way to lessen animosity between operatives and employers, and, in the words of Leonard Horner, to show "the humbler classes" the "kind sympathy" of their superiors, which in turn would reduce the risk for industrial riots.[11] An uneducated proletariat was more likely to be moved by radical agitators. This was probably a powerful argument among the middle classes during the period of Chartist agitation.

In conclusion, the making of the half-time system was a process which took place in a political context where this type of regulated child labour combined with elementary education was a solution which was widely supported among the middle classes outside manufacturing. Even if the actual creation of the half-time system should be seen as the work of the operatives, parents, and manufacturers, it is still important to note that there was no real social or political movement militating against it.

## The System at its Zenith: Child Labour in the 1870s

The official factory statistics show a peak in the proportion of half-timers in the cotton factory workforce in the 1870s.[12] Clark Nardinelli has explained this as a side effect of the introduction of the 1874 Factory Act. The minimum age for the employment of children in factories was raised from 8 to 10 years of age, but those who were registered as working before the date of implementation would be allowed to continue even if they were below the new legal age limit. As a result, many 8 and 9 year olds were registered as half-timers before 1 January 1875.[13]

Even if this argument is basically correct, it obscures some far more important reasons behind the apparent zenith of the half-time system. Contrary to received opinion, child labour practices in cotton factories were

10 PP 1852-53 XL, 2nd Half-yearly Rep. 1852, p. 46.
11 See Horner's report in PP 1843 XXVII, RIF, 4th Quart. Rep. 1842, p. 6.
12 See table 6 in chapter 4 above.
13 Nardinelli (1980), p. 748. See also the statements of Sub-inspector Cramp, Bolton district, and Sub-inspector Bignor, Stockport, in PP 1875 XVI, RIF, 1st Half-yearly Rep. 1875, pp. 66 and 68.

actually reinforced by the interplay of compulsory schooling legislation and the Factory Acts. The Factory Act had been extended in 1864 and 1868 to comprise the large majority of branches of industry. However, in the new factories coming under the scope of the factory legislation, the main effect was the dismissal of the child workers.[14] The half-time system was practically only used in the textile industries; above all in cotton, worsted, and jute factories. The abandoning of child labour in other trades further increased the pressure on the labour market for juvenile full-timers.

Moreover, the Education Act of 1870, as far as it was enforced, struck hardest against children employed in domestic work and other non-factory tasks. The half-timers in cotton mills, on the other hand, were not subjected to the requirements of the Education Act. The half-day schooling which they received as a part of the factory legislation was deemed to be sufficient. The effects of the schooling requirements must be seen in a family-economy framework. Working-class parents who had earlier depended on their children for household tasks and odd jobs found that the only way to have some real benefit out of them was to send them half-time to factories. Having them in school was regarded as a pure loss, since it only hindered the children from contributing to the family in a more material way. Factory operatives as well as other working-class parents therefore became more induced to secure half-time employment for their young children. It is also probable that there was a drop in the price of half-time labour, which in turn made their employment more viable. Sub-inspector Bignold, reporting in 1872, provides some evidence on this:

There has been during the six months a very marked increase in the number of half-time children employed, especially in cotton mills. Many firms, who had done without them, have been compelled to try the system, and I have noticed that the increase has mainly occurred in children between the ages of 8 and 10. I do not think this increase is the result of any extraordinary activity in the cotton trade, which in most branches is fairly good, but is due to the great demand of boys of 13 years in other trades, and to the great number of children under 13 - heretofore working full time in such other

14 See PP 1868-69 XIV, RIF, 1st Half-yearly Rep. 1869, p. 36. In most trades regulated by the Extension Acts, children below 13 were largely replaced with juveniles. In some cases, factory legislation speeded up the mechanisation of the tasks performed by children. The spread of the cylinder press in calico printing is one example of this process. Similarly, the Scottish tobacco manufacturers introduced machinery to replace their child workers when their trade came under the factory legislation in 1868. See PP 1870 XV, RIF, 1st Half-yearly Rep. 1870, p. 9. However, this does not preclude the possibility that changes in the organization of work in some branches also had the effect of reducing the employment of children. Manufacturers could also evade the more stringent factory regulations simply by keeping their workforce below 50, which meant that in legal terms it constituted "workshop" employment. Similarly, the improvement in the factory legislation towards the end of the century had the effect of changing the exploitation of child and woman labour towards "sweating", i e unregulated outwork in the homes. See Schmiechen, J A (1984): Sweated Industries and Sweated Labor. The London Clothing Trades, 1860-1914, chapter 6.

trades - who have been put on half-time, and sent to school by the joint action of the school board and the factory inspectors. [15]

Sub-inspector Cramp, Bolton, spelled out the implications of the Education Act for the working-class family in a similar way:

> ...the school board enforces compulsory education, and will not allow half-time exemptions to any but children employed in factories, workshops and mines. Parents, therefore, finding that they cannot keep children at home to mind the house, or shop, or babies, without letting them attend school morning and afternoon, at once send them to the mills for half-time work, half-time school, and half-time wages, instead of having their help at home. [16]

The strategy of the Lancashire working-class parents when faced with regulations on compulsory schooling was evidently to try to send their children half-time to the cotton factories. Instead of reducing the level of child labour in this branch of industry, the actual effect of the Education Acts was therefore to promote it by enhancing the supply of half-timers.

Simultaneously, the operation of the new Factory Act of 1874 really had the effect of raising the half-time statistics by making it more difficult for 13 year olds to work full time. For the first time certain educational standards were combined with the age limits to form requirements for both half-time and full-time work. Young workers were allowed to start full-time at 13 only if they had passed the educational Standard IV. If they could not manage this they had to continue as half-timers until they were 14 years old.[17]

Complaints were soon made by manufacturers in several parts of Lancashire that the new regulations had made it much more difficult to recruit full-timers. For instance, the managers of the large weaving firms in the Ashton district complained that the scarcity of young full-timers had obliged them to employ children.[18] Similar expressions of dissatisfaction were reported from the Oldham, Rochdale, Manchester and Bury districts.[19] Sub-inspector Osborn in the Rochdale district claimed that very few 13 year olds in his area were able to pass the required fourth standard.[20] Of the 1,691 young Manchester cotton operatives who aquired full-time certificates in 1878, only 153 were in fact 13 years old. The rest were 14.[21]

---

15 PP 1873 XIX, RIF, 2nd Half-yearly Rep. 1872, p. 131.
16 PP 1875 XVI, RIF, 2nd Half-yearly Rep. 1874, p. 75.
17 See PP 1876 XXIX, Report of the Commissioners appointed to enquire into the Working of the Factory and Workshops Acts, pp. lxv-lxvi.
18 PP 1876 XVI, RIF, 1st Half-yearly Rep. 1876, p. 24.
19 Ibid., pp. 25, 65.
20 Ibid., p. 25.
21 PP 1880 XIV, RCIFW, p. 90.

There is no reason to believe that the situation was much different in other districts. The overt result was, of course, a general rise in half-time statistics. This means that a part of the observed increase in child labour figures in the factory returns is spurious in the sense that it only reflects a re-definition of the category of "half-timer". But there was probably also a real increase of child labour in cotton as a consequence of family responses to the new regulations. Since the special educational requirements initially only applied to the textile trades, working-class families found that it was much more advantageous to place their 13 year old children in other industrial occupations, because in that way they would be allowed to work full-time without any educational requirements. During the 1870s, a 13 year old child who was unable to pass the educational standard was allowed to work full-time in other industries but only half-time in a cotton mill. This further impeded the recruitment of juvenile workers to the cotton industry, and made them more reliant on the labour of children . The regulations were not extended to cover other types of factories until 1880.[22]

My overall conclusion is that the statistical peak of the half-time system in the mid-1870s was caused by specific family responses to compulsory schooling and changes in the factory legislation.

### Relative Decline, 1880-1900: The Impact of Changes in the Legislative Framework

After the mid-1870s there was a gradual decline in half-time statistics, a trend which continued for the rest of the century. One possible explanation is that the 1878 Factory Act reduced the usefulness of the half-timer. By this Act children were prohibited from cleaning machinery in motion, and this in turn made them less suitable as little piecers in mule-spinning. However, it is very debatable if this regulation was much enforced. Offences could only be detected by an inspector if they were committed on his entering a workroom. Indeed, the lack of proper enforcement of this clause is sadly evidenced by the continuous crop of accidents involving children cleaning machinery in motion.[23] The factory inspector in Oldham reported in 1901 that the half-time piecers still performed an "enormous amount" of illegal cleaning, a practice which was instigated by the minder but often tacitly condoned by management.[24]

---

22 Ibid., p. 89.
23 See, for instance, PP 1884-85 XV, RCIFW, pp. 3-4.
24 PP 1901 X, RCIFW, p. 13.

However, these regulations possibly had some effect in a longer perspective in tipping the scale of preference against the employment of half-timers. It is also possible that some employers used the regulations on cleaning as a reason for stopping the hiring of children. This seems to have been the case in Manchester, where the employment of half-timers had never been popular among the manufacturers.[25]

Of considerably more importance for the relative decline of the half-time system was probably the gradual raising of the minimum factory age. During the last two decades of the nineteenth century, amendments in the schooling and factory legislation increasingly narrowed the population of children which could be employed as half-timers. The general pattern was that a raise of the minimum age requirement was included in a new Factory or Education Act, and it was then confirmed by a corresponding change in the other branch of legislation. The Factory Act of 1891 set the minimum age of half-timers to 11, and the Education Act of 1893 consequently raised the age of exemption to this level. In a similar way, schooling legislation in 1899 and a new Factory Act in 1901 raised the minimum age for half-timers to 12.[26] The tightening legal constraints on factory child labour were of course an important part of the relative decline of the half-time system during these decades. It is also the main explanation of this process which has found its way into the historical textbooks.[27]

However, a parallel process which also tended to reduce the "official" number of half-timers has not been acknowledged. As I have indicated in the previous section, one important reason for the statistical peak of the half-time system in the 1870s was that educational requirements hindered a substantial part of the 13 year olds from working full time. However, these obstacles were largely removed during the following two decades. Having the incentive of getting their children early into the mills, working-class parents who had earlier shown little interest in school performance now became eager that their children should pass the required test. The result was that children were more often able to meet the educational require-ments and were therefore allowed to start working full-time in the mill at 13.[28]

Perhaps more importantly, after 1899 the whole question of passing the standard largely lost its point when a new clause in the Education Act made it possible for children to gain exemption merely if they had reached a certain level of attendance. Later called the "dunce's clause" by the opponents of the half-time system, it meant that a child was allowed to

25 PP 1888 XXVI, RCIFW, p. 13.
26 See PP 1902 XII, RCIFW, p. xi.
27 See Simon (1965), p. 290; Cruickshank (1981), p. 94.
28 See PP 1889 XVIII, RCIFW, pp. 117-18.

work full-time at 13 if he or she had achieved 350 school attendances in five years. The effect was to make the working-class parents interested in their children's regular attendance at school in order to get them into paid employment as soon as possible. Also, in terms of the relative decline of the half-time system, the effect was to lower the number of 13 year olds working as half-timers.[29]

Unfortunately, it is very difficult to estimate how much of the relative decline of the half-time system which can be explained by the greater propensity of the children to pass the required education standards. One of the few pieces of evidence available is an estimate from 1892 by Thomas Birtwistle of the Weavers' Amalgamation, showing that 16.2 per cent of the half-timers in weaving were 13 years of age.[30] On the other hand, the Lancashire factory inspectors reported in 1893 that the proportion of 13 year olds among the half-timers had by then gone down to 4.5 per cent in Oldham, 2.3 per cent in Bolton, and 3.3 per cent in Blackburn.[31] This was probably much lower than the level during the previous fifteen years.

Consequently, my suggestion is that a substantial part of the decline in half-time statistics between 1880 and 1900 was not caused by a change in actual age composition, but instead by the fact that 13 year old workers were more generally being allowed to go to the mills full-time. The statistical representation of child labour levels in Lancashire is therefore somewhat misleading both in its peak of 1878 and in its subsequent decline.

Another complication for an analysis of child labour levels is the control of the local school boards over the conditions for half-time exemptions. After the Education Act of 1880, the question of exemptions was laid under local bye-laws.[32] One of the effects was that regulations for half-time exemptions were made more severe in districts where the use of child labour was insignificant. In Manchester, where the half-time system had never been strong, the school board was negative to child labour and even exacted higher fees from the half-timers than from the full-time pupils.[33] The most common measure, though, was to raise the educational standard

---

29 See PP 1909 XVII, Report of the Inter-Departmental Committee on Partial Exemption from School Attendance, Vol I, p. 2; Ibid., Vol II, evidence of R. Waddington, headmaster, p. 9 Q. 211; Ibid., Vol II, evidence of H. Whittick, teacher, p. 31 Q. 762; Ibid., Vol II, evidence of F. A. Hargreaves, secretary of the Burnley employers' association, p. 118 Q. 3,326.
30 PP 1892 XXXV, Royal Commission on Labour, p. 51 Q. 1,219. The estimation was based on a sample of 25,969 half-time tenters in different parts of Lancashire. Birtwistle stated that the main reason for the 13 year olds to work half-time was that they had not been able to pass the education standard. Ibid., p. 51 Q. 1,222-23. Birtwistle's figures were challenged by Richard Waddington, a headmaster and leading opponent of the half-time system, but the latter was unable to produce an alternative set of figures. See ibid., p. 146 Q. 3,739.
31 PP 1894 XXI, RIF, p. 323.
32 See PP 1881 XXIII, RCIFW, pp. 24-25.
33 PP 1888 XXVI, RCIFW, report of Sub-inspector Meade-King, Manchester, p. 13.

for half-time exemptions, thus decreasing the number of children eligible for work.

On the other hand, in districts where the half-time system still dominated and was widely supported, the educational requirements were kept at a very low level. In Burnley, a centre of the tenter-system in weaving, the schooling standards were clearly lower than in the weaving district of south Lancashire. The outcome was a process of centralization of the half-time system to certain core areas, above all to the Oldham, Bolton, and Burnley districts.

## Chapter 7

# Industrial Relations, Authority Structures, and the Employment of Half-timers in Lancashire, 1850-1920

In the sphere of production, the use of factory children rested on rather subtle definitions of authority over recruitment in the relations between operatives and employers. As I have shown in earlier chapters, a large majority of the Lancashire half-timers were subcontracted by adult workers. The question whether they would be allowed a free choice in recruitment, or had to take full-timers, was contested terrain in workplace relations. It would seem that in the spread of the half-time system after 1850, the adult operatives largely aquired greater authority over this aspect of recruitment. It should be emphasized, though, that there may have been great variations in this respect between different regions or even within the same factory town.

However, it is very difficult to reconstruct phenomena like real authority in the subcontracting relationship. Agreements were often made on an informal or tacit level, and are not to be found overtly stated in historical records. My arguments on this line should be taken as suggestions rather than proven facts. Nevertheless, the nature of the problem which is being studied necessitates the formulation of this kind of suggestion in order to obtain a full picture of the processes involved.

The half-time system rested on a kind of agreement between operatives and employers on the rights and limits of recruitment within the sub-contracting relationship. When industrial relations deteriorated towards the end of the nineteenth century, this also affected the definition of the sub-contract. Limited liability companies and emerging parvenu capitalists proved to be much less favourable to the employment of half-timers.[1] Also, there seems to have been a marked decline in the proportion of firms run by the owners.[2]

In this context, it should be emphasized that the possible extra cost of employing a full-timer instead of two half-timers was not borne by the

---

1 See PP 1888 XXVI, RCIFW, pp. 14-15.
2 See PP 1890-91 XIX, RCIFW, pp. 5-7.

employer. The trade was governed by price lists which only took account of the numbers of assistants, not their ages. The subcontracting relationship meant that extra costs for piecers or tenters had to be met by the adult operatives. Consequently, the employer himself had only a very marginal interest in using cheap child labour. The employment of half-timers was also connected with the disadvantage of more onerous book-keeping and the responsibility for attendance at school.

In the old family firms, the agreement to use children should be seen in a wider context of paternalistic industrial relations. However, with the emergence of limited companies and new competitive firms, the foundations for the old agreement were to some extent removed. By the 1890s there is ample evidence that many employers were either indifferent or hostile to the half-time system. Josua Rawlinson, secretary of the North & North-East Cotton Spinners' and Manufacturers' Association, claimed in 1892 that the employers had little interest in the hiring of half-timers:

> ...the employer is responsible for the attendance at school for each child, and one main reason why there is a superfluity of child labour at the present time, is because many employers absolutely decline to employ half-timers, because of the risks they run of violating the Factory Act. [3]

This statement is strengthened by the fact that the employer representatives in the 1892 Royal Commission on Labour did not argue against the raising of the age for half-timers.[4] One of them also claimed that the use of factory children was not particularly advantageous for the manufacturers, but rather to the operative weavers and spinners.[5] Similarly, the factory inspector in Stockport in southern Lancashire stated in 1895 that half-timers were disfavoured by the employers, and that their number was decreasing:

> In this district, were it not for the weavers and spinners engaging these half-timers direct[ly], as helpers, very few would be employed. [6]

The Chief Inspector added that there was a "general expression of disapproval" from the manufacturers on the employment of half-timers, due to the trouble caused by the children being absent from school, failing to bring

3 PP 1892 XXXV, Royal Commission on Labour, p. 117 Q. 2,926.
4 Ibid., evidence of W. Noble, United Cotton Manufacturers' Association, pp. 158-59 Q. 3,992-98.
5 Ibid., p. 163 Q. 4,081. Naturally, if the manufacturers had been more dependent on the use of child labour, one would have expected a public defence of the system.
6 PP 1895 XIX, RCIFW, p. 200.

the school registers, or making false entries in them.[7]. This opinion was reiterated by the Oldham inspector in 1901:

> As a rule, occupiers do not want half-timers. It is the minders who want them for piecing at the mules...The half-timer is a very cheap labourer, and work can easily be got out of him. [8]

Still, child labour continued to be used in the Lancashire cotton factories up till 1920. Why, then, did the employers continue with this practice? My suggestion is that there were two main reasons; first, that child labour was still found to be advantageous in the most expansive districts. In Bolton, Oldham, and Burnley, the relative scarcity of juvenile workers made the mill-owners accept a continuation of the recruitment of children. Second, it was also a matter of power in the local relations of production. Bolton and Oldham contained the strongest local associations of the Spinners' Amalgamation, and Burnley assumed a similar position within the Weavers' Amalgamation, at least after 1900. Since the adult operatives wanted to retain the option of hiring half-timers, the really crucial matter was to what degree they could put pressure on the manufacturers to accept the practice. Therefore, the important thing was the definition of authority within the subcontracting relationship, and this has to be explained in terms of power in the relations between employers and operatives. Apart from union strength, explanations should also be sought in differences in positions and objectives among the manufacturers. The question of actual authority rested with the strategies and resources of both parties.

However, a substantiation of these suggestions would require closer studies on a local level, and systematic comparisons between different districts. While it has not been possible for me to realize such an ambitious project, I will in the following section at least provide some findings on the question of authority in the subcontracting relationship in the weaving section of the industry.

## Authority and Subcontracting in Weaving: Some Examples

There seems to have been a major difference in the use of half-timers between the weaving districts in north Lancashire and those of the South. This is indicated in the 1886 wage census, where it is possible to isolate the workers in the specific labour process of weaving. While the proportion of

---

7 Ibid.
8 PP 1901 X, RCIFW, p. 312. See also PP 1909 XXI, RCIFW, p. 99.

half-time tenters in this process was 18.0 per cent in Blackburn, 18.3 per cent in Preston, and 15.2 per cent in the Burnley-Colne district, all in north Lancashire, the corresponding figure was 13.1 per cent in the Ashton-Stalybridge district in the South. Manchester had of course the lowest figure, only 2.9 per cent.[9] This difference can probably be linked to the lower degree of unionization among the weavers in the South.[10]

However, it is not possible to exclude the alternative explanation: that the half-time system was stronger in the North due to a greater rate of industrial expansion and a corresponding strain on labour supplies. To some extent the latter suggestion supports the former. The relative scarcity of labour in the expanding districts probably served to increase the influence of the local unions. Also, a lack of weavers would probably make the employers somewhat more favourable to the employment of half-timers, since this would mean that young operatives would be trained to start weaving at a comparatively early age.[11]

The Burnley district is a good illustration of that connection. Burnley had for a long period been a low-paying district in north-east Lancashire where employers had resisted the establishment of a regional list. Several attempts were made by weavers' unions in the other northern towns to make the Burnley employers accept the normative Blackburn List, but not until 1884 did they give in to the concerted pressure of the Weavers' Amalgamation and the North Lancashire Manufacturers' Association.[12] Even after the recognition of the Burnley List, many manufacturers still continued to pay below the agreed rate. From the local union reports it emerges that this problem was felt very acutely up till 1900.[13]

One important difference between Burnley and Blackburn, the other major northern weaving centre, was in the class structure of the manufacturers. While Blackburn was dominated by a few very large mill-owners, Burnley employers were predominately small-scale.[14] This was probably one reason for the difficulty experienced by the Burnley weavers to make all the local mill-owners stick to the agreed list, but it also meant that these smaller

---

9 PP 1889 LXX, Return of Rates of Wages..., pp. 8-51. N for all districts: Blackburn: 10,141; Preston: 4,864; Burnley-Colne: 4,944; Ashton-Stalybridge: 6,912; Manchester: 2,207.
10 On the unionization issue, see Bullen (1984), p. 6.
11 PP 1892 XXXV, Royal Commission on Labour, evidence of D. Holmes, Burnley Weavers', p. 35 Q. 909-10.
12 LRO, Preston. Preston Weavers' Minutes, 10/10/71; 8/7/73. See also Bullen (1984), p. 17.
13 Burnley Weavers' Monthly Reports, 1899-1900.
14 PP 1892 XXXV, Royal Commission on Labour, evidence of D. Holmes, Burnley Weavers', p. 40 Q. 1,006. See also Trodd (1978), chap. 2-3, on the difference in composition of the manufacturer class in Blackburn and Burnley.

employers did not have the power to disregard the union in the same way as larger firms.[15]

Also, Burnley was by the turn of the century the most expansive weaving district in Lancashire. The need to secure a sufficient labour supply, and preferably one consisting of skilful operatives, must have put the local union in a good bargaining position.

An indication of the relative strength of the Burnley weavers is the comparatively high proportion of male operatives to females. The 1906 Census of Production shows that 46.5 per cent of the Burnley weavers were men, which was the highest proportion of male weavers in all Lancashire districts.[16] Women's responsibility for domestic work, as well as male prejudice, tended to give women operatives much less chance to take part in union affairs.

There are clear indications that the Burnley weavers were strongly committed to the half-time system. Partly because the Burnley powerlooms were slightly narrower than in other places, the number of looms per weaver was probably the highest in Lancashire.[17] This was one material reason for the strength of the tenter-system and the propensity to use child labour. During the last decades of the 19th century, officials of the Burnley weavers' union actively advocated the continuation of child labour in the Lancashire cotton mills. David Holmes, the local union president, several times defended the half-time system in public. Before the 1892 Royal Commission on Labour, Holmes complained that many employers were prejudiced against having children coming into their mills as half-time learners.[18]

On a local level, when suggestions of raising the age of half-timers were brought forward at union meetings, these were dismissed without discussion. A special meeting of the Burnley Weavers' Association in 1891 even

---

15 Craig Calhoun has recently suggested a connection between worker radicalism and small scale factories and workshops. Even if I agree that factory size may be a useful indication of power resources in the relations of production, it is only one part of a complex array of causes. See Calhoun, C (1982): The Question of Class Struggle. Social Foundations of Popular Radicalism during the Industrial Revolution, pp. 198-201.

16 PP 1909 LXXX, Report of an Inquiry by the Board of Trade..., pp. 32-57. N for Burnley was 12,146. In contrast, the corresponding figures were 34.3 per cent in Blackburn and a mere 4.5 per cent in Ashton ( N for Blackburn = 10,607; N for Ashton = 3,445). See also Jewkes and Gray (1935).

17 PP 1889 LXX, Return of Rates of Wages..., pp. 36-38. N = 16,139. See also PP 1892 XXXV, Royal Commission on Labour, evidence of D. Holmes, Burnley Weavers', p. 35 Q. 909. The situation was still the same in 1906. See PP 1909 LXXX, Report of an Inquiry..., pp. 32-57. William Mass has recently claimed that the practice of working six looms per weaver was prevented by strikes in the 1880s and by the structure of the Uniform List after 1892. After that, four looms per weaver became the norm. See Mass (1984), p. 212. However, these statements are not really correct. Six-loom weaving continued in Burnley. The 1906 census of production indicates that 17.7 per cent of the Burnley looms were run in a six-loom system. PP 1909 LXXX, pp. 32-57. As I will argue in a later chapter, Mass tends to exaggerate the rigidity of the piece-rate structure.

18 PP 1892 XXXV, Royal Commission on Labour, p. 36 Q. 927.

condemned "any action being taken to increase the age of children attending factories above the present standard viz. 10 years".[19]

The Burnley weavers' union also tried to put pressure on local employers to accept the hiring of half-timers. When a manufacturer in 1890 decided to disallow the employment of children and accordingly posted advertisements for full-time tenters, the occasion was deemed sufficiently extraordinary as to warrant a special article in the Cotton Factory Times. Moreover, its conclusion was that the action of this employer would hopefully turn the redundant half-timers into good trade unionists.[20] Similarly, in 1894 the union officials complained to the local employers' association that some manufacturers refused to admit half-timers, and demanded to have this rectified.[21] The local factory inspector likewise described the manufacturers as "indifferent" on the question of the continuation of the half-time system.[22]

The employment of children seems to have been regarded as a customary right among the Burnley weavers, and they appear to have been relatively successful in persuading the manufacturers to continue with the practice. This conclusion is underpinned by the results of the investigations of the union members' attitudes on child labour reform which were conducted by the United Textile Factory Workers' Association (UTFWA) in 1909 and 1918.[23] Even at that later point in time, the Burnley weavers stood out as major proponents of the half-time system.

My conclusion is that the combination of smaller manufacturers and strained labour supplies resulted in relatively weak employer resistance to the operatives' definition of authority in the recruitment of tenters. The option to use half-timers became regarded as a customary right and a part of the local working-class culture. This also tended to lessen the local restrictions on child labour. The educational requirements for half-time exemption were kept low by the Burnley school board.

The case of Preston in north-west Lancashire provides some interesting contrasts. This town was the site of a protracted lockout in 1853-54, which can probably be seen as the last flourish of the older type of industrial relations before the shift towards collective bargaining between the

---

19 LRO, Preston. Burnley Weavers' Minutes, 11/3/91.
20 Cotton Factory Times, 10/1/90.
21 Burnley Weavers' Minutes, 23/4/94. A few months later the Burnley Weavers' officials visited the employers who refused to allow half-timers in their mills in an effort to persuade them to change their position. Ibid., 24/8/94.
22 PP 1895 XIX, RCIFW, p. 202.
23 See chapter 10 below for a detailed account of these investigations, and also for a fuller discussion on the reasons for the strong support of child labour practices by the Burnley weavers.

organized interests.[24] A Preston List for weaving was recognized in the 1860s, albeit not paying quite as high as the Blackburn version. The list was won through a union strategy of staging strikes, one at a time, against employers who did not pay full list prices.[25] Consequently, Preston weavers were unionized and had gained a standard list twenty years before the Burnley operatives. On the other hand, the cotton trade in Preston did not expand very much towards the end of the century, and this meant that there was no great scarcity of workers.[26] Also, the composition of the mill-owning class was different. Preston had several large employers, among them the huge concern of Horrocks, Crewdson & Co. Both these factors must have worked against the weavers in the local production relations.

Indeed, there are some indications that the Preston weavers only had a relatively nominal authority over their tenters.[27] Unfortunately, due to a gap in union records, the only available evidence on this matter stems from the period after 1900. The clearest example of a low degree of workers' authority is the Horrocks' concern, where the weavers seem to have had little power to adjust the wages of their assistants.[28] One weaver complained that when her tenter had been sick and she had been obliged to do all the work herself, the company had still withheld the wage of the assistant.[29] In 1912, weavers at Horrocks' again complained of the system of payment for them and their tenters which was laid down by the firm.[30]

There is also some similar evidence from other factories. At the Manchester mill, one weaver was obliged to have a tenter against her will.[31] In another case, one female weaver had a tenter taken away from her by the overlooker, and replaced with one she did not like.[32] Weavers from several mills complained they were not allowed by management to reduce the wages of their tenters when they were short of work.[33]

Admittedly, it is very difficult to reconstruct a general picture on the basis of these indications. Most of the above examples were complaints from weavers to the union officials, which really suggests that the operatives

---

24 For an excellent account of the dispute, see Dutton and King (1981), passim.
25 Preston Weavers' Minutes, 6/10/65; 30/10/65
26 On the relative stagnation of the Preston cotton industry, see Smith (1954), p. 561.
27 Mike Savage has emphasized the powerful position of the overlooker in Preston weaving factories. See Savage (1985), pp. 181-82. However, he clearly apportions the overlooker too much weight in the recruitment process, while neglecting the informal network among, sisters, kin, and neighbourhood over free weaving positions. Savage also curiously disregards the main function of the overlookers in weaving: to act as "pace-makers" and pressure the operatives to keep up a certain level of output. See, for instance, PP 1892 XXXV, Royal Commission on Labour, evidence of D. Holmes and W. Booth, pp. 34-35 Q. 898-906.
28 Preston Weavers' Minutes, 5/3/07.
29 LRO, Preston. Preston Weavers' Book of Cases and Complaints, 30/3/05.
30 Preston Weavers' Minutes, 9/7/12.
31 Preston Weavers' Minutes, 31/12/07.
32 Preston Weavers' Book of Cases and Complaints, 16/7/04.
33 Preston Weavers' Minutes, 1/9/08; 23/11/08; 9/2/09.

were of the opinion that in these cases overlookers and management had overstepped their customary limits of authority. On the other hand, there are no indications that the union was able to deal successfully with the complaints. Even if this evidence should be used with some caution, my impression is still that the Preston weavers only had a very nominal authority over their tenters. This impression is strengthened by my investigation of the relatively feeble union reactions against some Preston manufacturers in their attempts to change the organization of the labour process after the turn of the century, a subject which will be dealt with in the following chapter. The general picture is that recruitment and supervision were fully in the hands of overlookers and management in Preston.

Unfortunately, there is very little statistical evidence on changes in the level of child labour in Preston weaving sheds. According to the 1886 wage census, the proportion of half-time tenters in the weaving workforce was relatively high, or 18.3 per cent.[34] On the other hand, the same source indicates that more than half of the tenting work was performed by full-timers, which was a considerably higher proportion than in Burnley: 48.6 per cent of the tenting in Preston was performed by half-timers, as compared to 71.8 per cent in the Burnley-Colne district.[35]

There are two possible explanations of this: first, that the authority over recruitment was less in Preston, and employers had to a larger extent decided not to employ children below 13; second, that the relative industrial stagnation in Preston had limited the demand for weavers. The result was that young workers had to stay longer as tenters before being promoted to weaving positions. These explanations do not exclude each other; in fact, both are probably valid.

A third case of interest is that of Ashton in south Lancashire. On the whole, the weaving industry in the southern part of the cotton district seems to have had generally lower levels of child labour. The reasons for this are not altogether easy to establish. In 1892, the secretary of the Ashton Weavers confirmed before the Royal Commission on Labour that half-timers were much more scarce in his district than in Burnley. As an explanation, he stated that the Ashton district was dominated by large firms weaving quality goods.[36] Following the Preston example, this could be interpreted as an indication that the large manufacturers in the area were not keen to support the half-time system, and that they had a major influence in the relations of production. The half-time system in neighbouring Hyde is

---

34 PP 1889 LXX, Return of Rates of Wages..., pp. 49-51.
35 Ibid., pp. 36-38, 49-51.
36 PP 1892 XXXV, Royal Commission on Labour, evidence of W. Booth, Ashton Weavers', pp. 36-37 Q. 945-54.

similarly said to have been ended on the initiative of the employers.[37] Research into the industrial relations of the Ashton-Stalybridge-Hyde area in the South does give the impression that the manufacturers were able to run things in a rather autocratic way.[38] Also, similarly to the Preston case, it could be argued that the relative stagnation of the cotton industry in the southern district did not put much strain on labour supplies.

On the other hand, it should also be noted that the secretary of the Ashton Weavers' regarded the half-time system as troublesome, and obviously did not regret its decline.[39] In obvious contrast to the Burnley case, this seems to imply that the half-time system did not have much support among the Ashton weaving operatives. How can this be explained? One suggestion is that the level of unionization and the structure of industrial relations based on price lists had been generally weaker in the South than in the North.[40] One consequence of this may have been a greater reluctance to accept minding more looms, and, in turn, that the use of tenters was less common. The 1886 wage census does give some indication that the number of looms per weaver in the Ashton district was considerably below the ratio in the northern towns. Only a third of the machines were run in a four-loom system.[41] The southern district continued to have weaker unions and a much lower proportion of male weavers in the workforce. This is the social context in which the evidence of W. Booth of the Ashton Weavers' has to be seen.

This is also why the use of children in factories never became an established part of working-class culture in the Ashton weaving district in the same way as in the North. There was evidently an interplay between the levels of production relations and culture. The relative weakness of the south Lancashire operatives in trade union organization and in the sub-contracting relationship was probably an important reason why cultural conceptions and support of child labour practices as a part of a family wage ideology became less pervasive. This also meant that the operatives were less keen to defend the half-time system when the manufacturers were

---

37 White, J L (1978): The Limits of Trade Union Militancy. The Lancashire Textile Workers, 1910-1914, p. 61.
38 John Rylands Library, Manchester. Ashton and District Cotton Employers' Association Minute Books; Glossop, Hyde and District Cotton Employers' Association Minute Books.
39 PP 1892 XXXV, Royal Commisson on Labour, evidence of W. Booth, Ashton Weavers', pp. 36-37 Q. 945-54.
40 In 1877 the Preston Weavers' Association sent a copy of the Standard List, a few leaves of a collecting book, and two collecting cards to the newly established Ashton branch as an introduction to trade unionist practice. Preston Weavers' Minutes, 23/11/77. On the low level of unionization in the South, see Bullen (1984), p. 6.
41 Of the 18,034 powerlooms in the Ashton-Stalybridge area sampled in the census, 32.7 per cent were used in a four-loom system, 53.3 per cent in a three-loom system, and 13.9 per cent in a two-loom system. PP 1889 LXX, Return of Rates of Wages..., pp. 8-10.

beginning to abandon it. As I will show in a later chapter, the decline of the half-time system after 1900 was much more rapid in the Ashton district than in Burnley.

## Authority in the Mule-spinning Process: Minder Power and the "Joiner-system"

The spinning section of the Lancashire cotton industry has been the subject of much historical, sociological, and economic research. However, one strange feature of this vast literature is the unvarying concentration on the spinning centres of Bolton and Oldham at the expense of the other districts. This is very clear when trying to reconstruct the nature of production relations in other parts of Lancashire. In fact, the general picture of the great authority of the operative spinner in the labour process is very much based on the Bolton case. In this passage, I will examine the traditional images of minder authority, and also present some contrasting examples.

As Harold Catling recounts it, the Lancashire minders made a "tacit assumption that it was a mere oversight that the hierarchy of mule spinning had not been set down in the first Book of Moses".[42]. A minder usually had full authority over his piecers. He recruited, supervised, and paid them out of his gross earnings. All piecers were paid time wages, but the scale and also the minder's possibility to make his own bargain seem to have differed between districts. In Oldham, the standard list specified the percentage of the gross earnings which should be paid to the piecers.[43] They also received wages which were higher than those of the Bolton piecers, a difference which was probably caused by the competition for young male workers from the Oldham machinery plants.[44] In Bolton, piecers' wages were fixed by the spinners at a customary level.

Apart from the minders' authority in the subcontracting relationship, they also exercised the right of adjusting the machinery. The authority of the mill mechanic stopped at the main shaft; from there on the spinner was in full control. As I have indicated earlier, the role of the overlooker in mule-spinning was marginal. His main function in the line of production seems to have been to check that the spun yarn was of the correct fineness. In other respects the work-teams at the mules were practically independent

---

42 Catling (1970), p. 178.
43 See PP 1886 XXI, Second Report of the Royal Commission.., Appendix A (7).
44 Ibid., evidence of S. Andrew and S. Taylor, Oldham employers, p. 154 Q. 4,533.

producers, receiving the roving and handing back the spun yarn. What happened in between was solely the business of the minder.

However, this general picture has to be qualified in several ways. The manufacturers seem to have retained the right to dismiss piecers who broke the mill rules.[45] Also, the right of a free choice of piecers was not generally accepted. In the new limited liability companies, management in most cases refused to condone the employment of half-timers. This seems to be the case also with other newly started firms. As I have argued in a previous chapter, this seems to have been occasioned by the fact that the new companies were not bound by customary rights and agreements to the same extent as the older firms. The refusal to acknowledge the half-time system was a part of the management's deal with the new operatives. On the other hand, spinners on the most modern machinery could expect to earn higher wages than the operatives on older mules, which meant that minders in the new firms could afford to pay slightly more to get older piecers. Mainly as a result of managerial policy, half-time piecers became increasingly associated with the older family firms.

A second qualification of the image of mule-spinner authority was the existence of "joiner-minding". In this organization of work, the minder and the big piecer were replaced by two joiner-minders with joint responsibility for the work. Their wages were still determined by the list, but split equally between them, while in the other system the minder generally earned more than twice as much than the big piecer.[46] Joiner-minding has been curiously disregarded in earlier research, possibly because it did not fit in with the general picture of minder authority.[47] Also, joining was not a common practice in the spinning centres in central Lancashire which have been most intensively covered by earlier research. Joiner-minders really dominated the smaller spinning industry in north Lancashire, especially in Blackburn. According to the 1906 Census of Production, 74 per cent of the Blackburn spinners were in fact joiner-minders.[48]

In areas where alternative employment in weaving or coal-mining made the recruitment of piecers more difficult, the spinners probably found it harder to check the spread of joiner-minding.[49] But it was also a matter which depended on union strength and strategy. The Preston spinners tried for a long period to block the adoption of joiner-minding by refusing to let minders who worked in the same mill as these joiner-minders to become

45 See Cotton Factory Times 31/12/97.
46 See Cotton Factory Times 12/7/01.
47 Joseph White, for instance, has stated that the two joiner-minders took charge of four mules. This is clearly not correct. See White, J (1982): Lancashire Cotton Textiles, p. 213.
48 PP 1909 LXXX, Report of an Inquiry..., p. xxxii.
49 Lazonick (1979), p. 249.

members. However, after some time they were forced to change strategy. In 1892 the union decided to allow joiner-minders to enter the association, and by 1898 they had more or less given up their resistance to joiner-minding.[50] This really illustrates the limited influence of the Preston spinners in the local relations of production.[51] Generally speaking, spinners' authority and control was much less in the northern towns than in Bolton and Oldham.

Around 1900, the employers seem to have introduced the practice in most parts of the cotton district, with the important exception of Bolton. In this town, union opposition prevented the mill-owners from introducing joiner-minding.[52] However, even if this system was stronger in the North, it did make some inroads in the southern part of the district outside Bolton. In Oldham, the union allowed joiner-minding at a certain proportion of mules in each mill. The Spinners' Amalgamation estimated in 1901 that 9.4 per cent of the mules in Oldham were staffed with joiner-minders, while the corresponding figure for the districts outside the Bolton and Oldham provinces was 20.4 per cent.[53] Joining became an intermediary step between the positions of big piecer and minder, and was mainly filled by big piecers who were not yet able to be promoted to minders.

Generally speaking, the position of joiner-minder seems to have been connected with less authority over the work than the position of minder. The Cotton Factory Times commented in 1903 that the growth of joiner-minding could undermine the custom of minder authority, and regretted that it had not been more strenuously opposed by the unions.[54] On the other hand, there are no indications that the employers were particularly interested in replacing the traditional minder-piecer system entirely with joiner-minding. The Cotton Factory Times published a short editorial in 1902 on the continued support from the manufacturers for the minder-piecer system:

> There can be no doubt that employers and managers are quite alive to what is best for them in working their mills, and if they could have got a better system of working than they are now content with it would not have been a question of considering the minders' interests. [55]

---

50 Preston Spinners' Minutes, 6/1/98; 15/3/98.

51 Another indication of this fact is that the Preston employers seem to have had a practice of dismissing complaining spinners, at least up to 1880. See PP 1892 XXXV, Royal Commission on Labour, evidence of J. Billington, Preston Spinners', p. 196 Q. 4,751.

52 Cotton Factory Times 12/7/01; 18/4/02. As late as 1935 there were no joiner-minders in Bolton. Jewkes and Gray (1935), p. 189.

53 Cotton Factory Times 25/10/01; 18/4/02. N for Oldham = 13,342 mules; N for the rest of Lancashire = 15,224 mules.

54 Cotton Factory Times 13/3/03.

55 Cotton Factory Times 14/2/02.

My suggestion is that the generally lower authority on the part of the joiner-minders also had an indirect effect on child labour practices. These operatives had less power resources and were less able to assert their right of free recruitment than the minders. If an employer wanted to stop employing half-timers, joiner-minders were probably not in a position to oppose this.

It is also possible that little piecers could more easily be dispensed with in joiner-minding than in the minder-piecer system. During the First World War there was a pervasive lack of little piecers in Oldham, and one suggested remedy was to organize the work at more mules according to the joining system.[56] This suggestion would only be rational if little piecers were somewhat less necessary in joiner-minding than on the traditional system. One possible explanation is that in the minder-piecer system, one important task of the little piecer was to take care of the minder's end of the mules when he was busy adjusting the machinery, while in joiner-minding it is probable that these adjustments were to a greater extent performed by the overlooker. In this perspective, I would suggest that the substantial growth of joiner-minding in the districts outside the central Bolton and Oldham areas would to some extent serve to weaken child labour practices in those districts.

My contention is that a general shift in industrial relations, the rise of limited liability firms, and the growth of the system of joiner-minding, all served to reduce the ability of the spinners to recruit half-timers. On the other hand, there are some indications that the minders at the same time were beginning to find the employment of children a less alluring prospect. This will be investigated in the following section.

## Minders' Changing Preference in Recruitment, 1880-1900

The minders' preference when hiring little piecers appears to have changed somewhat in the late 1870s. Full-timers who were above 13 years of age were gradually becoming more favoured than the half-timers.

Sub-inspector Coles, Oldham district, reported in 1879 that the minders in his area had lately shown a greater preference for older assistants. Together with the depression of the cotton trade, this had caused a decrease in the employment of half-timers.[57] The same kind of observation was later made in several quarters. Thus, even if the organization of the

---

56 Cotton Factory Times 5/3/15; 23/4/15.
57 PP 1880 XIV, RCIFW, p. 90.

labour process remained virtually the same, there was obviously a change in the spinners' conception of the piecers.

One major reason behind this were changes in speed, work intensity, and the size of the mules. As I have indicated earlier, one of the advantages of the minder-piecer system was its propensity to accomodate changes in work intensity and productivity. Mules were constantly built longer and driven at higher speeds. Towards the end of the century, work intensity was further increased by managerial strategies of cutting costs by using inferior and cheaper raw cotton. As a result of these processes, the work in the mule-gate became much more demanding. In this context, it seems that the minders' interest in hiring half-timers lessened. The greater capacity and precision of juveniles of 13 to 16 years seems to have made them a more likely choice. This can be illustrated by an editorial in the Cotton Factory Times in 1896:

> As far as the spinning branch is concerned, we do not think the half-time system is so prevalent as it was some years ago, and the reason for this is that in this department of the cotton industry there has been such a rage for long mules and quick speeds that half-timers are now of very little use, and spinners take less interest in employing them as assistants. [58]

The minder's other option was, of course, to bring in more half-timers, but this was evidently not done. The pressure exercised by the minder to minimize stoppages of production demanded great efficiency and control in the operations performed by the little piecer. Creeling (supplying new roving to the spindles) and doffing (removing the full cops of spun yarn) had to be performed with accuracy and speed in order to keep production going with minimal delay. The little piecer also had to be able to tend the minder's half of the mule-gate when the latter was busy adjusting straps or machinery.[59] Therefore, the increases in work intensity towards the end of the 19th century tended to favour the minders' employment of young juveniles as little piecers. Already by 1886, the wage census indicates that only 9.8 per cent of the little piecers on self-acting mules in Bolton were half-timers. The corresponding figure for Oldham was 15.5 per cent.[60]

However, this is only one half of the story. There was another long-term change which has to be considered. Between 1850 and 1900, the spinners' employment strategy towards the piecers appears to have altered. I believe

58 Cotton Factory Times 6/5/96.
59 PP 1909 XVII, Report of the Inter-Departmental Committee..., Vol II, evidence of W. Marsland, Spinners' Amalgamation, p. 129 Q. 3,686.
60 PP 1889 LXX, Return of Rates of Wages..., pp. 15-17, 21-24. Naturally, this means that only 4.9 per cent of the little piecer positions in Bolton and 7.7 per cent in Oldham were occupied by half-timers. N for Bolton = 893 little piecers; N for Oldham = 1,595 little piecers.

that this should be seen in the context of growing union strength over that period. Around 1850, the spinners seem to have employed younger piecers and only for a period of a few years each. The most clear quantitative evidence of this is in Michael Anderson's study of Preston in 1851. According to his figures, there was a massive peak in the age interval 11-14 years in the cotton factory workforce, and a dramatic decline in the subsequent age groups.[61]

My interpretation is that the spinners' general employment strategy was to limit the number of adult operatives in the trade by using young piecers and only for a very limited period. When a piecer reached the age of 15 or 16, he was dismissed and replaced by a younger one. The result was a very high turnover and an excessive demand for 13 and 14 year old workers, these being preferred because they were less hampered by the regulations of the Factory Act than was the case with the half-timers.

One important reason behind this strategy was the relative lack of union strength and workplace control among minders at mid-century. In trade unionist terms, the great weakness of the minder-piecer system was that it tended to create a great surplus of adult spinners. If a spinner is supposed to have had a working life of 20 years, and during that time employed two young piecers, it could be estimated that he had at his retiral trained at least five new spinners while leaving only one position vacant. Recognizing that a surplus of trained spinners would undermine their bargaining position, the main union strategy was to dismiss the majority of the piecers at a relatively early age. This was a way to stave off possible attacks from the employers.

Towards the end of the century, this pattern had changed completely. The age composition of the piecers had moved upward and the position of a "big piecer" had been firmly established. But the fundamental problem of the minder-piecer system remained, namely that there was never enough spinner positions for even a minority of the piecers to be promoted to mind their own pair of mules. However, in comparison with the situation around mid-century, it appears that the age of exit for most piecers was much higher. Indeed, there are indications that the main exit from the trade was that of big piecers in their late teens or early twenties. Facing bleak promotion possibilities in mule-spinning, these operatives turned to the growing metal industry or to casual labour. This phenomenon became known as "the piecer problem". In terms of employment strategy, the minders now accepted the existence of a great surplus of big piecers who were quite capable of taking over spinning positions.

---

61 Anderson, M (1971), pp. 26-28. However, Anderson interprets this process as a case of young factory workers finding better employment elsewhere, which rather misses the point.

How can this change be explained? The answer must be formulated in terms of union strength and self-reliance. The Webbs, for instance, found it remarkable that the mule-spinners had managed to retain their trade union position in spite of the fact that they had no formal control over recruitment while at the same time there existed a great surplus of trained big piecers with no real prospects of promotion.[62] James Mawdsley of the Spinners' Amalgamation clearly stated in 1892 that the minders' ability to maintain their position in spite of the surplus of qualified big piecers was due to the high degree of unionization in the trade.[63]

My contention is that the spinners to some extent allowed this situation to occur because they were towards the end of the century in a very strong trade union position. The building up of local associations and the foundation of an efficient Spinners' Amalgamation seem to have provided sufficient security for the minders to allow the emergence of a surplus of adult big piecers. Consequently, the spinners' strong trade union position was a precondition for the general lift in the age composition of the piecers which took place during the last decades of the 19th century.


# Conclusions

The great majority of Lancashire half-timers were subcontracted by older workers. This makes it necessary to try to estimate the authority over recruitment among the weavers and mule-spinners in order to see if they had the real option to hire half-timers.

A comparison between three Lancashire weaving towns shows that there were considerable differences in this respect. In Burnley, the half-time system was well established, and the strong local union actively pressured the local manufacturers to continue with the system. The Preston weavers were less able to gain influence over the recruitment of tenters, probably because the employers were larger and more in a position to disregard union demands. In Ashton, the half-time system was never as important as in the northern towns. Weak unions, lower machine assignments, and autocratic employers, contributed to this process.

On the mule-spinning side of the industry, a similar distinction can be made in the case of the joiner-minders. These operatives generally had a weaker position than the regular minders, and were probably less able to recruit half-timers.

---

62 Webb and Webb (1897), p. 475.
63 PP 1892 XXXV, Royal Commission on Labour, evidence of J. Mawdsley, p. 29 Q. 799.

Moreover, the mule-spinners' employment preferences changed towards somewhat older piecers after the late 1870s. This process was coupled with an acceptance of longer mules, higher speeds, and a general increase in work intensity. But it was also occasioned by a shift in union priorities. The increased strength of their unions induced the mule-spinners to gradually relax their previous measure of dismissing non-family piecers at a relatively early age. The result was a general rise in the age profile of the piecers, and less need for half-timers.

Chapter 8

# Changes in the Organization of Work: The Americanization of Production in Lancashire Weaving, 1890-1920

The apparent decline of the half-time system in the 1890s, above all in mule-spinning, led both factory inspectors and some cotton union officials to believe that the system would soon be practically extinct. However, the expected demise proved to be elusive. Around 1906-7 the use of half-timers seemed to stabilize again, albeit on a lower level. In the end, it was an Education Act in 1917 which finally broke the resilience of the half-time system. From 1920 the school-leaving age was raised to 14 without exemptions, and the factory work of children below that age was finally abolished.

Part of the reason for the persistent retention of child workers in the Lancashire cotton industry must be sought in the organization of the labour process. Subcontracted piecers and tenters were part of a specific way of staffing the machines, an organization of work which had become rare outside the Lancashire cotton district.The subcontracting relationship not only provided the adult operatives with a specific interest in hiring rather young assistants, it also served to some extent as a link between the spheres of work and family.

However, some attempts were made to change these traditional structures. Two important technological innovations were introduced, the ring-spinning frame and the automatic powerloom. There were also some initiatives to reorganize the work at the traditional type of machinery, above all in the weaving process. In this chapter, I will try to estimate to what extent the labour process was actually reorganized on the traditional type of powerlooms, and also see how this change affected the hiring of children.

As I have shown in a previous chapter, the main difference between American and Lancashire cotton-weaving lay in the division of labour. In the U.S., the ancillary tasks of cleaning, sweeping, and carrying were performed by special operatives, while the weaver's work was confined to operating the looms. In Lancashire, subcontracted tenters were used to help with the weaving operations and to perform the ancillary tasks.

The Lancashire manufacturers were early aware of the American methods. Already in 1894 the Textile Recorder commented on the differences between English and U.S. powerloom weaving, hoping that some experiments with the American methods would be staged in Lancashire.[1] After 1900 there are clear indications that the Lancashire employers were beginning to show some real interest in the American way of production. Visits by mill-owners to the U.S. and the publication of the Mosley Report in 1903 probably served as an inducement to try the American methods as a new way to increase work efficiency and profitability.[2]

This kind of reorganization of the weaving operations would probably have had a dramatic effect on the viability of the half-time system. The position of "tenter" was the most important occupation for child workers in the Lancashire cotton industry. An Americanization of the weaving process would end the employment of subcontracted tenters, and would therefore leave much less room for child labour practices. The ancillary tasks would be taken over by special operatives, who were generally older and also directly employed by management.[3] It is therefore crucial to establish to what extent the weaving process was actually reorganized in Lancashire.

The employers' attempts to introduce the American methods in Lancashire weaving have received very scant attention from researchers. One notable exception is William Mass, though he is primarily interested in the introduction of the automatic Northrop loom.[4] As a contribution to this rather neglected area of research, I have made two local studies in close detail of Burnley and Preston in north Lancashire. In order to get a more general picture, I have also tried to estimate the changes in the organization of production in other parts of the district. My intention is not merely to describe to which extent the new methods were implemented; I also have the ambition to provide an explanation as to why American methods were or were not chosen. Such an explanation must be made in terms of production relations, or more specifically in terms of strategies and power resources among both operatives and employers. The question really has four parts, namely: first, did the operatives resist the introduction of the American system in weaving; second, did they have the power to succeed in this endeavour; third, how eager were the employers to implement the new methods; and fourth, what power did they have to achieve it? All these aspects must be considered if simplistic explanations are to be avoided. In

---

1 Textile Recorder, June 1894, p. 70.
2 Mosely Industrial Commission (1903), passim; Textile Manufacturer 15/5/02; 15/6/02; Fowler, A (1979-80): Trade Unions and Technical Change: The Automatic Loom Strike, 1908, pp. 43-44.
3 Gray, E M (1937): The Weavers' Wage. Earnings and collective bargaining in the Lancashire cotton weaving industry, p. 40.
4 Mass (1984).

the following section, I will begin by evaluating the impact of the American methods in Burnley, the main centre of the Lancashire weaving industry.

## Burnley: Resistance and Permanence

The Burnley weavers' association was founded in the 1870s but this first attempt foundered in the 1878-79 depression. A functioning local union was therefore not in operation before 1880, which was rather late compared to other weaving towns in north Lancashire.[5] However, Burnley seems to have made up for its late start by developing a strong brand of trade unionism over the next decades. As I have indicated in an earlier chapter, one important factor in this development was the rapid expansion of the industry and the fact that the Burnley manufacturers were dominated by small employers. This relatively strong position of the local weavers' union should be kept in mind when dealing with proposed changes in the labour process.

The first sign of a reorganization of the weaving process in Burnley was an initiative by some manufacturers to employ special oilers for the looms, a task which had customarily been performed by the weavers themselves. In a list of Burnley operatives from 1886, 84 loom oilers were mentioned.[6] It is probable that the employers wanted to take over control of the oiling since any neglect of this task would damage the machinery. In itself, this was hardly a very contentious point. But since the oilers relieved the weavers from an operation which they had performed previously, the employers demanded that the wages of the former should be paid by the weavers themselves. In 1892, the union official David Holmes complained before the Royal Commission on Labour that the manufacturers deducted a part of the weavers' wages for the oiling. He also sharpened his attack by stating that the oilers were used for other kinds of odd jobs in the shed for the benefit of the employer, while their wages had to be met by the weavers.[7] In the following year, the association decided to call shop meetings in order to stop the employers from making deductions from the weavers' wages for oiling.[8] The outcome is not entirely clear, but it seems that the union was not in a position to stop the deductions.[9]

---

5 Burnley & District Weavers, Winders & Beamers' Association (1896), pp. 4-7.
6 LRO Preston. Burnley Weavers' Letter Book. Letter from the Burnley Weavers' Association to the Burnley Health Department, containing a list of the weaving operatives of the town, 4/2/86.
7 PP 1892 XXXV, Royal Commission on Labour, p. 44 Q. 1,104. A representative of the manufacturers denied the latter allegation.
8 Burnley Weavers' Minutes, 17/10/93.
9 See also Cotton Factory Times 12/11/97.

The same kind of conflict reappeared in 1902, but this time on a larger scale. The firm of Witham Brothers announced that they would reorganize the work at Plumbe Street Shed by using trolleys and special operatives to transport yarn and cloth.[10] In August 1902 a deputation from the Burnley Weavers' visited the firm to "protest against the proposed deduction of 1 d. per loom per week from the weavers['] wages for taking their pieces into the warehouse".[11] The union officials were not prepared to allow any deductions in wages, and demanded that the matter should be brought before the Joint Committee, the forum of negotiation between the Amalgamation and the North and North-East Cotton Spinners' and Manufacturers' Association.[12]

This was the first move towards a reorganization of work along the American lines. Other Burnley manufacturers viewed the experiment at Witham Brothers with great interest. Even before the matter was discussed in the Joint Committee, the Burnley employers had decided to support the firm of Witham Brothers if the union called a strike.[13] The two organizations discussed the question at two meetings in September 1902 and January 1903, but no agreement could be reached. The employers maintained that a deduction of 1 d. per loom was reasonable, while the union representatives could not agree to any deductions at all.[14] A ballot was made among the weavers of the firm in February 1903 to see if they were prepared to accept the proposed deduction, but the result is unfortunately not stated in the union records.[15] However, in the light of later events, it is probable that the operatives remained negative.

The situation became more complicated in April 1903 when another Burnley firm, Thornber & Sons, announced that they intended to reorganize the work in one of their weaving sheds. The company wanted each weaver to mind eight looms instead of the normal four, but with slightly reduced speed, high quality yarn, and special labourers to perform all the ancillary tasks. The form of payment was also to change from piece-rate to a set weekly wage of 26 s. plus a small bonus.[16] This would mean a complete reorganization along American lines. The tenter-system would be replaced by older ancillary operatives employed by the firm. In this context, it cannot

---

10 I have only been able to find one earlier example of this kind of reorganization of the labour process. In September 1899, the Cotton Factory Times reported that a firm had laid down tram lines in the shed and ran small wagons with the cloth and yarn between the ware-house and the weaving-rooms. However, the operatives successfully resisted the deduction of a half-penny per loom and week for this "improvement". See Cotton Factory Times 8/9/99.

11 Burnley Weavers' Minutes, 28/8/02.

12 LRO Preston. Burnley Masters' Minute Book, 20/11/02.

13 Burnley Masters' Minute Book, 14/10/02; 28/10/02.

14 Reports of Joint Committees, 30/9/02; 10/2/03.

15 Burnley Weavers' Minutes 16/2/03; 19/2/03.

16 Burnley Weavers' Minutes, 26/4/03; Rep. of Joint Committees, 3/7/03; Burnley Masters' Minute Book, 4/5/03; 11/5/03.

be excluded that a certain hostility towards the use of half-timers played some part in the decision to reorganize production. Thornber had been previously mentioned by the local factory inspector as an example of a manufacturer who was not in favour of the use of child labour in factories.[17]

Thornber received the full backing of the Burnley Masters' Association, who tried to persuade the weavers' representatives to allow an "experiment" with reorganized work and an eight-loom system for twelve months.[18] However, the union officials remained sceptical. The Thornber case was taken up twice in the Joint Committee in July 1903, but even though the firm raised its bid to a weekly wage of 30 s., the weavers' representatives would not agree to the system being tried. After a short strike in August 1903, the firm seems to have dropped the idea altogether.[19]

However, the firm of Witham Brothers proved to have more determination. In November 1903 they declared that they were going to implement the changes proposed by Thornber in their own shed. All ancillary tasks would be reorganized, and 3 d. per loom and week was to be deducted from the weavers' wages. Again the Burnley Masters supported the scheme, while the union officials refused to consider any trial period or any deductions in wages.[20] This time the conflict was brought to a head. Witham Brothers decided to start carrying out the proposed changes, and towards the end of the month the union called a strike.[21]

Commenting on the dispute, the Cotton Factory Times questioned the "utility and advantage" of the proposed reorganization of work.[22] On the other hand, periodicals connected with the manufacturers criticised the actions of the Burnley union. The Textile Recorder supported experiments with the American methods, arguing that it was a loss of time for the skilled weavers to take part in the ancillary tasks. Instead, they should specialize entirely on the weaving operations. The initiative of Witham Brothers was therefore "a step in the right direction". The Textile Recorder also criticised the Burnley operatives for their negative attitude towards innovations.[23] Similarly, the Textile Manufacturer found the weavers of Witham Brothers unreasonable and ignorant, and that the dispute was "one of the most childish strikes that have [sic] occurred for some time". The periodical

17 PP 1895 XIX, RCIFW, p. 202.
18 Burnley Masters' Minute Book, 15/5/03.
19 Rep. of Joint Committees, 3/7/03; 28/7/03; Burnley Weavers' Minutes, 4/8/03; 6/8/03; 13/8/03. See also the Textile Journal, Sept. 1903, p. 114.
20 Burnley Masters' Minute Book, 16/11/03; 19/11/03; Rep. of Joint Committees, 23/11/03.
21 Burnley Weavers' Minutes, 26/11/03.
22 Cotton Factory Times 4/12/03.
23 Textile Recorder, March 1903, p. 325.

maintained that the strike was directed against change, and that it savoured of "the old plug-drawing times".[24]

Nevertheless, the strike continued. In December the secretary of the Burnley Weavers' Association claimed that the new system had as yet only been applied at 476 looms, but the firm was trying hard to extend it to another 1,024 machines. Only 19 of the striking weavers were stated to have returned to work.[25] The strike proved to be very long. In June 1904 the Amalgamation took over the cost of strike payments to the 141 weavers who were still out of work after complaints from the Burnley union that voluntary contributions from other districts were insufficient.[26] This should be interpreted as an indication that the Amalgamation saw this as an important dispute. Striking weavers slowly obtained positions in other factories, but in November there were still 63 operatives on strike pay. The dispute only finished in January 1905 when the remaining strikers were allowed by the union to seek re-employment at Witham Brothers.[27]

The firm seems to have carried on the new organization of work in spite of the tense relations with the union. William Witham was even summoned before the Burnley magistrates for alleged "threatening behaviour" towards two strikers who had tried to collect contributions outside the factory.[28] But in the end, the strike clearly did not stop Witham Brothers from implementing the American methods. Sub-inspector Taylor specifically commented in 1905 on a Burnley firm which for the last two years had employed adult male labourers to perform the ancillary tasks in weaving:

> The occupier referred to asked their weavers to attend to the weaving of cloth only, and for the sum of 3 ½ d. per loom per week they would do all the necessary work, which in other similar works is done by the weaver herself; this work of which the weavers are relieved...comprises sweeping and cleaning of the looms, oiling of the looms, filling and carrying of the weft from the warehouse to the looms, and the carrying of the cloth from the loom to the warehouse. /.../ This new system causes the firm to employ 13 sweepers, 3 weft carriers, 1 weft filler, and 3 cloth carriers, or a total of 20 additional hands who are male adults. [29]

This seems to be a good illustration of the effects on the composition of the workforce which were occasioned by the shift to the American system in weaving. Adult males seem to have been preferred as ancillary labourers because they did not fall under the scope of the Factory Acts, and were therefore allowed to clean and sweep the looms during the weavers' meal

24 Textile Manufacturer, Dec. 1903.
25 Rep. of the General Council of the Weavers' Amalgamation, 19/12/03.
26 Rep. of the General Council, 11/6/04; Cotton Factory Times 10/6/04.
27 Rep. of the General Council, 19/11/04; Burnley Weavers' Minutes, 19/1/05.
28 See Cotton Factory Times 15/1/03.
29 PP 1906 XV, RCIFW, p. 175.

hours. The Textile Recorder claimed in 1906 that the American system at Witham Brothers had been a "considerable success", and that it had also done away with illegal cleaning and accidents.[30]

The American system, when implemented in full, obviously did away with the use of tenters. The half-time system was therefore virtually abandoned at Witham Brothers. In the specific Lancashire context, the implementation of the American methods and the accompanying discontinuation of the subcontracting relationship should therefore be seen as a process with a large potential to end the employment of children. But two questions require more deliberation: first, to what extent did the American system spread outside the above firm; and second, why were the weavers so strongly against it?

Beginning with the second question, it seems clear that the union feared that the proposed change in the organization of work would undermine the weavers' bargaining position. In 1903 David Holmes, president of the Burnley association, stated that the operatives had taken their stand against American labour-saving methods because these would probably entail a reduction in the weavers' wages. "Experiments" would not be accepted at the cost of the workpeople. Any trial period of the American system had to be paid for by the employer. Holmes also warned that the acceptance of deductions in wages for various "improvements" would have the effect of wiping out the price list.[31] The secretary of the Burnley Weavers', Fred Thomas, defended the union against allegations of "unreasonableness" on the question of American methods:

> ...when a proposal is made which does not at least guarantee the operatives as good a position as they formerly possessed, we shall resist such encroachment. We believe that the bulk of the operatives are with us and if we yield on any point it will only be to a superior force. In all three cases of supposed improvements, namely, the Barber Knotter, the eight loom system, and the sweeping and carrying arrangement, we have listened to the proposals of the employers, and in no instance have we a guarantee that the operatives will be in any better position, nay, we have contended that they would be worse off than now, and consequently we have been unable to accept their offers. /.../ Operatives cannot afford to risk their wages in experiments of this kind. [32]

Several considerations lay behind this position. The most important was that the breaking up of a uniform and well regulated structure of wage bargaining would make it much more difficult for the union to defend the existing levels of earnings and workloads. The weaving trade was at this

---

30 Textile Recorder, Nov. 1906, p. 193.
31 See Cotton Factory Times 29/1/03.
32 Burnley Weavers' Quarterly Report, 30/12/03. The Barber Knotter was a mechanical appliance in winding.

point regulated by an intricate system of lists covering all types of cloth production. This structure was very stable in the sense that it had become very difficult for the individual employer to lower the piece-rates in his factory. Underpaying of the list had been much less common after 1900, mainly through union endeavours but with important support from the factory legislation. The Particulars clause of the Factory Acts made it mandatory for the employers to supply the operatives with the actual calculations on which their wages were based. Since the list system was extremely intricate, one important managerial strategy of underpaying had previously been to refuse to specify how the weekly earnings had been calculated. This was counteracted by the Particulars clause, which not surprisingly was lauded by the unions as a most beneficial piece of legislation.[33] The Amalgamation's support of the status quo must be seen in this perspective.

Furthermore, price lists which regulated wages and workloads were practically their only asset in terms of trade unionism. The work was relatively unskilled, and the labour force was to a large extent composed of women. If the main structure of industrial bargaining were to be broken up, the union would probably find itself in a very awkward situation. The question of deductions in the list for the introduction of American methods was therefore not merely a defence of current earnings. If individual employers were allowed to make arbitrary deductions, the basic stability of the list system would be dissolved. In the case of Witham Brothers, there was no guarantee that the level of deductions would not be raised in coming periods of bad trade. The stability of the system was dependent on collective bargaining over wage levels. The prospect was now that the union would be back in a situation of having to face each employer separately. This is what David Holmes meant when he stated that deductions would have the effect of wiping out the price list.[34] In a sense, the whole structure of industrial bargaining was at stake.

Moreover, the weavers had two further objections. If the American methods were fully implemented, and the number of looms per weaver increased to eight, the effect would surely be unemployment for some operatives. Fred Thomas claimed that if the eight-loom system was introduced, the increased level of unemployment would undermine or nullify the union ability to defend the proposed level of wages:

---

33 In 1905 the Cotton Factory Times called the Particulars Clause "one of the most useful enactments in industrial legislation ever adopted." Cotton Factory Times 17/11/05. See also ibid., 3/5/07.
34 Cotton Factory Times 29/01/03.

With between five and six thousand weavers walking the streets of Burnley would the 30/- be maintained? Certainly not, and before very long we should have the eight loom weavers working for the same amount as the present four loom weaver. [35]

These findings underpin the relevance of the perspective of wage-effort bargaining. The list system was defended because it provided a reasonable security for the operatives in the conflict over workloads and efforts. The reorganization of work and deductions in piece-rate threatened the weavers' only pillar of strength in this bargaining process. If deductions and work alterations should be allowed to go ahead, the weavers would lose their control over both wages and workloads. The minding of eight or ten looms would necessitate much more walking and handling of yarn, which would probably intensify the work without guaranteeing any real rise in earnings. The Burnley weavers were therefore reluctant to abandon the status quo.[36]

On the other hand, if the American methods were only partially introduced, another kind of problem emerged. If only a part of the ancillary tasks were reorganized, the weaver was in a position of being subjected to deductions in wages while at the same time still requiring the assistance of a tenter. Being straddled between the two systems of work was clearly not a good prospect.

The weavers' resistance to the American system may also have been influenced by their desire to retain the tenter-system. The lack of clear evidence of this link can possibly be attributed to the fact that an open defence of the tenter-system would have been to advocate factory child labour, a position which was becoming untenable after the turn of the century. It is unlikely that the union representatives would voice such opinions, bearing in mind that the official line was that the half-time system should be allowed to expire at its own rate. Still, it should be kept in mind that Burnley was at the time a core area of the half-time system, and later ballots among the operatives showed very large support for its retention. A reorganization along American lines would have limited the prospects for child and juvenile labour, and in the weaving districts in the North-East there was a strong conception that as many family members as possible should work and contribute to the family resources. It is not improbable that the operatives perceived that a general abandoning of the use of tenters would tend to lower the family income. But also in a less direct way, the resistance towards the reorganization of the weaving process may be seen as a defence of a cultural system based on the family wage. However, in the absence of clear proof, this must remain a suggestion.

---

35 Burnley Weavers' Quarterly Reports, 30/12/03.
36 For expressed fears of intensified work with the new methods, see Cotton Factory Times 19/8/04.

What has been established is that the Burnley Weavers' Association as well as the Amalgamation resisted the deductions in the piece-rate which were part of the employers' proposals on the introduction of the American system. It was not really a minor point of supposed reductions in earnings for the weavers of Witham Brothers, but a determined defence of the deep structure of industrial bargaining. However, it remains to be seen how effective that resistance really was. The strike at Witham Brothers clearly did not stop the firm from carrying out the intended changes in production, and in the end the union had to allow the remaining strikers to apply for re-employment.

On the other hand, I have found no indication that the example of Witham Brothers was followed by other Burnley firms. William Mass has argued that the dispute at Witham Brothers shows that trade union resistance hindered the implementation of the American system in Lancashire.[37] While it is not unreasonable to assume that the resistance put up by the Burnley weavers may have discouraged employers from adopting the new system, there is still no positive proof in this direction. Furthermore, the manufacturers' strategies and objectives must be analysed as well as those of the union. There are no indications that any Burnley employers desired or attempted to introduce the American system in the period immediately after 1905.

Indeed, the general surge of interest in American methods among Lancashire manufacturers seems to have passed already by 1905. There is also no real evidence that the structure of price lists and industrial bargaining constituted the main obstacle to the implementation of the American methods. On closer scrutiny, there are no indications that the employers seriously wanted to break up the list systems which formed the basic structure of industrial relations. Expressing the view of the mill-owners, the Textile Manufacturer criticized the strike at Witham Brothers but nevertheless defended the list system as "the only method of obtaining the best work from the operatives".[38] After a brief period of experimentation and scrutiny, the employers opted for the continuation of the traditional organization of work.

When trying to explain this development, it is necessary to discuss it in terms of possible managerial strategies and available markets. From the late 1880s, the Lancashire cotton industry was very much geared towards the production of cheap cloth for Third World markets, especially India,

---

37 Mass (1984), p. 218. Mass bases his argument merely on the reports of the dispute in the Cotton Factory Times.
38 Textile Manufacturer 15/12/03; 15/5/07.

China, and Latin America. Tariff barriers had impeded exports to the Continent, Russia, and the U.S.A.

Finding the structure of industrial bargaining relatively rigid, individual employers started to explore alternative ways of cheapening production. As I have indicated in an earlier chapter, one of the main strategies of this kind was to use inferior qualities of yarn. Heavy "sizing", a compound consisting mainly of china clay, was also used to strengthen the bad yarn and to reduce the amount of the more expensive cotton in the cloth. Great reductions in production costs could be gained by these strategies. Moreover, the list systems did not take into account the effects of using inferior yarn. This meant that the structure of industrial bargaining was gradually undermined and circumvented by more manufacturers resorting to the use of cheap yarn. These tendencies were evident already in the 1890s, but they only became pronounced after the turn of the century.[39] From the point of view of the weaver, bad material increased the rate of breakages and intensified the work, and also lowered the level of production and actual earnings. The strategy of using cheap yarn was profitable to the employer, but detrimental in all respects to the workpeople.

It was also the case that other managerial strategies had become more difficult to implement after the turn of the century. As has been shown above, the strategy of underpaying was still used in the late 1890s, but had later become much less viable due to trade union organization and the enforcement of the Particulars Clause in the Factory Acts.[40] Another main device, that of "driving", or the overlookers harassing the operatives to increase output, was becoming less efficient. The weavers' unions had managed to form links and agreements with the overlookers' union with the objective of counteracting "driving", especially the much disliked practice of posting the earnings of the weavers by their looms.[41] In 1901 an agreement was reached with the employers' federation which ruled that this form of driving, called "the slate system", would no longer be allowed.[42] However, on local level the interpretation of what constituted "driving" and the slate-system continued to vary, and the problem partly remained.[43]

Still, the main managerial strategies which were left open to the individual employer after 1900 were either the reorganization of production

39 The first recorded discussion on the bad material issue in the General Council of the Weavers' Amalgamation was in 1899. See Report of Gen. Council, 23/9/99.

40 See Weavers' Amalgamation, Reports of the General Council Meetings, 16/11/95; 15/1/96; 8/2/96; 13/2/97; 13/8/98; 16/11/98; 19/11/98; Burnley Weavers' Minutes, 21/4/92; 4/5/92; 27/5/92.

41 LRO, Preston, Minute Book of the Burnley Textile Trade Federation, 9/12/92-28/9/94; Burnley Weavers' Minutes, 14/4/92; 13/4/93; 8/3/94; 29/3/94; 1/5/94; 17/5/94; 4/6/94; 28/6/94; 30/11/94.

42 Report of Joint Committees, 1/10/01.

43 See LRO Preston. Blackburn Master Cotton Spinners' and Manufacturers' Association Minutes, 25/1/11.

along the American pattern, or the use of cheap yarn. For instance, when writing to the secretary of the Burnley Weavers' in 1903 on the matter of the Thornber dispute, the secretary of the employers' association emphasized that if the firm was not allowed to introduce the American methods, the only alternative was to resort to cheaper yarn.[44]

However, these strategies were mutually exclusive. The use of bad yarn was incompatible with an increase in the number of looms per weaver. The increased rate of breakages when using cheap yarn made it virtually impossible to attend more than the traditional number of looms. This, I would argue, was the main reason why the interest in the American methods of production seemed to fizzle out after a few years. An efficiently run eight-loom system would require good yarn at a considerable expense. This simply did not fit in with the kind of cheap quality markets which the great majority of manufacturers were aiming at. The result was that the employers largely opted for the strategy of using bad yarn and leaving the organization of work intact. In Burnley, it can be seen that conflicts over the use of cheap yarn became endemic after 1904.[45] The same seems to have been the case in other northern weaving towns.[46]

Consequently, the lack of implementation of the American methods in Burnley was probably occasioned by both union resistance and employer indifference. But if the perspective is shifted to other parts of the cotton district, it should be noted that the dispute at Witham Brothers is not the best case on which to generalize about the impact of union resistance on the reorganization of production. After all, the Burnley Weavers' Association was probably the most powerful local union at the time. If union resistance was the main obstacle to the implementation of American methods, it would be reasonable to assume that this process would go ahead in areas where the unions were relatively weak. This suggestion will be investigated in the following section.

---

44 Letter from Hargreaves to Thomas, 25/5/03. Copy found in LRO, Preston, Weavers' Amalgamation Collection, DDX 1123/6/2/363a, More Loom Negotiations 1928-29.
45 Burnley Weavers' Quarterly Reports, 1905-1912; Burnley Weavers' Minutes, 25/11/04; 29/12/04; 24/1/05; Burnley Weavers' Letter Book, letters to Amalgamation officials complaining of bad material disputes, 19/1/07; 20/1/07; 31/1/07; 15/4/07; Burnley Masters' Minutes, 20/12/04; 12/5/05; 9/2/06.
46 Blackburn Master Cotton Spinners' and Manufacturers' Association Minutes, 27/11/05; 23/4/06; 5/4/07; 17/6/07; 30/6/11; Preston Weavers' Minutes, 8/12/03; 16/2/05; 21/2/05; 10/5/05; 23/5/05; 16/6/05; 18/7/05; 1/9/05; 19/12/05; 20/2/06; 24/2/06; 6/3/06; 27/3/06; 27/4/06; 19/6/06; 2/10/06; 13/11/06; 11/12/06; 1/1/07; 15/1/07; 12/2/07; 26/2/07; 5/3/07; 19/3/07; 22/3/07; 26/3/07; 9/4/07; 23/4/07; 2/5/07; 27/8/07; 1/10/07; 9/10/07; 3/12/07.

# Preston and the South: Signs of Change

In comparison with Burnley, Preston was dominated by a few large employers, and especially by the firm of Horrocks, Crewdson & Co. The cotton trade of the town was also stagnating compared to the rate of growth in the Burnley district. The indications are that the Preston weavers' union would be in a far less favourable position to resist changes in the labour process.

From 1904 there is some evidence of American methods being tried in Preston. The union records indicate that an eight-loom experiment was being staged at Horrocks, Crewdson & Co. The weavers were not paid on piece-rate, but at a set weekly wage of 23 s.[47] It should be noted that this was considerably less than the 30 s. offered by Witham Brothers in Burnley. Also, the time gap of seven months between the two pieces of evidence on the eight-loom experiment shows that it was not merely a short test. However, no strike or any other kind of industrial action is recorded. In 1907 the firm started to make deductions from the weavers' wages for the sweeping of looms, and in 1913 the ancillary tasks were completely re-organized. On the latter occasion, no further deductions were demanded.[48]

Horrocks, Crewdson and Co. was not the only Preston firm to make these kinds of alterations. When reporting about the case of Witham Brothers in 1905, Sub-inspector Taylor also mentioned that two factories in Preston had reorganized the work in a similar way.[49] The firms in question were probably Leigh Brothers and the Ashton Shed. In both these cases deductions were made for the sweeping of looms.[50] In 1909 special sweepers were introduced in Alexandra Mill, and 2 d. per loom was deducted. The weavers seem to have accepted the terms in a shopfloor ballot, but the union claimed that the voting had been carried out in an unfair manner. The operatives later complained that the sweeping was not done properly.[51]

These findings have several important implications. First, it is clear that more experiments with American methods were staged in Preston than in Burnley. The local weavers' union was not in favour of them, but seems to have been unable to interfere. I have found no indications of strikes being called over the use of American methods or the increased division of labour either in union or in employer records.[52]

---

47 Preston Weavers' Minutes, 9/8/04; Preston Weavers' Book of Cases and Complaints, 30/3/05.
48 Preston Weavers' Minutes, 5/3/07; Reports of Joint Committees, 9/3/20.
49 PP 1906 XV, RCIFW, p. 175.
50 Preston Weavers' Minutes, 29/11/04; 21/3/05.
51 Preston Weavers' Minutes, 29/1/09; 9/2/09.
52 However, it seems clear that the Preston employers had some anticipation of industrial disputes over this issue. In 1906 an employer from Bamber Bridge just outside Preston was allowed to join their association, but only on the express condition that he would not be eligible for financial support in a possible dispute

One main reason for this lack of open conflict, I would suggest, was that the Preston weavers lacked the power and organization required to challenge large employers like Horrocks, Crewdson & Co. There are some indications that the Preston union was relatively weak. When the persistent use of bad material in Oxhey's mill in 1907 raised the question of calling a strike, the union meeting concluded that it was not possible to take any action because there were not "sufficient members in the mill".[53] In this sense, the dispute at Witham Brothers at Burnley cannot be seen as typical for the Lancashire weaving industry.[54]

A second important conclusion is that the adoption of American methods in Preston was much less common than expected. Although there was no forceful union reaction against the reorganization of production, such changes were only carried out in a small minority of the Preston firms. The great majority of Preston employers did not make any initiatives in this direction.

As I have suggested above, the main reason for this lack of interest was that a more-looms system was only viable if the quality of yarn used was substantially improved. Already in 1902 one Preston manufacturer recently back from a trip to the U.S. stated to his colleagues in the North Lancashire Employers' Association that the American methods were interesting but only efficient in connection with the use of high quality yarn.[55] This strengthens my general argument that the main reason behind the tenacity of the traditional work organization in weaving was not union resistance, but the employer strategy of using bad material to cheapen production.

This can be illustrated by one further comparison. The weaving district of south Lancashire was more geared towards the production of high quality

---

over the reorganization of the ancillary tasks in his factory. See LRO Preston. North Lancashire Textile Employers' Association, Minutes, 26/4/06. According to William Mass, the employer in question tried to impose deductions for the reorganization of work, but this was successfully resisted by the operatives. Mass (1984), p. 218.

53 Preston Weavers' Minutes, 26/3/07.

54 This argument is supported by a case in Nelson in north-east Lancashire in 1909, where the union presence was relatively strong. There was a dispute at Laurel Bank Mill, Nelson, over deductions for reorganizing the tasks of sweeping and cleaning the looms. Even though the local union was against it, claiming that it would lead to "driving", they could not stop one part of the operatives from accepting the employer's terms. See Cotton Factory Times 17/9/09; 24/9/09; 8/10/09; 17/12/09. Similarly, a manufacturer in Haslingden successfully deducted half-penny per loom for cut-carrying. Cotton Factory Times 29/11/12. This evidence implies that weavers in many parts of the district lacked the union strength to withstand determined employer initiatives towards reorganization.

55. North Lancashire Textile Employers' Association, Minutes, 10/7/02. The employer in question, Smith, was later singled out by the weavers' association as the most consistent underpayer in Preston - a fairly traditional managerial strategy. He did not introduce American methods in his own factory. Preston Weavers' Minutes, 25/11/04.

cloth, and was also more weakly unionized than the North.[56] There is some evidence which indicates that the Americanization of production became more important in this district, both in the form of the reorganization of the ancillary tasks and an increase in the number of looms per weaver, and also by the introduction of automatic looms. In terms of the relations of production, what stands out in a comparison with Burnley and Preston is the low degree of union influence. Research into the industrial relations in the southern part of the cotton district conveys an impression of uncompromising employers and weak unions.[57]

This state of industrial relations is also evidenced by a strike over deductions connected with American methods in Marple, outside Manchester, in 1910. The management of Hollins Mill had imposed a 15 per cent reduction for reorganizing the ancillary tasks, using large shuttles, and increasing the machine assignment to six looms per weaver. The firm produced high quality calico cloth and used good ring-bobbin weft. While the weavers seem to have accepted the initial deduction, things came to a head when the firm announced that the reduction on list prices would be raised to 30 per cent. The result was a strike involving 600 operatives.[58]

The Cotton Factory Times repudiated the firm's demands, claiming that it was "difficult to believe that practical men are in earnest in putting forward so exorbitant a claim on the flimsy and shadowy hypothesis that these so-called advantages are so highly favourable to the weaver". The reduction could not be justified by either "precedent, fairness, or logic".[59]

This incident provides information of two kinds. The main objection was not the reorganization in itself, or even the making of deductions. 15 per cent had been cut off list prices without any kind of industrial action. The great risk involved which made the Cotton Factory Times and the union express such concern was the prospect of arbitrary increases in the level of deductions. In the southern districts, the unions were obviously trying to establish a "customary" level of deductions. The local secretary expressly used the argument that other mills in the area had not imposed higher deductions than 15 per cent when introducing the American methods.[60] If the "astounding claim" of 30 per cent was accepted at Hollins Mill, the risk was that other firms in the district would follow suit. The unavoidable result would be a downward trend of wages.[61] Not surprisingly, the Weavers'

---

56 See PP 1892 XXX, Royal Commission of Labour, evidence of W. Booth, Ashton Weavers', p. 37 Q. 952-54; Bullen (1984), p. 6.
57 Minutes of the Ashton and District Cotton Employers' Association; Minutes of the Glossop, Hyde and District Cotton Employers' Association.
58 Cotton Factory Times 4/3/10; 11/3/10.
59 Cotton Factory Times 4/3/10; 18/3/10.
60 Cotton Factory Times 18/3/10; 1/4/10.
61 Cotton Factory Times 1/4/10.

Amalgamation was adamant in its resistance. After the strike had continued for one month, the management of Hollins Mill accepted to limit the deductions to 15 per cent.[62] While not being able in most places to resist employers' attempts to introduce the American methods, the next line of defence was evidently to try to fix the level of deductions by "custom" or agreement.

The ability of the local weavers' unions to withstand employers who wanted to reorganize the labour process evidently varied markedly within the Lancashire cotton district. While the unions in the North-East were better organized and more able to withstand deductions, this was clearly not the case in the South. One, albeit rather crude, measure of union strength seems to underpin this general picture. The proportion of male weavers to females was much higher in the North-East than in the other parts of the district. Figures from the 1906 Census of Production shows that Burnley had 46.5 per cent male weavers, Blackburn 34.3 per cent, Preston 18.7 per cent, Ashton only 4.5 per cent while Manchester had none at all.[63] This should be seen as an indicative measure rather than a causal link. Women weavers were not encouraged to take part in union business, and very often enrolled on a lower scale of contributions. They were also expected to perform the housework after factory hours.[64] For these reasons the union came to be regarded as a male sphere. In the oral history material collected by Elizabeth Roberts, one former female weaver concluded that "the men were more union minded than [the] women".[65]

Consequently, it is not unreasonable to assume a correlation between union strength and the proportion of male weavers to female.[66] The above figures support the view that the Burnley union cannot be taken as typical, Burnley having the highest proportion of male weavers in the entire district. The general contrast between the North-East and the South is also emphasized. The south part of the cotton district seems to have been dominated by female weavers. Even if it could be shown that the American methods were to some extent countered by union resistance in Burnley, this actually says very little about such prospects in other parts of the district.[67]

---

62 Cotton Factory Times 8/4/10. William Mass has noticed the 15 per cent reduction at Hollins Mill, but believes that it was an exception to the rule. He has not discovered that this level of deductions seems to have been the custom in south Lancashire. See Mass (1984), pp. 232-3.
63 PP 1909 LXXX, Report of an Inquiry..., pp. 32-57. N for Burnley was 12,146, for Blackburn 10,607, for Preston 6,407, for Ashton 3,445, and for Manchester 1,560.
64 See Liddington and Norris (1978), passim.
65 North-West Oral History Project (NWOHP), Mrs H1, Preston.
66 White (1978), p. 40.
67 William Mass expressly uses the Burnley example as an illustration of the structure of industrial relations in Lancashire weaving. This is clearly a mistake. See Mass (1984), p. 212.

Previous research has clearly overstated the ability of the Weavers' Amalgamation to resist the introduction of American methods. One reason for these misapprehensions is that the Amalgamation's official line throughout this period was to refuse any deduction in list prices when work was reorganized. What has not been perceived in earlier research is that this policy did not reflect the practice in the poorly unionized districts. In 1914 the general council of the Amalgamation admitted that the official line of "no deductions" had not been successful. It had not hindered individual employers from imposing reductions or striking bargains with the operatives to this effect. Instead, the Amalgamation now wanted to negotiate with the employers in order to standardize the levels of deductions.[68] The Amalgamation had previously been unable to negotiate in these matters because the General Council "had not been able to make up its mind on the subject". Reports from the different localities now made it clear that the operative weavers generally wanted to be relieved of the "dirty drudgery" of sweeping and cleaning the looms.[69] Preferably, the Amalgamation wanted a settlement without deductions but, if this proved unattainable, that the payment should be fixed through central negotiations.[70]

However, the manufacturers preferred to leave the question undecided, and refused to make any agreements on deduction levels.[71] This is a clear indication that the employers as a body were not seriously interested in a general adoption of the American methods. It is also important to note that the manufacturers' refusal to negotiate about these matters left the door open to future disputes, and tended to undermine the structure of industrial bargaining which was embodied in the list system. The balance of power in industrial relations in weaving seems to have shifted markedly in favour of the employers during this period.

The manufacturers found that the structure of industrial bargaining could be turned to their advantage if it was combined with the strategy of using bad yarn. The machinery of conciliation which had been laid down by the Brooklands agreement did little to improve conditions for the operatives. While the employers did concede to stage inspections by joint committees, this never proved to be a real remedy. There were always delays which enabled the employer to finish off his supply of bad yarn, and there could never be any guarantee that the practice would not be repeated

---

68 Cotton Factory Times 28/8/14; 1/1/15.
69 Weavers' Amalgamation, Reports of General Council Meetings, 5/6/15. However, some delegates feared that adoption of the American system would lead to "driving".
70 Rep. of the Joint Committees, 23/7/15; Weavers' Amalgamation, Rep. of General Council Meetings, 4/10/20; 15/1/21.
71 Weavers' Amalgamation, Rep. of General Council Meetings, 15/1/21.

once the inspection of material had been carried out.[72] Compensation was seldom awarded, and in cases where it was it was never in proportion to the loss of earnings and the intensification of work on the part of the operatives.[73] The years before 1914 became marked by an increasing number of spontaneous strikes against the use of bad yarn.[74] The whole structure of industrial bargaining had been badly damaged.

It is slightly ironic that the piece-rate system, which the operatives had fought for fifty years to establish, was now turned against themselves. With the use of bad material the weavers were forced to work harder while at the same time receiving less wages. They had essentially lost their control of the wage-effort bargaining, which was the whole point of the list system.

After the First World War the Weavers' Amalgamation gave priority to the establishment of a minimum wage level, but the employers would not accept this proposal.[75] By 1920 local weavers' unions started to demand that the piece-rate structure should be abandoned in favour of set weekly wages.[76] The Amalgamation later tried once more to secure a certain level of minimum wages, but the employers refused to depart from the structure of flat piece-rates.[77] Without piece-rates, the bad yarn strategy would not be effective since the operatives would not be induced to increase their work efforts. The manufacturers had now turned into ardent defenders of the piece-rate structure.[78]

These were the reasons for the very limited adoption of the American methods in Lancashire cotton-weaving. The lack of employer initiatives in 1915 and 1920 to negotiate over the organization and payment for the ancillary tasks demonstrates that they were not interested in applying the American system.[79] Empirical evidence of operating more-loom systems is also very scant.

---

72 Bullen (1984), p. 20.

73 The profitability of the bad material strategy has not been generally appreciated. Joseph White, for instance, has stated that this strategy "far from representing best managerial practice, was essentially a throwback and an evasion of managerial functions". White (1982), p. 211.

74 Weavers' Amalgamation, Rep. of Gen. Council Meetings, 21/9/12; 19/10/12/; 14/12/12; 15/4/13; 14/6/13; 18/10/13; 10/1/14; Weavers' Amalgamation, Annual Report 1917, p. 3.

75 Reports of Joint Committees, 14/2/19.

76 The demands were put forward by the Burnley and Nelson unions, probably the strongest in the Amalgamation. This shows the extent of the crisis. Weavers' Amalgamation, Rep. of the General Council Meetings, 20/11/20.

77 Weavers' Amalgamation, Annual Report 1925, pp. 10-11.

78 In contrast, William Mass sees the stability of the list system in weaving as a "testimony to the strength of the worker organization relative to capitalist organization in Lancashire". Mass (1984), p. 210.

79 Weavers' Amalgamation, Reports of General Council Meetings, 9/10/20; Reports of Joint Committees, 24/9/20; 12/11/20. The employer representatives claimed that an agreement compelling manufacturers to provide sweepers and cleaners would constitute an "undue interference with the management of the mills", and also that there were differences in opinion among the employers about the usefulness of this reorganization of work. Ibid., 12/11/20. See also Weavers' Amalgamation, Annual Report 1921, p. 9.

Not until 1929 was a real eight-loom experiment tried in earnest in Burnley, once again involving the firm of Thornber's as one of the participants.[80] However, by that time the Lancashire cotton industry was in serious decline, and the unions were reluctant to increase the level of unemployment by working more looms per weaver.[81] Trade unionists also doubted if the piece-rates could be maintained if an eight-loom system was accepted, and they proved correct in their fears. Due to employer initiatives, the piece-rate on more-loom systems was cut in the early 1930s.[82] In the end, it took an Act of Parliament in 1935 to protect the wage levels of the Lancashire weavers.

The fact that more-loom systems remained very unusual is also indicated by Gray's investigation in 1937, which shows that only 0.6 per cent of all Lancashire weavers minded as many as eight looms.[83] Consequently, while it has not been possible to measure the precise extent of the reorganization of the ancillary tasks, there was clearly no major change towards an American eight-loom system. The tenter-system continued to dominate the Lancashire industry, which in turn made a continuation of child labour practices viable.

When explaining the failure of the American methods in the Lancashire context, recent research has mainly focussed on the signs of union strength in the 1890s, and on union resistance to the more-loom experiments in the late 1920s. William Lazonick and William Mass have seen the permanence of the industrial structure in Lancashire as occasioned by the cotton unions' resistance to change, and to a rigid system of industrial relations.[84] This means that they have essentially neglected the important changes which took place during this period. Lazonick fails to see that the balance of power within the structure of industrial relations had changed markedly in favour of the manufacturers between 1900 and 1930. In a recent contribution, he claims that by 1934 the Uniform List was broken by the employers on one third of the looms in the Lancashire industry, but this does not hinder him from concluding that the "cohesive workers' organizations" on the traditional technologies had held "the balance of power" against the more divided employers.[85]

This is logically inconsistent, as well as a serious misjudgement of the nature of industrial relations in Lancashire weaving. The ineffective union

80 Weavers' Amalgamation Collection, DDX 1123/6/2/363a More Loom Negotiations 1928-29. See also Gray (1937), pp. 15-16, 40, 48; Bullen (1984), pp. 52-53.
81 Gray (1937), p. 16.
82 Mass (1984), p. 218.
83 Gray (1937), p. 6, Table II.
84 Lazonick (1983); Lazonick (1986a); Mass (1984); Lazonick and Mass (1984).
85 Lazonick (1986), pp. 29-30. I will return to a more full discussion of Lazonick's postulation of "institutional rigidity" in the subsequent chapter.

opposition to reductions on the more-loom system and their failure to defend the Uniform List in the early 1930s really show how much the power resources of the Weavers' Amalgamation had eroded. In the words of a Darwen representative to the General Council in 1930, the employers were becoming both "list-maker and price-maker".[86]

My conclusion is that after 1905 the structure of industrial relations in Lancashire weaving remained only superficially the same. On a deeper level, the managerial strategy of bad material completely turned the tables in favour of the employers. This was the most potent reason for the remarkable structural permanence of the Lancashire industry after 1900.


# Conclusions

An introduction of American methods in Lancashire cotton-weaving after 1900 would have reorganized the work in such a way as to make child labour practices much less required. However, the American system never became implemented to any extent. The organization of work in Lancashire weaving remained remarkably permanent at least up to 1930.

Previous research has tended to explain this in terms of union resistance and a rigid structure of industrial bargaining. However, a closer study of the northern weaving towns of Burnley and Preston shows that union resistance cannot have been the real reason. The weavers' unions outside the Burnley district simply lacked the strength to withstand serious attemps to re-organize production.

Instead, the conclusion must be that the great majority of Lancashire manufacturers were never seriously committed to an adoption of the American methods. The most potent reason behind this was that a more-loom system was only viable if high quality yarn was used. For manufacturers who produced cheap cloth for Third World markets, this was never a real option. The cost of better yarn was simply too high to be offset by possible productivity gains through reorganization. Instead, the great majority of manufacturers opted for the alternative strategy, that of cutting production costs by using bad yarn and the traditional organization of work. The reason for the perceived "rigidity" of the industrial bargaining structure was primarily the fact that the employers had managed to turn it to their own advantage.

---

86 Report of the Special General Council Meeting on the More Looms Question, 29/11/30.

Chapter 9

# Production Relations and Technology Change: Automatic Weaving and Ring-spinning in Lancashire, 1900-1930

From the 1890s there emerged a new generation of textile technology, above all the ring-spinning frame and the automatic loom. In this chapter I will examine the spread of the new technology in the Lancashire industry during the early decades of the 20th century, and also see how child labour practices were affected where the new machines were brought into use.

## The Failure of Technological Transition: Automatic Weaving in the Lancashire Cotton Industry

The Northrop loom was developed by the American Draper Company in the 1890s. The major change compared to the traditional powerloom was that the Northrop re-threaded the shuttles automatically, and also had a warp-stop motion which stopped the machine when breakages occurred. The work of the Northrop weavers consisted mainly in replenishing the supplies of yarn and mending breakages. Since the manual re-threading of shuttles was no longer required, there was a great potential for increasing the number of looms per weaver. American practice soon showed that weavers on automatic looms could tend 16-20 machines each if the ancillary tasks were performed by special operatives. However, one important precondition was the use of good quality yarn.[1] The weavers could handle this machine assignment efficiently only if breakages were kept at a low level. Frequent stoppages lowered output, while the Northrops required a high level of production to offset the greater capital cost.

In this chapter I will argue that in the Lancashire context, the requirement of high quality yarn combined with high customary wage levels proved to be a major obstacle to the introduction of the Northrop loom. While 56

1 Smith (1954), pp. 111-12.

per cent of the looms in southern U.S. and 29 per cent in New England were automatic just before the First World War, the corresponding figure for Lancashire was a mere 2 per cent.[2] In 1937 the proportion of automatic looms in the English cotton weaving industry was still less than 5 per cent.[3] In the context of this study, the relative failure of the technological transition towards automatic weaving was an important part of the retention of the traditional organization of work. To be economical, Northrop looms required a separation of ancillary tasks from the weavers. The tenter-system was not a viable organization of work in connection with this type of technology, and the relative failure of the Northrop loom in Lancashire can therefore be seen as an important precondition for the continuation of the half-time system in weaving.

However, the reasons stated in previous research for the relaive failure of the Northrop loom have not been correct. Lars Sandberg has claimed that the main cause behind the very limited success of the automatic loom in Lancashire was union resistance to technological change.[4] More recently, Lazonick and Mass have argued that the stable piece-rate systems and institutional rigidities in the Lancashire industry made the shift towards new technology virtually impossible.[5] Those perspectives will be examined in the following sections.

Automatic weaving was one important factor in the general surge of interest in American methods in Lancashire after the turn of the century.[6] The prospect of greatly increasing the ratio of looms per weaver naturally appealed to many employers. On the other hand, the unions seem to have been more cautious. In September 1902 the Cotton Factory Times stated that it was time to make a provisional agreement with the employers on the piece-rate on the Northrop loom. Such an agreement would be "experimental" since the work effort required on the automatic looms was still unknown.[7] Later in the same year the paper asserted that the Northrops would need much better yarn than was normally used in Lancashire, and that this would dampen the high expectations of the new technology which had been expressed by the employers.[8]

---

2 Mass (1984), pp. 1-2.

3 Gray, E M (1937), p. 35.

4 Sandberg, L G (1974): Lancashire in Decline, p. 80. However, Sandberg still sees foreign tariffs as the main cause of the decline of the Lancashire cotton industry. See ibid., pp. 172-73, 185. But see also Alan Fowler's criticism of Sandberg in Fowler (1979-80), passim.

5 Lazonick (1986a); Lazonick and Mass (1984); Mass (1984), chapter 5.

6 See, for instance, the Textile Recorder, August 1900, pp. 130-32; July 1901, p. 65; August 1902, p. 97; May 1903, p. 1.

7 Cotton Factory Times 19/9/02.

8 Cotton Factory Times 7/11/02; 9/1/03.

However, there is also some evidence that the manufacturers were not unaware of the drawbacks connected with the Northrop technology. The fact that the automatic looms required a better quality of yarn was recognized by the Textile Recorder already in 1901-2.[9] Also, one Preston employer who had visited U.S. cotton mills stated that the Northrop loom was "very efficient for American productions", i.e. when using high quality yarn.[10] The secretary of the employers' federation also stated that the Northrop was hardly adapted to the requirements of British trade.[11] Finally, the Textile Manufacturer believed that the automatic loom was not suitable for the production of finer types of cloth.[12]

Employer expectations were probably also dampened by some contemporary investigations of the American cotton industry. In an article in 1904 describing the adoption of Northrops in a cotton mill in Vermont, T. W. Uttley calculated that the higher capital cost of automatic looms made the advantage of operating with Northrops very small.[13] In a book issued a year later, Uttley concluded that automatic weaving fitted best with the requirements of the American South, where wage levels were extremely low.[14]

As a consequence, there seem to have been few Lancashire manufacturers who were willing to experiment with the new technology. In 1905 the Textile Recorder commented on the Lancashire manufacturers' "conservatism" in reorganizing production and introducing new technology.[15]

At the same time, there is no evidence of overt resistance from the Weavers' Amalgamation to the introduction of Northrops.[16] In fact, the only strikes of this kind which have been recorded were among non-unionized weavers at the remote country mill of Quarry Bank, Styal, who struck in 1907 and 1908.[17] Moreover, the Weavers' Amalgamation never demanded that the same piece-rates should be paid on Northrops as were paid on the traditional looms. A period of trials and experiments was regarded as necessary before real negotiations on a list for automatic weaving could be started.

---

9 Textile Recorder, July 1901, p. 65; August 1902, p. 97. The same point was reiterated in 1909 as a major explanation as to why the Northrop loom had not succeeded in Lancashire. Ibid., April 1909, p. 385.
10 North Lancashire Textile Employers' Association, Minutes, 10/7/02.
11 Cotton Factory Times 4/9/03.
12 Textile Manufacturer 15/7/01. This is also the conclusion of Alan Fowler (1979-80), p. 52.
13 Textile Recorder, April 1904, p. 359.
14 Uttley, T W (1905): Cotton Spinning and Manufacturing in the United States of America, pp. 21, 24-25, 51, 67. See also Young, T M (1902): The American Cotton Industry, pp. 70, 111-12, 138-43.
15 Textile Recorder, February 1905, p. 289. In October the same year, this periodical again hinted that Lancashire manufacturers were generally critical of Northrop looms. See Textile Recorder, October 1905.
16 Naturally, it is possible that operatives and local officials were less inclined to accept the automatic loom. After discussing the matter with Blackburn employers, one observer concluded that the union officials made "all the opposition they can and manufacturers are hesitating to make the experiment". Shadwell (1906), Vol I p. 96.
17 See Rose (1986), p. 98.

The first major disagreement over the conditions of Northrop weaving occurred in 1904. The operatives at the firm of Ashton Brothers, Hyde, complained of hard work, low earnings, and too many breakages of the yarn when working on the automatic looms.[18] This firm was the major explorer of the potential of the Northrop loom. Situated in the very south tip of the cotton district, and geared towards the production of high quality cloth, it had already introduced 500 automatic looms in the Throstle Bank Mill, Hyde.[19] From the reports of the Cotton Factory Times it seems that the weavers minded 10-12 Northrops each, and that special operatives were used for the ancillary tasks. The main causes of dissatisfaction among the weavers were that the quality of the yarn was to low, which made the work too arduous, and that the piece-rate was unsatisfactory. They claimed that when working on ten Northrops they could not make a weekly wage of 25 s., which was the standard earnings for four-loom weavers on traditional machines.[20] When negotiations failed, 150 operatives came out on strike.

However, the dispute lasted only three days. After the weavers' piece-rate was raised 10 per cent, and the wages of the ancillary workers improved, the operatives resumed work.[21] But the number of Northrops per weaver continued to be unregulated, and working conditions still caused complaints.[22] Ashton Brothers initially tried to use only modest qualities of yarn on the Northrops while keeping the number of looms per weaver comparatively low. However, this created strong dissatisfaction among the weavers over the level of yarn breakages. Only gradually did the manufacturers accept that the Northrops needed good yarn in order to be run efficiently.

Automatic weaving continued to be less regulated by central negotiation than the work on traditional looms. In 1907 the Cotton Factory Times commented that it was high time to establish a uniform list for Northrop weaving. The main worry at this time seems to have been that some firms were experimenting with increases in the number of automatic looms per weaver, "almost more than they can reasonably look after".[23] Later in the same year, the Cotton Factory Times expressed its concern that working conditions on the Northrops were deteriorating, and that there was a risk that the operatives would be requested to mind an "exorbitant number" of

---

18 Weavers' Amalgamation, Rep. of Gen. Council Meetings, 29/10/04; Cotton Factory Times 7/10/04; 14/10/04.
19 Textile Manufacturer 15/5/02. The production at Ashton Brothers was geared towards high quality cloth markets in China. See Mass (1984), pp. 205-6.
20 Cotton Factory Times 21/10/04; 28/10/04.
21 Cotton Factory Times 4/11/04.
22 For the 1904 agreement, see Weavers' Amalgamation Collection, DDX 1123/6/2/41, Northrop Loom Agreements (printed sheet).
23 Cotton Factory Times 31/5/07.

looms. The new invention, it was stated, was not to be allowed to establish its reputation at the expense of the operatives' physique, comfort, and wages.[24]

At this time Ashton Brothers experimented with a loom assignment of 24 Northrops per weaver.[25] However, the manager of this firm responded to union initiatives to limit the number of machines per weaver by declaring that the Amalgamation was prejudiced against the Northrops and against inventions which would do away with "the old order of things".[26] At the same time, the union was under hard pressure from the operatives to achieve some improvement in working conditions.[27]

Things came to a head in 1908 when a large strike was staged over wages and workloads at the firm of Ashton Brothers.[28] With the prospect of automatic weaving spreading throughout the cotton district, the Amalgamation clearly wanted to establish central agreements over piece-rates and workloads. The strike of 1908 was therefore of great principal importance for the general regulation of automatic weaving within the framework of industrial bargaining.

In April 1908 2,600 operatives at Ashton Brothers were out on strike, demanding a raise in piece-rates and a maximum limit of 20 Northrops per weaver.[29] Negotiations proved to be very difficult. The firm of Ashton Brothers had chosen not to join the employers' federation, and were not familiar with the type of industrial bargaining conducted by the Weavers' Amalgamation. The tendency of the firm's directors to view the presence of union officials as "outside interference" probably served to prolong the strike.[30] It is also noteworthy that the chairman of Ashton Brothers, H. P. Greg, was not in favour of a structure of collective bargaining based on price lists.[31]

It took three months before a settlement was reached, and the outcome must be described as ambiguous. Even if the terms were described by the Cotton Factory Times as "satisfactory", it is evident that the union had only managed to achieve an increase in the piece-rates. The settlement specified that the employers were entitled to full control over both machinery speeds and the number of looms per weaver.[32] Evidently, the Amalgamation had

24 Cotton Factory Times 13/9/07.
25 Cotton Factory Times 20/3/08.
26 Cotton Factory Times 11/10/07.
27 Cotton Factory Times 29/11/07.
28 Cotton Factory Times 17/1/08.
29 Cotton Factory Times 3/4/08.
30 Fowler (1979-80), pp. 48-50. Ashton Brothers only joined the employers' association after the 1908 strike. Glossop, Hyde and District cotton Employers' Association Minutes, 24/10/98; 30/7/08; 16/12/08; 20/12/11.
31 See the Textile Manufacturer, May 1907.
32 Reports of Joint Committees, 29/6/08; Cotton Factory Times 3/7/08.

been forced to withdraw the original demand of a maximum limit to the number of Northrops per weaver. It is probable that the union officials felt that their main chance in winning the regulation of automatic weaving lay in the establishment of a uniform list.

However, a general list for Northrop weaving was never established. A survey conducted by the Weavers' Amalgamation in 1911 shows that outside the firm of Ashton Brothers, only 600 out of a total of 3,555 Northrop looms were covered by wages or piece-rates agreed to by the local union. Furthermore, 500 of the Northrops covered by agreements were in the Stockport district where the local union was extremely weak.[33]

Very surprisingly, William Mass has concluded from this evidence that the agreement with Ashton Brothers had set a pattern for the trade.[34] The important point that a uniform list for automatic weaving was never established is quickly brushed aside.[35] Mass is simply too anxious to find support for his general thesis that the introduction of Northrops was hampered by the trade unions' ability to keep up the piece-rate levels. On the contrary, the evidence shows that the Amalgamation was never able either to limit the number of looms per weaver, or to lay down a stable system of piece-rates for automatic weaving.

The opinion that automatic weaving was hampered by union actions must also be qualified. The Northrop loom was introduced in weaving districts where the local union was relatively weak. This was clearly the case in Hyde, Ramsbottom, Wigan, Bury, Stockport, and Bolton. By 1929 these districts contained 86 per cent of the 8,154 Northrops in Lancashire.[36]

In contrast, the weaving districts in the North-East hardly contained any Northrop looms at all. It is probable that the local unions in this relatively strongly unionized area tried to discourage manufacturers from adopting the automatic loom. Answering the Amalgamation's investigation into the use of automatic looms in 1911, the Nelson secretary stated that they had none and did not want any either.[37] In 1928 the secretary of the Burnley weavers made a statement to the central committee of the Amalgamation which clearly stated his opinion that it was the strength of the local union which had kept the Northrops out of the Burnley district. But he also specifically pointed out the firms of Ashton Brothers, Hyde, Hoyle's in

33 Amalgamated Weavers' Association (1911): Northrop Weaving. Replies to Questions, passim.
34 Mass (1984), p. 238.
35 Ibid, p. 243. In contrast, E. M. Gray stated in 1937 that the Weavers' Amalgamation had tried to establish a uniform flat rate for automatic weaving, but the employers did not recognize it and most firms made their own arrangements. Gray, E M (1937), p. 36.
36 Weavers' Amalgamation Collection, DDX 1123/6/2/314, Automatic looms. Replies from districts 1929, manuscript returns.
37 Weavers Amalgamation Collection, Northrop Loom Agreements, manuscript replies to the 1911 survey on automatic looms.

Ramsbottom, and Horrocks, Crewdson & Co in Preston as large concerns over which the local unions had precious little influence.[38]

The case of Horrocks, Crewdson & Co really illustrates the limited power of the Amalgamation over the conditions for Northrop weaving. In 1911 the operatives on the automatic looms were paid weekly wages set by the firm. When Whittaker automatic looms were installed in 1924, the firm devised a price list of their own without consulting the local union.[39] Consequently, while it might be argued that union resistance contributed to impede the introduction of automatic looms in the North-East, it is clear that the Amalgamation did not have that kind of power in the southern and western parts of the district. Union influence over piece-rates for automatic weaving was never sufficiently strong or widespread to constitute a serious obstacle.

One possible reason why earlier researchers have exaggerated the impeding effect of the unions on automatic weaving is the fact that the weavers frequently opposed deductions in wages when single "improvements" were made on the traditional looms. During the period when there was a considerable interest in American methods, many employers tried to make deductions for appliances like warp-stop motions or large shuttles on ordinary looms. The unions strongly objected to such innovations, mainly because they believed that the productivity gains would be small, and the earnings of the operatives would actually be lowered. The warp-stop motion, for instance, would stop the loom when serious breakages occurred. This was necessary when operating an American system of eight looms, but not when minding four as was the most common practice in Lancashire. Here a skilled weaver could mend minor breakages without stopping the loom, which in turn meant that the application of a warp-stop motion would actually lower the level of production and earnings.[40] Similarly, the use of larger shuttles required a lowering in machinery speeds which in turn meant a drop in output.[41]

The weavers naturally opposed deductions in the piece-rate for the introduction of such "improvements". In 1906 a major strike was fought in Bolton over deductions for the use of warp-stop motions.[42] The firm in

38 Weavers' Amalgamation Collection, DDX 1123/6/2/363a, More Loom Negotiations 1928-29, Statement of J. Hindle, Burnley Weavers', to the Central Committee of the Weavers' Amalgamation, 1/12/28 (litographed), pp. 1-2.

39 Amalgamated Weavers' Association (1911): Northrop Weaving. Replies to Questions; Reports of Joint Committees, 8/8/24; 22/5/25. Horrocks, Crewdson & Co. went on to introduce 700 automatic looms in 1929. See Savage (1985), p. 189.

40 Cotton Factory Times 21/4/05; 15/12/05; 23/3/06. This was also acknowledged by T. Pickle, a Burnley manufacturer. See the Textile Recorder, March 1906, p. 319.

41 Cotton Factory Times 19/8/04. See also Mass (1984), p. 232.

42 Cotton Factory Times 5/1/06; 23/3/06; 1/6/06. Two years earlier, a similar strike had been called at Guthrie's Mill, Todmorden. See Cotton Factory Times 5/2/04; 12/2/04; 19/2/04.

question had operated with female non-unionized weavers and a price list of their own. When the warp-stop motion was introduced, the firm increased the number of looms per weaver and cut the piece-rate by 35 per cent. The response of the largely female operatives was to join the union and demand assistance, complaining that workloads had become much heavier under the new system. The union officials managed to reduce the deductions to 15 per cent, which was the customary level in the area.[43] Naturally, the employers described the unwillingness to reduce list prices for the use of warp-stop motions in terms of the unions being averse to technological improvements.[44] This impression seems to have survived.

Did the structure of industrial relations actually impede the adoption of automatic looms? In this context it has to be remembered that the Amalgamation's power to enforce list prices was much more considerable in traditional weaving than on automatics. In one sense it could be argued that the more stable piece-rate system on ordinary looms would have tended to make the Northrops a more interesting prospect for the employers. There are some indications that employers who had earlier tried more-loom systems on traditional powerlooms later changed policy and started to use Northrops. Of the firms which have been investigated earlier, that was the case at Horrocks, Crewdson & Co, Preston, and Hollins Mill, Marple.[45]

On the other hand, some users of automatic looms did not find it worthwhile to continue. The Blackburn employer who had introduced 400 Northrops by 1911 had ceased using them by 1929. According to the local union secretary, he had scrapped them and reverted to the traditional powerloom.[46] Even the technically progressive firm of Ashton Brothers experimented with a 9-loom system with traditional looms fitted with warp-stop motions in 1932.[47]

There were no major initiatives among the Lancashire manufacturers to make the transition towards automatic weaving. Even when the loss of Asian markets in the 1920s induced the manufacturers to move away from their bad material strategy and interest themselves more seriously in reorganizing production, automatic looms were obviously not their first choice.[48] If union resistance had been the main obstacle one would assume

---

43 Weavers' Amalgamation Collection, DDX 1123/6/2/312, Tootal Broadhurst Lee's Dispute, Bolton, 1906. Transcripts of shorthand notes taken at a joint meeting 17/9/06.
44 Cotton Factory Times 4/9/03; 12/2/04.
45 Amalgamated Weavers' Association (1911): Northrop Weaving.
46 Ibid.; Weavers' Amalgamation Collection, Automatic Weaving 1929, manuscript reply.
47 Weavers Amalgamation Collection, DDX 1123/6/2/355, Letters exchanged with Ashton Brothers over conditions for a 9-loom system.
48 Weavers' Amalgamation Collection, More Loom Negotiations 1928-29, Statement by J. H. Hindle, Burnley Weavers', p. 2.

that the transition towards automatic weaving would simply have taken place in the weakly unionized districts in the South. However, there was no major tendency in this direction. In order to understand this lack of initiative, it is necessary to look for other reasons than trade union influence. The most important ones were the low requirement of skill in Northrop weaving, the relatively high wage level of the Lancashire operatives compared to weavers in other countries, and the dependence of the industry on Third World markets.

While the unions had very limited influence over the rates paid for automatic weaving, it was still not possible for the manufacturers to fix the wage levels arbitrarily. The major defence of the conditions of the Northrop weavers was simply that the employers could not reduce their wages or increase workloads beyond what was usual or customary in traditional weaving. The operatives still had the option to leave for better jobs elsewhere.[49] Consequently, the stabilizing factor in the conditions of the Northrop weavers was not union control over wage levels, but rather the fact that Lancashire was at this time in relative terms a high-wage district, and operatives were in demand. The Amalgamation surveys indicate that weavers on automatics were generally paid more than operatives on the ordinary looms.[50] Only in this very limited sense did the structure of industrial bargaining determine the wage levels at the Northrop loom in Lancashire.

Indeed, it is possible that it was the relatively high wage levels in the North-East which dissuaded employers from introducing Northrops, not merely union resistance. In 1930 the Bacup employers approached the Weavers' Amalgamation with the proposal to make the Hyde list for automatic weaving uniform for the whole district.[51] This would indicate that it was the lack of a clear agreement on automatic weaving and a standard list which made it more difficult to utilise Northrops in the North-East than in the Hyde region.

My conclusion is that the relative failure of the Northrop loom in the Lancashire industry was not caused by either union resistance to technological change or a rigid structure of industrial bargaining. After examining the potential of the new technology for a few years, most Lancashire manufacturers decided to keep the traditional machinery and organization

---

49 This is evidenced by a dispute on automatic weaving in a Glossop mill in 1909. Finding the work too arduous, the weavers left and sought employment in other mills. See Cotton Factory Times 23/4/09.

50 Weavers' Amalgamation Collection, Northrop Loom Agrements, manuscript replies; Automatic Looms 1929, manuscript replies. One possible exception was the Northrop weavers in Wigan, who in 1929 were stated to receive "poor wages".

51 Weavers' Amalgamation Collection, DDX 1123/6/2/170, Northrop Weaving, Letter from Bacup employers to the W A, 3/12/30.

of work.[52] One major obstacle was that the Northrop could only be efficiently run when supplied with high quality yarn. As William Mass has expressed it, "the labor-saving potential of the Northrop loom is much more dependent on reducing yarn breakage than on the common loom".[53] This requirement made it relatively unsuitable for the production of cheap and heavily sized cloth for Asian markets which were the main target for the Lancashire industry. The manufacturers who opted for Northrops were all geared towards the production of high quality cloth, but they were not really typical for the Lancashire trade. When the potential of the automatic loom had been tried, most employers decided to rely on the traditional loom and a cheap yarn strategy.

Automatic weaving was also much more vulnerable to foreign competition. The Northrop needed less skill and work intensity than the ordinary powerloom, the work mainly consisting of replenishing the supplies of weft and keeping the machinery running. Therefore, a low-wage strategy proved to be much more viable in automatic weaving than it had been on the old technology. In the Southern U.S. and in Japan, Northrop looms were operated with extremely cheap labour.[54] In contrast, Lancashire had a relatively high customary wage level, which made it virtually impossible to compete on the coarse end of the cloth market which constituted the staple product of those countries. While the English cotton industry had previously had some competitive advantages on the traditional technology, mainly in the form of an efficient organization of work and an effort-wage bargaining system which was amenable to increases in work intensity, no such advantages existed on the automatic looms. On the new technology, the use of cheap labour seems to have been of paramount importance.[55] Consequently, the chances of Lancashire automatic weaving gaining a lasting hold on export markets were very slim indeed. This was probably the

52 Cotton Factory Times 19/8/04; 5/5/05.
53 Mass (1984), p. 92. In his investigation of the firm of Ashton Brothers, William Mass comes to the conclusion that the unit cost on the Northrops was lower than on the traditional looms under the negotiated list prices, and that the vital point was the more expensive high quality yarn required on the automatics. But following Lazonick, he links this to the vertical specialization of the industry. Mass (1984), pp. 245-53. This is where he goes wrong. Contrary to the Lazonick thesis, it was not the vertical specialization of the industry which impeded the adoption of Northrop loom. As I will argue more fully in a later section of this chapter, it was rather the decision not to utilise the new technology which kept the Lancashire industry separated.
54 See Young (1902), p. 111.
55 This is evidenced in Mass' study of the adoption of the Northrop loom in Fall River, Massachusetts. He tries to show that the sliding scale of pay in Fall River impeded the transition to automatic weaving, but what it really boils down to is the fact that the wages of the Fall River operatives could not be reduced to the level of the "white trash" labour in the American South. The overriding importance of cheap labour on the new technology is also shown by the case of the Fall River Iron Works, the main user of Northrop looms in the city. In 1924, the firm simply dismantled the machinery and relocated to a plant in Tennessee in the South in a move to cut wage costs. See Mass (1984), pp. 166, 190. Generally speaking, the decline of the New England cotton industry after 1900 and its relocation to the South must be seen as an indication that it had become primarily a low-wage industry.

most important reason why the great majority of employers in the Lancashire cotton industry found it so impossible even over a long time period to make the transition to the technology of automatic weaving.

## Changes in Lancashire Mule-spinning, 1890-1920

The relative stability of the organization of work which has been found in the weaving sector was perhaps even more pronounced in mule-spinning. It has often been stated that the remarkable permanence of minder authority in Lancashire mule-spinning was a result of union strength.[56] Even if it is largely correct that the minders did build up a very strong union position during the last decades of the 19th century, the case definitely requires some qualification. As I have shown earlier, most spinners' unions were not able to resist the introduction of joiner-minding. Union influence was also considerably less outside the Bolton and Oldham provinces, and especially so on the outskirts of the cotton district. While in 1902 union membership was almost 100 per cent in Bolton and 96 per cent in Oldham, it was 88 per cent in Preston, 78 per cent in Ashton, 70 per cent in Burnley, 55 per cent in Huddersfield, and only 20 per cent in Wigan.[57]

While I accept the argument that union strength to some extent prevented the employers from staging experiments with the labour process in mule-spinning during this period, there is little evidence that the employers had any real alternative to the minder-piecer system which they were desirous to introduce. It should be kept in mind that the Lancashire model of organization in mule-spinning had for a long time seemed superior to any other. Yet, in this section I will deal with one question which was vital for the spinners' unions, namely the attempts by some employers to introduce "under-minding" or "multi-pair" systems in mule-spinning.

Under-minding or multi-pair systems generally meant that the minder was in charge of at least two pairs of mules instead of one. In effect, it was an attempt to have fewer highly paid spinners and more low-waged piecers. While the unions were always against it, there seem to have been instances of under-minding experiments in the outlying areas of the cotton district where the influence of the spinners' unions was much less tangible. This was the case in Mossley in the far South-East of the cotton district, where some local employers tried to introduce "under-minding" in 1902. Responsibility

---

56 For some recent examples, see Cohen (1985a); Lazonick (1981c), pp. 501-2. See also the previous discussion in chapter 4.
57 Cotton Factory Times 18/4/02. Still in 1909 the Yorkshire cotton spinners were said to be practically unionized and lacking a standard price list. Cotton Factory Times 21/2/09.

for the machinery was taken over by the overlooker, and "under-minders", paid slightly more than big piecers, were set to work the mules.[58]

A small spinning-mill in Burnley also departed from the normal minder-piecer system by requesting the minder to supervise two pairs of mules instead of one.[59] In 1904-6 there was a long dispute in Mossley over twiners being set to supervise three pairs of mules with the help of two under-minders.[60] No agreement could be reached with the employers, and in 1906 the remaining strikers were advised to seek employment elsewhere.[61] Further away from the pale of the Spinners' Amalgamation, a multi-pair system with female spinners dominated the trade in Glasgow.[62]

Two observations should be made from the above cases. First, the spinners' unions had actually very limited power outside the core area of the cotton district; and second, there is little evidence that under-minding or multi-pair systems were really more economically viable than the traditional minder-piecer system. If the unions had been the main obstacle to a vital reorganization of production, it would be logical to assume that new spinning centres would develop in non-unionized areas. This clearly did not happen. The central area of Bolton-Oldham continued to be the most expansive cotton spinning district, while weakly unionized areas like Blackburn, Burnley, and Glasgow gradually declined. The conclusion must be that the survival of the minder-piecer system owed less to union resistance than to its obvious efficiency.

However, in the same way as in weaving there was a perceptible change in the balance of power within the structure of industrial bargaining. The main managerial strategy in mule-spinning after 1900 was to use cheap qualities of raw cotton. This was especially the case in the coarse-spinning sector of the trade, which was under more pressure from foreign competition. The Oldham district soon became the centre for complaints and disputes over "bad spinning". The employers were taking advantage of the fact that neither the list system nor the Brooklands machinery of conciliation was devised to cope with disputes over the use of bad cotton. Finding their position untenable, the Spinners' Amalgamation withdrew from the Brooklands Agreement in 1913.[63]

---

58 Cotton Factory Times 7/3/02; 6/5/02.
59 Cotton Factory Times 20/5/04. The paper was strongly against this practice, and claimed that it had not been seriously attempted for many years.
60 Cotton Factory Times 28/10/04; 4/11/04; 10/3/05; 15/12/05. The same kind of experiment had also been staged among the badly organized Yorkshire twiners. Cotton Factory Times 10/3/05; 7/7/11. Twining was a process where mules were used to turn several fine yarns into sewing thread.
61 Cotton Factory Times 20/4/06.
62 Webb Trade Union Collection, vol 34 folios 386, 413. See also chapter 11.
63 A.A.O.C.S., Quarterly Reports, 31/1/13, pp. 3-4, 6-9; General Representative Meeting, 25/12/12, pp. 1-4, 10; A.A.O.C.S., Annual Report 1913, p. 3.

One important reason why the employers were generally not interested in changing the structure of industrial bargaining and the organization of work in mule-spinning was that those structures fitted excellently with their strategy of using cheap cotton.


## The Viability of New Technology: Ring-spinning in Lancashire

While the basic characteristics of mule-spinning remained very much the same up to the First World War, the major structural change was the appearance of the new ring-spinning technology. It was essentially an American invention based on the same principles as the old throstle.

From the employers' point of view, one important advantage with ring-frames was that they could be operated by cheap female and child labour. In the 1886 wage census sample, virtually all throstle and ring-spinners were females, most of them working for small weekly wages. The same material also indicates that half-timers were often used as doffers on ring-frames. In Rochdale, which was to turn into the most important centre of ring-spinning in Lancashire, the proportion of half-timers in the ring rooms was 17.2 per cent. Similarly, the corresponding figure in the Ashton-Stalybridge district was 17.5 per cent and in Oldham 13.1 per cent.[64]

This proportion of child labour in ring-spinning was considerably higher than on self-actors. In the same wage census material, the percentage of half-timers on the latter technology was 3.6 in Oldham and 2.4 in Bolton.[65] In general terms, the proportion of children in the ring-spinning workforce was more than three times higher than in mule-spinning, or 11.7 per cent compared to 3.6 per cent.[66] Accordingly, one factory inspector anticipated an increased demand for child labour if ring-frames were to replace mules.[67]

There was also an important difference in the mode of employment. Child labour in ring-spinning was the only form of direct employment of half-timers by the manufacturers in the Lancashire district. In the other processes where child labour was relatively common, above all in mule-spinning, weaving, and drawing-in, children were subcontracted by adult

---

64 PP 1889 LXX, Return of Rates of Wages..., N for Rochdale ring spinning and throstle operatives was 907, for Oldham 286 and for Ashton-Stalybridge 228.
65 Ibid. N for Oldham = 4,540; N for Bolton = 2,413
66 Ibid. This effectively disproves Clark Nardinelli's claim that child labour was not required in ring-spinning. See Nardinelli (1980), p. 747.
67 PP 1888 XXVI, RCIFW, p. 15.

operatives. The half-time doffers in ring-spinning constituted an important exception to the rule.

Apart from the obvious differences in staffing between mules and rings, there were also some important dissimilarities in technology. The spinning process on the ring-frame was continuous, and stopped if the yarn broke. This meant that high levels of breakages were not economical, since this tended to lower the level of production too much. Generally speaking, the ring-frame was best suited for the production of strong yarn from good raw cotton. While ring-frames were well suited to American standards of production, they proved to be less compatible with Lancashire conditions. Compared to the success of ring-spinning in, for instance, Japan and the U.S., the transition towards this new technology was remarkably incomplete in England.

The limited adoption of the ring technology in England has been the subject of much debate. Lars Sandberg has argued that this was the result of a "rational" managerial strategy of keeping still functioning mules.[68] However, he seems to have underestimated the extent of new investment in mules. Saxonhouse and Wright have recently shown that managers in Lancashire continued to order new mules well up to 1914, in spite of the fact that the ring-spinning technology was by then regarded as superior to the mule in most countries of the world.[69] The proportion of ring-frames rose slowly during the pre-war period, but they remained a junior partner compared with the mule. What, then, was the reason for the limited adoption of the ring-spinning technology in Lancashire? Saxonhouse and Wright have indicated that mules remained important in Russia and India because the manufacturers wanted to utilize their domestic short-staple cotton.[70]

In the Lancashire context, an obvious explanation is that the managers wanted to reduce costs by using cheaper qualities of raw cotton. The mule technology was superior to rings in that it was much more versatile and could spin inferior and shorter staple cotton, which made it perfectly suited for a managerial strategy of utilizing cheap cotton.

**The Lazonick Thesis: Vertical Specialization and Institutional Rigidity**

An elaborate theory on the limited spread of the new textile technology in Lancashire after 1900 has recently been presented by William Lazonick. He acknowledges that the mule was suitable in the context of a cheap cotton

---

68 Sandberg (1974), passim.
69 Saxonhouse and Wright (1984b), passim; Saxonhouse and Wright (1984c): New Evidence on the Stubborn English Mule and the Cotton Industry, 1878-1920, p. 507.
70 Saxonhouse and Wright (1984b), passim; Saxonhouse and Wright (1984c), p. 514.

strategy, but settles in the end for a quite different explanatory framework. He maintains that the limited breakthrough of ring technology in Lancashire was caused by the high degree of vertical specialization of the industry.[71] At the end of the 19th century the cotton district was very much separated into a weaving sector in the North and a spinning sector in the Bolton-Oldham region.[72] Lazonick argues that the geographical distance between the spinning and weaving districts made it difficult to utilise the new technologies of ring-spinning and automatic looms. The ring-frame spun the yarn on wooden bobbins, and the cost of shipping these bobbins or the alternative measure of rewinding the yarn was prohibitive.[73] The result was that the transition to the new technology was only viable on warp yarns, which had to be rewound in any case.

Lazonick has lately extended his explanatory framework and now sees the geographical separation of the different sectors of the industry as a part of a general pattern of "institutional rigidity" and a failure to make the transition towards the corporate capitalist firm.[74] The failure of the Lancashire managers to utilize the new and potentially more productive technologies of ring-spinning and automatic weaving was caused by an entrepreneurial ineptitude to overcome institutional rigidities and constraints. The new technologies required a vertical integration between spinning, weaving, and marketing. However, this new integrated form of enterprise did not emerge, and Lazonick shows instead that the vertical specialization of the Lancashire industry continued to increase even after the First World War.

Another very important feature of institutional rigidity was the general system of industrial bargaining. Lazonick claims that the relative immobility of the Lancashire piece-rate systems and work customs made it very difficult for the employers to find profitable ways of utilising the new technology. However, one important problem with Lazonick's approach is that the structure of industrial bargaining in Lancashire was built up around the

71 Lazonick, W (1981a): Factor Costs and the Diffusion of Ring Spinning in Britain prior to World War I, passim; Lazonick, W (1984): Rings and Mules in Britain: Reply, p. 396.

72 See Jewkes, J (1930): The Localisation of the Cotton Industry, passim.

73 Lazonick (1981a), passim. But see also Sandberg (1974), chapter 2, and Farnie (1979), p. 320, for this argument. Lazonick claims in this article that there were two reasons for the Lancashire manufacturers to continue favouring the mule. First, it was viable in connection with a cheap cotton strategy, and second, the transport cost of ring bobbins was too high. Finding that the saving on inferior cotton is difficult to estimate, Lazonick instead calculates that the transport costs for ring bobbins were prohibitive. He then goes on to claim that this was the causal factor behind the limited adoption of ring-frames. This, I would argue, is logically inconsistent. The possibility remains that ring-frames were not generally adopted entirely because they required a better and more expensive quality of raw cotton. Indeed, the very lack of interest shown by the Lancashire manufacturers in integrating their firms or overcoming the "constraint" posed by the wooden ring bobbins really indicates that this was the fact. In Lazonick's theory, general managerial ineptitude is an explanatory factor which has to carry far too much weight.

74 Lazonick (1983); Lazonick and Mass (1984); Lazonick (1986a).

older technologies of mule-spinning and traditional powerlooms, and did not regulate the workloads and wages on the new machines. It is evident that in sketching the "rigidity" of the structure of industrial relations, Lazonick has used evidence from the mule-spinning side of the industry to illustrate the "institutional" constraints for ring-spinning and automatic weaving.[75] But Lazonick naturally realizes that the viability of his theory must hinge on the "rigidity" of the bargaining structure which involved the ring-spinners and automatic weavers, and not that of the operatives on the older technologies:

> ...firms that contemplated the introduction of the new technologies, such as the ring-frame and automatic loom, had to contend with the power of the ring-spinners' union or the weavers' union to determine the levels of piece-rates and the number of machines per worker. [76]

This quote pinpoints one essential weakness in Lazonick's thesis. As I have shown in the previous section, the Weavers' Amalgamation was never in a position to determine the level of piece-rates or the number of Northrops per weaver. There was never a uniform list for automatic weaving, or any agreement over the number of machines per worker.

Automatic weaving simply never became a part of the regular structure of industrial bargaining in Lancashire. When one Kirkham manufacturer using Northrop looms applied for membership in the North and North-East Lancashire Cotton Spinners' and Manufacturers' Association in 1909, he was not admitted as member: "...as there is no list for Northrop looms the executive cannot entertain the question of membership at present, in the near future when there is a list the executive will be pleased to consider the application".[77] In other words, Northrop weaving never became integrated in the elaborate system of industrial bargaining which regulated traditional weaving. This goes diametrically against Lazonick's notion that the "rigid" structure of industrial relations had seriously impeded the adoption of the Northrop loom in Lancashire.

Similarly, Lazonick's reference to the "power of the ring-spinners' union" is hardly very constructive. The ring-spinners were generally regarded as the worst paid and worst unionized part of the cotton industry workforce.[78] The Cotton Factory Times stated in 1896 that in ring-spinning "the employers

---

75 This is especially the case with Lazonick's use of W. S. Taggart's "Cotton Mill Management". This book is clearly about conditions in mule-spinning mills, and has no relevance for the introduction of new technology. See Taggart, W S (1923): Cotton Mill Management. A Practical Guide for Managers, Carders and Overlookers, passim, but esp pp. xxix-xxx. Cf Lazonick (1983), p. 198; Lazonick (1986a), pp. 20-21.
76 Lazonick (1986a), p. 20. See also Lazonick and Mass (1984), pp. 17-18, 36-7.
77 LRO Preston. North and North-East Cotton Spinners' and Manufacturers' Association Minutes, 8/9/09.
78 See Turner (1962), p. 143.

and their agents have practically had the whole field to themselves in the matter of fixing prices and wages, and they have had no opposition from the trade unions".[79] The mule-spinners early refused to allow them to join their union, and they were instead organized as a part of the Cardroom Amalgamation. However, the ring-spinners remained badly unionized and equally badly paid. In 1907-10 the Amalgamation made some attempts to improve their conditions and to establish a uniform list for ring-spinning, but the resistance from employers proved abortive.[80] In 1909 the ring-spinners were still described as "probably the worst paid workers in the cotton trade".[81] A uniform list was not gained until 1912.[82]

In conlusion, it must be stated that Lazonick has much exaggerated the power of the automatic weavers and ring-spinners to determine the level of wages and workloads. His description does not fit with empirical facts. Also, it could be questioned whether the perceived rigidity of the industrial bargaining structure on the traditional technologies was really such an obstacle for the employers. In one sense, inflexible piece-rates on the old technology would rather tend to encourage employers to shift towards rings and automatic looms. Especially in the case of ring-spinning, this must have been really apparent.

Moreover, the "rigidity" of the industrial bargaining structure is really a misinterpretation. After 1900 the Lancashire manufacturers managed to turn this structure to their own advantage, and consequently wanted to maintain it. The employers wanted to keep the regular piece-rate structure because it was a vital part of the strategy of utilising cheap cotton and yarn. Lazonick acknowledges that this became the dominant managerial strategy after 1900, but seems to regard it as caused by other roads being closed by the rigid piece-rate structure. Instead, I would argue that Lazonick has underestimated the extent to which the employers were able to turn the system of industrial bargaining to their own advantage. On the other hand, he is not alone in this kind of misapprehension. Most researchers in the industrial relations of the cotton industry in this period have only perceived the superficial permanence of the structure, while missing the fact that the balance of power within that structure had changed completely.[83]

---

79 Cotton Factory Times 15/5/96. Two years later they stated that the ring-spinners were "miserably underpaid". Cotton Factory Times 1/7/98.
80 Cotton Factory Times 3/5/07; 16/8/07; 27/9/07; 13/12/07; 10/1/08; 3/12/09; 22/7/10; 21/6/12.
81 Cotton Factory Times 3/12/09. See also ibid., 25/3/10.
82 See Jewkes and Gray (1935), p. 117. The Textile Recorder found it "curious" that a uniform list in ring-spinning had not been established before, and claimed that the attempts on the part of the Cardroom Amalgamation to achieve it had not been very strenuous. Textile Recorder, June 1912, p. 35.
83 See Porter, J H (1967): Industrial Peace in the Cotton Trade, 1875-1913, passim; White (1978), pp. 85-88; Jewkes and Gray (1935), p. 135. The Webbs were much impressed by the conciliation machinery in the cotton industry, and their writings may have influenced later historians. See Webb and Webb (1897), pp. 195-6, 203-5, 258-60.

Similarly, Lazonick's emphasis on the vertical specialization between the spinning and weaving districs in Lancashire cannot explain why new combined firms did not emerge, or why the Lancashire manufacturers showed so little interest in overcoming the constraints connected with the ring-spinning technology.[84]

Vertical specialization was hardly the real issue. Instead, it should be emphasized that the main reason for the limited spread of ring-spinning was the even more limited adoption of Northrop looms. It is clear from the American case that cotton production was really organized around the process of automatic weaving, and ring-spinning with its stronger yarn and low-paid operatives was evidently the best complementary process.[85] As I have shown above, the reasons for the relative technological permanence of the Lancashire cotton industry should rather be discussed in terms of market dependence, high customary wage levels, and perhaps most importantly, a lack of competitive advantages on the new technology.

The Lancashire cotton industry was more dependent on export markets than any of its competitors, with the possible exception of Japan. Towards the end of the 19th century, tariff systems had seriously impeded their access to the American, Russian, and European markets. Production became geared towards Indian, Chinese, and Latin American markets, mainly in the form of cheap, heavily sized cloth.

Lazonick and Mass have argued that the Lancashire industry should instead have turned towards high quality markets in Europe and the U.S.A.[86] However, this suggestion is not very realistic. After 1900 exports constituted more than 80 per cent of the Lancashire production of cotton cloth. There were simply not high quality markets available which could have swallowed the great productive potential of the Lancashire cotton industry. Indeed, there were few real alternatives to the cheap Asian markets. As the Lancashire manufacturer Thomas Stuttard prophetically expressed it in 1886, "on India we rely, and if we lose India, Lancashire is practically ruined".[87]

The older technologies of mule-spinning and traditional powerlooms were well suited for this kind of production. Above all, they could be run on relatively cheap qualities of cotton. In the same way, the use of bad material proved to be a very efficient managerial strategy in the context of the prevailing industrial relations. An industrial bargaining structure based on

---

84 For criticism of Lazonick on these points, see Sandberg, L G (1984): The Remembrance of Things Past: Rings and Mules Revisited, p. 391; Saxonhouse and Wright (1984c), p. 516; Saxonhouse and Wright (1987): Stubborn Mules and Vertical Integration: A Disappearing Constraint?, passim. Lazonick's answers contain little new. See Lazonick (1984), p. 397; Lazonick (1987): Stubborn Mules: Some Comments, passim.
85 See Miles, C (1968): Lancashire Textiles: A Case Study of Industrial Change, pp. 30-31.
86 Lazonick and Mass (1984), p. 5.
87 PP 1886 XXI, Second Report from the Royal Commission..., p. 168 Q. 4,958.

piece-rates and high customary wage expectations proved to be an excellent setting for the strategy of using cheap cotton. The operatives were made to work harder with virtually no compensation. In this sense, markets, technology, and the industrial bargaining structure combined to single out the most advantageous prospect for the employers.

The new technologies of ring-spinning and automatic looms did not fit in this context. First, they required much better qualities of raw cotton and yarn in order to run efficiently. This was a serious obstacle for their adoption in the production of cheap cloth for Asian markets. Second, there is no indication that Lancashire had any competitive advantages on the new technology. In mule-spinning and traditional weaving, the English cotton industry had dominated the world markets because of its very efficient organization of production. The old technology was highly dependent on the work intensity of the operatives, and this had been favoured by the context of industrial relations. The stable piece-rate structure had encouraged technological improvements and increased work efforts.

However, the Lancashire industry did not have any such advantages on the new generation of textile machinery. The economic utilization of ring-frames and automatic looms was less dependent on work intensity, and more a question of keeping the machines running with the help of cheap labour. As a consequence, low-wage strategies became much more viable. With its high customary wage levels, Lancashire was clearly at a disadvantage. It was impossible for the employers to drastically lower the wages of automatic loom weavers and ring-spinners, simply because they would not have been able to recruit workers. Even if union influence over wage levels was minimal, it would still have been an extremely difficult and slow process to lower the workers' expectations of customary earnings. The Lancashire industry could simply not change over to low-wage conditions. There was no way that Lancashire operatives would accept work under conditions similar to those of the female Japanese workers or the cheap "white trash" labour in the Southern U.S. cotton factories.[88] Furthermore, low-wage competition in the Lancashire context was made difficult by the more developed British factory legislation which prohibited shift work for women and juveniles.[89]

My conclusion is that the permanence of the Lancashire industrial structure was not caused by vertical specialization, rigid industrial relations, or entrepreneurial failure. The main problem with the new technology was that it required good quality cotton and cheap labour. This did not fit in with either available markets, customary wage levels, or the existing factory

---

88 See Farnie (1979), p. 126.
89 A. Ormerod, a managing director, claimed in 1963 that multi-shift operation was an absolute necessity in order to meet foreign competition. See Ormerod, A (1963): The Prospects of the British Cotton Industry, pp. 13, 20.

legislation.[90] The viable managerial strategies which remained were to use the old technology on cheap cotton, and to gear the mule-spinning towards the production of finer yarn, or away from direct competition with the ring-frame. As a consequence of these managerial decisions, the industry remained vertically specialized.[91]

# Changes in the Labour Process and Child Labour: Some Conclusions

It is now time to emphasize the links between the changes in the labour process and the use of child labour. But at the same time, it is essential not to postulate any strictly deterministic connections. There was no direct causal relationship between the organization of the labour process and the actual level of child labour. Rather, the deep structure of work organization should be seen as leaving more or less scope or potential for the use of children.

In the case of powerloom weaving, the traditional organization of work was challenged by American methods of production and the introduction of the Northrop loom. Both these alternatives included the reorganization of the ancillary tasks of sweeping, cleaning, and carrying. Evidence from the actual use of Northrops or the American system on traditional looms

---

90 On the question of the importance of the integrated firm, Lazonick has to some extent built his argumentation on A. Ormerod's article referred to in note 89. Ormerod was the managing director of the firm of Ashton Brothers, and advocated increased governmental support for the integrated mills using ring-frames and automatic looms. To some extent, it has to be recognized that Ormerod tended to emphasize the viability of the type of integrated firm which he represented. Nevertheless, he indicated that the high capital cost of the new technology did not make the transition "an acceptable commercial risk", and that the U.S. and continental industries were protected by tariffs against Asian producers, which Britain was not. Ormerod also indicated that the situation in 1963 was rather different from that of the 1910s and 20s. Above all, textile wage-levels in Britain were now below those in Europe. See Ormerod (1963), passim but esp. pp. 3, 7. This change is even more marked today, when the remnant of the Lancashire cotton industry has finally made the transition to ring-spinning and automatic looms. A major strike in the spring of 1988 revealed not only that the firms paid extremely low wages, but also that they had turned into a major employer of cheap labour in the form of Asian immigrants, who now constitute the majority of the cotton workforce.
91 Naturally, this is also a major reason for the dramatic decline of the English cotton industry after the First World War. With the increasing perfection of the new technology, and with the development of the Casablancas high draft technique which made it possible to use cheaper cotton on the ring-frame, the Lancashire cotton industry was no longer competitive. This has, quite mistakenly, been attributed to the fact that the transition towards the new technology was not undertaken. However, it has not been recognized that Lancashire was not competitive on the new technology either. Simultaneously, many countries were putting duties on cotton imports in order to protect their own budding industries. Under this double pressure, the Lancashire cotton industry started its long decline. After the Second World War, the British political commitment to free trade left the Lancashire cotton industry wide open to foreign competition. On the Casablancas technique, see Saxonhouse and Wright (1984c), p. 519; Saxonhouse and Wright (1984b), p. 296.

indicates that there was very little scope for child labour in this model of work.[92] It also implied a change in the mode of employment. The adoption of the American methods meant that the subcontracting relationship between adult weavers and young assistants was abandoned, and consequently a very important link between work and family wage strategies was severed.

However, I have also shown that these new methods never became very widespread in the Lancashire district. The general picture is that the traditional organization of work largely remained, with weavers subcontracting tenters to carry out the ancillary tasks and help with the weaving. On the other hand, the new methods were implemented to a somewhat larger extent in some areas compared to others. Automatic looms were more common in the southern part of the district than in the North. The Amalgamation survey of Northrop looms in 1911 shows that more than half of these machines were in the Hyde district in the far South. In Burnley, Nelson, Darwen and other weaving centres in the North-East, there were hardly any Northrops at all.[93] Similarly, it is probable that the American methods on ordinary powerlooms were more frequently used in the high quality cloth factories of south Lancashire. This is one reason for the distinguishable regional pattern of the half-time system. Burnley and the North-East remained the most important centre for child labour in weaving.

In mule-spinning, the general picture is likewise one of essential permanence of the traditional structures of work. The minder-piecer system continued to dominate, and the position of little piecer remained a viable occupation for half-timers. Alternative forms of organization, like "under-minding", "multi-pair" systems, and the use of women minders, never became significant. They remained exceptions on the geographical fringe of the cotton district. However, one important change proved to be more permanent. "Joiner-minding" became an important feature in all spinning districts outside Bolton. While it probably did not remove the position of little piecer, it certainly reduced the spinners' authority in the subcontracting relationship and their chances to employ half-timers.

The most important structural change in the industry was occasioned by the growth of ring-spinning. Although ring-frames remained secondary to the mules, they did make a much greater impact on the industry than the technological changes in weaving. In the context of viable positions for child labour, the indications are that doffing at the ring-frames became a very important occupation for half-timers. The 1886 wage census shows that

---

92 This seems to have been the case with all types of automatic looms. See Textile Manufacturer, May 1903, for a detailed description of the reorganization of the ancillary tasks at Guthrie's mill, Todmorden, during an experiment with Hattersley automatic looms.
93 Amalgamated Weavers' Association (1911): Northrop Weaving.

throstle and ring-spinning had by that time a much higher proportion of half-timers in the workforce than self-actor spinning. With the growth of ring-spinning after 1900, one probable result was that the half-time system remained important in certain areas. Rochdale, the centre of Lancashire ring-spinning, had by 1907 turned into a core area of the half-time system. The available factory statistics indicate that the use of child labour in the Rochdale cotton factories now equalled the level in the northern weaving district.[94] However, the use of half-timers in ring-spinning differed in one important respect from the practice in the other parts of the labour process. The doffers in ring-spinning were not subcontracted by the spinners; they were hired directly by the employer. In this sense, the doffers constituted an important exception to the general rule in the Lancashire cotton industry.

In conclusion it can be said that there was no major structural change in the organization of production which would tend to make half-timers less required. There were slight changes in the organization and technology of weaving which tended to have this effect, but the reverse tendencies occasioned by the growth of ring-spinning were probably stronger. The half-time system in cotton was not made redundant by any major changes in the organization of production.

---

94 PP 1907 X, RCIFW, p. 379; PP 1909 LXXIX, Returns of Employment in Textile Factories, 1907, p. 5 Table 2.

## Chapter 10

# The Stubborn Half-Timer: Child Labour Practices and Working-Class Culture in Lancashire, 1890-1920

Towards the end of the nineteenth century, the employment of children in factories appeared to be in rapid decline. In most industrial trades where child labour had still been common the practice was largely abandoned shortly after the trade's inclusion in the Factory Acts. By 1899, 88 per cent of all half-timers in British factories were employed in the textile branches.[1] The employment of half-timers seemed to be steadily decreasing also in the Lancashire cotton industry, where successive issues of factory statistics show a falling proportion of children. While half-timers performed 4.1 per cent of the work in 1895, by 1901 the figure had dropped to 2.8 per cent.[2] The Factory Act of 1901 raised the minimum age for factory children to 12, and also reinforced the impression that these practices would soon be abandoned. By 1904 the child labour level in Lancashire textiles had been reduced to 2.3 per cent.[3]

However, after 1904 the downward trend seems to have stopped, and the proportion of half-timers in Lancashire cotton remained fairly stable. Factory statistics from 1907 show that 2.3 per cent of the work was still performed by half-timers.[4] General progress, rising standards of living among the operatives, and the increasing emphasis on education, were evidently not sufficent to erode the half-time system. In the end it took an Education Act in 1917 to finally raise the school-leaving age to 14 without exemptions.

The remarkable thing in this process was not so much the gradual upward movement of age levels as a part of educational reform, but rather the resilience and relative permanence of the half-time system in a period of social change. Most researchers, however, have concentrated on the

---

1 PP 1902 XII, RCIFW, pp. 11, 27. The total number of half-timers was 51,590.
2 PP 1897 XVII, RCIFW, pp. 169-71; PP 1904 X, RCIFW, pp. 7-14.
3 PP 1907 X, RCIFW, p. 379.
4 PP 1909 LXXIX, Returns of Employment in Textile Factories, 1907, p. 5. No further statistics on the cotton workforce are available before 1920.

political and social forces behind the gradual advances in school legislation.[5] The questions in this chapter will be somewhat different: how was the half-time system able to survive in Lancashire after 1900? What were the social forces and structures behind its retention?

From the investigation in the previous two chapters it is clear that there was no major reorganization of the labour process or any introduction of new technology before 1920 which tended to make young workers less required.[6] Indeed, the introduction of ring-spinning rather seems to have increased the propensity to use child labour. One possible exception was that drawing-in machinery had been invented in the U.S., and if introduced in Britain it would probably do away with the use of child reachers-in.[7] However, the very absence of such machinery in Lancashire raises the question whether the subcontracting of cheap child labour actually removed the incentive to find technological solutions to certain constraints in the labour process. Technology cannot be seen as an extraneous force outside the relations of production.

Even within the stable structures of labour there existed a certain degree of flexibility regarding workforce composition. Indeed, the statistical decline of factory child labour in the 1890s seems to have been mainly caused by a small upward shift in the age composition of the subcontracted young workers. The level of child labour was not wholly determined by the specific organization of production. As I have argued previously, one important determinant of the level of child labour in Lancashire was the degree of authority over recruitment within the subcontracting relationship, and the interest of the adult operatives to retain the right to hire half-timers. In the 1890s the operatives themselves constituted the main social force behind the retention of the half-time system, while the employers seem to have been relatively indifferent.

The support for the continuation of child labour in the cotton factories was strong both among union representatives and the rank-and-file. The Cotton Factory Times stated in 1890 that the operatives as a whole opposed any alterations of the child labour regulations.[8] When the cotton union officials gave evidence before the Royal Commission on Labour in 1892 they all defended the half-time system. In a language strangely similar to that of the employers in the Factory Commission of 1833, they claimed that the children had to start in the mill early in order to become proficient

---

5 See Griggs (1983); Frow, E and Frow, R (1970): A Survey of the Half-Time System in Education.
6 In contrast, there is some evidence that a self-doffing spinning frame was developed in worsted, which would lessen the need for young doffers. See PP 1909 XVII, Report of the Inter-Departmental Committee, Vol II, evidence of Lady Factory Inspector Squire, p. 51 Q. 1,414.
7 Ibid., evidence of F. A. Hargreaves, Burnley Masters' Association, p. 118 Q. 3,339, 3,351.
8 Cotton Factory Times 28/3/90.

workers. One official of the Blackburn Weavers' Association claimed that when children started work at an earlier age, "their fingers are more deft, and they can learn more easily".[9] George Silk of the Oldham Cardroom Association stated that it was considered normal and proper among the factory operatives to send their children to work in the mill as soon as they had passed the required educational standard.[10]

Expressing the union position in this matter, the Cotton Factory Times continued to support the half-time system. In 1896 it opposed suggestions to raise the minimum age to twelve, complaining that the operatives would be deprived of "some pecuniary assistance from their children for one year longer", and added that "the best textile workers are those who learn to work while they are young".[11] Later in the same year the paper asserted that children who remained at school would never reach the same level of efficiency in factory work as the half-timers, and also that the children's earnings were important contributions for poor families.[12]

There can be no doubt about the special attachment between the cotton workers and the use of half-timers. It is considerably more difficult to estimate the employers' attitude to the half-time system. In a previous chapter, I have indicated that in the 1880s and 90s, the manufacturers were becoming indifferent or even hostile to the use of children in their factories. This was especially the case in the new public limited companies, where managers generally would not allow the mule-spinners to hire half-time piecers. By the early 1900s the employers' defence of child labour practices can hardly be described as substantial. The Textile Recorder, a manufacturer periodical, actually welcomed the proposals to raise the age for half-timers as a step towards a better education for the operative classes and the establishment of technical secondary education.[13] Still, there were probably some differences of opinion. The Textile Manufacturer, a rival employer periodical, stated in 1902:

> There is no doubt that many robust children would be better off at the mill than at school, for their rustic intellect is only running to waste at a time when their healthy muscles might be profitably employed. There are many children who could never

---

9 PP 1892 XXXV, Royal Commission on Labour, evidence of G. Barker, Blackburn Weavers', p. 74 Q. 1,907. See also ibid., evidence of T. Birtwistle, Weavers' Amalgamation, p. 61 Q. 1,543; Ibid., evidence of W. Mullin, Cardroom Amalgamation, p. 12 Q. 355-77; Ibid., evidence of G. Silk, Oldham Cardroom Association, pp. 20-21 Q. 617-22, 629-32, 658-60.
10 Ibid., evidence of Silk, p. 20 Q. 617-20.
11 Cotton Factory Times 6/5/96.
12 Cotton Factory Times 18/9/96. See also Cotton Factory Times 6/11/96; 24/9/97; 21/1/99.
13 Textile Recorder, January 1896, p. 289; May 1896, p. 3; December 1898, p. 273; April 1909, p. 385; August 1909, p. 109. See also the Textile Journal, April 1905, p. 170. Naturally, this does not mean that all manufacturers necessarily shared this view.

earn their living by anything much more elevated than horsework, and who are only allowed to lapse into idle habits by enforced attendance at school. [14]

The remaining impression is still that the main support for the continuation of factory child labour was to be found among the workers themselves. In 1900 a critical factory inspector stated that the system was now only defended by 90,000 Lancashire operatives, and one of his colleagues described the use of factory children as "almost entirely encouraged and sustained by the operatives".[15] However, it remains to be explained more fully why they held that position, and also how they reacted when faced with criticism and pressure for child labour reform. In this chapter, I will try also to explain the survival of the half-time system up to its final abolition in 1920.

## Educational Pressure Groups and the Half-Timer

The lingering remnants of the half-time system of employment for children, which was rightly regarded at its initiation as a great achievement, and which moved the admiration of Karl Marx, are now the anathema both of educational and factory reformers. [16]

The above citation points to a complete change in attitude to the half-time system among educationalists which occurred after the implementation of compulsory schooling in 1870. Before that date, educationalists had generally supported the extension of the Factory Acts and the employment of half-timers simply because this was the only legal framework which provided working-class children with some schooling. In fact, one important argument in debates over the extension of factory legislation to encompass new trades was that it would enable the child workers to have some education.[17] Schooling would provide them with notions of morality, Christianity, and subordination.[18]

---

14 Textile Manufacturer, August 1902. Similarly, in 1907 the Textile Manufacturer advocated a more careful medical examination of half-timers, but did not want an abolition of the system. The employment of children as half-timers, the paper argued, would make them able to handle powerlooms at an earlier age. Textile Manufacturer, March 1907.
15 PP 1900 XI, RCIFW, p. 232; PP 1903 XII, RCIFW, p. 117.
16 Keeling, F (1914): Child Labour in the United Kingdom, pp. xxiv-xxv.
17 However, it seldom worked out that way because in most cases the children were dismissed when the Factory Acts were implemented. On the other hand, the relative failure of the schooling clauses of the Factory Act may have been an important precondition for the 1870 Education Act. Since factory legislation had proved insufficient to provide working-class children with some elementary education, separate legislation was required.
18 Silver (1977), pp. 144-5.

After the passing of the 1870 Education Act, the half-time system turned from a vehicle of schooling into an impediment. Factory work no longer meant some education for the children who would otherwise go without, it actually hindered them from attending school full-time.[19] From then on educationalists started their political and legislative campaign against the half-time system. Already in 1874 the minimum age requirement in cotton factories was raised from eight to ten years. That limit was subsequently raised to 11 in 1891 and 12 in 1899. The half-time system was to be gradually weeded out.

One important part of that campaign was staged by the National Union of Teachers (N.U.T.). Especially after 1895, Lancashire teachers agitated strongly against the half-time system. They claimed that it disrupted classes, lowered educational standards, and created unneccessary book-keeping. Half-timers who worked in the morning were too tired during the afternoon classes to actually learn something.[20]

One of the leading figures in this campaign was the Bolton headmaster Richard Waddington, who frequently agitated against the half-time system. He claimed that the main objective of the Lancashire parents regarding education was to make their children pass the required standard and get them into the mill as early as possible. These parents, he argued, were generally not poor, but sent their children to the factory as a result of "an exaggerated form of thrift" or want of consideration.[21] In a presidential address to the N.U.T. in 1898, he stated that factory inspectors, mill-owners, and Lancashire M.P.s were all against it, and severely criticised the cotton operatives for their support of child labour.[22]

The Cotton Factory Times often responded in kind by stating that the teachers only wanted to abolish the half-time system because they wanted to line their pockets with more government grants.[23] When Sir John Gorst in 1900 put forward a bill to end the half-time system, the Cotton Factory Times commented that he had "for a long time served as a travelling tinker to the schoolmasters' union...but his tinkering policy does not find favour with the working classes".[24] Richard Waddington and the N.U.T. were

19 See PP 1909 XVII, Report of the Inter-Departmental Committee, Vol I, p. 4; Simon, B (1965): Education and the Labour Movement, 1870-1920, p. 290.
20 See McMillan, M (c1896): Child Labour and the Half-time System; also PP 1909 XVII, Report of the Inter-Departmental Committee, Vol I, pp. 4-7; Ibid, Vol II, evidence of A. R. Pickle, teacher, p. 16 Q. 380.
21 PP 1892 XXXV, Royal Commission on Labour, evidence of R. Waddington, p. 143 Q. 3,683, p. 145 Q. 3,722, 3,724.
22 Frow and Frow (1970), p. 78.
23 Cotton Factory Times 22/4/98; 24/2/99; 27/4/99.
24 Cotton Factory Times 27/4/00.

advised to take more interest in the problem of street-selling and loitering children rather than in those who were usefully employed.[25]

Naturally, it is difficult to assess the real impact of the NUT agitation on the legislative process. Frow and Frow, for example, simply describe the several pressure groups in favour of educational reform without indicating any specific causal relationships.[26] A more interesting angle, I believe, would be to study the influence of the N.U.T. and other educationalists on the local level. After 1900 local school boards had the powers to define exemption requirements and also to compel school attendance up to the age of 14.[27] This meant that local towns and districts had the option to limit the use of half-timers by raising the requirements for exemption or even to abolish it altogether. The outcome was a great variation in the standards for school exemption among the different localities.[28]

My impression is that these requirements were raised in areas where the half-time system was relatively weak. One obvious example is Manchester, where it had never really taken root. Here the educational standards for half-time exemption were much higher than in other districts.[29] Similarly, the requirements seem to have been considerably higher in south Lancashire than in the North. This meant that in areas where the half-time system already was relatively unimportant, it was further restricted or even abolished by educational bye-laws. This was an important reason behind the gradual geographical concentration of the half-time system to a smaller area of Lancashire. However, in Bolton, Burnley, and Rochdale, where the system remained strong, the educational bye-laws were kept at a modest level.

While I find no general indications of school boards actively holding back half-time exemptions, the town of Bury may have been an exception. Here the local board refused to grant exemptions if they were not substantiated by evidence of poverty. The level of half-timers seems to have declined accordingly. While the number of factory children had risen in other districts, Bury saw a reduction from 602 in 1904 to 252 in 1908.[30] On the other hand, it may be the case that other causal processes were involved. Bury had, for instance, an unusually high number of automatic looms.[31]

25 Cotton Factory Times 9/9/98; 22/2/01; 16/6/05.
26 Frow and Frow (1970), passim.
27 Simon (1965), p. 141.
28 In 1903 Superintending Inspector Henderson described the varying standards for school exemption as "a state of chaos". PP 1903 XII, RCIFW, p. 119.
29 PP 1908 XII, RCIFW, p. 107. In contrast, there seems to have been no educational requirements at all in Oldham for half-time exemption. See PP 1913 XXIII, RCIFW, p. 93.
30 PP 1909 XVII, Report of the Inter-Departmental Committee, Vol I, pp. 12-13; Ibid, Vol II, evidence of A. R. Pickle, Burnley teacher, pp. 17-18 Q. 418-20.
31 Amalgamated Weavers' Association (1911): Northrop Weaving. Replies to Questions, shows that Bury contained 400 Northrops in 1911.

Another example is perhaps more straightforward. Huddersfield in the West Riding of Yorkshire had 200 cotton mule-spinners in 1909, but no half-time piecers. The local school board had decided not to grant any exemptions at all.[32]

More studies at a local level are no doubt required in order to obtain the full picture. Obviously, local actions on exemption requirements could have had a decisive impact on the use of half-timers. Still, the main conclusion must be that the educational bye-laws were used to reduce or abolish child labour where it was already relatively insignificant, and that the result was a concentration of the half-time system to a core area. In this process, teachers and educationalists probably played an important part.


## The Labour Movement and the Question of Child Labour

A different kind of pressure on the Lancashire operatives and their organizations on the half-time question emanated from other parts of the labour movement. The Independent Labour Party and the Social Democratic Federation both agitated strongly against child labour.[33] Perhaps more importantly, the Trades Union Congress (T.U.C.) proved to be against the half-time system and was critical of the attitude of the cotton unions on these matters. From 1897, resolutions for the raising of the school-leaving age were made at each T.U.C. congress against the isolated votes of the cotton unions. In many instances the debate over the half-timer issue became rather heated.[34] The cotton unions' continued defence of child labour became the target for much criticism, especially from the Gas-workers' and General Labourers' Union.

One reason for the apparent hostility which the question aroused was that most delegates from other trades held that it was a basic trade union principle to remove wage-reducing competition from young teenagers. Also, the majority of the T.U.C. delegates resented the defence of the half-time system because it would impede future educational reforms and improved schooling opportunities for working-class children. The representatives of the cotton unions, on their part, argued that this might be a good policy in other trades, but not in theirs. They pointed out that the high level of earnings among their members showed that the half-time system did not keep down the wages in the Lancashire cotton industry.[35] In response to the

---

32 PP 1909 XVII, Report of the Inter-Departmental Committee, Vol II, evidence of W. Marsland, Spinners' Amalgamation, p. 129 Q. 3,705-6.
33 See Frow and Frow (1970), chap. III and IV.
34 See Griggs (1983), p. 42.
35 See T.U.C. Congress Report 1897, pp. 41-42; Ibid., 1898, pp. 75-76; Cotton Factory Times 3/6/98.

T.U.C. resolutions on the child labour issue, the Weavers' Amalgamation organized a ballot of its members in 1897 which showed an "overwhelming majority" against the proposed raise of the age limit for factory work.[36]

The 1898 T.U.C. Congress produced new attacks on the half-time system, the elected chairman severely criticizing the cotton operatives for being "the greatest opponents of the abolition of the system". The main blame, he stated, lay with the union officials who had chosen not to "educate their members" but instead had tried to justify their position. By doing so they were "accessories of legalised child murder".[37] The cotton union officials rejected accusations of child slavery and parental heartlessness, maintaining that the critics were not aquainted with the real conditions in cotton factories. They also denied that child labour lowered the wages of the adult workers.[38] The Cotton Factory Times even insisted that the life of the half-timer in cotton was rewarding and pleasant:

> The minder and the big piecer vie with each other in making the lad expert in his job. When the ends are up and it is "spinning well", and there is neither creeling nor doffing, he has happy times, and is as cheerful as a lark. [39]

Joseph Cross of the Blackburn Weavers' even argued that child labour was necessary since the Lancashire industry had to compete with cheap foreign labour.[40]

This discussion within the trade union movement continued with varied intensity for the next ten years. Even if it had little immediate effect, it is probable that the T.U.C. pressure and the constant debates on the half-time issue in the long run had a pervasive influence on the representatives of the cotton unions. But at the turn of the century, the question was still unresolved. The representatives of the cotton unions held the official view that the half-time system was in gradual decline and needed no further

---

36 According to the Cotton Factory Times, 95.9 per cent of the voters were against the T.U.C. resolution to raise the school-leaving age to 15. Cotton Factory Times 12/11/97; 19/11/97. However, there are some indications that the cotton union officials were divided on this issue. In an editorial comment the paper advocated a gradual raise of the age limit for half-timers, and stated that some propagandist and educational work was needed to overcome the prejudice of the operatives on this issue. See Cotton Factory Times 12/12/97.

37 T.U.C. Congress Report 1898, p. 29. The address was held by J. O'Grady of the London cabinetmakers. In Cotton Factory Times' version of the event, O'Grady had denounced the parents of Lancashire half-timers as "moral murderers". Cotton Factory Times 2/9/98.

38 See the comments of David Holmes, Burnley Weavers, T.U.C. Congress Report 1897, pp. 41-42.

39 Cotton Factory Times 20/1/99.

40 T.U.C. Congress Report 1897, p. 42.

legislation.[41] For a while, the reports and statistics provided by the factory inspectors appeared to support them.

## Lancashire's Stubborn Half-Timers

With the passing of the 1901 Factory Act, the minimum age for half-timers was raised to 12. The law also contained a clause which prohibited half-timers from cleaning any part of a machine when it was in motion, and it was expected that this regulation would greatly lessen the number of half-time piecers in mule-spinning. The factory inspector in the Bolton district believed that the new clause would "go a great way to stop half-time employment in textile factories. The fact that a child will not be allowed to clean any place under any machinery other than overhead mill gearing, will prevent a child sweeping under the creel of a self-acting mule, and the minders will find that no half-timers would be of any use as little piecers." Similarly, little piecers in Oldham were mainly employed in cleaning tasks, not in piecing. Inspector Crabtree therefore predicted that the half-time system would soon lose most of its importance in that district.[42]

Undoubtedly, the 1901 Act restricted the activities and general usefulness of half-time piecers. The Cotton Factory Times commented several years later that if all regulations were followed, the half-timer could only be used to fetch hot water, do some tubing, and draw wages.[43] But the question is whether these regulations really were obeyed. As I have described in a previous chapter, clauses of this type were extremely difficult to enforce. The factory inspector could only detect offences by finding children actually in the process of cleaning machinery in motion, or by being notified of accidents. The child piecer could stop the illegal cleaning immediately it became known that the inspector was in the vicinity. I therefore find it unlikely that the clause on cleaning machinery in motion had much effect. The continued crop of children involved in accidents tells in a grim way that the practice was not generally abandoned. The half-timer was not the minder's first choice when recruiting piecers, and probably had not been for twenty years. However, when full-time piecers were difficult to find,

---

41 At the 1900 T.U.C. Congress, the delegate of the Blackburn Weavers' declared that the half-time system would die out on its own accord in a year or two. T.U.C. Congress Report 1900, p. 89. See also Cotton Factory Times 3/6/98; 16/12/98; 3/3/99; 12/9/02.
42 PP 1902 XII, RCIFW, pp. 121-2.
43 Cotton Factory Times 19/3/09; 3/4/08.

children would have to do. The new regulations did not stop half-timers from being a last resort when the minder was short of a little piecer.[44]

In a similar way, the 1909 Children's Act was used to prohibit half-timers from carrying heavy weights. The most obvious target in the cotton industry was the child tenters in weaving, who were often made to carry heavy cuts of cloth to the warehouse.[45] Even the Cotton Factory Times stated that the new law would soon discourage weavers from employing half-timers.[46] But in the same way as the clauses on cleaning, offences against these regulations were very difficult to detect.

Moreover, the employers could use the subcontracting relationship in such a way as to make the operative weaver responsible for the illegal use of half-time tenters. Burnley employers who had been cautioned by the factory inspector for letting children carry heavy weights of cloth simply responded that they had ordered the weavers to perform that task in the future, and that those operatives were responsible for the actions of their tenters.[47] Apart from some vague discouragement of the use of half-timers, these regulations probably had very little real effect.

These enforcement difficulties were not immediately perceived. After the passing of the 1901 Factory Act, the general impression was that the half-time system in the textile industry was in rapid and irreversible decline.[48] Also, child labour in factories was regarded as well-regulated in comparison with other forms of employment of school children.[49] As a result, social reformers and educationalists began to look in other directions. The most important social problem now appeared to be what was labelled "boy labour" outside school hours: street-sellers, newspaper boys, children used in small workshop production, as lather boys in shaving saloons or as performers in public houses.[50] Even a hardened opponent of the half-time system like Richard Waddington was made to admit that the gravest problem at the time was the usage of children outside factories.[51] This became the prime field for social reform during the next eight years.

However, the generally held expectation of a swift decline of the half-time system did not come true. In 1906 the factory inspectors reported a

44 See PP 1913 XXIII, RCIFW, p. 92.
45 PP 1909 XXI, RCIFW, p. 99.
46 Cotton Factory Times 4/6/09.
47 Cotton Factory Times 4/6/09; 1/7/10.
48 See PP 1902 XXV, Minutes..., evidence of R. Waddington, p. 95 Q. 4,412-13; Ibid., evidence of Lady Inspector Anderson, p. 238 Q. 9,963.
49 PP 1902 XXV, Report..., pp. 12, 18-19.
50 Ibid., pp. 5-8, 12, 19; Keeling (1914), p. viii; Alden, M (1908): Child Life and Labour, chapter VII; Bray, R A (1911): Boy Labour and Apprenticeship, chapter V ; Hird, F (1898): The Cry of the Children. An Exposure of Certain British Industries in which Children are Iniquitously Employed, passim.
51 PP 1902 XXV, Minutes..., p. 95 Q. 4,414.

general increase in the number of half-timers. Sub-inspector Rogers reported from Blackburn:

> The steady annual decrease in the number of half-timers which had been so noticeable, was arrested during 1904 by the increased demand for juvenile labour owing to the boom in the cotton trade which commenced that year, and the number employed rose from 7,876 in 1904, to 8,281 in 1906. [52]

It should be remembered that a rise in the absolute figure does not necessarily indicate a rise in proportion. But the impression of the factory inspectors seems to have been that the downward trend of the half-time system had stopped. The editors of the Cotton Factory Times, who had also confidently predicted the gradual demise of the half-time system, expressed some amazement:

> The number of half-timers has increased during the past three years. It is said that this has been brought about by the booming trade. It is surprising if that is so. We should have looked for an opposite effect. If parents are earning more wages, they are better able to keep their children at school. [53]

Factory statistics from this period are rather scant, but the impression is that the level of child labour in cotton did not sink significantly again before the First World War.[54] What was the reason for this resilience? Contemporaries obviously ascribed it to a period of good trade and a consequent scarcity of juvenile workers. In this chapter I will examine more specifically why children continued to be used in the processes of mule-spinning and powerloom weaving.

### Piecers and Creelers in Lancashire Mule-spinning, 1900-1920

The effect of labour scarcity was most noticeable in mule-spinning, and requires some explanation. Around 1900, complaints started to emerge about a scarcity of little piecers. The Cotton Factory Times stated that minders found it increasingly difficult to recruit little piecers, and often found themselves running the mules without the full complement of assistants.[55] The minders complained of being harassed and even threatened with dismissal by the management if they could not find juveniles to piece

---

52 PP 1907 X, RCIFW, p. 136. See also PP 1906 XV, RCIFW, p. 173; PP 1907 X, RCIFW, pp. 133-4; PP 1909 XVII, Report of the Inter-Departmental Committee, Vol II, evidence of A. R. Pickle, Burnley teacher, p. 17 Q. 412-15; Ibid., evidence of Factory Inspector Crabtree, Oldham district, p. 42 Q. 1,095.
53 Cotton Factory Times 24/7/08. See also Cotton Factory Times 3/4/08.
54 See PP 1913 XXIII, RCIFW, p. 92.
55 Cotton Factory Times 28/7/99; 25/8/99; 1/9/99; 11/5/00.

for them.[56] In some cases the firm withheld the wages due to the little piecer when the minder had had to work short-handed, which was really a contravention of the list system.[57]

These examples illustrate the employers' interest in the retention of subcontracting, and the superficial nature of this arrangement in some firms. Most of the open conflicts with management arose in districts with less strong spinners' unions, but the problem of piecer scarcity seems to have been general.[58] Management's harassment of minders on the recruitment issue seems only to have been checked by a strong trade union presence:

> Respecting minders being troubled for the want of little piecers, they are subject to much annoyance from the nasty manner in which they are treated by some of the managers and overlookers, and were it not for their trade unions their position would be made most uncomfortable indeed. Several attempts have been made to fine members for being without little piecers. [59]

The scarcity of little piecers proved to be a persistent issue. In the booms of 1906-7 and 1912-13 it reappeared in even greater force.[60] This chronic lack of juvenile workers caused a renewed interest in the employment of child labour. While many employers had previously been reluctant to allow the employment of half-time piecers, there was now an obvious change in attitude. In April 1907 the Cotton Factory Times stated that there was a large number of employers who would not employ half-timers because they were "too much trouble". However, due to the persistent scarcity of young workers, some of them had now withdrawn their objections.[61]

There can be no doubt about the link between the lack of juvenile workers and the manufacturers' readiness to accept half-timers. The factory inspector in Bolton stated in 1901 that the only reason for the employment of children in mule-spinning was the scarcity of full-time piecers. Even millowners who were "totally opposed" to child labour actually had half-timers employed in their factories.[62] Similarly, his Oldham colleague stated in 1909 that half-timers were only employed if older piecers could not be found.[63]

The continued use of child workers in Bolton and Oldham was probably caused by strained supplies of labour in combination with strong spinners'

---

56 For instance, the minders at Horrocks, Crewdson & Co., Preston, were threatened with dismissal if they failed to produce creelers. Preston Spinners' Minutes, 12/11/99.

57 Cotton Factory Times 30/6/99.

58 Cotton Factory Times 30/6/99; 1/9/99; 22/12/99; 11/5/00.

59 Cotton Factory Times 29/3/01. For the later period, see also Cotton Factory Times 25/10/12.

60 Cotton Factory Times 19/10/06; 4/1/07; 26/7/12; 25/10/12; 8/11/12.

61 Cotton Factory Times 12/4/07.

62 PP 1901 X, RCIFW, p. 313.

63 PP 1909 XVII, Report of the Inter-Departmental Committee, Vol II, evidence of Factory Inspector Crabtree, p. 42 Q. 1,099. See also PP 1909 XXI, RCIFW, p. 99; PP 1913 XXIII, RCIFW, p. 92.

unions. Roughly 70 per cent of the employers in those two districts continued to employ half-timers.[64] Furthermore, it seems as if the half-time system was strongest in the suburban areas outside Oldham and Bolton proper, in places like Shaw, Royton, Leigh, and Farnworth. This was probably caused by a more limited supply of young workers compared with the situation in the towns.[65]

There was also a difference in the use of half-timers between firms. New companies with the most modern machinery seldom employed half-timers. But this is in itself no proof that children were less required on the most modern mules.[66] Instead, the indication is that the minders on the new and more efficient machines were able to offer higher wages for their assistants, and consequently creamed off the supply of available full-time piecers.[67]

It should also be recognized that the minders in the new mills were in a less strong position to demand full authority over recruitment, while the owners on their part were not bound by customary agreements. But the main conclusion must be that the stabilization of the half-time system in mule-spinning was caused by a scarcity of juvenile workers.

However, the argument has to be taken one step further. The issue of labour scarcity was mediated by the existing production relations, and the solution of using half-timers was not the only viable one. Furthermore, it has to be considered why the process of mule-spinning required such extreme amounts of young workers, and also the reasons for this supply eventually drying up. In the following passages I will discuss three structural factors which contributed to the situation of piecer scarcity: first, the special requirements inherent in the minder-piecer system; second, the movement towards longer mules and a larger number of piecers per spinner; and third, the exclusion of women from the mule-spinning rooms.

The first consideration is the inherent problems of the organization of the minder-piecer system. A major weakness of this organization of work was that it required a much larger number of piecers than could ever become minders.[68] During the span of his working life, a minder trained at

---

64 77 per cent of the Bolton manufacturers in 1901 and 70 per cent of the Oldham employers in 1909 had half-timers in their factories. PP 1902 XII, RCIFW, p. 121; PP 1909 XVII, Report..., Vol II, evidence of Factory Inspector Crabtree, p. 45 Q. 1,207.

65 PP 1909 XVII, Report..., Vol II, evidence of Factory Inspector Crabtree, p 43. Q. 1,105-7. A detailed study of the Bolton district from 1898 shows that while 3.2 per cent of the spinning workforce in Bolton were half-timers, the corresponding figure for Leigh was 5.3 per cent, for Farnworth 5.9 per cent, and for West Houghton 6.3 per cent. PP 1900 XI, RCIFW, p. 70.

66 Factory Inspector Crabtree stated that the type of machinery did not make "the slightest difference" regarding the employment of half-timers. PP 1909 XVII, Report..., Vol II, p 46. Q. 1,254.

67 Ibid., p. 43 Q. 1,116-19, p. 46 Q. 1,239.

68 On this issue, see Thorpe (1969), p. 37; White (1978), p. 36; Jewkes and Gray (1935), pp. 172-3.

least eight piecers while leaving only one minder position vacant.[69] This problem was for a while made less imminent by the general growth of the cotton spinning industry, whereby the absolute number of minder positions increased. But as the growth of the industry levelled off, what was called "the piecer problem" became more serious. Big piecers found it increasingly difficult to be promoted to minders, and the large majority of them were forced to leave the cotton industry and seek employment elsewhere.[70]

The bad prospects of promotion caused a strong sense of dissatisfaction among the piecers. Since promotion was largely determined by seniority, the big piecers who were determined to stay in the trade found that they would perhaps be in their late twenties before they became minders. Their wages were relatively high compared to alternative juvenile employment, but wholly insufficient as a wage for an adult and a potential breadwinner. The dissatisfaction of the piecers was further exacerbated after 1905 when working conditions deteriorated due to the employers' increasing use of cheap cotton. The years before the First World War were marked by piecers' remonstrances and strikes over promotions, working conditions, and low pay.[71]

It is perhaps necessary to explain more fully why it was so difficult to move away from the minder-piecer system. The obvious solution of the "piecer problem" would have been the general adoption of the system of joiner-minding, but such a move was not approved of by the Spinners' Amalgamation since it would have seriously reduced the earnings of the minders working on the traditional system.[72] The fact that the piecers were subcontracted and dominated by the minders also made changes or expressions of discontent more difficult. The piecers also lacked an independent union. The Spinners' Amalgamation had laid down that all piecers should be organized in special piecers' unions connected to the local spinners' association. Attempts to form separate, independent piecers' unions were forcefully counteracted by the minders.[73]

---

69 The conclusion is a result of the following calculation: one minder working between the years of 20 and 52, and requiring two piecers between the ages of 12 and 20. During his working life, the minder was thus in a position to train four pairs of piecers.

70 See PP 1892 XXXV, Royal Commission of Labour, evidence of J. Mawdsley, Spinners' Amalgamation, p. 28 Q. 782-94; PP 1909 XVII, Report..., Vol II, evidence of W. Marsland, Spinners' Amalgamation, p. 126 Q. 3,578-79.

71 Cotton Factory Times 14/7/11; 29/9/11; 3/11/11; 12/1/12; See also White (1978), pp. 36, 99-100; White (1982), p. 226.

72 See 1909 XVII, Report..., Vol II, evidence of W. Marsland, Spinners' Amalgamation, p. 130 Q. 3,724.

73 See PP 1892 XXXV, Royal Commission on Labour, evidence of J. Mawdsley, Spinners' Amalgamation, p. 29 Q. 800-804; Cotton Factory Times 17/3/99; 21/4/99. See also Turner (1962), p. 142; Burgess, K (1975): The Origins of British Industrial Relations, p. 256.

The official line was that the relative privations which the piecers suffered would be compensated after their promotion to minders.[74] However, this must have been small comfort to the majority of big piecers who would never gain that promotion. The spinners' unions acknowledged that the piecers deserved better pay, but claimed that the money should come from the employers, not the spinners.[75] The manufacturers naturally did not share this view.

In fact, the development after 1900 highlights the important employer advantages connected with the continuation of the subcontracting system. The spinners were forced to exert themselves to recruit piecers in an increasingly difficult labour market, and also to meet the costs of rising juvenile wages. The latter phenomena was also felt in other parts of the industry where adult operatives subcontracted youngsters, like in reaching-in and weaving. Subcontracting was a convenient way for management to leave the increasing wage demands from the juvenile workers to be met by the adult operatives.[76] Also, when working conditions deteriorated as a result of the use of inferior cotton, the spinners had to discipline and cajole the piecers to accept the worsened conditions of work. In this sense, the minders constituted an important buffer between the management and the growing discontent of the piecers.[77]

This very ambiguous nature of the subcontracting relationship is also shown by cases of minders taking their piecers to court for breach of contract when staging spontaneous walk-outs.[78] The existence of this kind of internal discipline within the mule-spinning workforce was an important prerequisite for the managerial strategy of utilizing cheap cotton. In conclusion, there can be no doubt that the minder-piecer system was advantageous to the employers in several different ways. The continuation of this organization of work during this period should therefore be seen as caused by both union strength and employer connivance. Complaining of the very mixed blessings of subcontracting, one minder wrote to the Cotton Factory Times in 1912:

> The question...is whether it might not be a good thing on the whole if the spinners renounced their right of discharging piecers, and threw the responsibility on the employers? /.../ The present relation of spinner to piecer is neither one thing nor the other. The spinner has the right of engagement or discharge of his own piecers

74 Cotton Factory Times 12/5/99.
75 Cotton Factory Times 15/1/01; 15/1/09; 10/11/11.
76 Commenting on this problem in 1902, the Cotton Factory Times stated that the big Oldham strike in 1878 had been partly caused by the spinners' unwillingness to take over the full responsibility for their piecers' wages. Cotton Factory Times 14/2/02. See also Jewkes and Gray (1935), pp. 65-69.
77 Cotton Factory Times 7/6/01.
78 Cotton Factory Times 3/5/01.

theoretically, but in practice it is found that his rights under this head dwindle down to very small proportions indeed. /.../ The time is now opportune when the position of the minder and employer in regard to piecers should be definitely settled, and in renouncing all claim to engage and discharge piecers, minders would be free from responsibilities which have greatly increased of late years, and would only be giving up a privilege which has long ceased to have any value. [79]

However, the Spinners' Amalgamation was not interested in changes in the status quo. Without either minder or employer support for an essential re-organization of the work in mule-spinning, the piecers were in no position to achieve any change in conditions. In the end, "troublesome piecers" were not likely to be allowed promotion, either by the management or by the spinners' union.[80] These are the reasons behind the apparent rigidity of the organization of work in mule-spinning.

One important conclusion is that the scarcity of little piecers which became so pronounced after 1900 should be seen in the context of the structural imbalance of the minder-piecer system in connection with a retarded growth rate of the Lancashire industry. The very small prospects of promotion served as an important discouragement to sending boys into the cotton spinning industry.

There are some indications that even the minders themselves preferred to send their sons into engineering or other skilled trades due to the bad promotion opportunities in cotton spinning. W. Marsland of the Spinners' Amalgamation stated in 1909 that a large majority of mule-spinners did not put their sons to the same trade if they could avoid it.[81] A small sample from Oldham in 1909 also suggests that the great majority of half-time creelers in that town were children of casual labourers.[82] Clearly, this situation should be seen in the specific context of constraints implied in the minder-piecer system. But this is only one of the structural reasons behind the piecer problem. Another was the tendency after 1900 to construct longer mules staffed by one minder and three piecers.[83] The increasing ratio of assistants per spinner further exacerbated the "piecer problem".

Perhaps more importantly, piecer scarcity should also be seen as an effect of the deliberate exclusion of women and girls from the mule-spinning rooms. The exclusion of female operatives from mule-spinning was mainly occasioned by trade union policy. In the late 1880s, attempts were .

---

79 Cotton Factory Times 25/10/12.
80 Cotton Factory Times 21/4/99.
81 PP 1909, Report..., Vol II, p. 128 Q 3,669, p. 131 Q 3,755.
82 Out of fifty half-time creelers in Oldham, only four had spinners or joiner-minders as fathers. Thirty were classified as children of casual labourers. Ibid., Appendix II, pp. 266-69, figures produced by Factory Inspector Crabtree. These families were probably attracted by the relatively high juvenile wages in cotton spinning while disregarding the bleak long-term prospects.
83 Cotton Factory Times 10/11/11.

made by some Bolton employers to use women as mule-spinners. Female piecers had previously been commonly used in some districts, and with the increasing perfection of machinery it was believed, or hoped, among the mill-owners that women minders would prove to be a more economical choice than the highly paid men. The union reacted by adopting a strict policy of exclusion. In order to cut off the future supply of female minders, women and girls were no longer accepted as piecers. This policy soon became general in the areas outside Bolton, with the exception of a few marginal spinning districts.[84] For instance, female piecers continued to be used in Manchester. Employers in Wigan on the very outskirts of the cotton district even proceeded to use women as minders. In the latter case, the unions admitted that they were not in a position to do anything about it. Still, apart from in these very marginal areas, mule-spinning became an exclusively male domain.

The policy of barring women from mule-spinning was officially defended along two lines: first, that the work was much too arduous for females; and second, that it was morally wrong to let men and women work close together while scantily dressed. Already in 1873 the Burnley spinners had objected to the use of girl piecers on grounds of decency, referring to the "postures frequently rendered necessary by the work, and the scanty clothing commonly worn in consequence of the high temperature".[85] Of course, these arguments merely served to obscure the exclusion policy. It is hard to understand, for instance, why the work was too arduous for a woman but perfectly suitable for a boy of thirteen. Nevertheless, the Cotton Factory Times defended union policy by stating that "on physical grounds the work is pre-eminently that of a male...the work is unfitted for a female".[86]

The extent and strength of the exclusion policy only surfaced during the First World War. During the preceding period, the decision not to use girls as piecers was tacit and left little trace in the records. During the war-time conditions, however, the government started to put pressure on the Spinners' Amalgamation to release more men to the front by accepting women in the mule-spinning rooms. This brought the situation to a head, and also threw some light on the exclusion policy which had dominated the previous decades. In January 1915, the Cotton Factory Times reported that suggestions had been made that the crippling scarcity of piecers should be solved by the employment of young women. But such a scheme would have meant an inroad for female minders, and the paper remarked that "we do

---

84 See Thorpe (1969), p. 75; White (1978), p. 39; Clarke, A [1899]: The Effects of the Factory System, p. 83.
85 PP 1873 LV, Report..., p. 10.
86 Cotton Factory Times 10/4/14.

not think that any responsible person will contend that the minding of mules is fit occupation for women".[87]

A month later the general secretary of the Spinners' Amalgamation declared that any attempt to introduce female minders would be "strenuously resisted" in peace or in war.[88] Rather than introducing women into mule-spinning, the Amalgamation officials suggested that all restrictions on 13 year-olds to work full-time should be lifted. Such a measure would ease the piecer scarcity somewhat.[89] Only when this request was refused by the government, and after having received guarantees from the employers that this was a temporary measure which would be discontinued after the war, did the Spinners' Amalgamation finally accept the recruitment of young women as piecers.[90]

This war-time dispute over the employment of women in mule-spinning is interesting in two respects. First, it casts some light over the general policy of excluding women from mule-spinning which had probably been in force since the 1890s. Second, it shows that child labour continued to be important in mule-spinning as a reserve supply of young workers in times of scarcity of little piecers. Since the general policy excluded girls from this type of occupation, the boy half-timer continued to be an important resource in mule-spinning. Instead of hiring females, children were used. In this way, the preservation of the minder-piecer system in conjunction with a policy not to employ females created a structural niche for the half-timer. Also, this case clearly shows the relevance of the gender dimension in the study of child labour.

So far I have dealt with structural reasons for the piecer scarcity in terms of the social constructs of work. But there were also processes working in the same direction outside the spinning mills. The opportunities and possible choices of occupation had widened, at least for boys. Engineering, the post office, and the railway began to be more cherished occupational choices among working-class youths than cotton spinning.[91] These tendencies had a more specific effect on the organization of work in mule-spinning since girl piecers were generally not accepted.

The remarkable thing about the persistence of the half-time system in mule-spinning after 1900 is that it seemed to have been made wholly redundant both by changes in the labour process and by more restrictive factory regulations. The intensity of work and the speed of the mules

87 Cotton Factory Times 29/1/15.
88 Cotton Factory Times 12/2/15.
89 A.A.O.C.S., Quarterly Report 31/7/15; Cotton Factory Times 13/8/15.
90 A.A.O.C.S., Quarterly Report 31/10/15; Annual Report for 1915, p. 7; Anual Report for 1916, p. 4; Cotton Factory Times 29/10/15; 5/11/15.
91 Cotton Factory Times 25/8/99.

required a high degree of accuracy and stamina from the piecers, which would seem to make half-timers a less likely choice. This was clearly also the opinion of the minders already in the 1880s. Nevertheless, they continued to use half-timers, either to give their sons an early start in their mill careers, or in cases of piecer scarcity when full-timers could not be found at reasonable prices.

Similarly, stricter rules on the employment of children seemed to contemporaries to be practically prohibitive. But due to piecer scarcity and enforcement difficulties, it seems very doubtful if those regulations were much obeyed. Consequently, the demands of the labour process and the factory regulations were not sufficient to abolish the use of half-timers. Due to the persistence of the peculiar structure of the minder-piecer system, the subcontracting relationship, and the ensuing minder strategies on the recruitment of piecers, the half-time system was given a chance to survive.

However, one possible beneficial effect of the piecer scarcity was that the minders were obliged to treat their young assistants with more consideration. Brutal or difficult minders probably had less chance of keeping their little piecers. One Cotton Factory Times cartoon accordingly portrayed the little piecer as the "monarch of the mill", ordering his minder to "pick that cop up, or I'll go whoam".[92]

### Half-time Tenters in Lancashire Weaving, 1900-1920

Turning to the other main sector of the industry, it could be said that the reasons for the persistence of the half-time system in weaving were somewhat different. As I have shown in the previous two chapters, the fundamental precondition for the continuation of the half-time system in weaving was the survival of the traditional organization of work and the subcontracting relationship, and also the relative failure of the American methods of production and the automatic loom. But even if the older technology was retained, the employers could disallow the recruitment of half-time tenters. The continued use of child tenters depended on the local relations of production.

The evidence of one certifying surgeon supports this kind of argument. Dr Musson, Clitheroe, stated in 1909 that in one part of his district, the greater part of the children worked as half-timers, while in the other, the employers would not take them.[93]

---

92 Cotton Factory Times 13/3/08.
93 PP 1909 XVII, Report..., Vol II, p. 103 Q. 2,973.

However, there were also some important differences regarding child workers in weaving compared to mule-spinning. Weavers did not use half-time tenters as a last resort when juvenile workers were difficult to get. The indications are that the weaving operatives in many cases preferred using half-timers.[94] One reason for this was that the work of the tenter was less hectic than that of the little piecer, and permanent attention was not required. The tenter mainly performed ancillary tasks, looked for breakages of the yarn, and helped to re-thread shuttles. The most important function of the tenter was probably to clean the loom machinery. In the oral evidence collected by Elizabeth Roberts, Mrs B1, Preston, recollected how she performed that work in the years after 1913:

> ...you had to sweep and clean and polish your looms and oil them. I can smell all the oil, and on the floor they'd sand, like gritty sand, and Saturday dinner time you spread all this sand and you had to go early before 6 and get it all swept away and the floor looked white then and you had to oil all the looms, oh I can smell that oil. I used to dread Monday mornings. [95]

The cleaning was done at one loom at a time, allowing the weaver to keep the other three running while most of the cleaning work was done by the tenter. Since the powerlooms were generally cleaned three times per week, many weavers seem to have found it convenient to employ half-time tenters to help out during those days.[96] Saturday was the main cleaning day, and there are some indications that children sometimes were taken in illegally on that day to help weavers without regular tenters.[97]

The relative stability in the use of half-timers in weaving has largely been unnoticed. The observations on the general decline of child labour before 1900 were mainly based on the case of mule-spinning in south Lancashire. The use of half-time tenters in the weaving district in the North-East proved to be much more stable. Apart from the reason stated above about the relative usefulness of the half-time tenter in weaving, several processes combined to create a veritable "half-time culture" in the weaving centres in north-east Lancashire. A high rate of expansion and the predominance of relatively small-scale employers contributed to create a system of produc-

---

94 David Shackleton of the Weavers' Amalgamation stated in 1909 that weavers customarily preferred to have one half-time tenter, except when minding six looms, in which case two half-timers or one full-time tenter would be employed. Ibid., p. 58 Q. 1,595-96, p. 63 Q. 1,728-29.

95 NWOHP, Mrs B1, Preston. Needless to say, starting work before 6 o'clock in the morning was illegal for "protected persons" under the Factory Act.

96 PP 1894 XXI, RCIFW, p. 324. See also PP 1876 XXX, Report of the Commissioners..., evidence of E. Schofield and R. Williams, schoolmasters, Darwen, pp. 497-98 Q. 10,047-51.

97 See the report of Lady Factory Inspector Paterson, PP 1896 XIX, RCIFW, pp. 118-19, who complained that management often did not assume any authority over the child workers. The extent of the illegal cleaning performed by children during Saturday afternoons is of course almost impossible to estimate.

tion relations where the local unions were relatively influential.[98] In this situation, employers were more prone to condone or accept the employment of half-time tenters. The secretary of the Burnley Masters' Association was in favour of the retention of the half-time system as late as 1909, regarding it as a suitable introduction to mill life.[99]

The relative stability of the half-time system in weaving should also be seen in the context of gender, family, and cultural expectations that children start work early.[100] Among the weaving operatives in the North-East, the half-time system was seen as a way to get the children some useful employment and an early start in their mill careers.[101] In 1892, a representative of the Burnley weavers stated that half-timers generally worked without getting paid for a short period simply in order to be lined up when a tenter vacancy arose.[102] This was still the case seventeen years later.[103] To send the child as early as possible to the weaving shed seems to have been regarded as the normal thing. Even some factory inspectors saw half-time tenting as a good introduction to factory employment, quite on a par with attending technical classes at school.[104]

In this context it has to be pointed out that most half-time tenters were girls. They were not affected by the widening of occupational prospects which had contributed to the severing of the links between factory and family in mule-spinning. Working-class girls in north-east Lancashire did not have the opportunity to go into apprenticeships leading to well-paid occupations, or to attend technical colleges. The cultural expectation was that they should start earning wages as early as possible and contribute to the family economy before getting married.[105]

Supporting evidence of this link can be found in the oral material collected by Elizabeth Roberts. In the family of Mrs B1, Preston, all the sisters went early as tenters in a weaving factory, while the brothers went into

---

98 For indications of labour scarcity in weaving, see Cotton Factory Times 18/10/12; 13/12/12.

99 PP 1909 XVII, Report..., Vol II, evidence of F. A. Hargreaves, pp. 117-18 Q. 3,302-05, 3,331-34.

100 See Roberts (1985), chapter 2. D. A. Farnie has also suggested that the weaving district in north-east Lancashire should be seen as culturally different from the Southern part of the cotton district, and that the institution of family was actually strengthened by the dominating pattern of child and juvenile employment. See Farnie (1979), pp. 295-96, 323.

101 See PP 1892 XXXV, Royal Commission on Labour, evidence of G. Barker, Blackburn Weavers', p. 74 Q. 1,902-06; PP 1909 XVII, Report..., Vol II, evidence of D. Shackleton, Weavers' Amalgamation, p. 58 Q. 1,587.

102 PP 1892 XXXV, Royal Commission on Labour, evidence of D. Holmes, Burnley Weavers', p. 36 Q. 929; Ibid., evidence of T. Birtwistle, Weavers' Amalgamation, p. 62 Q. 1,593.

103 According to the secretary of the Burnley employers, F. A. Hargreaves, half-timers worked the first two months without wages. PP 1909 XVII, Report..., Vol II, p. 119 Q. 3,368.

104 See PP 1902 XXV, Minutes..., evidence of Superintending Inspector Richmond, p. 6 Q. 165-71.

105 See Liddington and Norris (1978), pp. 57-59; Roberts (1985), chapter 2.

apprenticeships.[106] In this way, the stability of the half-time system in weaving was underpinned by family and gender patterns. What is more, these cultural conceptions proved to be very resilient, and seem to have prevailed well into the 1930s. Mrs C5 and Mrs H7, Preston, both started work in a weaving shed at 14 in the early 1930s. They both disliked the mill work, but Mrs C5 stated that "you had to do it in them days as your mother was waiting for the money".[107] Obviously, the dimension of gender is essential for an understanding of the resilience of the half-time system in weaving after 1900.

In conclusion, several reasons have been indicated for the retention of the half-time system after 1900 in the mule-spinning and weaving processes. To this should be added the growth of ring-spinning and the increasing prevalence of half-time doffers in that process. The combined effect was to halt the decline of the half-time system in conjunction with the boom of 1906-7.

The half-time system was mainly retained in the expansive weaving districts in the North-East, in the ring-spinning district of Rochdale, and in the still growing mule-spinning towns of Bolton and Oldham. In the other parts of the cotton district, relative industrial stagnation, a lesser degree of union authority, and more strict educational bye-laws combined to lessen the extent of factory child labour. In the Hyde district in the South, the introduction of a considerable number of Northrop looms probably contributed to the weakening of the half-time system.

On the other hand, in 1909 the process of educational reform started rolling once more. Further parliamentary investigations were made into the question of school exemptions and the effects of the half-time system.[108] Perhaps more importantly, by this time most of the officials of the cotton unions had shifted position and were now in favour of the abolition of child labour. But the process of reform still proved to be difficult.

# The Last Defence of the Half-Time System

The 1909 Committee on school exemptions strongly recommended the abolition of the half-time system, setting 13 as the minimum age for factory

---

106 NWOHP, Mrs B1, Preston. In Elizabeth Roberts's Preston sample, only one girl went into apprenticeship. See Roberts (1985), pp. 64-65. In Oldham in 1920-21, 80.8 per cent of the girls leaving school entered a cotton mill as compared to 58.2 per cent of the boys. Jewkes and Gray (1935), p. 179 Table III.
107 NWOHP, Mrs C5 and Mrs H7, Preston.
108 See PP 1909 XVII, Report..., Vols I and II.

work. The Committee connected the two problems of factory half-timers and other forms of child labour, claiming that in local communities where factory half-timers were prevalent, other forms of school exemptions were also more common. The only way to solve the problem was to abolish exemptions altogether.[109] Probably to show that the manufacturing interest was not backing the half-time system, the cotton employers were described as not favouring the use of child labour.[110] The necessity to use child labour was questioned by the Committee in the light that this practice was very unusual outside a few textile trades:

> We feel compelled to doubt whether there is anything in the processes of cotton and worsted spinning and weaving which differentiates them so completely from other industries as to make it essential to have children at 12 to commence labour. [111]

Similarly, the absence of factory child labour in the Scottish cotton industry was brought forward as an argument against the alleged necessity to employ half-timers.[112]

On the surface the case seemed clear for reform. Parliamentary Bills to this effect were brought forward every year up to the First World War, but in spite of having the backing of a majority of M.P.s, the measures were never allowed to pass. The government seems to have been very reluctant to implement the suggested reforms.

One reason for this may have been the resistance from the Lancashire workpeople to the abolition of the half-time system. At least, this was given as a reason for not pressing the matter. In a meeting with a Labour delegation arguing for educational reform, Prime Minister Asquith simply referred to the negative opinion among the Lancashire operatives.[113] It is possible that the government calculated that political ground in Lancashire would be lost if they chose to go ahead with educational reforms. But it is also a firm possibility that they were not genuinely interested in reform and simply used the opinions of the Lancashire operatives as an excuse for doing nothing. However, I will not pursue this question further. Instead, the main perspective in this section will be on the stubborn defence which was

---

109 Ibid., Vol I, pp. 3, 8, 13-14.
110 Ibid., p. 10. However, the continued support for the half-time system on the part of the Yorkshire worsted masters was also mentioned. See ibid., pp. 10-11; and also Textile Recorder, April 1908, p. 370; April 1909, p. 385; and Textile Manufacturer, March 1907. I have not searched actively for the position of the jute manufacturers on this issue, but the evidence of the Dundee mill-owner J. H. Walker in 1892 indicates that these manufacturers also defended the half-time system. PP 1892 XXXV, Royal Commission on Labour, p. 451 Q. 10,862-63.
111 PP 1909 XVII, Report..., Vol I, p. 11.
112 Ibid., Vol II, evidence of Mary Paterson, lady Factory Inspector, p. 50 Q. 1,354-55, 1,360.
113 Cotton Factory Times 26/2/09.

put up by the Lancashire operatives in support for the retention of the half-time system.

Historians who have dealt with the Lancashire cotton operatives and the half-time question have generally seen it in terms of ideological and political backwardness. Clive Griggs states that it was "disheartening and embarrassing" for the T.U.C. to find defenders of child labour within their own ranks.[114] Indeed, this was probably the general opinion of the labour movement of the day, since the Lancashire operatives' resistance to change was an effective check on further educational reform. It was also the opinion of the International Textile Workers, who in 1914 severely censored the Lancashire section for their continued support for child labour.[115] But this does not mean that "backwardness" is the best historical explanation of the phenomenon. In this section, I will try to describe and explain more fully the reasons for the conflicting attitudes on the half-time system between the Lancashire operatives and the rest of the English labour movement.

As I have shown earlier, the child labour question had aroused much heated sentiments at T.U.C. congresses from 1897 onwards. Around 1908 the cotton union officials changed their position and were now coming round to endorse the T.U.C. view that the half-time system should be abolished. David Shackleton, an M.P. and a top official of the Weavers' Amalgamation, held meetings together with the educationalist Sir John Gorst in favour of the abolition of child labour. Stating that all other trade unions wanted an end to the half-time system, Shackleton claimed that the Lancashire operatives could no longer be a "brake in the wheel of progress".[116] In 1909 he reminded a Nelson audience that the T.U.C. and the Labour Party were solidly against the half-time system, and that the cotton unions were now its only supporters.[117] The secretary of the Nelson Weavers' also agitated openly against the half-time system.[118]

They do not seem to have been unrepresentative for the cotton union officials. An annual meeting in 1908 of the United Textile Factory Workers' Association (UTFWA), a body consisting of delegates from all cotton unions, voted a clear 186 to 27 in favour of the abolition of child labour in

---

114 Griggs (1983), p. 40. While considering the half-time as a "great blot" on the cotton industry, Alan Fowler has recently indicated that the operatives themselves saw it mainly in terms of family economy. Fowler, A (1987a): War and Labour Unrest, p. 163.

115 Cotton Factory Times 19/6/14. Already in 1908, the Lancashire cotton unions had been criticized by their German counterpart for their "reactionary" position on the question of factory child labour. See Cotton Factory Times 19/6/08.

116 Cotton Factory Times 16/10/08.

117 Cotton Factory Times 30/7/09.

118 Cotton Factory Times 18/9/08. Nelson was something of a special case in the sense that it was a stronghold of the Independent Labour Party, which agitated strongly against the half-time system.

factories.[119] The result was later forwarded to the 1909 Parliamentary Committee as a proof that the opinion among Lancashire operatives on educational reform had changed.[120]

In order to substantiate this claim, the UTFWA organized a ballot among all Lancashire textile factory workers on the raising of the age of half-timers from 12 to 13 years. However, there was some early premonition that rank-and-file opinion was against any change in the minimum factory age. The result of previous inquiries into the opinion of the local associations had prompted some of the union officials, like William Marsland of the Spinners' Amalgamation, to defend the existing half-time system before the Parliamentary Committee.[121]

The Cotton Factory Times stated that the writings of "outsiders" on the working conditions of children in the cotton industry had been "amusingly exaggerated", and that their existence was much preferable to that of street children, whose numbers would swell if the factory age was raised. But the paper also defended the UTFWA executive in saying that their stance against the half-time system was taken in a genuine belief that this was in the best interest of their members.[122]

The result of the ballot was a resounding setback for the union officials who favoured a change. The operatives voted solidly against the raise of the minimum age for half-timers. Of the 196,887 operatives voting, 76.7 per cent were against any change of the half-time system, 6.0 per cent were neutral, and only 17.3 per cent advocated the raising of the age to 13.[123]

This occasioned a new wave of criticism from reformers of the "heartlessness" of the Lancashire operatives, but the Cotton Factory Times stubbornly disavowed the opinions of "outsiders" without real knowledge of the half-time system, and claimed that the people whose children were affected were the ones most entitled to consideration.[124] As I have indicated earlier, the result of the ballot also became an excuse for the government not to go ahead with educational reform. In February 1909, a Labour deputation to Asquith on this subject was told that the present feeling among the Lancashire operatives made it impossible to raise the school-leaving age.[125]

119 Cotton Factory Times 7/8/08.
120 PP 1909 XVII, Report..., Vol II, evidence of D. Shackleton, Weavers' Amalgamation, pp. 57-58 Q. 1,577, 1,583. Shackleton advocated the abolition of half-time work under 13. Ibid., p. 59 Q. 1,607.
121 Cotton Factory Times 27/11/08. 20 out of 29 local spinners' meetings had voted for the retention of the half-time system. PP 1909 XVII, Report..., Vol II, evidence of W. Marsland, Spinners' Amalgamation, p. 126 Q. 3,589.
122 Cotton Factory Times 27/11/08; 4/12/08.
123 UTFWA (1909): Analysis of Voting on Age of Half-timers, passim. It should be noted that the vote was not even on the full abolition of the half-time system, but merely on the raising of the minimum age to 13.
124 Cotton Factory Times 12/2/09; 26/2/09.
125 Cotton Factory Times 26/2/09. The same situation was repeated two years later. See Cotton Factory Times 24/2/11.

Naturally, the ballot also placed the cotton union officials in a very awkward position. While being personally against the half-time system, they were now under an obligation to represent the views of their members. At the same time, the stance of the Lancashire operatives was disparaged by all other parts of the labour movement. At the 1909 annual meeting of the UTFWA, the secretary Joseph Cross described the outcome of the ballot as "a great surprise", and continued:

> That the system had a deep and strong hold on the textile workers it was useless to deny, and the reason was difficult to explain. The present situation is rather embarrassing and very discouraging, as it shows that the textile workers still favour the system of child labour in the cotton trade. [126]

But, he went on, the question had now become one of national concern, and general public opinion was clearly against the half-time system. On all sides, the continued use of child labour was criticized and condemned. A resolution was carried "respectfully appealing" to the parents to stop sending their children half-time, and urging the Amalgamations to take the initiative and "educate" their members in favour of a minimum age of 13.[127]

However, the UTFWA campaign against the half-time system fizzled out after a few meetings. Most of the officials seem to have held the view that they were bound to respect the opinion of their members. At the 1909 T.U.C. congress, the cotton unions' votes against the abolition of child labour were greeted with cries of "shame!".[128]

Hoping that the opinions among the operatives had changed, the UTFWA decided to take a new ballot in 1911.[129] However, the result was largely the same: 116,573 operatives, or 79.6 per cent, voted for the retention of the half-time system, while 29,933, or 20.4 per cent, voted for a raise in the minimum age to 13.[130] Moreover, the result did not include the Burnley and Clayton districts, and especially the former was expected to be strongly in favour of the existing half-time system.[131]

The UTFWA had again failed to get the membership to endorse the abolition of the half-time system. On the other hand, the cotton unions were urged by the labour movement to give a lead and educate their members. A third ballot was decided upon in 1914, but it seems to have been aborted by the outbreak of the First World War.[132]

---

126 Cotton Factory Times 6/8/09.
127 Cotton Factory Times 6/8/09.
128 Cotton Factory Times 17/9/09.
129 Cotton Factory Times 1/9/11; 17/11/11.
130 Cotton Factory Times 23/2/12. The paper believed that more ballots on this issue would be futile for many years to come.
131 Cotton Factory Times 23/2/12.
132 Cotton Factory Times 31/7/14.

In the end, the half-time system was finally abolished by an Education Act in 1917 as a part of Lloyd George's programme of "a land fit for heroes" for post-war Britain. While the cotton union officials were in favour of raising the school leaving age, the Lancashire operatives seem to have been recalcitrant to the very end.[133] A special ballot was called in 1918 over the proposed Education Bill, and the union members were asked to give it their consent. On the ballot forms it was expressly stated that the UTFWA was in favour of the reform, and that it was hoped that the ballot would express the determination of the Lancashire operatives to improve the educational opportunities for working-class children by voting for the abolition of the half-time system and a minimum age of 14.[134] Again their pleas were unanswered. Of the 141,424 weavers, mule-spinners, and twisters & drawers who expressed any opinion, 68.7 per cent voted against the proposed educational reform.[135] The Spinners' Amalgamation noted the result, but added that "this expression of opinion has but little influence on those responsible for the proposal".[136] Indeed, the Lancashire cotton workers' defence of the half-time system was no longer given much heed by the political actors.

Nevertheless, the Lancashire cotton operatives' stubborn defence of child labour in factories was in many senses remarkable. The pressure from the T.U.C., the Labour Party, and even from their own union officials, does not seem to have had any major effect.

It is not altogether easy to reconstruct the reasons why the operatives defended the use of child labour. The main sources are of trade union origin, and the officials were after 1908 more keen to argue against the system than try to understand the operatives' rationale for adhering to it. Typically, Joseph Cross of the UTFWA found the members' support for factory child labour embarrassing and difficult to explain.[137] This is also an attitude which has been adopted by later historians.[138]

One exception is Joseph White, who has tried to salvage the reputation of the Lancashire operatives by arguing that they were not altogether alone in their defence of the half-time system. The senior factory inspector in charge of the Lancashire district saw little reason to abolish child labour in cotton factories. Before the 1902 Committee, Superintending Inspector

---

133 PP 1917-18 XI, Final Report of the Departmental Committee on Juvenile Employment after the War, Vol II, evidence of J. Cross and W. Marsland, pp. 37-38. See also Cotton Factory Times 22/9/16, where it is claimed that nearly all union officials were in favour of abolition, but the majority of operatives were against it.

134 LRO Preston, Weavers' Amalgamation Collection, DDX 1123/6/2/98, Half-time Ballot 1918, ballot forms.

135 Weavers' Amalgamation Collection, Half->time Ballot 1918, manuscript returns.

136 A.A.O.C.S., Quarterly Report 31/4/18, p. 5.

137 Cotton Factory Times 6/8/09.

138 Griggs (1983), pp. 40, 43, 47; Frow and Frow (1970), p. 57; Bullen and Fowler (1986), p. 125.

Richmond claimed that this type of regulated child labour was a good introduction to mill work, and that half-timers generally were quick and intelligent children.[139] The Bolton factory inspector also reported in 1900 that a raising of the minimum age to twelve would only increase the number of street-selling children in the district. In Wigan, where only 214 half-timers were employed, "children from 11 to 13 years of age are in abundance in the streets begging, selling papers, matches &c.".[140]

Inspectors Richmond and Tinker were clearly worried that the street, not the school, would take over the children made redundant by more restrictive Factory Acts. Even if this shows that the inspectorate were divided on this issue, it was probably the case that Richmond and Tinker represented a minority. Most factory inspectors seem to have anticipated and welcomed the decline of the half-time system.[141] There is therefore not much reason to emphasize the support from the inspectorate for the half-time system. It is far more constructive to view it in terms of the work, family patterns, and culture of the operatives themselves.

One important difficulty when trying to reconstruct the workers' perception of child labour is the scant and misleading character of the public discourse on the issue. The voices of the operatives themselves are seldom to be found. In the debate between reformers and cotton union officials before 1908, the latter mainly resorted to the defensive line of stressing the necessity of the earnings of half-timers for the sustenance of poor families.[142] This is hardly a valid explanation of the wide support for factory child labour in Lancashire. Poverty existed in all manufacturing areas in Britain, but child labour was almost exclusively used in the textile trades.

It is also very doubtful if the majority of half-timers came from poor families. In his investigation of the system in 1907, Sandiford estimated that 75 per cent of the cases of school exemption were not based on poverty pleas.[143] The critics of the half-time system repeatedly stated that the practice was based on custom, not on poverty.[144] In the opinion of Factory

---

139 White (1978), pp. 58-59; PP 1902 XXV, Minutes..., evidence of Superintending Inspector Richmond, p. 6 Q. 165-74, 181, 194.
140 PP 1900 XI, RCIFW, p. 71.
141 See PP 1902 XXV, Minutes..., evidence of Lady Inspector Anderson, pp. 236-37 Q. 9,883, 9,887, 9,895, 9,906; PP 1909 XVII, Report..., Vol II, evidence of Factory Inspector Crabtree, p. 44 Q. 1,147; Ibid., evidence of Lady Inspector Paterson, p. 49 Q. 1,329-30.
142 See, for instance, the evidence of David Holmes, Burnley Weavers', in PP 1892 XXXV, Royal Commission on Labour, p. 37 Q. 959.
143 Sandiford, P (1907): The Half-time System in the Textile Trades, p. 344. The 1909 Committee found that there was, if anything, rather an inverse relationship between child labour and poverty. PP 1909 XVII, Report..., Vol I, p. 12. See also Factory Inspector Crabtree's demolition of the poverty argument in PP 1901 X, RCIFW, pp. 312-13.
144 See PP 1909 XVII, Report..., Vol II, evidence of R. Waddington, p. 2 Q. 9; Ibid., evidence of A. R. Pickle, Burnley teacher, p. 19 Q. 450; Ibid., evidence of H. Whittick, teacher, p. 23 Q. 562; Ibid., evidence of Lady Factory Inspector Paterson, p. 49 Q. 1,324.

Inspector Crabtree, who had himself worked in an Oldham spinning mill as a child, the large majority of parents who sent their children half-time did so because it had been customary since "their Grandfather's days".[145]

However, it has to be discussed what formed the basis for this custom. In this context, it is necessary to refer to some fundamental characteristics of the organization of production and reproduction, and see them as a background to the development of a special culture or ideology of work and the family.

## Working-Class Culture and the Organization of Production

The most important characteristic in this context was the subcontracting relationship between the adult operative and the half-timer.[146] Subcontracting existed in all labour processes where children were employed, with the sole exception of ring-spinning. As I have shown in the previous chapter, the subcontracting relationships which were embedded in the minder-piecer system and the use of tenters in weaving continued to dominate the Lancashire cotton industry. Similarly, the drawers undoubtedly subcontracted half-time "reachers-in" because they wanted cheap assistant labour.[147] In contrast, where children were employed directly by the manufacturer, the latter also seems to have been the main defender of the half-time system. Such was the case in cotton ring-spinning as well as in worsted and jute.

Some contemporary reformers, like the teacher Richard Waddington and the Bolton journalist Allen Clarke, did emphasize that the operatives had vested interests in getting their subcontracted assistants as cheaply as possible.[148] However, these observers slightly missed the point. The real issue for the minders was not to get piecers at a very low price. Indeed, after at least 1880 they seem to have preferred full-timers if only they could find them. Their main interest in this matter was to have an alternative source of

---

145 PP 1901 X, RCIFW, pp. 312-13.

146 Surprisingly, only H. A. Turner has stressed the link between the subcontracting relationship and the continued support for the half-time system among the Lancashire operatives. See Turner (1962), p. 257.

147 See PP 1909 XVII, Report..., Vol II, evidence of W. C. Robinson, Association of Beamers, Twisters, and Drawers, p. 132 Q. 3,804. The drawers by that time wanted the employers to take over the responsibility for the employment of the young workers, since the scarcity of that type of labour had driven up their wage demands. Ibid., p. 133 Q. 3,858.

148 Clarke [1899], pp. 78, 98-99; PP 1892 XXXV, Royal Commission on Labour, evidence of R. Waddington, p. 147 Q. 3,749-50; PP 1902 XXV, Minutes..., evidence of Superintending Inspector Richmond, p. 6 Q. 175; PP 1909 XVII, Report..., Vol II, evidence of Waddington, p. 4 Q. 846-86; Ibid., Vol I, p. 12. This argument has been taken up by Frow and Frow (1970), p. 26.

labour which they could tap if recruitment proved difficult. The subcontracting of children as a form of cheap labour is probably a more correct description in the cases of weaving and drawing.

It also has to be recognized that the operatives were providers of child labour as well as subcontractors. Up to at least 1900, the minders very generally employed their own sons as piecers. In weaving, I would argue that a major force behind the half-time system was the cultural expectation on girls to go to work early and contribute to the family economy. The Lancashire operatives' continued support for the use of child labour must be analyzed on the level of culture, in terms of the prevailing conceptions of work and family.

At the same time, this culture was heavily influenced by a long tradition of subcontracting of child labour. As I have shown in earlier sections, subcontracting had existed in mule-spinning since the end of the 18th century, and in weaving at least since 1850. In the second half of the 19th century, the practice of subcontracting was incorporated in and buttressed by the structure of industrial bargaining which dominated the cotton trade.

The subcontracting relation implied a large measure of control on the part of the adult operatives over the use of child labour, which meant that half-timers could not be used as a means by employers to depress wages and undermine the bargaining position of the adult workers. This was an important precondition for the integration of child labour in the operatives' cultural perception of work. The result was that the support for the half-time system spilled over from the operatives engaged in subcontracting children and became a part of a general culture of work and family among all cotton factory workers. The dominating perception was that children should start mill work early in order to contribute to the family economy and to be lined up for promotions to better positions in the factory.

There is some quantitative evidence which substantiates the claim that the support for the half-time system among the operatives was on a cultural level rather than an immediate effect of the subcontracting system. The UTFWA ballots on child labour in 1908 and 1918 have left a quantitative material which gives several important clues. If the ballot result is grouped according to occupation, the following pattern emerges:

Table 8.  Half-time ballots 1908 and 1918. Proportion of individual union votes against raising the age of half-timers. [149]

| Union | 1908 | N | 1918 | N |
|---|---|---|---|---|
| Spinners | 82.9 | 18,462 | 60.8 | 11,886 |
| Weavers | 81.4 | 120,482 | 69.7 | 126,678 |
| Drawers | 84.1 | 3,946 | 58.5 | 2,860 |
| Cardroom op. | 83.0 | 35,124 | - | - |

Sources: UTFWA (1909): Analysis of Voting on Age of Half-timers; LRO Preston, Weavers' Amalgamation Collection, DDX 1123/6/2/98, Half-time Ballot 1918, manuscript returns.

The voting pattern of the UTFWA ballots shows that the support for the continuation of factory child labour had a broader base than simply the operatives who were actively taking part in the subcontracting relationship. Very few children were employed in the card- and blowing room operations. As far as I have been able to ascertain, the practice among female frame tenters in the cardroom to subcontract back-tenters was relatively weak.[150] Yet, the ballot result shows that the members of the Cardroom Amalgamation were equally strong in their support for the half-time system in the 1908 ballot as the minders and weavers.

Another illustration of the importance of culture is the geographical distribution of the votes. It is possible to see in the ballot material that the support among the operatives for the half-time system was weaker in areas where the system itself was less dominant, which is perhaps only to be expected. In 1908, the only local union which recorded a majority vote against the half-time system was the weavers in Manchester, where the custom of factory child labour had been very weak for decades.[151] A more interesting pattern which emerges is a stronger child labour culture in the North compared to the south part of the cotton district, a difference which cuts across occupational lines. This is indicated by the geographical distribution of the negative votes among the spinners:

149 Only votes for or against have been considered. It is not possible to estimate the number of neutral votes or abstentions, since such figures were only provided by a few of the local unions. It is therefore possible that these figures do not show a growing disinclination towards the half-time system as mirrored in an increased number of abstentions. On the other hand, the turnout in 1918 is not drastically below that of 1908, at least not in the Weavers' Amalgamation.
150 North and North-East Cotton Spinners' and Manufacturers' Association Minutes, 16/7/06, indicates that creelers and back-tenters in the carding rooms were generally not subcontracted.
151 UTFWA (1909): Analysis of Voting...

Table 9. Proportion of votes against the raising of the age of half-timers recorded in the Spinners' Amalgamation, 1908 and 1918. per cent.

| District | 1908 | N | 1918 | N |
|---|---|---|---|---|
| The North-East* | 86.3 | 1,044 | 76.7 | 438 |
| Preston | 75.4 | 678 | 49.1 | 161 |
| Bolton | 80.5 | 4,641 | 55.4 | 3,830 |
| Oldham | 84.0 | 7,368 | 65.6 | 4,827 |
| The South** | 83.1 | 2,214 | 53.3 | 1,265 |

\* Blackburn and Burnley.
\*\* Stalybridge, Ashton, Mossley, and Stockport.

Sources: See table 8.

The support for the half-time system was strongest in the North-East, where the actual use of child piecers was relatively modest. The mules in this district were generally shorter than in the South, and were often worked solely by a minder and a big piecer or two joiner-minders.[152] As I have indicated in a previous chapter, a combination of industrial stagnation, relatively weak union authority, shorter mules, and a greater prevalence of joiner-minding, had all tended to make the half-time piecer relatively unimportant in the North-East. It is also noteworthy that the decline of support over the decade between 1908 and 1918 was considerably less in the North-East than in any other spinning district.

The figures for Bolton and Oldham, where the half-time system in mule-spinning was stronger, show a consistent support for the continuation of child labour, but a more substantial reduction in the later ballot. In the southern district, where the actual use of half-time piecers was relatively modest, the defenders of the status quo nearly saw their majority disappear in 1918 after a reduction of almost 30 per cent.

One possible explanation of the overall pattern is that culture and actual strength of the half-time system in the spinning process were both highly relevant factors. The long tradition of factory child labour and subcontracting in the cotton industry had created a cultural perception that it was normal and desirable that children should be sent to the mill already as half-timers. However, that cultural perception crumbled much faster in the South, where the actual use of factory children was relatively low in spinning as well as in weaving.

---

152 See Smith (1954), p. 714.

A similar pattern emerges when looking at the ballot results of the Cardroom Amalgamation in 1908 and the Association of Beamers, Twisters and Drawers on both occasions. The districts in the North-East consistently show a higher degree of support for the half-time system than other areas.[153] What has to be considered, therefore, is an explanation as to why the "child labour culture" was stronger in the North-East. One key element, I believe, was the importance of the half-time system in the weaving industry in those districts. As can easily be shown, the defence for the use of child tenters was strong among the northern weavers:

Table 10.   Proportion of votes against the raising of the age for half-timers recorded in the Weavers' Amalgamation, 1908 and 1918.

| District | 1908 | N | 1918 | N |
|---|---|---|---|---|
| The North: | | | | |
| Burnley | 85.2 | 15,752 | 83.0 | 19,493 |
| Blackburn | 79.9 | 15,409 | 67.5 | 15,790 |
| Bacup | 93.0 | 1,393 | 77.6 | 651 |
| Clitheroe | 73.6 | 2,174 | 60.8 | 1,745 |
| Colne | 76.3 | 4,237 | 70.0 | 5,295 |
| Rossendale | 90.8 | 2,447 | 84.5 | 1,964 |
| Darwen | 88.3 | 6,754 | 78.3 | 6,849 |
| Nelson | 69.6 | 10,080 | 59.7 | 10,981 |
| Preston | 81.6 | 5,098 | 54.8 | 6,394 |
| The South: | | | | |
| Ashton | 78.9 | 3,899 | 50.1 | 3,716 |
| Hyde/Hadfield | 78.3 | 5,588 | 42.8 | 5,042 |
| Glossop | 66.7 | 790 | 66.7 | 1,155 |
| Bolton | 87.5 | 4,828 | 63.8 | 5,476 |
| Manchester | 27.5 | 171 | - | - |

Sources: See Table 8.

Naturally, several processes may have had an impact on the voting result. The relatively low poll in favour of the half-time system in Clitheroe and Nelson could be at least partly ascribed to specific political reasons. Nelson was a stronghold of the Independent Labour Party, and the M.P. for Clitheroe was David Shackleton, the official of the Weavers' Amalgamation who had campaigned strongly in favour of a raise of the factory age. However, the main impression is that there was a much stronger "child labour culture" in the North-East compared to the South. The level of votes

---

153 UTFWA (1909): Analysis of Voting...; Weavers' Amalgamation Collection. Half-time ballot 1918, manuscript returns.

in favour of the half-time system was consistently higher in the North-East, and the decline of support between the two ballots was much more perceptible in the South.

Burnley seems to have been a remarkable case, with the votes against the abolition of the half-time system remaining on a consistently high level. As I have shown in earlier chapters, the custom of using child tenters was uncommonly strong in Burnley. Relatively strong unions, an adherence to the traditional organization of work, and a very limited introduction of automatic looms in the North-East, were all important factors in this development. In Preston, it is interesting to note that the support for the half-time system eroded relatively quickly both among the spinners and the weavers. This could possibly be connected with a relatively low degree of authority over the recruitment of piecers and tenters in Preston compared to other areas.[154] In the South, it is notable that the Hyde district, which contained the greater part of the automatic looms in Lancashire, swung round strongly and voted for a raising of the age in 1918. Where the actual practice of using child tenters was relatively weak, the cultural support for the half-time system seems to have eroded more quickly.

My suggestion is that the more substantial half-time culture in the North-East had its foundations in the ability of the tenter-system in those districts to tie together the organization of work and the requirements of the family in a strong and well-functioning way.

The dominating cultural expectation on young girls was that they should go tenting as early as possible and contribute to the family economy. Such a perception of childhood actually rested on three different preconditions: first, the prevailing opinion that children should be "useful" as early as possible; second, that schooling was held to be relatively unimportant[155]; and third, that the mill career was the natural and unchallenged option for the children. These preconditions were well met by the young girls in the north-east weaving districts. Education was commonly regarded to be less necessary for girls. It was more important to send them tenting as early as possible in order to have them quickly promoted to weaving. The tenter-

154 The Preston spinners, who had strongly opposed the raising of the age for half-timers in 1891, and had voted 511 to 167 against it in 1908, dramatically changed position and voted with a majority for reform both in 1911 and in 1918. Joseph White believes that this was caused by having a union offical who was in favour of reform, but he does not consider that this was the case in most local unions at the time. A more interesting angle is the simultaneous shift among the Preston weavers, which indicates a more general change away from the previously dominant "child labour culture". See Preston Spinners' Minutes, 17/3/91; 2/4/91; 2/5/95; 3/5/95; UTFWA (1909); Weavers' Amalgamation Collection, Half-time Ballot 1918, manuscript return; White (1978), p. 61.

155 According to an investigation in 1904, the attaining of school levels was normally not a requirement for employment in the Lancashire cotton factories, and the school record was not considered to have any impact on work performance. Early experience of mill work seems to have been more important than schooling. PP 1904 XIX, Report on the School Training and Early Employment of Lancashire Children, pp. 29-30.

system therefore met the requirements of the family and gender patterns in the local working-class culture.

This was less the case in mule-spinning. The increasingly bad prospects of promotion for piecers after 1900 made this trade a less obvious option for sons of minders and other relatively high status factory operatives. The half-time system in mule-spinning became increasingly reliant on the recruitment of children of casual labourers and other "lower" segments of the working class. These latter families had low expectations of future work prospects for their children and were more interested in the relatively high juvenile wages which piecers could demand. In this sense, the half-time system in mule-spinning was held together by the family wage strategies of the unskilled workers. In comparison with weaving, the use of child labour in mule-spinning did not blend the requirements of work and the family pattern of the factory operatives. However, it should also be remembered that half-time piecers were more of a last resort than a positive choice. There can be no doubt that the design of the tenter-system was more amenable to the use of children. The conclusion must be that the "half-time culture" was the result of both work, family, and gender.

In this context, the question should also be asked how the children themselves responded to the cultural expectations of being young wage-earners. Were they, as the contemporary critic Allen Clarke believed, at the mercy of parents who only regarded their children as commercial speculations who were to be turned into wage-earning machines as early as possible?[156] Naturally, it is very difficult to reconstruct the children's reactions to the prospect of starting work at the mill. It is nevertheless probable that when the half-time culture was flourishing, most children welcomed their entry into the world of work and their being able to contribute to the family economy. Going half-time and earning wages meant being treated less like a child and more like a young adult, while at the same time it provided them with some pocket money for their own use. Going to work meant leaving the total dependency of childhood, and served as an initiation to the adult world.[157]

Teachers readily perceived this change, and complained about it in no uncertain terms. The half-timers, they asserted, soon assumed adult manners like smoking and swearing, and became loud-voiced and undisciplined. Girls soon lost their "delicacy and reserve".[158] Of course, their concerns were those of middle-class observers. What really should be noted is the separation of the half-timer from the world of childhood.

---

156 Clarke [1899], op cit p. 105.
157 Sandiford (1907), pp. 338-39.
158 Ibid., p. 334; PP 1909 XVII, Report..., Vol II, evidence of R. Waddington, p. 1 Q. 3-4.

However, the actual work experience of young half-timers should not be painted in too bright colours. From the oral material collected by Elizabeth Roberts it emerges that most of the women had bad memories of their early tenting experiences. Several of them complained of harsh treatment from adult weavers and overlookers.[159] It is also probable that as the specific Lancashire factory culture slowly eroded, children were becoming less keen to go early to the mills.[160] Sending children half-time was increasingly seen as a sign of backwardness or low class.

The half-time culture was really a phenomenon among the textile factory workers and did not include other industrial trades. The local trades' councils in Lancashire often issued resolutions against the half-time system, and criticized the cotton unions for their support of child labour. In 1908 the trades' councils in Oldham, Burnley, Rochdale, Stockport, Accrington, and Leigh issued resolutions in favour of the raising of the factory age to 13. The year after, the Burnley trades' council voted for a minimum age of 14.[161] This shows that even in the areas where the half-time culture was strong, the workers in other industrial trades did not support it. The use of child labour was a part of the work culture in the cotton factories, not a more general phenomenon.

This brings us back to a re-examination of the child labour controversy within the English labour movement. The last problem to be addressed in this chapter is the contrast in the perception of child labour between the "factory foaks" in Lancashire and the other members of the T.U.C. My suggestion is that there was a definite difference of work ideology between the cotton operatives and workers in other trades. In Lancashire, the perception of work remained centered on the family wage and the contribution of all its members. Among workers in other industrial trades, the dominating ideology was that of the male breadwinner, and sending children half-time was not compatible with notions of "respectability".

Among the Lancashire cotton operatives the perception of respectability was not, or only very slowly, connected with the child labour issue. But they obviously constituted something of an exception. The perspective of the breadwinner wage became increasingly dominant during the nineteenth century in other sections of the working class, and also became a keystone in T.U.C. policy. This major difference in the perception of work and family was the essential background to the persistent quarrels between the Lancashire operatives and the T.U.C. at the turn of the century.

---

159 NWOHP, evidence of Mrs B1, Lancaster, Mrs B1, Preston, and Mrs H2, Preston.
160 Mrs C5 and Mrs H7, Preston, who were both sent to the factory at 14 in the early 1930s, really did not want to go. NWOHP.
161 Cotton Factory Times 5/5/08; 30/4/09.

# Family Wage versus Male Breadwinner Ideology

In most industrial trades in Britain during the second half of the 19th century, calls for factory legislation on woman and child labour constituted one way for male operatives and their unions to curtail the possibility of competition from cheaper forms of labour. Outside the textile trades, the use of child labour was generally abandoned by the employers when the industry came under the Factory Acts.[162] A regular half-time system only emerged in the cotton, worsted, and jute factories.

Moreover, in other industrial trades the processes connected with factory legislation were compounded by a trade union strategy to limit the recruitment of women and juveniles.[163] The ideology which epitomized this perception of work and family was the notion of a male breadwinner.[164] This ideology became dominant in all trades where men were substantially employed, with one single exception. That exception was the Lancashire cotton industry.

Several historical and structural reasons may be given as an explanation for the specific development in Lancashire. Factory legislation was implemented very early in the cotton industry. Already in 1834 the working day of children and juveniles was limited by law, and in 1844 adult women were added to the list of "protected persons". This happened before the male breadwinner ideology could be said to dominate the trade union movement. Indeed, it is arguable whether anything like a trade union movement existed at that time. Consequently, the very early timing of restrictive legislation should be given some importance.

Moreover, in the organization of work after 1844 women, juveniles, and children continued to play vital parts. In the case of the latter, the important connection with the subcontracting system of employment has already been pointed out. As for women workers, one of the most marked characteristics of the Lancashire cotton industry was the extreme degree of segmentation according to gender which existed between the different occupations.[165] Overlookers, mule-spinners, blowing-room operatives, mill engineers, and strippers-and-grinders were always males. In contrast, frame tenters in the carding room, winders, and ring-spinners were always females. The only important exception to the rule was in powerloom

---

162 PP 1868-69 XIV, RIF, 1st Half-yearly Rep. 1869, p. 36.
163 Webb and Webb (1897), pp. 482-83, 487.
164 Davin (1982), passim; Humphries, J (1979): Class Struggle and the Persistence of the Working-Class Family, passim; Levine, D (1985): Industrialization and the Proletarian Family in England, pp. 178-81; Seccombe (1986), passim.
165 PP 1892 XXXV, Royal Commission on Labour, evidence of W. Mullin, Cardroom Amalgamation, p 1. Q. 23-4.

weaving, which remained a mixed occupation employing both men and women.[166]

The main picture was one of extreme segmentation. In this context, there were no major threats to the position of the skilled male operatives. Child and juvenile labour was largely controlled in the subcontracting relationship, and women were employed in special occupations which were socially defined as fitting for females. Furthermore, the skilled male operatives like mule-spinners and strippers-and-grinders had considerable strength in the wage bargaining with the employers. In such industrial and social contexts, the foundation and support for a male breadwinner ideology were relatively insubstantial. In one sense, since industrial reforms were still carried out to the sole benefit of the "protected persons", the male operatives actually needed the presence of women and juveniles for the limitation of their legal working day.

The outcome was that the perspective of the family wage continued to dominate among the Lancashire operatives. The ideology of the male breadwinner simply did not fit very well with either work structures, gender roles, or family requirements.[167] This is essentially the reason why the Lancashire operatives continued to defend the practice of factory child labour right up to 1918, to the evident embarrassment of the T.U.C. What happened after 1908 was above all that the cotton union officials shifted positions and adopted the general T.U.C. stance. The notion of a male breadwinner was finally accepted, as can be evidenced by the position of the Cotton Factory Times in 1914:

> All trade unionists believe that a man should receive a wage that would enable him to keep his wife and children in decency without being under the necessity of sending the children to the mill at an immature age to make up the family income. [168]

Commenting later in the same year on a mill strike in Georgia, U.S.A., the paper stated that it was becoming more and more recognized that child labour was "false economy".[169] By 1917 the officials of the Spinners' Amalgamation confidently stated that the improvement of the educational facilities for working-class children had always been "one of the principal objects of labour organizations".[170]

---

166 The Webbs actually used the Lancashire weaving industry as an indication that it was not necessary to exclude women operatives in order to obtain a standard rate of wages. Webb and Webb (1897), p. 507.
167 For an illustration of the cotton union officials' reluctance to embrace the notion of the male breadwinner before 1900, see the evidence of T. Birtwistle, Weavers' Amalgamation, in PP 1892 XXXV, Royal Commission on Labour, pp. 59-60 Q. 1,496-1,512.
168 Cotton Factory Times 1/5/14.
169 Cotton Factory Times 11/9/14.
170 A.A.O.C.S., Quarterly Rep. 31/10/17, p. 3.

This shift in policy was undoubtedly occasioned by the long period of discussion and persuasion which the officials of the cotton unions had spent with the representatives of other trades. But it proved to be a much slower and more difficult process to get the rank-and-file of the cotton operatives to follow the example of their leaders. The rationale for the abolition of the half-time system was framed in the language of another ideology of work, which had only a very limited relevance for the actual labour and family lives of the cotton operatives. There was a clear discrepancy between the opinions of the officials and the social reality of the members. David Shackleton, President of the Weavers' Amalgamation and a leading abolitionist, publicly embraced the tenets of the male breadwinner and the woman's role in the domestic sphere, while at the same time representing a union whose majority consisted of women workers.[171]

This may serve to illustrate as to why the union leaders found it so hard to "educate" the rank-and-file. The popular base of the breadwinner ideology in the cotton industry was probably very narrow. Only those who were committed to the ideals of the labour movement or were convinced of the long term good of the extension of elementary education were inclined to support the abolition of the half-time system. Such sentiments dominated among the union officials, but were evidently less prominent among the members. Among the Lancashire operatives, the perception of the child as a young wage-earner remained dominant. Even though the half-time system was finally abolished with relatively little friction in 1920, the inordinate demand for young juvenile labour remained a feature of the Lancashire cotton industry well into the 30s. The persistent structures of work and family made the changes in ideology and culture remarkably slow.[172]

# Conclusions

In spite of the agitation of educationalists and the T.U.C., and the increasingly tighter regulation of industrial child labour, the half-time system in the Lancashire cotton industry proved to be remarkably resilient. The cotton union officials changed their opinion on these matters around 1908,

---

171 Indeed, part of the union strategy connected with the implementation of the automatic Northrop loom was to make weaving relatively highly paid work, thus enabling the male weavers to take over and establish the breadwinner position in their trade. See Fowler (1979-80), passim.

172 PP 1922 VII, RCIFW, p. 85; PP 1923 XI, RCIFW, p. 50. The labour process in mule-spinning was not reorganized until the late 1930s, and was until then dependent on the "closed alley" employment of young juvenile piecers. In their investigation of the cotton industry in 1935, Jewkes and Gray indicated that the only solution of the problem was to increase the proportion of joiner-minders and to reorganize the work along American lines. Jewkes and Gray (1935), pp. 179-81, 185-87.

but the members remained in favour of the retention of industrial child labour up to its final abolition in 1920.

The reasons for this are to be found in work structures, family patterns, and the local working-class culture. In mule-spinning, half-time piecers continued to be recruited in times of scarcity of juvenile workers, a condition which became chronic after 1900. The structural imbalance of the minder-piecer system, which meant that very few piecers could actually be promoted to minders, was making recruitment of young workers difficult. As a result, half-time piecers continued to be used, in spite of the fact that the work requirements actually favoured older operatives.

The labour scarcity was in a way created by a union policy of excluding women and girls from the mule-spinning rooms. If the mule-spinners' unions had accepted the recruitment of young women as assistants, the piecer scarcity would probably not have occurred.

The half-time system remained even stronger in the weaving side of the industry. The use of child tenters continued to dominate the trade, above all in the districts in the North-East. Relatively strong unions, a scarcity of weaving operatives, and the virtual non-existence of automatic looms and American methods in these districts were all important factors in this development. In the southern part of the cotton district, the half-time system in weaving eroded much faster than in the North-East.

The subcontracting of tenters in weaving constituted an important link between work and family. Daughters or younger sisters were brought early into the mills as tenters. But it should also be seen in the perspective of gender. Tenters were predominantly girls, while apprenticeship and a longer education were generally reserved for the boys. Girls were supposed to contribute to the family economy until they got married and formed a household of their own. The tenter-system in weaving fitted very well with this family pattern.

The long tradition of subcontracting of young operatives in the Lancashire cotton industry is a major explanatory factor of the veritable "child labour culture" which remained strong among the operatives well into the 20th century. The notion of a "family wage", where both adults and children contributed as much as possible to the family economy, remained dominant. The "male breadwinner" norm, which was a very important part of T.U.C. policy, did not have any strong backing among the Lancashire cotton operatives. These workers continued to view it as normal and even desirable that children should start working in the mills as early as possible in order to bring home some money and to develop into proficient operatives. In regional terms, the "child labour culture" was strongest in the North-East, where the use of child tenters in weaving was most common.

Chapter 11

# A Different Development: Scotland, 1840-1910

This chapter, in which developments in the Scottish cotton industry after 1840 will be investigated, really has a dual purpose: to describe the organization of production in the Scottish district, but also to present a contrast to the Lancashire industry which will hopefully add to the understanding of the specific developments in that area.

While the chapters on Lancashire have been very much centered on the development and permanence of the half-time system, this chapter will deal with its relative failure in the Scottish cotton district. As I have indicated in an earlier chapter on the implementation of the early factory legislation in Scotland, the use of factory children in Glasgow was discontinued shortly after the passing of the 1833 Factory Act. I will now make an attempt to put this phenomenon in a general context of production methods, managerial strategies, union presence, and the labour market conditions which prevailed in the Scottish district.

One important difficulty in this endeavour has been the relative scarcity of relevant sources as well as secondary literature. Very little has been written on the Scottish cotton industry after 1840. All the main contributors to the history of the cotton industry in Scotland have chosen not to go beyond that year.[1] What remains is a handful of articles touching on the reasons for the decline of the Scottish cotton industry after 1860.[2] However, these contributions generally lack analytical depth. While most historians agree that Lancashire competition was a vital factor behind the decline of the Scottish cotton industry, no attempt has been made to compare the way production was organized in these two areas. It remains to be explained why the Lancashire industry was the more competitive; an undertaking which has not as yet been seriously made by historians. The most recent

---

1 Brassay (1974); Fraser (1976); Butt (1976); Butt (1987); Ward, J T (1987): Textile Trade Unionism in Nineteenth-Century Scotland.
2 Mitchell, G M (1922): The English and Scottish Cotton Industries. A Study in Interrelations; Marwick, W H (1924): The Cotton Industry and the Industrial Revolution in Scotland; Hamilton, H (1932): The Industrial Revolution in Scotland; Henderson, W O (1951): The Cotton Famine in Scotland and the Relief of Distress, 1862-1864; Campbell, R H (1967): The Industrial Revolution. A Revision Article; Robertson, A J (1970): The Decline of the Scottish Cotton Industry 1860-1914.

contributors tend to favour the view that the Scottish decline was due to "entrepreneurial failure" and lethargic management, an explanation which is hardly satisfactory.[3]

The approach in this chapter will be entirely different. An attempt will be made to reconstruct the organization of production and the nature of industrial relations which dominated in the Scottish cotton district after 1840, and compare these structures with those prevailing in Lancashire. The differences in the organization of work and in union authority found in the Scottish district will then be used to explain why the half-time system for child workers never really developed north of the Border.

As I have shown in an earlier chapter, in 1836 the cotton manufacturers in the Glasgow district drastically reduced the number of children below 13 in their mills. This seems to have been a concerted response to the announcement in Parliament that the education clauses of the Factory Act would be stringently enforced. The manufacturers simply prohibited the operative spinners to hire children below 13 years of age as piecers.[4] The level of child labour in the Glasgow cotton factories was immediately reduced to a mere fraction.

There were probably several reasons why the Glasgow manufacturers adopted this strategy. They clearly objected to being held responsible for the schooling of their child workers, and to the prospect of being prosecuted for offences against the education clauses. This was the main reason put forward by the mill-owners themselves as to why they were so negative towards the use of half-timers in their factories.[5] The insufficient number of schools in the industrial districts clearly added to this problem.[6] The only Glasgow firm which persisted in employing children into the 1860s, Clark's thread factory, ran a school of its own for half-timers.[7]

Still, the reaction of the Glasgow manufacturers seems to have been very drastic. James Stuart, the local factory inspector, claimed that the mill-

---

3 Robertson (1970), passim; Slaven, A (1975): The Development of the West of Scotland 1750-1960, pp. 163-65.
4 See PP 1837-38 VIII, First Report from the Select Committee on the Combinations of Workmen, evidence of James McNish, operative spinner, p. 64 Q. 1,278-80; PP 1839 XIX, RIF, p. 57.
5 See PP 1850 XXIII, RIF, 1st Half-yearly Rep. 1850, pp. 35-36.
6 Studies on Scottish schooling and literacy in the 19th century have emphasized the poor educational facilities in the industrial districts. R. K. Webb has estimated that in 1842 80 per cent of the Glasgow children between 10 and 15 years were unable to write, a subject which was not often taught in the Sunday Schools. Webb, R K (1954): Literacy among the Working Classes in Nineteenth Century Scotland, p. 110. R. D. Anderson has maintained that there was a considerable "educational deficiency" in the Scottish industrial districts up to the Education Act of 1872. Anderson, R D (1983): Education and the State in Nineteenth Century Scotland, passim.
7 PP 1876 XXX, Report of the Commissioners..., Vol II, evidence of Daniel Walker, Assistant Factory Inspector, pp. 927-28 Q. 19,576, 19,587.

owners were a superior class of people who were extremely sensitive to the prospect of being publicly prosecuted for offences against the Factory Act. The children were dismissed in order to minimize this risk.[8] While it should be recognized that Stuart was partial to the mill-owners, his explanation should perhaps not be totally rejected. The other inspectors seem to have agreed with him on this point, concluding at a meeting in 1840 that the differences observed in the Glasgow district were due to the high class of persons running the factories.[9]

However, instead of comparing the manufacturers in terms of moral sensibility, it is perhaps more fruitful to see this phenomenon in the perspective of different ownership structures. The Scottish cotton industry was run much more on a partnership basis than was the case in Lancashire, where owner-managers and family firms were the dominant forms of ownership. The Scottish legal system was at this time more conducive to partnership structures than the English.[10] As a consequence, many members of the Glasgow commercial elite were partners in cotton mills, but without any real managerial functions. Yet, according to the Factory Act, they were legally responsible for the observance of the law in their factories. It is therefore possible that non-managing partners were not keen to allow the employment of children, since even "accidental" transgressions were likely to expose them to prosecution.

Naturally, this is not an exhaustive explanation of the employers' strategy. One important precondition was the relatively large supply of juvenile workers in the Glasgow district. As I have shown in an earlier chapter, the whole problem of recruiting slightly older piecers was transferred to the operative mule-spinners. Child workers could therefore be replaced with juveniles with certificates of being 13 years of age without any problems for the manufacturers. James Stuart claimed in 1839 that this was the situation in all the Scottish industrial cities:

> In my district the Factory owners and occupiers in the large towns, viz. in Glasgow, Paisley, Dundee, Aberdeen and Belfast, have little or no difficulty in procuring a sufficient number of young persons above 13 years of age who are not liable to the educational provisions of the Act; and accordingly they employ so few children..., who alone are liable to those provisions, that no school has been established in consequence of the Act in any town in my district... [11]

---

8 PP 1840 X, Second Report from the Select Committee..., evidence of James Stuart, pp. 77-78 Q. 3420.
9 LAB 15/1. Minutes of the Meetings of the Inspectors of Factories, 3/2/40.
10 Butt (1976), p. 117. See also Mitchell (1925), p. 105.
11 PP 1839 XLII, Return on the Educational Provisions of the Factories Act, p. 63. See also Stuart's report in PP 1845 XXV, 1st Half-yearly Rep. 1845, p. 57; PP 1840 X, Fourth Report from the Select Committee..., evidence of Cunninghame, a Glasgow surgeon, p. 45 Q. 5,767-68; Ibid., evidence of Daniel Walker, Superintendent, p. 15 Q. 5,212-13.

There are also other indications of a large supply of unskilled juveniles in Glasgow. In 1838 it was estimated that 1,305 children of handloom weavers worked as piecers to 950 Glasgow mule-spinners.[12]

The relative stagnation of the Scottish cotton industry during the following decades probably ensured that labour supplies were not much strained. In this context, the eventual decline of Glasgow cotton is not without interest. In the expansive Lancashire districts it is evident that a scarcity of young workers was one tangible reason for the manufacturers to accept the half-time system. The stagnation and decline of the Scottish industry and the relative availability of juvenile labour meant that the manufacturers did not feel any pressure to adapt to the requirements of the half-time system.[13]

The effects of the manufacturers' decision not to employ children were soon observable in the form of a "loitering problem". While remaining a supporter of the mill-owners, James Stuart did not approve of the lack of useful employment for children. Since neither the city nor religious authorities made much effort to send working-class children to school, he maintained that the greater part of them were brought up "in ignorance, loitering about the streets unemployed, and of course contracting vicious habits" [14]

John Kincaid, who succeeded Stuart as factory inspector in 1849, criticized the policies of the Glasgow manufacturers for not leaving children below 13 any better option than the street. In order to solve the loitering problem, Kincaid even suggested that the age limit should be lowered to 11 and combined with a literacy test to make working-class parents more interested in the education of their children.[15] In 1853 Kincaid complained once more of the "disfavour" of half-timers among the Scottish manufacturers, an attitude which he put down to the "imaginary trouble" of the educational clauses of the Factory Act.

During the boom of 1853, Kincaid noted an increased scarcity of cotton operatives in the Glasgow industry, and also a tendency to employ more children. He stated his hopes that more schools would be erected and that

---

12 PP 1837-38 VIII, First Report from the Select Committee..., evidence of A Gemmill, lawyer to the Spinners' Union, p. 215 Q. 2,846. Neil Murray has claimed that even more children of handloom weavers assisted their fathers or worked in casual trades. Murray, N (1978): The Scottish Handloom Weavers 1790-1850: A Social History, p. 200. See also Treble, J H (1979): Urban Poverty in Britain 1830-1914, pp. 66, 87, 97, and Treble, J H (1978): The Market for Unskilled Male Labour in Glasgow, 1891-1914, passim.
13 In a similar way, the textile manufacturers in the relatively unimportant districts of southern England and Ireland also seem to have dismissed their child workers below 13. See PP 1844 XXVIII, RIF, 1st Quart. Rep. 1844, p. 14.
14 PP 1841 X, RIF, 3d Quart. Rep. 1840, p. 12.
15 PP 1850 XXIII, RIF, 1st Half-yearly Rep. 1850, pp. 35-36; PP 1852-53 XL, RIF, 2nd Half-yearly Rep. 1852, pp. 46-47; PP 1857-58 XXIV, RIF, 2nd Half-yearly Rep. 1857, pp. 29.

the half-time system would finally be accepted by the manufacturers.[16] However, a regular half-time system along the Lancashire pattern never developed in Glasgow. Only three years later, Kincaid concluded that

> ...the educational clause of the Factory Act, contrary to the benevolent intentions of its framers, has virtually excluded children under 13 years of age from employment in the Scotch factories...[17]

This situation proved to be stable until the mid-1870s. In spite of an increased demand for weaving operatives in 1860, the Glasgow manufacturers would not consider hiring children. Half-timers were still only employed in Clark's thread factory.[18] However, the implementation of a new Factory Act in textiles in January 1876 occasioned something of a crisis. Young workers could now only be employed full-time at the age of 13 if they had passed the educational Standard IV. In view of the poor attendance of working-class children in the Glasgow schools, it is evident that very few 13 year-olds were able to qualify for full-time work.[19] An important supply of juvenile labour was suddenly cut off. The Sub-inspector in the Glasgow and Paisley district reported in 1876:

> I find that very many of the textile factories have discontinued taking young people under 14 years of age since 1st January 1876; that many others, finding that those between 13 and 14 were very generally utterly unfit to pass the Fourth Standard, have put all such taken on since 1st January on half-time; that very few examinations by school inspectors have taken place; but where they have taken place, certainly not more than 1 in 20 has succeeded in passing. [20]

Daniel Walker, Assistant Inspector, also reported a great scarcity of young juveniles, claiming that the new regulations in combination with the state of education in the manufacturing towns of Scotland had virtually prohibited full-time employment below the age of 14.[21] A Glasgow manufacturer wrote to the local Sub-inspector:

---

16 PP 1854 XIX, RIF, 2nd Half-yearly Rep. 1853, p. 35.
17 PP 1856 XVIII, RIF, 1st Half-yearly Rep. 1856, p. 33.
18 PP 1860 XXXIV, RIF, 1st Half-yearly Rep. 1860, p. 10. See also PP 1871 XIV, RIF, 2nd Half-yearly Rep. 1870, p. 61, where Daniel Walker, Assistant Inspector, claimed that the half-time system would not develop in Glasgow because juvenile labour was "abundant".
19 Daniel Walker, Assistant Inspector, stated in 1876 that the Glasgow schools were "inferior" to those in England, and that the "adventure schools" of Glasgow and Dundee were "a disgrace to the country". PP 1876 XXX, Factory Commissioners, Vol II, pp. 227-29 Q. 19,574, 19,582, 19,599.
20 PP 1876 XVI, RIF, 1st Half-yearly Rep. 1876, p. 16.
21 PP 1877 XXIII, RIF, 2nd Half-yearly Rep. 1876, p. 27.

252

You must really put in a strong word in your report to get the standard lowered. You can understand the difficulty we have to face in getting girls not under 14. We never have had half-timers and are very unwilling to begin. [22]

Alexander Redgrave, successor to Kincaid as factory inspector in Scotland, for his part hoped that this would prove to be the break-through for the half-time system in the Glasgow district.[23] Similarly, the 1876 Factory Commissioners hoped that the half-time system would now be "fairly tried" in Scotland as educational facilities were improving.[24] Indeed, the Factory Returns indicate that the proportion of half-timers in the Scottish cotton workforce almost doubled between 1874 and 1878.[25] There is also some evidence that the use of half-timers in Glasgow proper increased somewhat in 1876.[26]

However, this trend proved to be short-lived. When the recruitment situation stabilized, the Glasgow manufacturers would no longer consider using half-timers. Within a few years the child workers in the Glasgow cotton factories had vanished, this time never to return.

So far I have concentrated on the actual use of child labour in the Glasgow cotton district, and the manufacturers' rationale for not adopting the half-time system. Labour market conditions, the working of the educational clauses of the Factory Act, the poor school facilities in Glasgow, and the partnership structure of ownership, have been indicated as probable reasons for the determination among the manufacturers to avoid using child workers. However, this is not the full story. As I have suggested in the sections on Lancashire, the actual use of half-timers was not a simple reflection of managerial intentions and labour market conditions. The organization of the labour process, the extent of workers' authority over recruitment, the degree of subcontracting relationships, and the gender composition of the workforce, have all been shown to have had a clear impact on the half-time system in Lancashire. The question is, how much did the structures and relations of work differ in the Scottish district compared to Lancashire?

---

22 PP 1876 XVI, RIF, 1st Half-yearly Rep. 1876, p. 17.
23 Ibid., p. 17.
24 PP 1876 XXIX, Factory Commissioners, Vol I, pp. lxiii-lxv.
25 PP 1875 LXXI, Factory Returns; PP 1878-79 LXV, Factory Returns.
26 PP 1876 XXX, Factory Commissioners, Vol II, evidence of Daniel Walker, p. 811 Q. 17,066-67.

## Industrial Relations in Glasgow Mule-spinning, 1837-1870

The most apparent difference between the Glasgow spinning industry and its Lancashire equivalent was the hostile and antagonistic quality of industrial relations in the Scottish district. The Glasgow mule-spinners had had a powerful grip on the trade during the decade after 1825, and the masters were becoming increasingly anxious to break down their trade union and the prevailing piece-rate list. The decision of the Glasgow manufacturers in 1836 to disallow the employment of children must be seen in this perspective. Practically all child workers were piecers subcontracted by the mule-spinners, and this meant that the extra trouble and cost of finding slightly older piecers was handed on to the operatives. The mule-spinners were forced to find older piecers, or risk losing their jobs.[27]

The structure of industrial relations changed dramatically when the Glasgow cotton spinners' union was broken after the strike of 1837. While the union continued to exist "below ground", it nevertheless seems clear that from now on the manufacturers exercised a very high degree of control over recruitment, wage levels, and machine assignments. The piece-rate system which the operative spinners had successfully defended for a decade was now broken, and short mules were joined together to form longer ones.[28] According to a later description of events by an operative spinner, after 1837 the wage rates were fixed arbitrarily by the manufacturers:

> Then every employer paid just at whatever rate of prices he thought proper, and this system continued for some years, until the operatives felt reduction following reduction almost every week, and in many instances every day.[29]

Even if the frequency of reductions may be exaggerated, there is no reason to disbelieve the statement that the spinners were subjected to arbitrary wage cuts. After a strike in 1844 involving 19 mills there was an agreement on prices, but it only seems to have been kept for two years. The managers of mills containing longer mules felt disadvantaged by the agreed list, and were reluctant to adhere to it. Finding it impossible to force these manufacturers to pay according to the list, the spinners instead proposed a new one which was more favourable to the owners of longer mules. In reply the manufacturers drafted a list of their own which they submitted to the operatives in August 1853. The spinners duly accepted the proposed list, only to find that some masters abandoned it "the moment it became unfavou-

---

27 See PP 1837-38 VIII, First Report of the Select Committee..., evidence of James McNish, mule-spinner, Glasgow, p. 64 Q. 1,278-80.
28 Ibid., evidence of Patrick McNaught, Glasgow mill-owner, p. 28 Q. 617; Montgomery (1840), p. 77.
29 Glasgow Sentinel 17/12/53.

rable".[30] In December 1853, seven Glasgow manufacturers running mills with long mules broke the agreement and demanded a 7 ½ per cent reduction. The result was a partial strike followed by a lockout which lasted at least until February 1854.[31] The outcome of the dispute is not altogether clear, but in the light of later events it is very probable that the operative spinners were the main losers.

The Glasgow mule-spinners and self-actor minders never managed to establish a uniform list of prices. In fact, the structures of industrial bargaining remained rudimentary and fragmented. There was a masters' association which decided on raises and reductions in the wage rate, but many manufacturers remained outside this organization and continued to determine their own price lists. For instance, when the Glasgow Masters' Association agreed to a 5 per cent increase in 1859, this initiative was not followed by the unassociated mill-owners. The members of the Masters' Association consequently threatened to withdraw the raise unless it was paid by all.[32] According to the Glasgow Sentinel, one of the principal unassociated masters had stated that he would refuse to grant the wage raise "on principle against all combinations, and would rather sacrifice ten or twelve thousand pounds before he would yield".[33] Manufacturers owning long mules were among those who remained outside the Masters' Association.[34]

The result of these processes was that the spinners were unable to gain any control over the wage-bargaining process. Since a uniform list could not be established, or existing rates defended with reasonable certainty, the element of arbitrary wage reductions remained. It was this, rather than the reductions themselves, which the operatives reacted strongly against. This distinction is clear in a statement by the operative spinners during the strike of 1853:

> The cause of the strike...is an attempt on the part of the employers to reduce the present wages to the extent of 7 ½ per cent., with the prospect of still further undefined reductions, to which the cotton-spinners would not agree. The men state that they were quite willing to submit to any reasonable reduction, which the exigencies of the trade may require, upon the scale formerly fixed by the employers; but they wished that reduction, whether it might amount to ten, fifteen, twenty, or thirty per cent., to be made known to them, and the agreement held as binding on both parties for the time to come. [35]

30 Ibid.
31 Glasgow Sentinel 31/12/53; 7/1/54; 21/1 54; 28/1/54; 18/2/54; 25/2/54.
32 Glasgow Sentinel 19/11/59; 14/1/60.
33 Glasgow Sentinel 14/1/60.
34 Glasgow Sentinel 27/4/61.
35 Glasgow Sentinel 17/12/53.

However, this was not to be. The unassociated manufacturers retained the right to set the wage rates more or less at their pleasure, which naturally made binding agreements impossible. Many employers probably held it an advantage to be able to impose wage cuts if they felt the need. The Glasgow Sentinel sarcastically remarked about one cotton manufacturer: "Mr. Buchanan had for 38 years always considered a reduction of wages as a cure for every ill".[36]

Moreover, the manufacturers never accepted the spinners' union as a bargaining party. Each manufacturer negotiated with representatives of his own workpeople, who then met to compare the replies from the different employers.[37] Delegates to the meetings of the spinners' union would not have their names printed in newspaper reports for fear of victimization.[38]

The marked hostility on the part of the Glasgow manufacturers towards union influence was an important obstacle to formalized industrial relations. The general picture which emerges is one of employer domination, a very low degree of union authority, and an absence of collective agreements on price lists. The contrast to the structure of industrial relations which simultaneously emerged in the Lancashire cotton industry is very clear. The gradual acceptance of trade unions and the establishment of regional price lists and a formalized bargaining structure, which were distinct features of industrial relations in Lancashire, did not emerge in the Glasgow district.

The same contrast is evident in the case of workplace influence and authority over recruitment. From 1836 onwards, the Glasgow manufacturers would not let their mule-spinners hire children below 13 years of age as piecers. Subcontracting was allowed to remain, but only in such a form as would suit the needs of the mill-owners. The Glasgow Sentinel described in 1861 the general Scottish authority structure in mule-spinning in the following terms:

> ...the masters had the entire power of employing and paying off piecers, and...their number and wages are settled by an arrangement between the master and the spinner at the starting of the wheels... [39]

The operative spinner obviously did not have the power to determine the wages of his piecers. Also, employers generally kept the wages of piecers

---

36 Glasgow Sentinel 2/3/61.
37 Glasgow Sentinel 9/8/51; 11/10/51; See also the statements of the chairman of the Glasgow Masters' Association in An Account of the Discussion at Glasgow, on Thursday Sept. 27th, 1860, on the Motion that the Report of the Committee on Trades' Societies be Received (1860), p. 614.
38 Glasgow Sentinel 9/8/51.
39 Glasgow Sentinel 29/6/61.

who left without notice.[40] The conclusion must be that the mule-spinners in the Glasgow district had very limited influence in the subcontracting relationship and a low degree of authority over recruitment compared to the Lancashire operatives. This is corroborated by a statement of the chairman of the Glasgow Masters in 1860, who claimed that the employers only negotiated with their workmen about wages, and not at all on employment matters.[41]

What emerges is a substantial difference in authority and power resources between the Glasgow and Lancashire mule-spinners. A separate study would be required to explain the development of the set of industrial relations which prevailed in Glasgow, but an important part of this process must have been the determined resistance of the manufacturers to all attempts at renewed union activity. Possibly, the insistence of the Glasgow masters to run their own firms "unhindered" by the spinners' union may be seen as an outcome of the period of sharp conflicts and union dominance before 1837. But it should also be seen in a general Scottish context of a weak trade union movement, a long tradition of managerial strategies geared towards low-wage competition, and a local bourgeoisie which was not inclined towards compromises or social conservatism.

So far I have dealt with the question of authority and union presence in Glasgow hand-mule cotton spinning. It had an immediate impact on the use of child labour in the sense that the operatives were not able to resist the manufacturers' decision to dismiss all children below 13 years of age. But the low degree of union power was also an important factor when the organization of work at the new self-acting mules was determined.


## Workforce Composition at the Self-acting Mule in Glasgow, 1837-1900

The source material on the matter of workforce composition at the self-actors after the fateful strike of 1837 is unfortunately very scanty. Nevertheless, Margaret Freifeld is certainly wrong in her recent claim that women were excluded from working the self-actors in Scotland until the 1880s.[42] The initial strategy of the Glasgow manufacturers was to have the self-actors operated by juveniles of both sexes. According to the evidence of a Glasgow mule-spinner in 1854, the self-actors had initially been staffed with "boys and girls".[43] Similarly, according to the manuscripts of the Webb Trade Union Collection, the self-actors brought to Glasgow after the 1837

---

40 Ibid.
41 An Account of the Discussion...(1860), p. 614.
42 Freifeld (1986), pp. 335-41.
43 Glasgow Sentinel 18/2/54.

strike were worked by "young lads & women", all assisted by young piecers.[44] The same source states that around 1860 there were as many female as male minders in Glasgow, with the women working on the shorter mules.[45]

The difference in this respect to the Lancashire district is very sharp. After a few years of experimentation, female minders became very unusual in Lancashire. But it is also important to note that male minders existed in Glasgow even though they had virtually no trade union power. This is an indication that the skill requirements on the early self-actors were still substantial enough to persuade the manufacturers to hire male minders.

However, by 1880 there was a marked shift towards an increased use of female operatives in self-actor spinning. A multi-pair system with one skilled male operative supervising 3-4 pairs of mules, each staffed by 2-3 females, was first introduced in Grant's mill and, according to the Webbs, "purely out of economy".[46] This organization of work was also adopted by the Glasgow Cotton Spinning Co. when it started production in 1885-86.[47] The Webbs described the operation of the multi-pair system in the latter firm like this:

> On [No] 40s, with self-actors carrying 1,000 spindles, there are two adult women ("piecers") & one girl ("rove-piecer") - with one adult male "doffer" for every three pairs of mules. The "piecers" spin, the "rove-piecers" piece the rovings, and the "doffer" sets the machine & redoffs, meanwhile walking to & fro superintending the women. [48]

The senior factory inspector in Scotland, Henderson, remarked in 1883 that the Glasgow cotton industry was becoming "more and more exclusively a woman's industry".[49] This process was not only occasioned by the tendency towards the multi-pair system, but also by the gradual decline of the older hand-mule technology. The last hand-mules in Glasgow were abandoned about 1887, and by the early 1890s the multi-pair system was almost universal in Glasgow self-actor spinning.[50] Margaret Irwin, an assistant commissioner to the 1892 Royal Commission on Labour, found that in Glasgow

> the spinning is done entirely by the women, while men are employed merely as overseers and in keeping the machines in order, piecing the bands and belts, &c.[51]

44 Webb Collection, Vol 34, folio 413.
45 Ibid., folio 413.
46 Ibid., folio 413.
47 On the establishment of the Glasgow Cotton Spinning Co., see PP 1886 XIV, RCIFW, p. 4.
48 Webb Collection, Vol 34 folio 429.
49 PP 1883 XVIII, RCIFW, pp. 44-45.
50 Webb Collection, Vol 34 folio 385.
51 PP 1893-94 XXXVII, Pt 1, p. 193.

In this new organization of work, the tasks which required skill were transferred from the spinner to the male "doffer", who did all the adjustments to the machinery as well as performing the supervisory tasks. The work of minding the self-actor was reduced to mainly piecing the broken threads, and this position was entirely filled with young females.[52] The position of spinner was drained of its requirement of skill and designated as fitting for females.

Naturally, this was a clear deviation from the minder-piecer system which dominated so completely in Lancashire. While the English cotton spinning industry relied on skilled male minders and their subcontracted piecers, the Scottish manufacturers turned increasingly to cheap female labour. The male self-actor minders in Glasgow had fruitlessly tried to resist this change, and their attempt to form a union was finally abandoned in 1875.[53]

My conclusion is that the virtual breakdown of union power and influence after 1837 gave the Glasgow manufacturers the option to go for cheap labour solutions in the form of young female operatives. This became the predominant managerial strategy during the rest of the century. Uniform piece-rates were never accepted, and reductions were immediately imposed during periods of bad trade.

The development of the multi-pair system in self-actor spinning should be seen as a way to utilize cheap female labour in a situation when technological improvement had made the machine easier to handle. In one sense, the Glasgow manufacturers chose to exploit one form of cheap labour rather than another. Having the option to recourse to young female operatives without being hindered by union resistance, they did not have much reason to adopt the half-time system. This may be one part of the explanation as to why the Scottish mill-owners showed so little interest in using child labour.

In a comparative perspective, it is also important to note that the Glasgow mode of self-actor spinning was hardly a commercial success. Contemporary observers like the senior factory inspector, Henderson, even thought that the slow decline of Glasgow cotton spinning was caused by the increasing use of female spinners, who could not stand "the strain and

---

52 Freifeld's emphatic distinction that the female operatives in Glasgow were piecers, not minders, is pointless in the sense that the multi-pair system was entirely different in its organization compared to the traditional minder-piecer system. The female operatives were neither spinners nor piecers; they constituted a separate category of workers. Freifeld's only supporting evidence, the classification made in the 1886 Wage Census, is easily explained. The operatives on the multi-pair system simply did not fit in with the categories of the investigation, and therefore the Glasgow female workers were registered along with the piecers in the regular minder-piecer system. See Freifeld (1986), pp. 340-41, and PP 1889 LXX, Return of Rates of Wages..., pp. x, 59-61.
53 Webb Collection, Vol 34 folio 385.

fatigue involved in attending a pair of modern self-acting spinning frames".[54] As a result, Henderson claimed that productivity was much lower in Scottish mills than in Lancashire:

> A very much larger proportion of women are to be found in the spinning department of a cotton factory in Scotland than in England, and as a consequence the output from the same kind of machinery is very much less. Even although lower wages may be paid in Scotland, it is doubtful if the cost of production is not even greater. [55]

In a report in 1890, Henderson explained the decline of the Glasgow cotton industry in terms of inefficient operatives, pointing to the fact that all the spinning and weaving operations were performed by women and young girls.[56] However, the main explanatory factor is hardly the gender difference, but rather the varying contexts of industrial relations. Productivity remained low in the Glasgow mills because the operatives lacked organizational means to defend wage increases. Their main objective was to attain the customary wage level - beyond that they had no further expectations. Naturally, this situation made the workers unwilling to increase their work effort, since there was no guarantee that any increment above the customary wage would be permanent.

The manager of the Glasgow Cotton Spinning Co, the one firm which has been lauded for being progressive and keeping up with improvements in technology, found the attitude of the operatives very difficult to understand. Being trained in the Lancashire context of industrial relations, he found it strange that the Glasgow female operative had much less drive to earn more wages than was the case with the factory women in Lancashire. A female operative in Scotland, he claimed, was content when she earned half the wages that would satisfy an Oldham lass.[57] My contention is that the structure of industrial relations in the Glasgow district made the operatives stick to notions of customary wages and workloads.

It is naturally very tempting to link the low level of productivity in Glasgow mule-spinning with the eventual decline of the industry. By 1910, mule-spinning had been virtually abandoned in Scotland.[58]

---

54 PP 1883 XVIII, RCIFW, p. 45.
55 Ibid.
56 PP 1890-91 XIX, RCIFW, p. 7.
57 PP 1893-94 XVII, RCIFW, p. 102. For the positive appraisal of the Glasgow Cotton Spinning Co, see MacIntyre, I (1901): The Textile Trades, p. 145.
58 Wood (1910), p. 95. The 1906 census of production similarly gives no indication of mule-spinning in Scotland. See PP 1909 LXXX, Report of an Inquiry..., pp. 32-57.

# Glasgow Powerloom Weaving, 1850-1910

In the Lancashire section I have shown that child tenters in weaving became by far the dominant form of half-time work during the second half of the 19th century. The Scottish case is entirely different: the tenter-system was simply never adopted. The evidence on this matter is very clear. A male machine dresser in a Glasgow weaving factory stated to the 1876 Factory Commissioners that he had never known of a half-timer in the weaving process in all his life.[59] The 1886 Wage Census comprised 3,122 Scottish powerloom weavers, but no tenters at all.[60] Similarly, the 1895 Annual Return provided separate statistics for the weaving sector which show that child labour was virtually unheard of in Scottish weaving factories. Only 39 half-timers were reported in a total workforce of 16,020 operatives.[61] Finally, Mary Paterson, a factory inspector, told a parliamentary committee in 1909 that Glasgow powerloom weavers did not use tenters at all.[62]

How can the difference between Glasgow and Lancashire weaving be explained? First, it must be said that there was hardly any difference in technology. Paterson stated in 1909 that there was "no difference in machinery", yet there was no operative below 14 in the Glasgow weaving factories.[63] But there were definitely other important differences: in work-force composition, authority structures, and union presence.

Cotton-weaving in Scotland never became a mixed occupation like in Lancashire. The weavers were invariably female. As Superintending Inspector Henderson put it in 1883, "such a thing as a male powerloom weaver is not to be met with so far as I have seen in Scotland".[64] This work-force composition remained completely unchanged during the following decades.[65]

Another difference was that the Glasgow weavers completely lacked trade union organization, and uniform price lists along the Lancashire pattern were never established. An early attempt was made by the female powerloom weavers in 1832-33 to organize in a regular society, but it appears to have been shortlived.[66] Towards the end of the 19th century attempts were made by the Glasgow Trades' Council and the Women's

---

59 PP 1876 XXX, Factory Commissioners, Vol II, evidence of A.B., p. 788 Q. 16,557, 16,560.
60 PP 1889 LXX, Return of Rates of Wages..., pp. 60-62.
61 PP 1897 XVII, RCIFW, pp. 169-71.
62 PP 1909 XVII,Report of the Inter-Departmental Committee..., Vol II, evidence of Mary Paterson, lady factory inspector, p. 49 Q. 1,355.
63 Ibid., p. 49 Q. 1,348.
64 PP 1884 XVIII, RCIFW, p. 45.
65 See Irwin, M H (1896): Women's Industries in Scotland, pp. 72-73; PP 1909 XVII, Report of the Inter-Departmental Committee..., Vol II, evidence of Mary Paterson, lady factory inspector, p. 49 Q 1,354.
66 PP 1833 VI, evidence of William Graham, Glasgow manufacturer, p. 323; PP 1833 XX, evidence of John Stephen, cotton mill manager, Glasgow, p. A2 54.

Protective and Provident League to unionize the female weaving operatives, but there seems to have been no lasting organization before 1907.[67]

The absence of unions and the weak wage-bargaining position of the Glasgow weavers do not mean that they did not occasionally resist and challenge the authority of the manufacturers.[68] It would be more correct to say that the resistance of the Glasgow weavers was expressed in a different way to the case in Lancashire. Above all, it took the form of a determined defence of customary wage levels, workloads, and practices. The customary organization of production was perceived as a fundamental right, and transgressions from managers or overlookers could meet with an explosive response, either in the form of short "spontaneous" strikes, symbolical processions, or occasional violence. The Glasgow Sentinel reported in 1852 about a procession of Glasgow lappet-weavers directed against a much disliked former overlooker:

> The lappet-weavers in a factory about Graham Street having got up an effigy as the representative of an obnoxious ex-tenter, carried it along Bellgrove and Duke Streets, to Glen factory, where the flogging process was gone through with ropes, the female workers, in particular, striking hard. After being satisfied with the flogging the effigy had received, the weavers carried the unfortunate victim to a place in Duke Street, where, amid deafening cheers, it was consumed to ashes. [69]

The great importance which the operatives attached to customary work practices is evidenced by the strike of powerloom weavers at Galbraith's factory in 1858. This manufacturer had tried to change the customary work assignment of two looms per weaver, and instead put one operative to mind four looms with the assistance of a young girl. According to the Glasgow Sentinel, this "innovation" had immediately caused the weavers to strike work and to harass the two overlookers who were trying to implement the new system. These men were followed to and from work by hundreds of strikers and sympathizers from other mills, shouting and yelling, notwithstanding the presence of the police.[70] At a meeting the following week the weavers expressed their determination never to submit to the "debasing system" of working four looms.[71] They would not accept to mind more looms than the traditional two.

Apart from a pledge by the manufacturer that the matter of the proposed four-loom system could be left "on his honour", I have found no

---

67 Glasgow Trades Council Annual Reports, 1890-91, p. 18; 1891-92, p. 17; 1904-5, p. 16; 1907-8, p. 24.
68 On the difficulty to make the Glasgow manufacturers accept organized industrial bargaining, see A Letter to A. Galbraith, Esq., Lord Dean of Guild, Explanatory and Descriptive of the Present Dispute between the Manufacturers, and the Power-loom Weavers of Glasgow. By an Operative (1849), passim.
69 Glasgow Sentinel 24/1/52.
70 Glasgow Sentinel 14/8/58.
71 Glasgow Sentinel 21/8/58.

more information on the outcome of this strike.[72] However, it is clear from later material that the customary two-loom system continued to dominate in the Glasgow weaving industry. The 1886 wage census listed 2,512 two-loom and 560 three-loom weavers in the Scottish sample.[73]

Margaret Irwin, an assistant commissioner on the 1892 Royal Commission on Labour, found the Glasgow powerloom weavers "very tenacious of their habits, and lacking in adaptability to new circumstances and methods, and there is no point on which the Glasgow weaver is more fiercely combative than this of the two-loom versus the three-loom system, and none on which it is more difficult to convince her than any system but her own is practicable".[74] The tenacity of the two-loom system in Glasgow seems to have been remarkable. An attempt by a manufacturer in 1890 to increase the work assignment to three looms per weaver immediately produced a strike. Margaret Irwin commented:

> After the strike had gone on for some days the Glasgow Trades Council and the Council of the Women's Protective and Provident League took the matter up and entered into negotiations with the employer. The latter offered very fairly to provide new machinery, to introduce the change gradually, and to pay the wages due to increased production. /.../ The workers, however, refused even to allow a single experiment of three looms being tried in the weaving-shed, and only went back to their work on condition that such should not be enforced. The workers concerned in this strike are, as a class, among the least intelligent of the Glasgow weavers, but the same opinion prevails among all weavers on this question. [75]

Being the organizing secretary of the Women's Protective and Provident League, Margaret Irwin was a very well-placed observer.[76] Her depiction of events is also corroborated by Henderson, the senior factory inspector, who reported that an effort had been made to getGlasgow weaving operatives to attend more looms than the customary two, but after a long strike the workers had returned on the old conditions. Henderson, on his part, found it difficult to understand why the operatives were so much against the prospect of minding more machinery and obtaining more wages.[77]

However, the actions of the operatives were in no way irrational. The Glasgow weavers defended customary workloads in a situation where they had no real control over piece-rates or wage levels. Since weaving piece-rates were more or less fixed arbitrarily by each individual employer, there

---

72 Ibid.
73 PP 1889 LXX, Return of Rates of Wages..., pp. 60-62.
74 PP 1893-94 XXXVII, Pt I, Royal Commission of Labour. Reports on the Employment of Women, Pt I, p. 174.
75 Ibid., p 174. See also Irwin (1896), p. 75.
76 Glasgow Trades Council Annual Report 1890-91, p. 18.
77 PP 1893-94 XVII, RCIFW, p. 102.

was no coherent structure of industrial bargaining which could guarantee that wage increases would be permanent. The acceptance of minding more looms for higher wages could be followed more or less immediately by a reduction of the piece-rate which would lower wages to the previous level. In terms of effort-wage bargaining, the operative had to feel reasonably certain that an increased work effort would result in permanently higher earnings. Otherwise there was no point in accepting a higher workload.

The conclusion must be that the structure of industrial relations in Glasgow was not conducive to gains in productivity. This was to some extent recognized by Irwin, who put down the difficulties between the mill-owners and operatives in Glasgow to the absence of a uniform and stable piece-rate system:

> The chief source of difficulties between employers and workers in the textile industry in Glasgow is apparently the want of a declared and uniform rate of wages for the same work throughout the trade. /.../ There is no guarantee that any firm may not reduce wages as it pleases without the workers being able to compare those they receive with those current elsewhere. I find that the female operatives constantly complain that under this system of arbitrary fixation there must be great temptation to reduce wages on the part of the zealous manager, anxious to give a good account of his stewardship, and also on the part of the unscrupulous employer who "cuts" prices, trusting to recoup himself at his workers' expense. /.../ On the other hand the workers having had in the past no organisation strong enough to combat this evil and no centre to appeal to for support, or even for accurate information as to current rates, have in most cases been obliged to submit... [78]

There seems to have been no dramatic change during the decades to come. The 1906 wage census sample shows that 75.8 per cent of the Scottish weavers still minded the traditional complement of two looms, 7.7 per cent worked on one machine, and only 16.5 per cent minded three looms each.[79]

The contrast with Lancashire conditions is very sharp. Regional price lists for weaving emerged during the period after 1850, and by the 1880s the whole Lancashire district was covered by such agreements. The gradual growth of weavers' unions was an important precondition for this development, and the adjustment of the lists became the focal point in a formalized structure of industrial bargaining between the Weavers' Amalgamation and the two employer federations.

In Lancashire, this created a context of industrial bargaining which induced the weavers to accept increases in work assignments. The normal workload for an adult weaver quickly rose from two to four looms, often minded with the help of a subcontracted child "tenter". The wage increase

---

78 PP 1893-94 XXXVII, Royal Commission on Labour, Pt I, p. 174.
79 PP 1909 LXXX, Report of an Inquiry..., pp. 32-57.

which was connected with the taking up of an additional loom was so firmly protected by the list and the industrial bargaining structure that it was regarded as wholly secure. "Go slow" tactics were avoided, and the ability to mind more looms actually enhanced the weaver's position within the working-class community. It is therefore quite understandable that Superintending Inspector Henderson found such a difference in work intensity between the Lancashire weaving operatives and those in Scotland:

> The Lancashire weaver works with a will, she earns a high wage (on an average double that of her Scotch sister on the same class of work), and is anxious to maintain it. She will take charge of four power looms without hesitation; and indeed, her energetic industry is not unfrequently an embarassment to the inspector, for it makes her indifferent to the provisions of the Act of Parliament which has been passed for her protection. She has practically to be driven from her work, and, I believe, if a weaving shed in Lancashire were to be opened at five in the morning it would soon be filled with workpeople. In Scotland, on the other hand, it is common to find weavers of long experience with only two power looms, and it is with difficulty that they can be persuaded to take a third. [80]

Consequently, the reasons why it was so difficult to induce the Scottish operatives to mind more looms are strongly tied to the structure of industrial relations. Moreover, since there was no development towards a four-loom system, there was hardly any reason to start using young tenters. In the Glasgow weaving factories, the organization of production was geared towards the employment of women and young girls, but no children. The Glasgow cotton mills became firmly associated with the use of young female operatives, generally between 14 and 23 years of age.[81]

On the other hand, it is also possible that the weavers themselves saw the use of tenters as a possible threat to the customary organization of production. Child labour in Glasgow weaving therefore never became a real option. In a comparative perspective, the half-time system in Lancashire weaving was based on preconditions which were entirely absent in Scotland.

### Child Labour in the Country Mills

So far I have only described the processes connected with the child labour issue which took place in the Glasgow district. However, there were also several important country factories outside this district where the development was somewhat different. In these works child labour was not immediately abandoned after 1836, partly because the country factories had much

---

80 PP 1890-91 XIX, RCIFW, p. 7.
81 See Margaret Irwin's report in PP 1893-94 XXXVII, Royal Commission on Labour, Pt 1, p. 173.

more limited supplies of labour and could not easily replace the children with juvenile workers. Early in 1837, in the textile mills in the West of Scotland outside the city of Glasgow, children below 13 constituted 4.7 per cent of the workforce, and juveniles between 13 and 18 50.9 per cent.[82] This reinforces the impression that the country managers above all tried to utilize the cheap labour of children, juveniles, and women. There are also some indications that family employment structures still existed to some extent in the country mills.[83]

There were practically no unions in these mills. They also contained a large element of female mule-spinners, and probably did not have sub-contracting relationships between the operatives. Recruitment difficulties could therefore not be handed on to the adult workers as had been done in Glasgow. Instead, most of the larger country works started factory schools and continued to use child labour. In 1838 the factory children constituted roughly 10 per cent of the workforce in the concerns at Deanston, Catrine and Duntocher, while Ballindalloch and Stanley lay slightly higher and New Lanark a bit below this figure.[84]

However, already in the early 1840s it is evident that the level of child labour was decreasing in the country factories. In 1843 James Stuart reported that the number of child workers at the Deanston and Stanley cotton works was now less than half that in the late 1830s.[85] Within a few years the extent of child labour in these factories was practically insignificant.[86]

The reasons for this development are not difficult to guess. The manufacturers found child labour cumbersome, since it forced them to organize schools and increase the amount of book-keeping. It was therefore only resorted to as a response to labour scarcity. As soon as the supply of workers increased, a process which was undoubtably hastened by the period of bad trade in the early 1840s and the general stagnation of the Scottish cotton industry, the use of children was discontinued. Instead, the country factories which kept working were geared more heavily towards the use of cheap female labour.

---

82 PP 1837-38 XXVIII, RIF, p. 11. N = 13,159.
83 PP 1840 X, Fourth Report from the Select Committee..., evidence of Daniel Walker, Superintendent, pp. 20-21 Q. 5,333-35.
84 See PP 1839 XLII, Return on the Educational Provisions of the Factories Act..., pp. 65-68.
85 PP 1843 XXVII, RIF, 2nd Quart. Rep. 1843, p. 45.
86 PP 1844 XXVIII, 4th Quart. Rep. 1843, p. 29; Ibid., 1st Quart. Rep. 1844, p. 9; Ibid., 2nd Quart. Rep. 1844, p. 17. See also Donnachie, I (1987): The Textile Industry in South West Scotland 1750-1914, p. 26.

# Child Labour in Scotland: the General Context

While child labour disappeared very early in the cotton industry, there were no absolute obstacles to industrial child labour in Scottish culture and society. The half-time system became established in the Dundee jute industry and the Paisley thread factories, and remained so until the early 20th century.[87] But in comparison with Lancashire, there were some important differences in the mode of employment of half-timers. In both Dundee and Paisley, half-timers were hired directly by the manufacturer and constituted a part of an almost exclusively female, non-union workforce. The Lancashire pattern of subcontracted half-timers, a high-intensity organization of work, and a strong trade union presence, did not have any counterpart in Scotland.

Finally, it should be pointed out that the Scottish legislation on compulsory schooling was somewhat less conducive to the operation of the half-time system than the English. For instance, the Scottish Education Act of 1883 set the attainment of Standard III as a requirement for half-time work.[88] The Glasgow factory inspector reported in 1901 that the recent Scottish Education Act would "practically do away with half-time labour in his district".[89] The new Act laid down that half-time exemptions could only be granted on grounds of poverty and necessity, and gave the school boards absolute discretion to turn down applications.[90]

This seems to have created an impression that more restrictive schooling legislation had caused the decline of the half-time system in Scotland. Mary Paterson, a factory inspector, believed that Scottish "public opinion" had recognized that education was of more advantage to the child than factory work. She also stated that the Paisley school board had abolished the half-time system in that district.[91] These claims were probably exaggerated. It is very doubtful if the burgh of Paisley took any action of this kind against the wishes of the powerful thread manufacturers.

Moreover, the reason why the Scottish Education Acts were less accommodating to the half-time system must be seen in the context of a comparatively low level of industrial child labour. In the Glasgow textile district,

---

87 PP 1873 LV, Report...on Proposed Changes in Hours and Ages of Employment in Textile Factories, p. 27; PP 1892 XXXV, Royal Commission on Labour, evidence of J. H. Walker, a Dundee manufacturer, p. 451 Q. 10,862-63; PP 1893-94 XXXVII, Royal Commission on Labour, Pt 1, pp. 305-6; PP 1909 XVII, Report of the Inter-Departmental Committee..., Vol II, evidence of Paterson, lady factory inspector, p. 48 Q. 1,304, 1,307; Blair, M (1907): The Paisley Thread Industry, chapter 9. See also Smout (1986), pp. 96-97.
88 PP 1884-85 XV, RCIFW, p. 33.
89 PP 1902 XII, RCIFW, p. 145-46.
90 PP 1909 XVII, Report of the Inter-Departmental Committee..., Vol II, evidence of Mary Paterson, lady factory inspector, p. 48 Q. 1.310-11.
91 Ibid., p. 48 Q. 1,305, 1,308.

which long remained the most important, the half-time system was practically never adopted. It could therefore be argued that the legislation on education became more stringent in Scotland in a situation where industrial child labour was relatively unimportant. Outside the Dundee district, the half-time system never became firmly embedded in the organization of production or in popular custom.

# Conclusions

Child labour in the Scottish cotton factories was already relatively insignificant by 1840. In the Glasgow district, the manufacturers responded to the implementation of the 1833 Factory Act by prohibiting the employment of children below 13. A major reason for this decision was that the employers did not want to be legally responsible for the schooling of the factory children. An important precondition for this strategy was the large supply of juvenile workers in the city of Glasgow. In a general context of hostile industrial relations, the subcontracting relationship in mule-spinning was used to force the spinners to exert themselves to find older piecers.

The investigation has shown the importance of the power structure in industrial relations for the composition of the workforce in the Glasgow cotton industry. In mule-spinning, it is clear that the manufacturers' insistance on full authority over wage levels and recruitment made it impossible for the spinners to subcontract child piecers. The situation was similar in self-actor spinning, but in addition there was a reorganization of work in the 1880s. The minder-piecer system was replaced by a multi-pair system, and young female operatives took over all the spinning operations. The practice of subcontracting piecers was entirely abandoned under the new system. Finally, in the weaving process the arbitrary nature of managerial power provoked a stubborn defence of customary workloads among the operatives, which in turn meant that there was no place for a tenter-system with child workers similar to the Lancashire pattern. The predominant managerial strategy in the Scottish industry remained that of utilizing cheap female labour whenever possible. In turn, this made unionization extremely difficult.

Furthermore, in a family perspective, it must also be said that the high degree of mill-owner dominance in matters of recruitment left little scope for the realization of family wage strategies in the Glasgow factories. Working-class parents had to find other ways to make use of their children than having them employed in cotton factories. A more general culture of child or family employment in the factories was not allowed to develop.

# Chapter 12

# Two Contrasting Cases: Massachusetts and the U.S. South

In this chapter I will deal with child labour practices in American cotton mills between 1840 and 1920. However, my ambition to provide a full picture of the processes involved is more limited here than in the sections on England and Scotland. Using a comparative perspective, my main intention has been to establish interesting differences and contrasts to the developments in the British cotton industry. Above all, I will try to reconstruct the changes in the labour process over this period, and to some extent assess the structure and enforcement of factory legislation. I will also point out differences in labour recruitment and organization in the American mills compared to the British.

## Massachusetts, New England

After 1840 the recruitment strategy of the New England manufacturers changed quite markedly. The Lowell system, based on the employment of young females drawn from small New England farms, was discontinued in favour of the recruitment of immigrant Irish. The mode of employment shifted slowly towards "free" wage labour and family employment structures.

Since the Lowell system had primarily dominated in the northern half of New England, the shift was more tangible there. By 1875, 46.6 per cent of the Lowell operatives still lived in boarding-houses, as compared to 33.0 per cent in Lawrence and 14.8 per cent in Fall River.[1] The mills in Lowell and Lawrence, which had previously relied almost completely on young female labour, now developed a more varied age profile in their workforce, employing both children and older operatives to a greater extent than previously.[2] This major change in recruitment patterns naturally increased

---

1 Massachusetts Bureau of the Statistics of Labor (MBSLAR), Annual Report 1882, p. 293.
2 See MBSLAR, 1870, p. 91.

the level of child labour considerably. However, in the southern part of Massachusetts where family employment structures and child labour practices had dominated early in the century, it is probable that the increased availability of immigrant labour after 1840 actually served to lessen the employment of children.[3]

There were also other developments which tended to reduce the demand for child labour. Above all, the labour process was being reorganized in such a way as to reduce the influence of the adult operatives over recruitment and to leave less room for the use of children. When the self-acting mules were introduced in New England in the 1840s, the operative spinners were no longer allowed to hire any piecer assistants. The manufacturers demanded that they should perform all the piecing operations themselves, and that specific organization of work at the self-actors dominated for the rest of the century.[4]

One important exception was the minders in Fall River, who were assisted by one piecer each at the turn of the century. This was probably the only way for the manufacturers to utilize modern and longer self-acting mules of English make. However, these piecers were directly employed by management, not subcontracted by the minders.[5]

In a similar way, the "back-boys" who supplied the spinning machines with rovings were no longer subcontracted by the spinners, but were instead put under the full authority of overlookers and management. The only exception to this rule was the Fall River and New Bedford mule-spinners, who subcontracted the back-boys. This appears to have been caused by recruitment difficulties. Subcontracting was retained because the rapid expansion of the Fall River cotton industry made it very difficult for the manufacturers to recruit juvenile operatives. Subcontracting was used in such a way as to force the mule-spinners to exert themselves in order to find juvenile back-boys. As the operative spinner Thomas O'Donnel testified in 1883,

...if a man has not got a "back-boy" it is very hard for him to get along. In a great many cases they discharge men in that work and put in men who have boys. /.../ There are so many men in the city to work, and whoever has a boy can have work, and whoever has no boy stands no chance. [6]

---

3 See Tucker, B M (1980): The Family and Industrial Discipline in Ante-Bellum New England, pp. 73-74. However, this article is marred by its simplistic emphasis on the "harmonious" nature of the family employment structure.

4 MBSLAR, 1882, pp. 304-5; Lazonick (1979), p. 243; Cohen (1985a), pp. 53, 73.

5 Uttley (1905), p. 32.

6 Garraty, J A (ed): Labor and Capital in the Gilded Age: Testimony taken by the Senate Committee upon the Relations between Labor and Capital - 1883, p. 33. On New Bedford, see Uttley (1905), p. 32. See also Lazonick (1981c), p. 507.

In the Massachusetts mills, special teams of "doffers" were employed to remove the full cops of yarn, and in some mills "tubing-boys" were also used to put paper tubes on the empty spindles.[7]

In other words, all the operations which in Lancashire were performed by piecers and creelers under the supervision of the spinner, were in the Massachusetts mill performed by special operatives under the authority of the overlooker. Work was both more divided and under a greater degree of control by management.[8] The response of the operatives was to try to control the pace of the work and not let "greenhorns" or inexperienced young men put in excessive levels of work intensity, a practice called "rate busting".[9] This caused a constant conflict over the actual work-effort, which is one important reason why the American methods in mule-spinning required a far higher level of supervision than was the case in Lancashire. Thomas Ashton of the Oldham Spinners' estimated in 1902 that the proportion of overlookers in Massachusetts mills was two and a half times higher than the English custom.[10]

The end of the subcontracting form of employment meant that the various reasons for spinners to hire rather young assistants were no longer relevant - like the desire to employ their own sons at an early age, or to hire as cheap assistant labour as possible, or to minimize the risk to bring up too many spinners to the trade. Direct employment by management also meant that family wage strategies had less impact on workforce composition.[11]

---

7 See MBSLAR, 1880, p. 7, on the increased division of labour in Fall River spinning mills. The employers claimed that this "improvement" gave the spinner more time to perform the actual spinning operations. For later descriptions of the organization of mule-spinning in Massachusetts, see the report of Thomas Ashton, Oldham Spinners', Lancashire, in Mosely Industrial Commission (1903), p. 125; Uttley (1905), pp. 16-17; Lazonick (1981c), pp. 506-7.

8 However, this is not to say that this organization of work was very efficient. The secretary of the Ashton Spinners', Lancashire, was bemused during an American trip in 1909 by the slack activity among the juvenile back-boys and doffers in the mule-spinning process: "These youngsters, between doffing and creeling, think nothing of going outside for half an hour and coming back leisurely when the doffing and creeling has to be done." Cotton Factory Times, 16/4/09. Thomas Ashton of the Oldham Spinners' also found that the Lancashire methods in mule-spinning were superior to the American, but emphasized that in the Massachusetts mills the overlookers had "full management in the spinning rooms", and the power to discharge any person working there. Mosely Industrial Commission (1903), pp. 125-26.

9 Montgomery (1980), pp. 39, 42.

10 Mosely Industrial Commission (1903), p. 129. Commenting on this report, the Cotton Factory Times stated that "the expense of overlooking in an American mill is enormous". Cotton Factory Times 24/4/03. See also Textile Recorder, June 1905, p. 34. But there seems to have been no difference in supervision levels in the weaving process. See the report of W. H. Wilkinson, Weavers' Amalgamation, in Mosely Industrial Commission (1903), p. 145.

11 Tucker also sees that the abandoning of subcontracting structures of employment in the southern Massachusetts mills after 1840 was an important reason for the decline of child labour. Tucker (1980), p. 73. Lazonick has claimed that subcontracting practices had been less pervasive in the U.S. cotton industry even before 1840 than was the case in Lancashire, and management control more emphasized. See Lazonick (1979), p. 243.

While the managerial control over back-boys and doffers did not necessarily mean that child labour was abandoned, it nevertheless gave management a greater possibility to organize the work in such a way as to favour the employment of juveniles rather than children.[12] During the course of the 19th century, the work requirements for creeling and doffing became more geared towards the use of juvenile operatives. While the workforce in Massachusetts spinning in 1884 still contained more children below 14 than juveniles between 14 and 18, by 1907 it seems that the normal age for back-boys and doffers was 16 to 17 years rather than 14 to 15.[13]

Why, then, was self-actor spinning organized differently in Massachusetts than in Lancashire? The most important reason is probably that the manufacturers were determined to abolish the practice of subcontracting since they saw it as a vital requisite for the spinners in their domination of the other factory operatives. The mule-spinners were generally perceived by the employers as the most "troublesome" category of workers, being more often involved in unions and strike actions.[14] The requirement that the self-actor spinners should perform all the piecing, and not have the authority over the back-boys, was clearly part of a managerial strategy to reduce their relative independence and turn them into ordinary factory operatives. The Massachusetts manufacturers were simply not prepared to allow subcontracting forms of employment to remain. Instead, their main strategy was to increase managerial control over the labour process, and to raise work intensity by means of close supervision.

English operatives who emigrated to Massachusetts often found the overlookers more authoritarian and overbearing than had been the case in Lancashire.[15] The strike of the Fall River spinners in 1850 was, according to the operatives, caused by the "numerous petty tyrannies and unjust actions on the part of the overseers".[16]

The frequent strikes in Fall River were generally blamed on the preponderance of English cotton operatives, who were trying to introduce their work customs and union practices in the new country.[17] P. T. Silvia has

12 The same seems to have been the case at the roving frames. Uttley reported in 1905 that American mills did not have "back tenters" at the roving frames, but instead organized teams of doffers to perform that work. Uttley (1905), p. 12. W. Mullin of the Cardroom Amalgamation made the same observation during his American visit in 1902. See Cardroom Amalgamation, Annual Return for 1903, p. 45.

13 MBSLAR, 1884, pp. 195-96; Report on the Condition of Woman and Child Wage-earners, p. 81. However, the 1884 sample is not altogether reliable since it comprises both ring- and mule-spinning, and the 1907 sample is relatively small - N of back-boys and doffers = 160.

14 See MBSLAR, 1871, evidence of D. A. Brayton, mill director, Fall River, p. 50; MBSLAR, 1882, p. 313.

15 MBSLAR, 1870, pp. 114-15; MBSLAR, 1882, p. 338; Cohen (1985b).

16 MBSLAR, 1880, pp. 6-7. The men also complained that recent alterations of work had increased their labour. Ibid., p. 7.

17 MBSLAR, 1880, p. 59; MBSLAR, 1882, pp. 201-2, 340-41.

shown that the English operatives in Fall River, above all the mule-spinners, had organized the worker resistance to wage-cuts during the 1870s.[18] The manufacturers perceived this as an attack on their right of full authority in the mills. One Fall River employer remarked in 1882 that the strikes were not about wages, but a "question as to who shall rule".[19]

In a similar manner, the Massachusetts manufacturers remained for a long time hostile to any kind of union influence. They would not recognize or negotiate with representatives of a union.[20] Known trade unionists and prominent strikers were dismissed and blacklisted.[21] One Fall River employer maintained that the blacklist was mainly used against the mule-spinners' union, "for they cause us the most trouble".[22] Union initiatives were also made difficult by the relative ease with which the employers could replace striking workers with "newcomers". In the disputes in Fall River in 1850, in Salisbury in 1852, in Chicopee in 1858, and in Lawrence in 1867, the operatives on strike were replaced by "newcomers".[23]

The Fall River mule-spinners were the only ones able to form a relatively stable union, but not even they were always able to handle this problem. During the strike of 1879, for instance, strenuous attempts were made by the Fall River operatives to keep strike-breakers out of the city, either through persuasion or threats. One company of French Canadians brought in by the employers was even stoned by the local inhabitants. But in the end the spinners had to return to work wherever positions could be obtained.[24]

Still, Fall River stands out as the only town where unions were relatively strong.[25] In the other Massachusetts cotton towns, trade union organization proved to be even more difficult. Typically, one Lawrence employer maintained that "if we have any troublesome people they are told to go to the office, collect their money, and get out. Our agents will not submit to any dictation on the part of the operatives".[26]

There were also some specific factors which tended to increase the power resources of the employers. The New England manufacturers were

---

18 Silvia (1975), p. 232.

19 MBSLAR, 1871, evidence of D. A. Brayton, p. 50. See also Montgomery (1980), pp. 17-18; Cohen (1985b), passim.

20 MBSLAR, 1870, pp. 114-15; MBSLAR, 1871, evidence of D. A. Brayton, p. 50; MBSLAR, 1880, p. 60.

21 MBSLAR, 1870, pp. 13-14, 122; MBSLAR, 1871, evidence of a mule-spinner, p. 485. One Fall River employer stated in 1882: "We never employ a man who belongs to a trades union if we know it; we root them out wherever we find them." MBSLAR, 1882, p. 341. See also ibid., p. 345.

22 MBSLAR, 1882, p. 347. See also Silvia (1975), p. 237.

23 MBSLAR, 1880, pp. 8-22.

24 MBSLAR, 1880, pp. 55-57.

25 Thomas Ashton of the Oldham Spinners', Lancashire, found in 1902 that all Fall River mule-spinners were members of the union, while the weavers' and carders' unions only comprised 40 per cent of the operatives. See Mosely Industrial Commission (1903), p. 124. In 1913, Fall River was still described as the only "distinctly trade-union locality in the industry in New England". MBSLAR, 1913, p. 43.

26 MBSLAR, 1882, p. 219.

fewer, owned larger mills, and co-operated better than the Lancashire employers.[27] Consequently, while it could be argued that the American spinners had less resources of power than the English in a defence of the traditional minder-piecer system and their authority in the workplace, the main difference between the two countries was perhaps still one of managerial strategy, cohesiveness, and determination.[28] The intention of the American manufacturers to gain a more complete control over the labour process, and to increase the division of work, did not have any Lancashire equivalent. It is in this context of production relations and managerial strategies that the different organization of self-actor spinning in Massachusetts has to be seen.

An even clearer case of a different way of organizing work in Massachusetts compared to Lancashire was in powerloom weaving. The American system in weaving implied a much greater division of labour than was the case in Lancashire. Massachusetts weavers only performed the actual weaving operations, while ancillary tasks like cleaning and weft and cut carrying was done by special operatives. This is one reason why the Massachusetts weavers were able to manage more machinery than was the norm in Lancashire. A sample from Massachusetts in 1884 indicates that the normal loom assignment at that time was 5-6 machines per weaver.[29] Soon the normal workload had been increased to eight looms per weaver.[30] But it was also clearly the case that this organization of work, coupled with the evident managerial dislike for subcontracting forms of employment, simply left no room for the tenter-system which was the dominant form of child labour in Lancashire. Indeed, the avilable evidence indicates that children below 14 were not employed at all in the weaving process in the Massachusetts mills.[31] This is also shown in the 1884 sample:

---

27 Lazonick (1981c), p. 497.
28 In this context I am critical of Isaac Cohen, who has maintained that the reason for the differences between Lancashire and New England spinning was mainly trade union strength and tradition. See Cohen (1985a) and (1985b), passim.
29 MBSLAR, 1884, p. 196.
30 Young (1902), pp. 10-11.
31 MBSLAR, 1870, p. 121;  MBSLAR, 1871, pp. 258-60, 267-68.

Table 11. Child and juvenile workers in different labour processes in Massachusetts cotton mills, 1884. per cent.

| Occupation | Age | | N |
| | 10-13 years | 14-17 years | |
| --- | --- | --- | --- |
| Carding | 14.4 | 8.5 | 1,181 |
| Spinning | 19.1 | 16.8 | 1,500 |
| Weaving | 0.0 | 0.4 | 3,256 |

Source: MBSLAR, 1884, p 195-96.

The virtual absence of young operatives in the weaving process in Massachusetts must be regarded as remarkable. As I have shown earlier, the 1886 wage census in Britain indicated that 75 per cent of all half-timers in the Lancashire cotton industry were employed in weaving.[32] Similarly, there are some evidence which suggests that at least by the turn of the century, reachers-in were not used in the drawing process in Massachusetts mills.[33]

The relatively high figure for child labour in the spinning process is explained by the fact that the statistics did not separate mule-spinning and ring-spinning. As I will show below, ring-spinning remained a substantial employer of child labour in the American industry.

In the comparative perspective, it is noteworthy that a sizeable proportion of child workers in Massachusetts were employed in the carding room, a practice which was very weak in Lancashire.[34] This also argues against a purely "technological" explanation of child labour practices. Massachusetts child workers were not employed in the same tasks as in Lancashire mills, even though the machinery was very similar.

The main issue seems to have been a fundamental difference in the organization of production in England and America. While the Lancashire manufacturers condoned subcontracting in both spinning and weaving, and relied on an "inner incentive" structure based on stable piece-rates and relatively independent operatives, the American managers instead opted for a tighter control of the labour process, an increased division of labour, and the use of "driving" to force the operatives to work harder.[35]

Possibly, the greater tendency among the New England manufacturers to divide and deskill the operations of work may be seen in the context of a

---

32 PP 1889 LXX, Return of Rates of Wages..., pp. 9-58.
33 Young (1902), p. 10. See also Textile Recorder, September 1905, p. 130.
34 PP 1889 LXX, Return of Rates of Wages.., pp. 9-58. Only 2.2 per cent of the Lancashire half-timers were employed in the carding room, nearly all as sweepers and back-tenters at roving and slubbing frames.
35 On the differences in the organization of work between Lancashire and New England, see Uttley (1905), pp. 16-17. On the subject of "driving" or "grinding" in Fall River spinning, see MBSLAR, 1882, pp. 235-39, 301-6, 350-51; Cohen (1985a), p. 73.

very high labour turnover.[36] But it should also be seen as a part of mana-gerial strategy which the British manufacturers could not readily employ: that of replacing their workforce with newly arrived immigrants. This was a social process which clearly separates the Massachusetts experience from the British.

The ethnic composition of the New England cotton workers shifted several times between 1840 and 1920. The Irish in 1840 were followed by French Canadians a couple of decades later, who in turn were replaced by Portuguese, Poles, and Greeks in the early 20th century.[37] Indeed, the succession of ethnic groups was probably the most important change in the Massachusetts cotton industry during the second half of the 19th century.[38] Already by 1871, foreign born operatives constituted 72 per cent of the workforce of Massachusetts cotton mills; a figure which was practically the same in 1905.[39]

Immigrant workers were often preferred because they accepted less wages and worse conditions, and also because they were less prone to form unions. Being alarmed by the fact that English and Irish operatives were quickly adopting American "demands and ideas", some Fall River employers even contemplated importing cheap Chinese labour as a way to reduce wages.[40] However, the main ethnic minority to be recruited were the French Canadians, who were regarded as docile and slow to take part in strikes and riots.[41]

The inevitable result was ethnic conflicts within the working-class community. The Fall River mule-spinners were reportedly hostile towards the French Canadians, since the latter would accept the lowest wages for their work, and would not join the union.[42] But the case should not be over-stated. The manufacturers probably also saw the advantages of having a trained workforce and an established social network among the operatives.

---

36 T. M. Young estimated in 1902 that the turnover in a New England mill was five per cent every week. Young (1902), p. 12. See also Textiie Recorder, October 1904, p. 162.

37 MBSLAR, 1885, p. 192; MBSLAR, 1913, pp. 35-36.

38 Montgomery (1987), pp. 123-25.

39 MBSLAR, 1871, pp. 256-57. The sample comprised 38 cotton mills, N = 16,875; MBSLAR, 1913, pp. 35-36, shows that 72.7 per cent of the cotton operatives in Fall River, New Bedford and Lowell in 1905 were foreign born. N = 33,846.

40 MBSLAR, 1871, pp. 263-64. See also ibid., pp. 461-62. Chinese contract labour was indeed imported by one factory owner in North Adams, Massachusetts. Leiby, J (1960): Carrol Wright and Labor Reform: The Origin of Labor Statistics, p. 43.

41 MBSLAR, 1881, p. 470; MBSLAR, 1882, pp. 18-19, 25-26.

42 MBSLAR, 1882, pp. 206-7. The second generation of the French Canadians later became strong trade unionists. See MBSLAR, 1913, p. 44.

It is also probable that the newcomers were mainly set to perform the tasks which required the least skill.[43]

Still, in cases of serious industrial disputes, the managers do not seem to have been slow to replace strikers with newly arrived immigrants. This was the case, for instance, in the great Fall River strike in 1904-5.[44] The option to recruit immigrant labour was convenient when managers felt that they had to impose a major wage cut, a need which probably grew substantially towards the end of the 19th century. The increasing competition from the southern U.S. cotton mills after 1890 put more pressure on the manufacturers to impose repeated wage cuts, increases in workloads, and to look for cheap immigrant labour.[45] Also, in the context of industrial relations, it cannot be doubted that ethnic fragmentation made trade union organization much more difficult.[46]

It is also possible that the shift to new ethnic groups had some impact on workforce composition and the use of child labour. As Herbert Gutman has described it, the newcomers were often carriers of conceptions of work and the family which were derived from a primitive rural or "pre-industrial" culture.[47] One of the recurrent demands of the immigrants was to have the whole family employed, not just the adult members. This was clearly the case with the French Canadians, whom Carrol Wright found to be in many ways alien to American ways of life:

> With some exceptions the Canadian French are the Chinese of the Eastern States. They care nothing for our institutions, civil, political, or educational. They do not come to make a home among us, to dwell with us as citizens, and so become a part of us; but their purpose is merely to sojourn a few years as aliens... They are a horde of industrial invaders, not a stream of stable settlers. /.../ they will not send their children to school if they can help it, but endeavor to crowd them into the mills at the earliest possible age. To do this they deceive about the age of their children with brazen effrontery. They deceive also about their schooling...when at length they are cornered by the school officers, and there is no other escape, they move away to some other place where they are unknown, and where they hope by the repetition of the same deceits to escape the schools entirely, and keep the children at work right on in the mills. [48]

Obviously, there is a rather prejudiced strain in this description, and it accordingly caused protests from the French Canadian community. But

---

43 Uttley found that the French Canadian operatives in Fall River were mainly employed in the ring-rooms, the English and Irish in mule-spinning, and the Poles and Portuguese in the blowing and carding rooms. Uttley (1905), p. 31. See MBSLAR, 1913, p. 43.

44 MBSLAR, 1913, p. 39.

45 Textile Recorder, October 1904, p. 162.

46 Young (1902), p. 3.

47 Gutman, H (1973): Work, Culture and Society in Industrializing America, passim.

48 MBSLAR, 1881, pp. 469-70.

even the spokesman of this ethnic group admitted that newly arrived French Canadians were eager to send their children to the mills even if they were below the legal age.[49]

Frances Early has investigated the family economy of the French Canadians in Lowell in 1870, and she concludes that this ethnic group was particularly prone to have their children employed in order to improve the family economy. Work habits and customs from their farming background in rural Quebec influenced family strategies also in the new industrial setting. Children were preferably employed as early as possible, while mothers were generally not allowed to work outside the domestic sphere.[50]

This strengthens the suggestion that the recruitment to the cotton mills of ethnic groups with cultural notions of family employment could to some extent influence child labour levels. In her study of the Amoskeag mills in Manchester, New Hampshire, Tamara Hareven found a much higher degree of factory employment of children among immigrant workers than among the American operatives.[51] Naturally, much still depended on whether the manufacturers could be induced to receive the children. One suggestion is that employers aiming at hiring certain immigrant groups would presumably agree to make such arrangements. Another possibility is that it was easier for the operatives to influence recruitment decisions when these were made by overlookers rather than an employment office. Tamara Hareven has found such patterns, and she also stresses the importance of ethnic and family networks when applying for work in the mill.

However, it has only been possible to find sketchy evidence for the actual impact of the family employment culture among the French Canadians. In an investigation of the cotton mill workforce in Fall River in 1878, there was a clear discrepancy between the English and Irish as compared to the French Canadians regarding the proportion below the age of 16. While 18.7 per cent of the English and 12.4 per cent of the Irish operatives were below 16, the corresponding figure for the French Canadians was 38.7 per cent.[52]

---

49 MBSLAR, 1882, pp. 20-21. However, the representatives of the French Canadians put the main blame on the manufacturers who accepted the factory children, not on the parents who sent them.
50 Early (1982), pp. 180-85.
51 Hareven (1982), pp. 208-14.
52 MBSLAR, 1878, p. 215. N for the English = 4,237; N for the Irish = 2,591; N for the French Canadians = 2,159. However, the problem with this material is that children of foreign parents born in America are classified as American. Especially for the older generation of immigrants, this probably meant that their children were labelled as American to a greater extent than was the case with the newly arrived ethnic groups. Still, even if *all* the child workers labelled as Massachusetts born were to be counted as having English or Irish parents, the level of child labour among this group would still not be more than 20.4 per cent. It is also interesting to note that adult female operatives seems to have been much more prevalent among the Irish than in any other ethnic group. This might have been the result of a different conception of work and the family, or the result of an immigration pattern geared towards single women. See also MBSLAR, 1913, p. 36.

Naturally, there are several possible explanations. First, I have argued that the French Canadians were carriers of a family employment culture which made them seek positions in the factories for their children to a greater extent than operatives of other ethnic backgrounds. Second, the more newly arrived French Canadians were probably in a different life cycle stage than the more established groups, having more children of employable ages. Third, the French Canadians generally had larger families than the other ethnic groups. Fourth, male household heads among the French Canadians were primarily employed as casual labourers, and were therefore more dependent on their children's earnings. Irrespective of which of these suggestions has the greatest explanatory value, it was still the case that the recruitment of French Canadians would tend to increase the levels of child and juvenile labour.

However, the ethnic factor was not the only or even the major cause behind the changes in child labour levels. For instance, the state of the local labour supply must also have had some influence over the manufacturers' choice of workforce. There seems to have been a connection between the proportion of child workers, the French Canadian presence, and the growth rate of the local cotton industry in three Massachusetts cities:

Table 12.   Child labour, ethnic composition, and industrial growth rate in Fall River, Lowell, and Lawrence, 1878.[53]

| City | % Workers below 16 | % French Canad. | Growth rate |
|------|--------------------|-----------------|-------------|
| Fall River | 24.3 | 17.3 | 419 |
| Lowell | 11.1 | 12.6 | 92 |
| Lawrence | 14.0 | 7.9 | 20 |

Sources: MBSLAR, 1878, pp. 215-38; MBSLAR, 1880, p. 61.

Silvia maintains that the rapid growth rate and the accompanying labour scarcity in Fall River during the 1870s induced the manufacturers to demand that the tenants of company housing should provide the firm with a stipulated number of young workers.[54] The level of child labour was therefore a result of both company strategy, the ethnic factor, and priorities within the working-class family.

---

53 The growth rate figure is the proportionate increase in spindelage in these cities between 1865 and 1875. Other evidence also indicates that the growth rate in Fall River in the 1870s was far higher than in the older cotton towns of Lowell and Lawrence. Of the Fall River corporations in 1882, 24 out of 36 had been established after 1870. The corresponding proportion in Lowell was 4 out of 16 and in Lawrence 4 out of 12. MBSLAR, 1882, p. 229.
54 Silvia (1975), p. 247.

In the context of my comparative study, one specific feature of the Massachusetts example was the ethnically connected diversity of family ideologies. My suggestion is that the family employment culture of the French Canadians may have been shared by later immigrants.[55]

Still, the absence of subcontracting forms of employment made the process of labour force composition less dependent on family wage strategies than was the case in Lancashire. The division of work and the high degree of control over the labour process which was exercised by the Massachusetts manufacturers also made adjustments relatively easy when factory laws started to regulate the use of children in the cotton industry.

The early factory legislation in New England appears to have been comparatively inefficient. The first substantial factory law, the Massachusetts Factory Child Law of 1867, was described by the chief of the bureau of labour statistics as "wholly ineffective" and "a mere parade of strong words".[56] The law prohibited factory work for children below 10, and proscribed three months' schooling for children between 10 and 15. However, only one deputy of the constable was appointed to enforce the legislation in all the factories of Massachusetts.

There were also several structural weaknesses in the law. The inspector did not have the legal right to enter the mills, and the law did not proscribe a system of time books and registers of workers, or certificates of age and schooling, which he could check during the course of inspection. The law did not even explicitly prohibit some violations against its provisions, and convictions could only be made if the offence had been committed "knowingly". The loose structure of the legislation and the very low level of inspection made the 1867 law practically impossible to enforce.[57]

In a comparative context, this impression is strengthened by the evidence of an English senior factory inspector who visited Massachusetts in 1876 and 1884, who remarked specifically on its inefficient factory and school legislation.[58]

This also means that reliable statistics on child labour are hard to find. For instance, the 1871 sample of 38 Massachusetts cotton mills indicates that children below 15 years of age constituted 4.7 per cent of the workforce. But Henry Oliver, the chief of the Massachusetts Bureau of Statistics

---

55 Naturally, this depended wholly on the specific family culture of the new ethic group, and also on the pattern of immigration. The newcomers working in the Massachusetts mills after 1900 seem to have predominantly been young single men, and this in turn influenced the composition of the workforce. Report on the Condition of Woman and Child Wage-Earners..., Vol I, pp. 29-32; MBSLAR, 1913, p. 36.
56 MBSLAR, 1870, p. 136.
57 MBSLAR, 1870, pp. 134-37.
58 PP 1892 XXXV, Royal Commission on Labour, evidence of Henderson, Superintending Inspector, p. 376 Q. 9,030-58.

of Labor, held the view that these figures were very unreliable, since "mill-owners and parents combine in overstating the ages of the children employed".[59] In 1872, Oliver specifically pointed out the Pacific mills in Lawrence for including no children in their statistical return, even though investigations had shown that the mill in fact regularly employed many children below 15, and even some below 10 years of age. One Lowell firm had even stated that no children were employed, and that 55 of them attended school![60] The following year, Oliver gave this description of evasion practices in Lowell:

> There are probably several hundred children under fifteen years of age employed in the mills. It is well known that parents often overstate the ages of their children for the purpose of securing employment for them, and of evading the school laws. Overseers, superintendents, and employers are often guilty of collusion with such parents in this regard. It is the rule on all the corporations not to employ children under fifteen years of age. This rule was adopted in consequence of the enactment of the Children's Ten Hour Law of 1867. But neither the law of 1867, nor the rule to which it gave rise, is generally enforced... [61]

Oliver's successor, Carrol D. Wright, held the same opinions on the prospects of enforcement. Due to the evasion practices of managers and parents, the Massachusetts child labour law was not and could not be enforced. The only remedy was compulsory education.[62] Wright found that the situation was worst in the rapidly expanding town of Fall River:

> There is scarcely a corporation in Fall River but that employs children under ten years of age. The responsibility of hiring them, so far as could be ascertained from various sources, is owing as much to parents as manufacturers. In some cases the parents compelled manufacturers to hire their children under threats of leaving their work. [63]

A Fall River mule-spinner stated in 1882 that many parents made false oaths in order to get their children into the mills below the legal age, and that this was especially the case in the neighbouring Rhode Island factories "where they employ young people to do adults' work".[64] The case does not seem to have been much different in the town of Lawrence, as one citizen testified:

---

59 MBSLAR, 1871, p. 264. See also ibid., pp. 256-57, 466-67.
60 MBSLAR, 1872, pp. 162-63.
61 MBSLAR, 1873, p. 281.
62 MBSLAR, 1874, p. 5.
63 MBSLAR, 1874, p. 154.
64 MBSLAR, 1882, p. 202.

There is a large number of children in the mills, and, of course, there are some parents who will lie about their ages, and there are also a number of overseers who are willing to wink at it, thinking they can get work done cheaper by so doing. [65]

The general impression is that the 1867 child labour law was relatively inefficient. Henry Oliver and Carrol Wright continued all through the 1870s to press for improved factory legislation, repeatedly pointing to the British example. The English factory inspectorate, and the structure of the British Factory Acts, were used as models of efficiency.[66] Oliver even strove to establish a system of half-time education in accordance with the English pattern as a better solution than the Massachusetts law on three months schooling per year.[67]

I have not made any closer study of legislative developments, but it seems clear that both surveillance levels and factory laws were improved during the last decades of the 19th century. A Ten Hour Law was passed in 1874, and by 1891 children below 13 were excluded from factory employment.[68] Certificates of age and schooling were required for all workers below 16. These certificates contained a description of the child in order to reduce the risk of fraud, and had to be shown to the inspector on demand. 20 weeks schooling per year was required, and minors between 14 and 18 who could not read or write in English had to attend evening classes. At the same time, an Act of 1888 had increased the number of inspectors to at least two, and had given them the right of free access to factories and workshops, and to make investigations into the employment of children, young persons and women.[69]

The efficiency of the current factory legislation was assessed by the 1910 Senate Committee on the condition of woman and child wage-earners in the United States, on the basis of an inquiry performed in 1907-8 comprising 198 cotton factories.[70] The conclusion of the Committee was that only the state of Massachusetts had attained a reasonable degree of enforcement of its factory regulations.[71] All the New England states had laws which prohibited the employment of children below 14 years of age, but only Massachusetts had developed a reasonably efficient system of

---

65 MBSLAR, 1882, p. 209.
66 MBSLAR, 1870, p. 78; MBSLAR, 1872, p. 540; MBSLAR, 1873, p. 502. See also Leiby (1960), pp. 55-58.
67 MBSLAR, 1871, pp. 489-98; MBSLAR, 1873, p. 502. However, half-time schools were very seldom established. See MBSLAR, 1878, pp. 15-23.
68 MBSLAR, 1875, p. 180; MBSLAR, 1891, p. 78.
69 MBSLAR, 1891, pp. 7-8, 67-79.
70 Report on the Condition..., pp. 13-14. The inquiry covered 18.3 per cent of the mills and 25.4 per cent of the spindles in the U.S. cotton industry.
71 Ibid., pp. 157-69. The secretary of the Ashton Spinners', Lancashire, reported from an American visit in 1909 that factory inspection was less rigid in New England compared to Lancashire. Cotton Factory Times, 16/4/09.

certificates and factory inspection. Massachusetts had 26 factory inspectors by 1902, which was considerably more than any of the other states.[72]

Maine had only one factory inspector with no assistants, and the investigators found that 40.4 per cent of the young workers examined by them were employed contrary to law, and mainly without certificates of age.[73] New Hampshire had no special factory inspectors at all, and the labour laws were only enforced by truant officers. These officials only entered factories when requested to do so by the school boards, but according to the investigation New Hampshire was the only state where the truant officers actually went into the factories to any extent in the search for children who were absent from school. However, fines were seldom imposed even if illegally employed children were discovered - the manufacturers were merely required to send the children to school. Before 1901, the level of enforcement had been rather low.[74]

This picture is corroborated by the work of Hareven and Langenbach on the Amoskeag Mills in Manchester, New Hampshire. They also describe the child labour laws as fairly inefficient, and that overlookers were sometimes persuaded by adult operatives to receive their children even if they were below 14.[75]

In Rhode Island, one of the three appointed factory inspectors visited each mill at least once every year, but their practice of checking the age certificates seems to have been rather lax. A custom had been established that the inspectors would only demand to see the certificates if they believed that a child was actually below 14 years of age. The result was that the Rhode Island manufacturers never bothered to aquire age certificates for the larger or older children, since these documents were never demanded by the inspector. The responsibility for the employment of the young workers often rested with the overlookers, and the investigators were of the opinion that this was only effective if inspection was as stringent as in Massachusetts. In Rhode Island they found that a very large proportion of the young workers did not have the required certificates. 47 per cent of the examined Rhode Island juveniles were illegally employed, as compared to 3.1 per cent in Massachusetts.[76]

---

72 Young (1902), p. 4.
73 Report on the Condition..., pp. 158, 164.
74 Ibid., pp. 166-68.
75 Hareven, T and Langenbach, R (1979): Amoskeag. Life and Work in an American Factory City in New England, p. 119. However, Hareven and Langenbach also rather simplistically state that the ages of the children employed were generally higher than in the early 19th century, "because improvements in the machinery had ended their usefulness". As I will show in a later section, very young children were used on the same machinery in the Southern U.S. cotton factories. See also Hareven (1982), pp. 214, 226.
76 Report on the Condition..., pp. 164, 169-70.

Still, even if Massachusetts stands out in terms of factory law enforcement, it has to be recognized that the inspectors faced very difficult problems. Since a great proportion of the young workers were not born in the U.S., it was difficult to find reliable evidence of age. Foreign born children, who constituted the great majority of the young workers, were not entered in the baptismal records.[77] Parents were mainly interested in having their children employed as early as possible, and even their sworn statements were not regarded as reliable.[78] Incorrect passports and forged documents were sometimes produced to prove a child's age.[79]

The conclusion must be that a substantial number of young workers were really below the legal age, but were officially designated as 14 or 15. Exactly how large this proportion was is very difficult to say. The 1907-8 investigation made an estimation based on a thorough inquiry into the ages of the young workers in the group below 16 years, finding that 9 per cent of that group was actually below the legal age in New Hampshire, 10 per cent in Rhode Island, and 13 per cent in Maine. The corresponding figure for Massachusetts was 0.2 per cent.[80] These figures confirm the impression that the level of illegally employed children was much lower in Massachusetts than in the other New England states.[81]

Even during the period when the enforcement level of the factory laws was only moderately high, there is some evidence that it was enough to induce company managers to reorganize certain work practices involving children. For instance, the custom of using boys to oil the spinning mules seems to have been largely abandoned after the passing of the 1874 Ten Hour Act. According to this law, the protected categories of operatives were not allowed to work during the lunch hour. The managers therefore ordered that the adult male spinners, who were not covered by the law, should do the oiling during the lunch break. This seems to have been the case in Fall River at least by 1882:

---

77 Ibid., pp. 15, 152. In the New England sample of the investigation, 89 per cent of the female and young workers were born outside the U.S. Ibid., p. 17. N = 5,562.

78 Ibid., pp. 147-55.

79 Greeks, who formed an important ethnic minority in Lowell at least by 1912, did not have any passports and were suspected of forging birth certificates for their children in order to have them employed. Report on the Condition..., p. 160; MBSLAR, 1913, p. 35. On forged birth certificates in Fall River in the 1880s, see Silvia (1975), p. 239.

80 Report on the Condition..., pp. 40-41. N for New Hampshire = 111; N for Rhode Island = 498; N for Maine = 497; N for Massachusetts = 605. On the procedure of the investigation, see ibid., p. 15.

81 The Fall River operatives told Thomas Ashton of the Oldham Spinners', Lancashire, in 1902 that the factory laws were fairly well carried out. Mosely Industrial Commission (1903), pp. 126-27.

> Since the taking out of the boys from the spinning room, the spinners are compelled to do their own cleaning and oiling, which makes the work run so much the harder. [82]

This practice had also been introduced in a few mills in Lawrence:

> ...the spinners also complained of a practice that they say has been imported from Fall River, that is, compelling the spinners to oil and clean their own machines, a duty that was formerly done by boys...formerly all that was necessary was to call a boy and have him do the work while the spindles were in operation. [83]

One part of the managerial strategy aimed at intensifying the work of the adult operatives was obviously to reduce the number of young assistant workers. The combination of protective legislation and a set of hostile industrial relations therefore caused the abandoning of work customs which involved child workers, and instead management forced the adult male operatives to perform these tasks on top of their normal duties. This development must be seen in the context of industrial relations in the Massachusetts cotton industry.

However, there was no apparent change in technology which made child labour superfluous. If anything it was rather the reverse. The transition to ring-spinning at the end of the 19th century actually seems to have made it more viable to employ very young workers.[84] The mule-spinner Thomas O'Donnel maintained that the pressure for juvenile operatives in Fall River had been occasioned by the manufacturers' decision to introduce ring-spinning and that all the "small help" were being transferred to that process.[85]

Working as spinners and doffers in ring-spinning soon became the most important positions for children in the Massachusetts cotton factories. According to the 1907-8 investigation, 37.8 of all the New England operatives below 16 were employed in the ring-spinning process.[86] In Massachu-

---

82 MBSLAR, 1882, p. 308. See also Ibid., pp. 301 and 307. Lazonick claims that the tasks of oiling and cleaning the mules were transferred from the back-boys to the spinners in the 1870s. Lazonick (1981c), p. 507.

83 MBSLAR, 1882, p. 344. However, the majority of the Lawrence mills still used oiling boys in 1882. Ibid., p. 353.

84 The transition from mule-spinning to ring-frames was at least to some extent influenced by the manufacturers' desire to get rid of the male mule-spinners and replace them with more docile female operatives. See MBSLAR, 1882, pp. 313-14; Young (1902), p. 4; Uttley (1905), p. 4; Sandberg (1974), p. 34; Silvia (1975), pp. 235-37; Cohen (1985a), pp. 81-84. However, William Lazonick and William Mass are sceptical of this explanation, and see the transition to the ring-frame technology in more strictly "economic" terms. See Lazonick (1981c), p. 514; Mass (1984), p. 38.

85 Testimony in Garraty (1968), p. 33.

86 Report on the Condition..., p. 82. This made it by far the most important occupation for young workers. N = 1,689.

setts, youths below 16 constituted 9.3 per cent of the ring-spinning work-force, as compared to 1.5 per cent in weaving.[87]

Still, young children were not used to the same extent as in the American South. Legal restrictions and the development of the Massachusetts factory inspection by the turn of the century probably made it impossible for the manufacturers to fully utilize cheap child labour in the ring-spinning process. It is interesting to note that an automatic doffer soon appeared, allegedly in response to the restrictions of factory legislation.[88]

The 1907-8 investigation concluded that the extent to which the factory laws were violated was correlated to the efficiency of the inspector force.[89] However, another possible factor is the differences in labour supply. Massachusetts was very well-placed to receive a substantial part of the European immigrants, while labour supplies in New Hampshire and Maine were less proficient. In this perspective, it is plausible that the Massachusetts managers found it relatively easy to gear their production methods and work assignments towards the use of juveniles rather than children. In New Hampshire and Maine, somewhat tighter labour supplies probably made this shift more difficult, and the manufacturers therefore tended to disregard the child labour laws.

This also explains to some extent why child labour early became rela-tively unimportant in Massachusetts. The 1907-8 investigation estimated that 3.4 per cent of the Massachusetts operatives were below 16 years of age, as compared to 4.9 per cent in New Hampshire and 8.4 per cent in Maine. However, the relatively high figure for Rhode Island, 7.3 per cent, indicates that it was not only a question of labour supply.[90] A long tradition of child labour in the Rhode Island cotton mills, and a relatively inefficient factory legislation, are possible reasons for this comparatively high figure.[91].

The various managerial strategies aimed at gaining control over work and recruitment, in combination with tightening legal restrictions, were probably the most important forces behind the gradual decline of child labour in Massachusetts. But it should also be acknowledged that the trade unionists in the New England cotton industry were not in favour of the employment of children. In Massachusetts, it is probable that the early loss

---

87 Ibid., pp. 48-49. N for ring-spinning = 2,152; N for weaving = 4,950.
88 Cotton Factory Times, 6/8/09.
89 Report on the Condition..., p. 166.
90 Ibid., p. 16. N for Massachusetts = 18,001; N for New Hampshire = 2,246; N for Maine = 5,934; N for Rhode Island = 6,810.
91 In 1902 T. M. Young found that a Rhode Island mill still used boys between 12 and 14 years of age to perform the ancillary tasks in automatic weaving. There were also some even younger children who were taken in as "helpers" by their parents with the tacit approval of the management. Young (1902), pp. 23-24. The contrast with Massachusetts is remarkable, but not having done any research on the conditions in Rhode Island I can only suggest that an important element may have been the very long tradition of cheap labour strategies and the employment of children in that state.

of the position as a subcontractor of young assistants led the operative spinners to oppose child labour to a much greater degree than was the case in Lancashire. It is reported that Fall River mule-spinners, who had the strongest union in the New England cotton industry, would take their hats and coats and leave if "boys and girls" were set to mind the self-actors.[92] The United Textile Workers of America, an organization which in spite of its grand name was mainly based in Massachusetts, campaigned against factory child labour in the early 20th century, and this position was also assumed by the American Federation of Labor.[93] The 1907-8 investigators concluded that the New England cotton unions had exerted their influence to restrict child labour, and that their vigilance had in fact increased the efficiency of the factory inspection.[94] Even if the New England unions were perhaps less powerful than their Lancashire equivalents, it is still noteworthy that they did not support child labour practices.

In contrast to the Massachusetts example, child labour levels rose to unprecedented hights in the Southern states at the turn of the century. This phenomenon is to be examined next.

## The Southern U.S. States

The cotton industry in the South expanded dramatically during the last decades of the 19th century. The Southern manufacturers were initially very much geared towards the production of coarse yarn and fabrics, where skill requirements were relatively low. While not being very successful on the older mule-spinning and powerloom technologies, the great opportunity of the southern mill-owners was connected to a major technological change. In the transition to the ring-spinning and automatic loom technologies, the South proved to be more competitive than the old New England industry, and as a result American cotton gradually relocated to the South during the early decades of the 20th century.

The Southern manufacturers had one major advantage: access to extremely cheap labour.[95] In 1905, the Textile Recorder stated on the growth of the Southern U.S. cotton industry:

---

92 MBSLAR, 1871, evidence of D. A. Brayton, Fall River manufacturer, p. 55.
93 See the report of Thomas Ashton, Oldham Spinners', in Mosely Industrial Commission (1903), p. 133; Cotton Factory Times, 9/11/06; Walker, R W (1970): The A.F.L. and Child Labor Legislation: An Exercise in Frustration, passim.
94 Report on the Condition..., p. 608.
95 See Uttley (1905), p. 67, for a calculation of the profitability of automatic looms in the South.

> The cheap labour seems to be the paramount reason for capitalists exploiting the Southern states for spinning and manufacturing purposes, the close proximity of the mills to the cotton fields being only a secondary consideration. [96]

The operatives of the Southern mills were mainly recruited among the small mountain farmers in the "backwoods" Appalachian regions.[97] Blacks were seldom employed, apart from some instances in the picker room where working conditions were uncommonly dusty and disagreeable. Having blacks in the workforce would probably have reduced the prospects of recruiting poor whites.[98]

European immigrants rarely turned towards the South, discouraged above all by the low level of wages. One attempt in 1905 to ship European immigrants directly to Charleston in order to recruit them to the cotton factories ended as a failure.[99] Instead, the cotton industry in the South relied almost completely on the recruitment of the families of impoverished small farmers from the rural hinterland, who were severely pressed by the diminishing prospects in agriculture during this period.[100]

As a part of this process, recruitment to the Southern mills became increasingly geared towards the employment of whole families. The workforce composition immediately after the Civil War was slanted towards the use of female and child labour, but towards the end of the century the adult males were also included.[101] Recruitment patterns seem to have changed from utilizing the women and children of poor farmer househoulds in the vicinity to a more general employment of whole families.[102]

One effect of this shift was an increased employment of adult males. Census figures for the Southern states show that males of 16 years and older increased their proportion of the cotton workforce between 1880 and 1900 from 28.4 to 41.6 per cent. The proportion of children below 16 was virtually unchanged, or roughly 25 per cent.[103] The increasing participation of adult males was occasioned by the development of a more complete family employment structure, not by any changes in the process of production.[104]

---

96 Textile Recorder, Oct. 1905, p. 162.
97 MBSLAR, 1906, p. 42; Report on Condition..., pp. 120-23.
98 MBSLAR, 1906, pp. 44-45; Report on the Condition..., pp. 118-19; Pope, L (1971): Millhands and Preachers. A Study of Gastonia, p. 12.
99 Report on the Condition..., p. 125.
100 See the important article by Hall, Korstad, and Leloudis (1986), pp. 249-51.
101 MBSLAR, 1906, pp. 43-44, 54.
102 See Ward, D C (1987): Industrial Workers in the Mid-Nineteenth Century South: Family and Labor in the Graniteville (S C) Textile Mill, 1845-1880, pp. 336-44.
103 Report on the Condition..., p. 28. N for 1880 = 16,317; N for 1900 = 97,494.
104 Ibid., pp. 34, 58. Saxonhouse and Wright (1984a), p. 16.

The poor farmers who migrated to the factory villages brought with them strong cultural notions of family employment. All family members were supposed to find work in the mill. In the same way as the children had been set to work on the farm, they were now expected to be employed in the mill and contribute to the family economy. The specific context of the Southern mill village was largely designed in such a way as to allow a relative permanence of rural habits and customs.[105] Pre-industrial notions of work and the family therefore remained strong in the factory villages, a process which was underpinned by the fact that the migrants did not confront any older segment of factory operatives with different cultural notions. Family employment structures were therefore very persistent in the Southern mills. T. W. Uttley concluded that the child labour problem in the South had been caused by labour scarcity and the employment of entire families, "but in many cases the fault has been with the parents, who have insisted on employment being found for their children as well as themselves".[106]

Naturally, this situation would not have occurred without the interest of the manufacturers. The persistent scarcity of factory labour in the South was undoubtably the main reason why the mill-owners supported the system of family employment.[107] The hiring of poor landless families supplied the manufacturers with both younger operatives and adults at hardly more than subsistence costs, which was probably cheaper than finding "free" workers in a labour market.[108] Moreover, the low wage levels and the cultural "otherness" of the mill village operatives made recruitment difficult.[109] Quarrels between manufacturers for "stealing help" from each other were common, and some firms even employed private police to throw out recruiting agents from other mills.[110]

The persistence of family employment practices in the Southern mills must be seen as the major reason why the workforce comprised such a high proportion of children. The 1905 Census of Manufactures recorded the proportion of children below 16 in the cotton workforce as 12.0 per cent in Virginia, 22.5 per cent in North Carolina, 23.7 per cent in South Carolina, 22.4 per cent in Georgia, 27.0 per cent in Alabama, and 25.7 per cent in Mississippi. The corresponding level in Massachusetts was 6.3 per cent.[111]

---

105 Hall, Korstad, and Leloudis (1986), pp. 250-51.
106 Uttley (1905), pp. 45-46.
107 On the labour scarcity in Southern mills, see MBSLAR, 1906, pp. 45, 71, 74.
108 Saxonhouse and Wright (1984a), pp. 7-8, 18.
109 Report on the Condition..., p. 32. On the isolation of the operatives in "mill villages", see ibid., p. 585; Newman, D (1978): Work and Community Life in a Southern Textile Town, p. 207.
110 MBSLAR, 1906, p. 55; Report on the Condition..., pp. 126-27; Hall, Korstad, and Leloudis (1986), pp. 262-63.
111 Report on the Condition, p. 26. N for Virginia = 3,456; N for North Carolina = 36,356; N for South Carolina = 37,271; N for Georgia = 24,130; N for Alabama = 11,480; N for Mississippi = 2,161; N for Massachusetts = 88,033. The sample from the 1907-8 investigation shows a general reduction of a few per

The utilization of child labour was to some extent facilitated by the technology shift towards ring-spinning, which seems to have been fairly adaptable to the use of children. Factory statistics show that most children were found in the ring-spinning process, the girls as spinners and the boys as doffers:

Table 13. The proportion of child workers below 16 in the separate labour processes in the Southern U.S. states, 1907-8. per cent.

| Gender | Doffers | Ring-spin. | Speeders | Spoolers | Weavers | Other |
|--------|---------|-----------|----------|----------|---------|-------|
| Boys   | 31.0    | 3.7       | 0.4      | 0.1      | 3.0     | 14.3  |
| Girls  | 4.9     | 31.1      | 0.4      | 4.9      | 3.5     | 7.1   |

Source: 61st Congress 2nd Session. Senate Document No 645. Report on the Condition of Woman and Child Wage-Earners in the United States, Vol I, p. 83. [112]

Ring-spinning was the major position for child labour also in the younger age group. Of the child workers below 14 in the above sample, 70.4 per cent were employed as doffers and ring-spinners. There was definitely a managerial preference for placing the youngest workers in the ring-spinning rooms.

However, it should be recognized that the organization of work in the Southern mills was designed to utilize all the labour provided by the family employment structure.[113] Adult males were usually set to mind the speeder and roving frames, an occupation which in New England, Lancashire and Japan was entirely female.[114] Children were even used as "helpers" in automatic weaving, a process where no younger operatives were used either in Massachusetts or in Lancashire.[115] This indicates that the technology as such did not have a decisive impact on the use of children in the mills.

These findings naturally question whether there was any predominantly "technological" cause of child labour in the American cotton industry. On the same kind of machinery, children were employed in the South and juveniles or adults in New England.

The Southern method of production was definitely not a case of using cheap labour on old technology. The ring-frames and automatic looms in

cent in all states except Virginia, where the result was a rise of similar size. Ibid., p. 16. These are official figures which probably underestimate the real level of child labour.
112 N = 9,665. The relatively large "other" category comprised 38 different occupations, like band boys, bobbin boys, sweepers, warp hand helpers, and spare hands. Report on the Condition..., p. 84.
113 See Saxonhouse and Wright (1984a), pp. 13-14, 17.
114 Ibid., p. 17; Report on the Condition..., pp. 48-50, 57.
115 See Young (1902), p. 93; Uttley (1905), pp. 23, 57, 65; MBSLAR, 1906, p. 77.

the South constituted the most modern generation of textile machinery.[116] Instead, the Southern case illustrates the importance of the social and cultural context, and the processes and structures connected with the supply side of the child labour equation.[117]

In one sense, the substantial use of child labour in the Southern mills may have been the result of the removal of ideological barriers. David Ward has recently suggested that before the Civil War, cotton manufacturers had to show that working in the mills was not tantamount to "factory slavery". Relying on a workforce composed of poor whites, they had to impress the picture that the lives and conditions of the cotton operatives were much different from those of the blacks. This meant that children could not be employed before the age of 12, since this was the culturally defined age for young slaves to commence work. However, after the Civil War this situation dissolved, and all restrictions on child labour were lifted.[118]

There were also other preconditions for the strong child labour element in the Southern mills. One important reason why the child labour practices could persist was the virtual absence of factory and school legislation. There were no regulations on child labour before the early 20th century, and schooling was generally cut short by mill employment.[119] By 1910 all the Southern states had laws prohibiting the employment of children below 12, except North Carolina where the limit was 13 and Virginia where it was set to 14.[120] However, contemporary inquiries show that these laws were not enforced. Investigators from the Massachusetts Bureau of Statistics of Labor concluded in 1906 that laws and agreements on child labour in the South were "honored more in the breach than the observance".[121] One of them reported from a South Carolina cotton mill:

> ...the spectacle of child-labor with all its evils presented itself. There were not one or two, but scores of girls and boys, and a number of them did not appear to be more than eight years of age. [122]

---

116 See MBSLAR, 1906, pp. 81, 88.

117 It has been argued that the coarse qualities of the cotton products in the South would favour the employment of children, while the finer qualities manufactured in New England would require the employment of older workers. However, this argument should rather be reversed. The kind of work produced in the South was above all determined by the class of operatives they could recruit. Persistent labour scarcity and low levels of skill among the adult operatives, together with the implications of the family employment structure, made coarse products the only viable choice for the Southern manufacturers. See ibid., pp. 21, 58-61. See also Saxonhouse and Wright (1984a), pp. 16-17.

118 Ward, D C (1987), pp. 332-33.

119 Newman (1978), p. 207.

120 Report on the Condition..., p. 171.

121 MBSLAR, 1906, p. 55. See also ibid., p. 72.

122 Ibid., p. 72. See ibid., p. 77, for a similar report from a Georgia mill.

The Senate investigation in 1907-8 also found that children were very commonly employed below the legal age of 12, and concluded that the child labour laws were "openly and freely violated in every State we visited".[123] Naturally, this should be seen in the context of a virtual absence of factory inspection. By the time of this investigation, only the states of Virginia and Alabama had any provisions at all for the enforcement of the child labour laws. Virginia had instituted a probably rather feeble machinery for factory inspection in 1906. In Alabama, the inspector of jails and almshouses had also been given the task of inspecting the factories.[124]

The effect can hardly have been substantial. In the reports from the Southern states in 1907-8 it emerged that the real child labour level was clearly higher than the official figures. The investigations showed that wage books and census figures did not reflect the real extent of child labour, since the younger children were often brought in as "helpers" to older siblings, and did not receive separate wages. The manufacturers claimed that they were not responsible for the work practices which were used within the families, and would not regard these children as being employed by them. The investigators saw the "helper" system as a subterfuge which was used to evade the legal age limits.[125] The statistics on child labour in the South therefore seriously underestimate the real extent of child labour.[126]

The question of factory legislation also had regional and political implications. There was strong agitation in the Northern states for federal initiatives against child labour practices in the South. On the other hand, Southerners like Broadus Mitchell saw child labour not as an evil, but as a part of a nation struggling to lift itself out of the void occasioned by the Civil War:

> ...cotton manufacturing was hailed as a boon especially because it gave means of livelyhood to women and children. Poverty-stricken, the South was mustering every resource to stagger to its feet. All labor power was empirically seized upon; response was eager. At that critical juncture, later results of the employment of children could not be looked to. The great morality then was to go to work. The use of children was

---

123 Report on the Condition..., p. 171. 107 of the 143 inspected Southern mills were reported as employing children below the legal age.
124 Ibid., p. 214.
125 Ibid., pp. 189-90. The use of "helpers" was most common in North and South Carolina. See also Uttley (1905), p. 46, where he claimed that the employment of very young children as "helpers" was "a point where the Southern manufacturer is peculiarly blind". T. M. Young was told that the youngest girls in a South Carolina mill came in to help their sisters. Young (1902), p. 72.
126 In at least ten Southern mills the investigators found out that the mill manager had tried to conceal the true number of children employed, either by not producing the relevant wage-rolls or simply by sending the children home at the time of the inspection. Report on the Condition..., pp. 192-95.

not avarice then, but philanthropy; not exploitation, but generosity and cooperation and social-mindedness. [127]

Northeners, no doubt, viewed the matter less apologetically. However, they had also weighty economic reasons for imposing factory legislation on the South. The New England unions saw the competition from the cheap labour mills in the South as the most important threat to their existence. The New England manufacturers also supported attempts to introduce federal legislation which would limit the freedom of the Southern mill-owners to employ children.[128] Southern manufacturers and politicians violently resisted the prospect of state factory inspection, and often accused labour reformers of being instruments of the Northern manufacturers.[129]

However, the legislative initiatives were hardly successful. The Keating-Owen Act on child labour in 1916 was ruled to be "unconstitutional" by the Supreme Court in a verdict two years later, and federal legislation on this issue was not achieved until the late 1930s.[130]

Still, it is possible that the reliance on child labour in the Southern mills lessened somewhat over time.[131] As Saxonhouse and Wright have argued, the workforce in the Southern mills became slightly older when the factories had been in operation for a few decades.[132] In the first phase of establishment, the manufacturers were not keen to employ unskilled adults who had no experience from cotton factory work. Children and juveniles were most often preferred. The 1907-8 investigators concluded that older women were seldom employed in the South, "because they have not learned the work while young".[133] But as the first generation of young workers grew up, some of them remained in the mill as adults. The heavy reliance on child labour during the early period could therefore to some extent be seen as an effect of the initial process of industrialisation, a phase which most countries went through at one point or other. Entering late into industrial capitalism, the American South was still in this transitional state in the early 20th century.

The persistence of child labour practices and family employment notions also corresponded with a very limited development of trade union organiza-

127 Mitchell, B [1921]: The Rise of the Cotton Mills in the South, p. 95. For a recent criticism of this type of description of Southern child labour practices, see Beatty, B (1987): Lowells in the South: Northern Influences on the Nineteenth-Century North Carolina Textile Industry, p. 61.
128 Lea, A J (1975): Cotton Textiles and the Federal Child Labor Act of 1916, passim.
129 MBSLAR, 1906, pp. 67, 73; Report on the Condition..., p. 609.
130 See Walker, R W (1970), pp. 330-32, 340.
131 Southern mill operatives claimed in 1906 that child labour levels were lower than previously. See MBSLAR, 1906, pp. 55, 74.
132 Saxonhouse and Wright (1984a), pp. 13-14; Wright, G (1981): Cheap Labour and Southern Textiles, 1880-1930, pp. 624-28.
133 Report on the Condition..., p. 35.

tion and consciousness. The cotton workers in the South were not able to form stable unions, to the great disappointment of the organizers from New England. The massive hostility towards union activity displayed by the manufacturers was naturally an important part of this process, together with the primitive rural background of the workers. The manufacturers suspected that unions would not only raise wages, but also agitate for factory inspection and child labour legislation.[134] Quitting the job and moving away remained the viable way to express dissatisfaction and protest.[135]

In most cases the cotton operatives remained locked in a quasi-paternalist relationship with the manufacturers. This situation was perhaps facilitated by the prevailing practice of building separate factory villages around the mills, which made the operatives dependent on the manufacturers in all parts of their daily lives.

However, employer dominance was never complete. While the mill village structure served to isolate the cotton workers from the rest of Southern society, it also created strong quasi-familial ties within the factory community which in turn could be used to limit the social influence of the employer.[136] The Southern kind of mill-owner paternalism also required that the owner would act as a buffer between the operatives and the supervisors by listening to grievances concerning overlooker actions and behaviour.[137]

For the employers, the building of separate mill villages was a way to increase their control over the workforce, and to minimize "outside interference".[138] Strong employer control and relative deprivation were at least at some larger establishments coupled with "welfare institutions" which were mainly intended to induce discipline and lessen the labour turnover.[139] Alternative conceptions of work, family, and trade unionism, were difficult to introduce in this social context. Factory schools were described by one Georgia mill-owner as a "losing investment", because when the operatives realized their condition they would no longer accept working in the mill.[140] Family employment and child labour remained an issue in the Southern mills well into the 1930s.[141]

---

134 Ibid., p. 608. This was the New England pattern of union activity.

135 Hall, Korstad, and Leloudis (1986), p. 260.

136 Indeed, the radicalisation of the Southern mill villages in the 1930s seems to have been one reason for the manufacturers to abandon the system and rely more on dispersed rural labour. See Hall, Korstad, and Leloudis (1986), passim.

137 Ibid., pp. 255-57.

138 Uttley (1905), p. 47. Rates were also lower in the countryside than in the towns.

139 Report on the Condition..., pp. 126-27, 608; Hall, Korstad, and Leloudis (1986), pp. 263-65.

140 MBSLAR, 1906, p. 76.

141 Saxonhouse and Wright have argued that child labour in the Southern mill "virtually disappeared" after the passing of the Keating-Owen child labour act in 1916. Saxonhouse and Wright (1984a), pp. 13-14.

The rather primitive nature of industrial relations in the Southern mill villages also had its drawbacks. In the same way as in Scotland, the structure of production relations created a situation where the operatives defended customary workloads and efforts. Manufacturers often complained over the low intensity of work, comparing their mill-people unfavourably with the New England operatives. One Southern mill-owner stated in 1906 that he found it impossible to make his operatives work harder: "The moment you commence to drive them, they become hostile, and often quit their work". The investigator from the MBSL found that the mill operative in the South did not have the same "ambition to earn money" as the New England workers.[142] Indeed, the very low work intensity in the Southern mills may have been an additional reason why the manufacturers were reluctant to give up the very cheap labour of children.

# Conclusions

The American example shows a clear discrepancy between Massachusetts and the Southern states, and also with Britain. The diminishing use of child labour in the Massachusetts cotton mills was the outcome of several processes, both in the sphere of production and in the wider societal context. The lack of subcontracting forms of employment in both self-actor spinning and weaving separated the spheres of work and family wage strategies, and did not give the Massachusetts minder or weaver the option to choose cheap child assistants. It also made it easier for the employers to adapt the tasks of doffing and back-tenting to the employment of juveniles rather than children.

The organization of work was different than in Lancashire in both spinning and weaving; labour was more divided and under more firm control by management. The Lancashire "tenter-system" in weaving had no counterpart in Massachusetts, and child labour in this process was virtually unknown. On the other hand, child labour in the carding processes was more common in Massachusetts than in Lancashire, at least until the 1880s.

Another important difference was that the Massachusetts factory legislation did not regulate child labour in a half-time system. Instead, the structure of the law was to prohibit entirely the employment of children

---

However, I remain doubtful if the act really had this dramatic effect on child labour levels. J. P. Felt has maintained that the effect of the act of 1916 was small. Felt, J P (1970): The Child Labor Provisions of the Fair Labor Standards Act, p. 471.

142 MBSLAR, 1906, p. 68. See also Ibid., pp. 71-72, 78. The Southern operatives earned 50-60 per cent less than the Massachusetts workers.

below 13, later 14, years of age. Child labour was not "institutionalized" in the same way as in the Lancashire half-time system. I would also suggest that the relatively efficient enforcement of the Massachusetts law by 1900 had a real effect on child labour levels. By the time of the transition to ring-spinning technology, factory legislation was relatively stringently enforced, and the manufacturers were no longer in a situation to utilize cheap child labour. Instead, the predominant recruitment strategy continued to be the employment of recently arrived immigrants.

The American example shows a great contrast between the early decline of child labour levels in Massachusetts and a simultaneous rise in the South. While the Northern manufacturers ended subcontracting, increased the division of labour, and changed work assignments towards the employment of juveniles, women, and immigrants, the Southern manufacturers opted for a cheap labour strategy and family employment structures. The recruitment of "poor whites" to isolated mill villages tended to buttress a culture of family employment and child labour. In the virtual absence of factory and school legislation, the use of children in the Southern mills continued into the 1930s.

# Chapter 13

# Conclusions and Results

At the outset of this investigation, I proposed that the problem of industrial child labour should be studied in the triangle drawn up by the process of production, the working-class household, and the regulations imposed by the state. The societal structures and processes within or between these fields influenced child labour levels. Special consideration has been paid to the organization of the labour process, the spread of new technology, trade union aims, the employment strategies of working-class parents, the recruitment systems used by the manufacturers, labour market structures, and the efficiency of factory legislation.

Where previous research has primarily tried to establish the impact of factory legislation and technological change on industrial child labour within the boundaries of one country, I have applied a comparative perspective in order to see how child labour practices in the same industrial trade changed between different societal contexts.

A comparison between England, Scotland, and, to some extent, the United States, has shown that very different patterns existed in these countries regarding the use of child labour in cotton factories. The great variation between these patterns questions the notion that child labour was above all preconditioned by the use of a certain technology, a notion which has dominated research during the past decade.

## A Summary of the Findings

In the British cotton industry, production was initially very much geared towards the use of children. The early manufacturers were unwilling to hire adults who had no previous experience in cotton manufacturing. Labour scarcity and a preference for very cheap workers led them to rely on the use of poor parish apprentices, a practice which was common in the early water-powered mills in both England and Scotland.

However, it was probably also the case that the manufacturers over-estimated the advantage of cheap child labour. Believing that the machinery needed no more than occasional supervision, the recruitment of children was the initial priority. Only gradually did the mill-owners recognize that the productivity of adult workers was much higher.

Simultaneously, there were also important changes in technology and the labour process. The preparatory processes of picking and carding, tasks which had previously been performed by women and children, were fully mechanized. Adult males were increasingly employed as carders and, by the 1790s, on the new mule-spinning machines.

By the 1820s the system of hiring parish apprentices had virtually ceased, and the mode of employment had shifted towards "free" wage labour in the towns, and family employment structures in the country mills. The development of steam technology made possible an increasing urbanisation of the British cotton industry, which in turn strongly enhanced the available labour supply. Drawing on the children and juveniles of the whole working-class population, some urban manufacturers tried to cheapen production by recruiting a very young and low-paid workforce.

On the other hand, in the country mills the establishment of factory villages and the relatively tight labour supplies tended to promote a work-force which was considerably older than in the towns. Evidence from 1816 suggests that this was the case in country factories which had been in operation for a few decades, where the manufacturers had access to adult cotton operatives who had been trained in the mill since they were young.

The different age structures of the cotton workforce in town and country can hardly be explained in terms of new technology reducing the need for child labour. The machinery in the country factories was generally older and more primitive than in the urban mills. Instead, managerial recruitment strategies and labour market characteristics must be emphasized.

Still, in the context of the labour process, it is clear that there had been a major change between 1790 and 1830. While children had earlier been pre-dominant in the preparatory processes and in throstle-spinning, at the later date they were mainly employed as piecers and scavengers in mule-spinning. This was very clear in the urban mills geared to the spinning of relatively fine yarn, where mules predominated. Throstle-spinning was at this time primarily an occupation for young women, but certain variations no doubt existed.

This also meant another very important change in the mode of employ-ment of young workers. Practically all piecers and scavengers in mule-spinning were subcontracted by the adult spinners, while child workers in carding and throstle-spinning had previously been hired directly by the manufacturer. The subcontracting relationship gave the adult spinner a certain power to determine the ages of his assistants. This had two important consequences. First, it gave him the option to hire his own sons or daughters as piecers. This augmented the family wage, and created a link between work and the household. Second, subcontracting was also used as part of a union strategy to keep down the ages of non-family piecers in order to avoid a great surplus of adult spinners. Children from other working-class households were generally dismissed after a few years and replaced with younger ones.

By the 1830s, the use of children in the cotton factories had declined compared to the late 18th century. Nevertheless, perhaps prompted by an increasing use of child piecers in mule-spinning, a factory reform movement demanded the regulation of child labour. The eventual result was the 1833 and 1844 Factory Acts, which limited the working day of children, prescribed some daily schooling, and created a government inspectorate to ensure their enforcement. My investigation shows that evasions were common at least up to 1840, and that reasonable enforcement was probably not achieved until 1845, when the work of children below 13 was organized in a regular half-time system. After this date, the child labour clauses of the Factory Acts were well enforced in Lancashire.

These findings are contrary to the position of recent research on the British factory legislation, above all the work of P. W. J. Bartrip and P. T. Fenn. They have not recognized that the Factory Acts contained clauses which differed very markedly in enforcement viability and policy. Where they have seen a general low observance of the law, and an attitude of gradual resignation among the inspectors, I have shown that some parts of the law were more effectively enforced than others. The clauses on child labour were substantially enforced already by 1845, while safety measures and overworking remained considerably more difficult for the inspectors to handle.

One important effect of the factory legislation was to induce the British manufacturers to give priority to the recruitment of children who could pass for being 13 years of age. The use of children below that age was accompanied by the demands of increased book-keeping, and also a legal responsibility for the schooling of the factory children. The initial response of many manufacturers was to stop hiring children below 13.

However, in the Lancashire cotton industry the half-time system grew perceptibly in importance after 1850, and was only abolished by an Education Act in 1917. The growth of the system should be seen in the context of changing industrial relations, and a general climate of compromise between manufacturers and unions in the second half of the 19th century.

The operative mule-spinners supported a continued recruitment of children, partly in order to be able to employ their own sons and daughters as piecers, and partly to lower their own costs when hiring assistants from other working-class families. The general growth of the industry during this period and an accompanying scarcity of labour also played some part in this development. As a result of a more general compromise between the mill-owners and the operative spinners, the latter were increasingly allowed to hire children below 13 years of age.

Similarly, the new segment of self-actor minders which emerged in the 1840s soon took over the pattern of subcontracting piecers which had been the rule in hand-mule spinning. While this has previously been seen primarily as a result of union strength, this investigation has shown that for the manufacturers, too, there were considerable advantages connected with the retainment of subcontracting. Above all, this development should be seen in the context of managerial responses to the early factory legislation. The difficulty of recruiting juvenile labour in the wake of the 1833 Act served as an important reason for the mill-owners to accept the practice of subcontracting at the new self-actors. The spinners were in this way made responsible for the recruitment of their own piecers.

Another important part of the rise of the half-time system in the Lancashire industry was the use of subcontracted tenters in powerloom weaving. As part of a general managerial strategy to encourage the weaving operatives to mind more looms, half-time tenters were allowed to help the adult weavers with ancillary tasks, watching the looms, and re-threading shuttles. For the operatives this was a way to earn more wages, as well as to employ their own children or younger siblings. The half-time system in weaving became especially strong in the north-east corner of the English cotton district. By the 1880s, the weaving process had clearly passed mule-spinning as the main employer of children.

The organization of work in the minder-piecer system in mule-spinning and the tenter-system in weaving proved to be remarkably stable. During the course of the late 19th century, these structures became embedded in and buttressed by the structure of industrial bargaining. They were also strongly defended by the unions. But the survival of these forms of work should also be seen as a result of managerial strategies, preferences, and options. The minder-piecer and tenter-systems, combined with the structure of price lists which were devised to determine wages, proved to be very efficient. Work productivity was high and stoppages relatively few. Moreover, when the Lancashire industry came under increasing pressure from foreign competition towards the end of the century, this organization of work proved to be optimal in connection with a strategy of using cheaper qualities of raw cotton. This should also be seen in the perspective of a strong dependence on Third World markets. These were the reasons why the Lancashire manufacturers never in any real sense challenged the traditional way of organizing production. Previous research has, somewhat mistakenly, ascribed this permanence to union strength and institutional rigidity.

The support of the great majority of manufacturers for the tenter-system in weaving combined with the use of cheap yarn is also an important part of the explanation why the automatic loom failed to spread in Lancashire after 1900. Where applied, the new technology tended to be run entirely with adult operatives, but since its introduction never became more than fragmentary, the traditional tenter-system continued to dominate the Lancashire industry.

Still, it cannot be doubted that the level of child labour declined somewhat after a high point in the mid-1870s. There were several reasons for this development. The preferences of the operative mule-spinners shifted markedly in favour of older piecers after 1880. This was probably caused by the work becoming more arduous on the ever longer and faster mules, which demanded a great deal of stamina and precision of the young piecers and creelers. But it was also caused by a long-term shift in union priorities. Previously, the mule-spinners had tried to keep down the ages of the piecers in order to avoid a surplus of skilled spinners. However, towards the end of the 19th century, the union position of the spinners was sufficiently strong to induce them to allow a gradual rise in the ages of their assistants. The normal age of exit for superfluous big piecers now became the early twenties. The result was a general rise in the age profile of the piecers.

However, there were also other processes involved. As part of a general shift in industrial relations towards the end of the century, employers were becoming less willing to accept the hiring of half-timers as part of the subcontracting relationship. This was especially the case with the new public limited companies. New firms were not bound to customary agreements on subcontracting in the same way as old family concerns with "paternalistic" traditions. Moreover, the minders employed in the new firms were less in a position to demand the right to hire children but, working on longer and more modern mules, they were also more able to pay the higher wages of older piecers.

Finally, changes in the legal structure narrowed the recruitment of half-timers. The minimum factory age was raised successively from eight in the 1870s to twelve in 1901, leaving only the year between twelve and thirteen for half-time work.

Still, the use of children in the Lancashire cotton factories proved to be remarkably resilient in the core area comprising the Burnley, Oldham, Rochdale, and Bolton districts. After years of steady decline, the half-time system stabilized again during the boom of 1906, and appears to have remained on that level during the subsequent decade. The long tradition of subcontracting children in mule-spinning, weaving, and drawing-in had created a "half-time culture" among the Lancashire cotton operatives which proved to be relatively persistent. The general perception was that it was normal and desirable to send the children to the mills as early as possible in order to turn them into good operatives and to have some contribution to the family economy.

While the continuation of subcontracting practices in mule-spinning and powerloom weaving is seen as the most important precondition for the permanence of this kind of working-class perceptions, it should also be pointed out that this "culture" remained strongest in a core area character-ised by union influence, industrial expansion, and a relative scarcity of operatives. In the weaving district in the North-East, the use of children as half-time tenters was uncommonly persistent. However, it should also be noted that the half-time system was probably also strengthened by the gradual growth of ring-spinning, a process where children were commonly employed as "doffers" by the manufacturers.

Taken altogether, this meant that the half-time system remained at a stable level in the Lancashire district, above all in the central and northern parts, until it was finally abolished by an Education Act in 1917.


The Scottish development was very different. As a response to the 1833 Factory Act, the Glasgow cotton manufacturers disallowed the hiring of children below 13. The mule-spinners were no longer permitted to recruit piecers below that age. This was not an effect of the law in iself; rather, it was a combination of the legal restrictions on child labour and the specific managerial strategies which were formed at its implementation. The response of the mill-owners should above all be seen in the light of the very strained industrial relations which characterised the Glasgow cotton trade. The refusal to allow the employment of children below 13 meant that the trouble of finding older workers could be transferred to the operative mule-spinners.

As a part of this study I have reassessed the enforcement of the early factory legislation in the Glasgow cotton district. Ursula Henriques has maintained that enforcement levels were low due to the unreliability and slackness of James Stuart, factory inspector between 1836 and 1849. How-ever, she has not realized that the 1833 Act was met with very different managerial strategies in Glasgow compared to Lancashire. Due to the very strained industrial relations in the Glasgow cotton trade, the manufacturers decided to make their operative spinners responsible for the hiring of young operatives. The whole trouble of adapting to the child labour clauses was transferred to the adult workers. Due to these specific circumstances, the potential conflicts in the relationship between Stuart and the Glasgow mill-owners were largely removed. The mule-spinners were designated as the offending party when breaches of the law took place.

What is more important, this co-operation meant that the law was much more stringently enforced in the Glasgow district than in Lancashire. The operative spinners were not in a position to disguise their breaches of the law, and the punishment was very severe. Stuart soon adopted the policy of having the operatives found at fault discharged, a method which was not in accordance with the legal text. However, in terms of enforcement this measure proved to be uncommonly efficient. The manufacturers' reactions to the 1833 Act, and their co-operation with the factory inspector, ensured that the law was substantially enforced in the Glasgow district. This continued to be the case at least until the 1860s, long after the death of James Stuart.

There were also some important differences in the organization of production between Scotland and Lancashire. In the 1880s, the Glasgow manufacturers dissolved the traditional minder-piecer system. After that, the self-acting mules were operated entirely by young female operatives. Consequently, child labour below 13 was virtually prohibited by the Glasgow manufacturers already in the 1830s, and a half-time system in mule-spinning was never allowed to emerge.

Similarly, a tenter-system in weaving never developed in the Glasgow industry. Since the manufacturers could not provide the weavers with an incentive to mind more looms, the normal machine assignment remained the traditional two per weaver at least until the early 20th century. The sub-contracting of child "tenters" never became an issue under these circumstances. Child labour was hardly ever used in Glasgow powerloom weaving.

The key issue in the Glasgow case seems to have been the manufacturers' refusal to allow the employment of half-timers, and their virtually autocratic rule over the trade after the large spinners' strike in 1837. The kind of compromises and the regular structure of industrial bargaining which characterised the Lancashire industry after mid-century never emerged in Glasgow. The manufacturers insisted on personal control over wages and conditions.

Naturally, an important precondition for the Glasgow line of development was the access to relatively large supplies of juvenile workers who could take the place of the children, and also that it was possible for the manufacturers to gear the composition of their workforce increasingly towards young female operatives. Male workers were replaced with females as soon as it was deemed viable. Consequently, while avoiding the utilization of cheap child labour, due to the restrictions imposed by legislation, the mill-owners instead utilized the cheap labour of young women.

Outside the city of Glasgow, the situation was slightly different. Child workers were used somewhat longer in the large country mills, probably due to a greater scarcity of labour in those locations. But these young workers were soon marginalized, and the workforce geared more heavily towards young females. Already by the 1840s, children were seldom used in the country mills.

In comparison to the Lancashire example, it is obvious that child labour practices very early lost their importance in the Scottish industry. The most important differences seem to have been in authority structures and managerial strategies. Even though subcontracting was retained in Glasgow mule-spinning until the 1880s, the spinners were simply not allowed to hire piecers below 13. This meant that subcontracting could never become a link between work and family in the same way as in Lancashire. The manufacturers' exercise of power, and their preference for juvenile workers, ensured that children were not employed.

The American case also offers some interesting contrasts. In the early phase of industrialisation, the Massachusetts cotton factories were organized in two very different ways. In the southern part of the state, the early cotton mills were dominated by family employment. The workforce consisted mainly of male adults and children of various ages, while the adult women remained at home. Child labour levels were high in this setting. In contrast, the cotton factories in the northern part of the state were organized in a "boarding" system, relying heavily on the recruitment of young females from the surrounding agricultural districts. In the cotton town of Lowell, the workforce became wholly dominated by young females between 15 and 25 years of age, while child labour remained insignificant. This discrepancy was primarily caused by differences in recruitment strategies and societal contexts.

After 1840, the whole Massachusetts cotton industry turned gradually towards "free" wage labour, above all in the form of newly arrived immigrants. In this context I have suggested that the cultural conceptions of family employment among the new ethnic groups could possibly have influenced the use of children in factories. Male household heads among the newly arrived immigrants were also mainly employed in unskilled or casual occupations, and the family was therefore more reliant on the children's wages. This appears to have been the case with the French Canadians, who constituted a very important group of operatives in the New England mills after mid-century. The French Canadians appear to have insisted on the employment of their children when seeking work.

Naturally, the precondition was that the manufacturers were ready to accept such demands. My suggestion is that the employers granted these requests when they were eager to recruit a specific ethnic group, for example during industrial struggles. Differences in work culture between ethnic groups in New England therefore have some relevance for the study of industrial child labour.

However, this should not overshadow the fact that the main line of development within the Massachusetts industry was an increasing marginalization of child labour. Changes in work procedures and the ending of subcontracting forms of employment constituted important parts of this process. Self-actor minders in Massachusetts mills were generally not allowed to subcontract their assistants. In most cases they were not even allowed to have piecers, and were supposed to do all the piecing operations themselves. The creel-filling was performed by special "back-boys", who often attended several pairs of mules. Similarly, the task of "doffing" was performed by gangs of juvenile operatives. The organization of work was geared away from the use of very young operatives.

The contrast to the Lancashire example is evident. As I have argued above, the continuation of subcontracting constituted the backbone of the half-time system in Lancashire cotton. The termination of this form of employment in the Massachusetts mills already by mid-century removed an important mechanism for the employment of children. The adult operatives could no longer choose to hire children out of family wage considerations, union aims, or simply for economic reasons. The manufacturers gained a more complete control over employment.

In terms of the labour process, powerloom weaving constitutes a very clear example of the difference between Massachusetts and Lancashire. While child labour in weaving was the main prop of the half-time system in Lancashire by the 1880s, it is obvious that child labour was not used at all in this process in the Massachusetts mills. Instead of developing a system of operative weavers subcontracting their own tenters as a way to enhance productivity, the Massachusetts employers separated the weaving operations from the ancillary tasks of cleaning and maintenance, and increased the machine assignment. As a result of managerial initiatives, the labour process became much more divided than was the case in Lancashire.

Obviously, the dimension of power is essential. The insistence of the Massachusetts employers on gaining a full control over recruitment and the labour process was a major force behind the declining use of factory children. Subcontracting was disallowed, and instead the work was reorganized in such a way as to fit with the employment of juveniles and adults rather than children.

The Massachusetts factory laws probably had some part in this process. While initially rather weak in structure, and not very much enforced, they appear to have been somewhat improved towards the end of the century. By 1906 the factory inspection in Massachusetts was by far the most efficient in all the U.S. states. It is therefore possible to argue that the restrictions imposed by the factory laws to some extent influenced the Massachusetts manufacturers to move away from the utilization of child labour. But it should also be emphasized that this kind of reorganization does not seem to have caused the employers a great amount of trouble.

A final contrast is provided by the Southern U.S. states. Here the transition to industrial capitalism occurred relatively late. The cotton industry in the South expanded during the last decades of the 19th century, and slowly replaced the older centre in New England. The workforce was dominated by family employment. Poor white farmers from the Appalachian regions formed a main source of recruitment. Bringing with them cultural notions of family employment, they appear to have demanded the employment also of their children in the Southern mills. In a context of general labour scarcity, the employers were not slow to take advantage of the situation. The Southern mill villages were dominated by a culture of family employment and an early working life for children. Older siblings used younger ones as assistants.

To some extent, this development may have been facilitated by the transition to ring-spinning, where most of the children were employed, at the expense of the old mule-spinning technology. On the other hand, children were also used as "helpers" in automatic weaving, a process where child workers were never employed in Lancashire or in Massachusetts. In the case of the Southern mills, the practice and culture of family employment, combined with labour scarcity, seem to have provided the main reason for the employment of children. The only question was in which specific labour process they were to be employed.

The Southern example is also characterised by a lack of factory and school legislation. Investigations have shown that in those Southern states where child labour laws had been passed, enforcement was virtually non-existent. Consequently, there was very little pressure from the state authorities, at least before 1920, to abandon the practice of factory child labour. The relative absence of union organization, and the concentration of the cotton operatives in distinct and sometimes isolated mill villages, also contributed to the prolongation of the family employment culture. Child labour in the Southern mills remained an issue at least to the 1930s, while those practices had been virtually abandoned in the Massachusetts industry before the First World War.

## Consequences for the Theoretical Discussion

The very different patterns which have been obtained in the compared cases indicate that it is not fruitful to postulate one causal process which alone would be able to explain the decline of industrial child labour. The technological explanations which have been suggested in previous research have been either falsified or qualified. Nardinelli's claim that child labour in the Lancashire cotton industry was abandoned due to the adoption of the self-acting mule has been shown to be incorrect. Empirical evidence has been produced to show that there was no substantial link between the spread of self-actors and a lessened need for children. Consequently, the considerable decline in the proportion of child workers in the British cotton industry between 1830 and mid-century must primarily be seen as the result of factory legislation, not technological change.

In the case of Ludwig and the decline of child labour in the German cotton industry, it may well be correct that children were not used on the new powerlooms imported from England. Indeed, evidence from Scotland, Sweden, and the U.S.A. indicate that children were virtually never employed on this type of machinery. Still, in the Lancashire district, child workers were common on the very same kind of machines. Consequently, it has to be questioned whether the absence of child workers on the German power-looms was caused by the technology *as such*.

If instead work is considered as a social construct, the result of complicated bargaining between management and operatives, it is possible to see that child labour was used in some circumstances but not in others. The formation of the labour process was open-ended in the sense that several forms of organization were possible. The comparative approach used in this study has shown that work in self-actor spinning and powerloom weaving was organized very differently in Lancashire, Scotland, and the U.S.A. This, rather than technology, should be the level of analysis when determining the links between child labour and the process of production.

The comparative perspective has also indicated that there were several possible routes or patterns regarding factory child labour within the general frame of developing industrial capitalism. The declining use of children in the cotton mills of the three countries was obviously occasioned by very different social processes. While child labour virtually disappeared in the

Glasgow cotton district as a result of specific managerial responses to factory legislation already in the 1830s, children continued to be used in the Lancashire district for more than eighty years. Here, the use of factory children gradually came under pressure from restrictive legislation, hostile employers, and local bye-laws on schooling. Still, the half-time system remained strong in a core area in central and north-east Lancashire, and was only abolished by an Education Act in 1917.

In Massachusetts, on the other hand, the main force behind the decline of child labour seems to have been changes in the process of production which were imposed by the manufacturers. Subcontracting was disallowed and the work reorganized to fit with the employment of juvenile operatives. Combined with this process was also a gradual tightening of the factory legislation.

Another example is provided by the cotton industry in the American South, where child labour remained much longer than in New England, mainly due to scarcity of labour and weak legislation. Only with a gradual maturation of the workforce, and the passing of federal legislation in the 1930s, did the custom of factory child labour finally die out in the South.

Consequently, very different patterns were found in the three countries. As I have argued above, there was a considerable amount of flexibility involved in the formation of the labour process. Different processes and structures in this area developed in the four locations, primarily due to the general contexts of industrial relations. Similarly, the factory laws were not only different in structure in Britain and the U.S., their actual result also varied considerably due to their general societal setting. The early British Factory Acts did not have the same effects in Lancashire and Scotland, precisely because they were implemented in very different contexts of industrial relations and society. A general conclusion is that it is impossible to separate the causal processes from their societal context.

This investigation has shown that the relationship between factory legislation and child labour is more complicated than has previously been assumed. The actual effect of such laws must be seen as a complex process involving both the structure of the legal text and the actions of several agents - factory inspectors, manufacturers, local magistrates, and the operatives themselves.

In a wider comparison, this study provides some contrasts to the findings of Lars Olsson and Colin Heywood on the relative inefficiency of factory law enforcement in Sweden and France. In the context of the British cotton industry, it has been shown that the child labour clauses were stringently enforced already by 1845, and must be seen as a vital part of the substantial decline in child labour practices at mid-century. The existence of an independent and relatively well-provided inspectorate, as well as the fact that legislation at first only comprised the textile trades and not factories of every description, are probable reasons for the relative success of the British factory inspection.

Moreover, previous research on industrial child labour has not taken account of the effects of different recruitment strategies and employment patterns. I have, for instance, made a distinction between different forms of employment of children: "apprentice" labour, "free" wage labour, sub-contracting, and child labour as a part of family employment structure. This dimension is essential for an understanding of the actions of the different agents, and also of the general development or retainment of child labour practices. In the Lancashire example, I have suggested that a very important factor behind the sustained retention of factory child labour was the long tradition of subcontracting of the younger and assistant operatives.

Similarly, I have argued that the predominant pattern of family employment in the southern U.S. cotton mills around 1900 was an important factor behind the very high level of child labour.

However, there is hardly an absolute correlation between the form and degree of child labour. In the case of family employment, the American South had a very high level of child labour, while the British country mills organized on a family employment basis employed relatively few children after 1840. What is important here is probably the life cycle stage of the cotton operatives, the general state of labour supplies, and, naturally, the restrictive force of factory legislation.

Similar inferences can be made on the influence of the family-wage ideology of working-class parents on child labour levels. While family strategies towards employment appear to have had an impact in some cases, the precondition seems to have been either the support of the manufacturers for child labour, or a strong bargaining position of the operatives.

In the American example, the Southern employers supported the family work culture of the operatives. The case of the French Canadians in the Massachusetts industry appears to have been somewhat similar, although employer acceptance of child labour was never very general in the North. The most common attitude among the Massachusetts manufacturers was to remain fully in control of employment.

Similarly, the Glasgow manufacturers would not allow the hiring of children as part of a family-wage strategy. Operatives and working-class parents were not able to influence the employers to accept the half-time system. In contrast, the stronger unions in Lancashire, above all in the central and north-east parts of the district, were able to put some pressure on the local manufacturers to continue using half-timers. In parts of

Lancashire, as well as in the American South, forms of "child labour culture" emerged which were relatively persistent.

The results of this study therefore show a very complex picture of causality. Not only were there several different processes involved in the context of factory child labour, ranging in the triangle drawn up by the process of production, the working-class household, and the regulations imposed by the state. These processes and structures also developed in specific societal contexts; in combination with certain structures of family ideology, power, and socio-economic settings.

# Bibliography

## Manuscript Sources

**Public Record Office, Kew, London**

LAB 15 Minutes of the Meetings of the Inspectors of Factories

HO 45 Home Office Correspondance and Papers

HO 87 Home Office Letter Books on Factories

**London School of Economics, London**

Webb Trade Union Collection

**Manchester Central Library, Manchester**

Greg Collection

**John Rylands Library, Manchester**

Ashton and District Cotton Employers' Association Minute Books

Glossop, Hyde and District Cotton Employers' Association Minute Books

**Lancashire Record Office, Preston**

Association of Master Cotton and Flax Spinners of Preston Minute Book

Blackburn Master Cotton Spinners' and Manufacturers' Association Minute Books

Burnley Master Cotton Spinners' and Manufacturers' Association Minute Books

Burnley Textile Trade Federation Minute Books

Burnley Weavers' Minute and Letter Books

North and North-East Lancashire Cotton Spinners' and Manufacturers' Association
    Minute Books

North Lancashire Textile Employers' Association Minute Books

Preston Factory Law Amendment Association Minute Book

Preston Weavers' Minute Books and Books of Cases and Complaints

Weavers' Amalgamation Collection

Harris Library, Preston

Preston Spinners' Minute Books

# Typescript Sources

**Lancaster University Library**

North-West Oral History Project (NWOHP). Transcripts of interviews.

# Printed Sources

**British Parliamentary Papers**

Reports of the Inspectors of Factories (RIF), 1834-1877.
Reports of the Chief Inspector of Factories and Workshops (RCIFW), 1878-1923.
Factory Returns, 1836-1890.
Returns of the Number and Names of Persons Summoned for Offences against the Factory Act, 1837-1846.

PP 1816 III, Minutes of Evidence taken before the Select Committee on the State of the Children employed in the Manufactories of the United Kingdom.
PP 1824 V, Artizans and Machinery: Six Reports of Minutes of Evidence.
PP 1825 IV, Minutes of Evidence taken before the Select Committee on Combination Laws.
PP 1832 XV, Report from the Committee on the Bill to Regulate the Labour of Children in the Mills and Factories of the United Kingdom.
PP 1833 VI, Report from the Select Committee on Manufactures, Commerce and Shipping.
PP 1833 XX, First Report of...Commissioners...[on] the Employment of Children in Factories.
PP 1833 XXI, Second Report of...Commissioners...[on] the Employment of Children in Factories.
PP 1834 XIX, Factories Enquiry Commission. Supplementary Report Part II.
PP 1834 XX, Factories Enquiry Commission. Supplementary Report Part I.
PP 1836 XLV, A Return of the Number of Children of the Ages of 12, 13 and 14 Years, who are now Employed in the Mills and Factories of the United Kingdom.
PP 1836 XLV, A Return of the Names of all Persons Fined under the Factory Acts.
PP 1837-38 VIII, First Report from the Select Committee on Combinations of Workmen.
PP 1837-38 XXVIII, 1st and 2nd Memorial of the Short-Time Committee of Factory Operatives of Manchester and the Surrounding District.
PP 1839 XLII, Return of the Number of Mills Visited by each Inspector.

PP 1840 X, Reports from the Select Committee on the Act for the Regulation of Mills and Factories, together with the Minutes of Evidence.

PP 1841 IX, Report from the Select Committee on the Act for the Regulation of Mills and Factories.

PP 1873 LV, Report...on Proposed Changes in Hours and Ages of Employment in Textile Factories.

PP 1876 XXIX, Report of the Commissioners appointed to enquire into the Working of the Factory and Workshops Acts, with a view to their Consolidation and Amendment... Vol I. Report.

PP 1876 XXX, Report of the Commissioners... Vol II. Minutes of Evidence.

PP 1886 XXI, Second Report of the Royal Commission Appointed to Inquire into the Depression of Trade and Industry. Part I.

PP 1889 LXX, Return of Rates of Wages in the Principal Textile Trades ofthe United Kingdom.

PP 1892 XXXV, Royal Commission on Labour. Minutes of Evidence. Group C.

PP 1893-94 XXXVII, Pt 1. Royal Commission on Labour. Reports on the Employment of Women.

PP 1902 XXV, Report of the Inter-Departmental Committee on the Employment of School Children.

PP 1902 XXV, Minutes of Evidence taken before the Inter-Departmental Committee on the Employment of School Children.

PP 1903 LXIV, Return of the Number of Cotton Factories...and the Number of Spindles and Looms..., 1903.

PP 1904 XIX, Report on the School Training and Early Employment of Lancashire Children.

PP 1909 XVII, Report of the Inter-Departmental Committee on Partial Exemption from School Attendance.

PP 1909 LXXIX, Returns of Employment in Textile Factories, 1907.

PP 1909 LXXX, Report of an Inquiry by the Board of Trade into the Earnings and Hours of Labour of Workpeople of the United Kingdom. I. Textile Trades in 1906.

PP 1917-18 XI, Final Report of the Departmental Comittee on Juvenile Education in Relation to Employment after the War.


## Other British Printed Sources

Amalgamated Association of Operative Cotton Spinners (A.A.O.C.S.) Annual and Quarterly Reports.

Burnley Weavers' Monthly and Quarterly Reports.

*Burnley & District Weavers, Winders & Beamers Association* (1896), Burnley.

Cardroom Amalgamation Quarterly Reports.

Glasgow Trades Council Annual Reports.

Oldham and District Price List for Self-actor Minders, 1876.

Reports of Joint Committees (Weavers' Amalgamation and the North & North-East Cotton Spinners' and Manufacturers' Association)

Trades Union Congress. Annual Congress Reports.
UTFWA: *Analysis of Voting on Age of Half-timers*, Blackburn no date.
Weavers' Amalgamation. Annual Reports.
Weavers' Amalgamation. Reports of General Council Meetings.


**American Printed Sources**

Massachusetts Bureau of the Statistics of Labor, Annual Reports (MBSLAR), 1870-1920.
61st Congress 2d Session. Senate Document No 645. Report on the Condition of Woman and Child Wage-Earners in the United States.
Garraty, J A (ed): Labor and Capital in the Gilded Age: Testimony Taken before the Senate Committee upon the Relations between Labor and Capital - 1883. Boston 1968.

# Newspapers and Periodicals

Cotton Factory Times
Glasgow Argus
Glasgow Sentinel
Herald to the Trades' Advocate, and Co-operative Journal
Textile Journal
Textile Manufacturer
Textile Recorder
Textile Trade Review

# Contemporary Pamphlets and Books (before 1924)

"An Account of the Discussion at Glasgow, on Thursday Sept. 27th, 1860, on the Motion that the Report of the Committee on Trades' Societies be Received", in The National Association for the Promotion of Social Science (1860): *Trades' Societies and Strikes*, London.
Alden, M (1908): *Child Life and Labour*, London.
Amalgamated Weavers' Association (1911): *Northrop Weaving. Replies to Questions*.
Ashworth, H (1838): *An Inquiry into the Origin, Progress, and Results of the Strike of the Operative Cotton Spinners of Preston, from October, 1836, to February, 1837...*, Manchester.
Ashworth, H (1854): *The Preston Strike. An Inquiry into its Causes and Consequences*, Manchester.

Baines, E (1835): *History of the Cotton Manufacture in Great Britain*, London.

Banks, T (1888): *A Short Sketch of the Cotton Trade of Preston for the last 67 years*, Preston.

Bray, R A (1911): *Boy Labour and Apprenticeship*, London.

Bremner, D [1869]: *The Industries of Scotland. Their Rise, Progress and Present Condition*, Trowbridge 1969.

British Association for the Advancement of Science (1887): *On the Regulation of Wages by Means of Lists in the Cotton Industry*, London.

Brown, H (1840): *The Cotton Fields and Cotton Factories*, London.

Chapman, S J (1904): *The Lancashire Cotton Industry*, Manchester.

Clarke, A [1899]: *The Effects of the Factory System*, Otley.

Cooke Taylor, W [1842]: *Notes of a Tour in the Manufacturing Districts of Lancashire*, London.

Fielden, J (1836): *The Curse of the Factory System*, London.

Finlay, K (1833): *Letter to the Right Hon. Lord Ashley, on the Cotton Factory System and the Ten Hours' Factory Bill*, Glasgow.

Fredholm, J H G (1890): *Arbetarelagstiftningen och fabriksinspektionen i utlandet*, Stockholm.

Gill, A H: "The Organisation of Labour as a Political Force", *Transactions of the Manchester Statistical Society*, 1904-5.

Greg, R H (1837): *The Factory Question, Considered in Relation to its Effects on the Health and Morals of those Employed in Factories...*, London.

Hammond, J L and Hammond, B [1917]: *The Town Labourer*, Bungay 1978.

Hammond, J L and Hammond, B [1919]: *The Skilled Labourer*, Bungay 1979.

Hird, F (1898): *The Cry of the Children. An Exposure of Certain British Industries in which Children are Iniquitously Employed*, London.

Horner, L (1840): *On the Employment of Children, in Factories and other Works in the United Kingdom and in some Foreign Countries*, London.

Hutchins, B L and Harrison, A (1911): *A History of Factory Legislation*, London.

*Infant Slavery. Report of a Speech delivered in favour of the Ten Hours' Bill by Richard Oastler, Esq, at a numerous meeting held at Preston, on the 22nd of March, 1833...*,(1833), Preston.

Irwin, M H (1896): "Women's Industries in Scotland", *Proceedings of the Philosophical Society of Glasgow*, Vol XXVII, 1895-96, Glasgow.

Jevons, W A (1860a): "Account of the Weavers' Strike at Padiham in 1859", in The National Association for the Promotion of Social Science: *Trades' Societies and Strikes*, London.

Jevons, W A (1860b): "An Account of the Spinners' Strike at Ashton-under-Lyne in 1830", in The National Association for the Promotion of Social Science: *Trades' Societies and Strikes*, London.

Keeling, F (1914): *Child Labour in the United Kingdom. A Study of the Development and Administration of the Law relating to the Employment of Children*, London.

Lowe, J (1860): "An Account of the Strike in the Cotton Trade at Preston in 1853", in The National Association for the Promotion of Social Science: *Trades' Societies and Strikes*, London.

MacIntyre, R (1901): "Textile Industries", in British Association for the Advancement of Science: *Local Industries of Glasgow and the West of Scotland*, Glasgow.

McMillan, M: *Child Labour and the Half-time System*. Undated, c 1896.

Marx, K [1867]: *Capital Vol 1*, Aylesbury 1979.

*Memoir of Leonard Horner* (1890), Lyell, K M (ed). London

Merttens, F (1893-94): "The Hours and the Cost of Labour in the Cotton Industry at Home and Abroad", *Transactions of the Manchester Statistical Society*, 1893-94.

Merttens, F (1903-4): "Productivity, Protection, and Integration of Industry", *Transactions of the Manchester Statistical Society*, 1903-4.

Mitchell, B [1921]: *The Rise of Cotton Mills in the South*, New York 1968.

Montgomery, J (1835): *The Cotton Spinner's Manual; or a Compendium of the Principles of Cotton Spinning...*, Glasgow.

Montgomery, J (1840): *The Cotton Manufacture of the United States of America Contrasted and Compared with that of Great Britain*, Glasgow.

*Mosely Industrial Commission to the United States of America, Oct.,-Dec. 1902. Report of the Delegates*, (1903), Manchester.

*Narrative of the Late Occurrances at the Cotton Mills in Glasgow: In Answer to the Statement of these Occurrances by the Proprietors* (1825), Glasgow.

*The New Statistical Account of Scotland* (1845), Edinburgh.

*A Report of a Delegate Meeting of the Operative Spinners of England, Ireland and Scotland, Assembled at Ramsey, Isle of Man* (1829), Manchester.

Robinson, S (1854): *Friendly Letters on the Recent Strikes from a Manufacturer to his own Workpeople*, London.

Rose, H (1825): *Manual Labour, versus Brass and Iron: Reflections in Defence of the Body of Cotton Spinners, Occasioned by a Perusal of the Description of Mr. Roberts's Self-Acting Mule*, Manchester.

Sandiford, P (1907): "The Half-time System in the Textile Trades", in Sadler, M E (ed): *Continuation Schools in England & Elsewhere*, Manchester.

von Schulze-Gaevernitz, G (1895): *The Cotton Trade in England and on the Continent*, Manchester.

Senior, N (1837): *Letters on the Factory Act*, London.

Shadwell, A (1906): *Industrial Efficiency. A Comparative Study of Industrial Life in England, Germany and America*, London.

Shaw, Sir Charles (1843): *Replies of Sir Charles Shaw to Lord Ashley, M.P. Regarding the Education and Moral and Physical Condition of the Labouring Classes*, London.

Shuttleworth, J (1843): "On the Vital Statistics of Spinners and Piecers Employed in the fine Cotton-Mills of Manchester", in *Report of the twelfth meeting of the British Association for the Advancement of Science* (1843), London.

*Statement of the Proprietors of Cotton Works in Glasgow and the Vicinity; Case of the Operative Cotton-Spinners, in Answer to that Statement; Reply by the Proprietors...* (1825), Glasgow.

*The Statistical Account of Scotland 1791-1799. Edited by Sir John Sinclair* [1800], Trowbridge 1973.

Taggart, W S (1923): *Cotton Mill Management. A Practical Guide for Managers, Carders, and Overlookers*, London.

*The Trial of James Stuart, Esq., younger of Dunearn, before the High Court of Justiciary, 10 June 1822* (1822), London.

Ure, A (1836): *The Cotton Manufacture of Great Britain*, London.

UTFWA (1922): *Inquiry into the Cotton Industry, 1921-1922*, Blackburn.

Uttley, T W (1905): *Cotton Spinning and Manufacturing in the United States of America*, Manchester.

Webb, S and Webb, B [1894]: *The History of Trade Unionism*, London 1920.

Webb, S and Webb, B (1897): *Industrial Democracy*, London.

Wood, G H (1910): *The History of Wages in the Cotton Trade during the Past Hundred Years*, London.

Young, T M (1902): *The American Cotton Industry*, London.

# Secondary Works

Anderson, M (1971): *Family Structure in Nineteenth Century Lancashire*, Cambridge.

Anderson, M (1976): "Sociological History and the Working-Class Family: Smelser Revisited", *Social History*, 1976:3.

Anderson, M (1978): "Household structure and the industrial revolution; mid-nineteenth-century Preston in comparative perspective", in Laslett, P (ed): *Household and Family in Past Time*, Trowbridge & Esher.

Anderson, M (1980): *Approaches to the Western Family 1500-1914*, Bristol.

Anderson, R D (1983): "Education and the State in Nineteenth Century Scotland", *Economic History Review*, 1983:4.

Bartrip, P W J (1982): "British Government Inspection, 1832-1875: Some observations", *The Historical Journal*, 1982:3.

Bartrip, P W J (1985): "Success or Failure? The Prosecution of the Early Factory Acts", *Economic History Review*, vol 38, 1985:3.

Bartrip, P W J and Fenn, P T (1980a): "The Administration of Safety: The Enforcement of the Early Factory Inspectorate, 1844-1864", *Public Administration*, 58, 1980:1.

Bartrip, P W J and Fenn, P T (1980b): "The Conventionalization of Factory Crime - A Re-assessment", *International Journal of the Sociology of Law*, vol 8, 1980:2.

Bartrip, P W J and Fenn, P T (1983): "The Evolution of Regulatory Style in the Nineteenth Century British Factory Inspectorate", *Journal of Law & Society*, vol 10, 1983:2.

Beatty, B (1984): "Textile Labor in the North Carolina Piedmont: Mill Owner Images and Mill Worker Response, 1830-1900", *Labor History*, 25, 1984:4.

Beatty, B (1987): "Lowells of the South: Northern Influences on the Nineteenth-century North Carolina Textile Industry", *Journal of Southern History*, 53, 1987:1.

Berglund, B (1982): *Industriarbetarklassens formering. Arbete och teknisk förändring vid tre svenska fabriker*, Göteborg.

Bolin, P (1987): "Paternalism och underkastelse", *Arkiv för studier i arbetarrörelsens historia*, nr 38, 1987.

Boyson, R (1970): *The Ashworth Cotton Enterprise*, Oxford.

Brassay, Z G (1974): *The Cotton Spinners in Glasgow and the West of Scotland c. 1790-1840: A Study in Early Industrial Relations*, M Litt thesis, University of Strathclyde.

Braverman, H (1974): *Labor and Monopoly Capital. The Degradation of Work in the Twentieth Century*, New York.

Bull, E (1958): *Arbeidermiljö under det industrielle genombrudd*, Oslo.

Bullen, A (1984): *The Lancashire Weavers Union. A Commemorative History*, Manchester.

Bullen, A (1987a): "The Founding of the Amalgamation", in Fowler, A and Wyke, T (ed): *The Barefoot Aristocrats. A History of the Amalgamated Associaton of Operative Cotton Spinners*, Otley.

Bullen, A (1987b): "A Modern Spinners Union", in Fowler, A and Wyke, T (ed): *The Barefoot Aristocrats*, Otley.

Bullen, A (1987c): "The Making of Brooklands", in Fowler, A and Wyke, T (ed): *The Barefoot Aristocrats*, Otley.

Bullen, A and Fowler, A (1986): *The Cardroom Workers Union. A Centenary History of the Amalgamated Association of Card and Blowing Room Operatives*, Manchester.

Burgess, K (1975): *The Origins of British Industrial Relations*, Guildford.

Butt, J (1971): "Robert Owen as a Businessman", in Butt, J (ed): *Robert Owen Prince of Cotton Spinners*, Newton Abbot.

Butt, J (1976): "The Scottish Cotton Industry during the Industrial Revolution 1780-1840", in Cullen, L M and Smout, T C (ed): *Comparative Aspects of Scottish and Irish Economic and Social History 1600-1900*, Glasgow.

Butt, J (1987): "Labour and Industrial Relations in the Scottish Cotton Industry during the Industrial Revolution", in Butt, J and Ponting, K (ed): *Scottish Textile History*, Aberdeen.

Cage, R A (1981): *The Scottish Poor Law 1745-1845*, Edinburgh.

Calhoun, C (1982): *The Question of Class Struggle. Social Foundations of Popular Radicalism during the Industrial Revolution*, Oxford.

Campbell, R H (1967): "The Industrial Revolution. A Revision Article", *Scottish Historical Review*, Vol 46.

Carson, W G (1970): "White Collar Crime and the Enforcement of Factory Legislation", *British Journal Criminology*, vol 10.

Carson, W G (1974): "Symbolic and Instrumental Dimensions of Early Factory Legislation: A Case Study in the Social Origins of Criminal Law", in Hood, R (ed): *Crime, Criminology and Public Policy*, London.

Carson, W G (1979): "The Conventionalization of Early Factory Crime", *International Journal of the Sociology of Law*, vol 7, 1979:1.

Carson, W G (1980): "Early Factory Inspectors and the Viable Class Society - A Rejoinder", *International Journal of the Sociology of Law*, vol 8, 1980:2.

Catling, H (1970): *The Spinning Mule*, Newton Abbot.

Chapman, S D (1967): *The Early Factory Masters. The Transition to the Factory System in the Midlands Textile Industry*, Newton Abbot.

Clark, G (1987): "Why Isn't the Whole World Developed? Lessons from the Cotton Mills", *Journal of Economic History*, 1987:1.

Cohen, I (1985a): "Workers' Control in the Cotton Industry: A Comparative Study of British and American Mule Spinning", *Labor History*, 26, 1985:1.

Cohen, I (1985b): "American Management and British Labor: Lancashire Immigrant Spinners in Industrial New England", *Comparative Studies in Society and History*, 27, 1985:4.

Collier, F (1933): "An Early Factory Community", *Economic History*, Vol II, 1930-33.

Collier, F (1943): "Samuel Greg and Styal Mill", *Memoirs and Proceedings of the Manchester Literary and Philosophical Society*, Vol 85, session 1941-43.

Collier, F (1965): *The Family Economy of the Working Classes in the Cotton Industry 1784-1833*, Manchester.

Cruickshank, M (1981): *Children and Industry*, Manchester.

Cunningham, H (1987): "Child Labour in the Industrial Revolution", *The Historian*, 14, Spring 1987.

Davin, A (1982): "Child Labour, the Working-Class Family, and Domestic Ideology in 19th Century Britain", *Development and Change*, 13.

Donnachie, I (1987): "The Textile Industry in South West Scotland 1750-1914", in Butt, J and Ponting, K (ed): *Scottish Textile History*, Aberdeen.

Driver, C (1949): *Tory Radical. The Life of Richard Oastler*, London.

Dublin, T (1979): *Women at Work. The Transformation of Work and Community in Lowell, Massachusetts, 1826-1860*, New York.

Dutton, H I and King, J E (1981): *Ten Per Cent and No Surrender. The Preston Strike 1853-1854*, Cambridge.

Dutton, H I and King, J E (1982): "The Limits of Paternalism: The Cotton Tyrants of North Lancashire, 1836-54", *Social History*, 7, 1982:1.

Early F H: "The French-Canadian Family Economy and Standard-of-Living in Lowell, Massachusetts, 1870", *Journal of Family History*, 7, 1982:2.

Edwards, M M and Lloyd-Jones, R (1973): "N J Smelser and the Cotton Factory Family: A Reassessment", in Harte, N B and Ponting, K G (ed): *Textile History and Economic History. Essays in Honour of Miss Julia de Lacy Mann*, Manchester.

Ekdahl, L (1983): *Arbete mot kapital. Typografer och ny teknik - studier av Stockholms tryckeriindustri under det industriella genombrottet*, Lund.

Elson, D (1982): "The Differentiation of Children's Labour in the Capitalist Labour Market", *Development and Change*, 13.

Farnie, D A (1979): *The English Cotton Industry and the World Market 1815-1896*, Oxford.

Felt, J P (1970): "The Child Labor Provisions of the Fair Labor Standards Act", *Labor History*, 11, 1970:4.

Finer, S E (1952): *The Life and Times of Sir Edwin Chadwick*, London.

Fitton, R S and Wadsworth, A P (1958): *The Strutts and the Arkwrights 1758-1830*, Manchester.

Fowler, A (1979-80): "Trade Unions and Technical Change: The Automatic Loom Strike, 1908", *Bulletin of the North West Labour History Society*, 6, 1979-80.

Fowler, A (1987a): "War and Labour Unrest", in Fowler, A and Wyke, T (ed): *The Barefoot Aristocrats*, Otley.

Fowler, A (1987b): "Spinners in the Inter-War Years", in Fowler, A and Wyke, T (ed): *The Barefoot Aristocrats*, Otley.

Fowler, A (1987c): "Decline of the Amalgamation", in Fowler, A and Wyke, T (ed): *The Barefoot Aristocrats*, Otley.

Fraser, W H (1976): "The Glasgow Cotton Spinners, 1837", in Butt, J and Ward, J T (ed): *Scottish Themes. Essays in Honour of Professor S. G. E. Lythe*, Edinburgh.

Freifeld, M (1986): "Technological Change and the "Self-Acting" Mule: A Study of Skill and the Sexual Division of Labour", *Social History*, 11, 1986:3.

Frow, E and Frow, R (1970): *A Survey of the Half-time System in Education*, Manchester.

Gadian, D S (1978): "Class Consciousness in Oldham and the other North-West Industrial Towns 1830-1850", *The Historical Journal*, 1978:1.

Ginzburg, C (1981): *The Cheese and the Worms. The Cosmos of a Sixteenth-Century Miller*, Old Woking.

Ginzburg, C (1983): *The Night Battles. Witchcraft and Agrarian Cults in the Sixteenth and Seventeenth Centuries*, Bodmin.

Glen, R (1984): *Urban Workers in the Industrial Revolution*, Beckenham.

Gray, E M (1937): *The Weavers' Wage. Earnings and Collective Bargaining in the Lancashire Cotton Weaving Industry*, Manchester.

Gray, R (1987): "The languages of factory reform in Britain, c. 1830-1860", in Joyce, P (ed): *The historical meanings of work*, Trowbridge.

Grew, R: "The Case for Comparing Histories", *American Historical Review*, 85, 1980:4.

Griggs, C (1983): *The Trades Union Congress & the Struggle for Education, 1868-1925*, Basingstoke.

Gutman, H (1973): "Work, Culture and Society in Industrializing America, 1815-1913", *American Historical Review*, 78, 1973:3.

Göransson, A (1988): *Från familj till fabrik. Teknik, arbetsdelning och skiktning i svenska fabriker 1830-1877*, Lund.

Göransson, A and Schön, L (1976): "Teknologi och barnarbete", *Scandia*, 1976:1.

Hall, J D, Korstad, R, and Leloudis, J (1986): "Cotton Mill People: Work, Community, and Protest in the Textile South, 1880-1940", *American Historical Review*, 91, 1986:2.

Hamilton, H (1932): *The Industrial Revolution in Scotland*, Oxford.

Hareven, T K (1982): *Family Time and Industrial Time. The Relationship between the Family and Work in a New England Industrial Community*, Cambridge, U.S.A.

Hareven, T and Langenbach, R (1979): *Amoskeag. Life and Work in an American Factory City in New England*, London.

Hart, J (1965): "Nineteenth Century Social Reform: A Tory Interpretation of History", *Past and Present*, no 31.

Henderson, W O (1951): "The Cotton Famine in Scotland and the Relief of Distress, 1862-1864", *Scottish Historical Review*, Vol 30.

Henriques, U R Q (1971a): "An Early Factory Inspector: James Stuart of Dunearn", *Scottish Historical Review*, vol 50.

Henriques, U R Q (1971b): *The Early Factory Acts and their Enforcement*, London.

Henriques, U R Q (1974): "Jeremy Bentham and the Machinery of Social Reform", in Hearder, H and Loyn, M R (ed): *British Government and Administration. Studies presented to S. B. Chrimes*, Cardiff.

Henriques, U R Q (1979): *Before the Welfare State. Social Administration in Early Industrial Britain*, Bungay.

Heywood, C (1988): *Childhood in nineteenth-century France. Work, health and education among the "classes populaires"*, Trowbridge.

Hobsbawm, E (1968): "Custom, Wages and Work-load in Nineteenth-century Industry", in Hobsbawm, E: *Labouring Men. Studies in the History of Labour*, Trowbridge & Esher.

Holbrook-Jones, M (1982): *Supremacy and Subordination of Labour. The Hierarchy of Work in the Early Labour Movement*, Guildford.

Hordern, F (1983): "Les Industriels Alsaciens et la Loi de 1841 sur le Travail des Enfants", *Revue d'Alsace*, vol 109.

Howe, A (1984): *The Cotton Masters 1830-1860*, Oxford.

Huberman, M (1987): "The Economic Origins of Paternalism: Lancashire Cotton Spinning in the first half of the Nineteenth Century", *Social History*, 12, 1987:2.

Humphries, J (1977): "Class Struggle and the Persistence of the Working-Class Family", *Cambridge Journal of Economics*, 1977:1.

Humphries, J (1981): "Protective Legislation, the Capitalist State, and Working Class Men: The Case of the 1842 Mines Regulation Act", *Feminist Review*, 7, Spring 1981.

Humphries, S (1981): *Hooligans or Rebels? An Oral History of Working-Class Childhood and Youth 1889-1939*, Oxford.

Hurt, J S (1979): *Elementary Schooling and the Working Classes 1860-1918*, Thetford.

Hutter, B M (1986): "An Inspector Calls. The Importance of Proactive Enforcement in the Regulatory Context", *British Journal of Criminology*, vol 26.

Jeremy, D J (1981): *Transatlantic Industrial Revolution: The Diffusion of Textile Technologies between Britain and America, 1790-1830s*, Cambridge, Mass.

Jewkes, J (1930): "The Localisation of the Cotton Industry", *Economic History*.

Jewkes, J and Gray, E M (1935): *Wages and Labour in the Lancashire Cotton Spinning Industry*, Manchester.

Johansson, I (1982): *Strejken som vapen. Fackföreningar och strejker i Norrköping 1870-1910*, Kristianstad.

Johnson, R (1970): "Educational Policy and Social Control in Early Victorian England", *Past and Present*, no 49.

Jonsson, U (1987): "Komparation: en strategi för att fånga breda samhälleliga förändringsmönster och processer", in *Från vida fält. Festskrift till Rolf Adamsson*, Stockholm.

Joyce, P (1975): "The Factory Politics of Lancashire in the Later Nineteenth Century", *The Historical Journal*, 18, 1975:3.

Joyce, P (1982): *Work, Society and Politics. The culture of the factory in later Victorian England*, Bristol.

Joyce, P (1984a): "Labour, capital and compromise: a response to Richard Price", *Social History*, 9, 1984:1.

Joyce, P (1984b): "Languages of reciprocity and conflict: a further response to Richard Price", *Social History*, 9, 1984:2.

Joyce, P (1987): "The historical meanings of work: an introduction", in Joyce, P (ed): *The historical meanings of work*, Trowbridge.

Karlsson, L and Wikander, U (1987): "Om teknik, arbetsdelning och ideologi som formare av kvinnors - och mäns - arbetsvillkor", *Historisk Tidskrift*, 1987:1.

Kirby, R G and Musson, A E (1975): *The Voice of the People. John Doherty, 1798-1854. Trade Unionist, Radical and Factory Reformer*, Manchester.

Kirk, N (1985): *The Growth of Working Class Reformism in Mid-Victorian England*, Champaign.

Kuczynski, J (1958): *Geschichte der Kinderarbeit in Deutschland*, Berlin.

Lazenby, W (1949): *The Social and Economic History of Styal*, MA thesis, University of Manchester.

Lazonick, W (1979): "Industrial Relations and Technical Change: The Case of the Self-acting Mule", *Cambridge Journal of Economics*, 1979:3.

Lazonick, W (1981a): "Factor Costs and the Diffusion of Ring Spinning in Britain Prior to World War I", *Quarterly Journal of Economics*, 1981:1.

Lazonick, W (1981b): "Competition, Specialization, and Industrial Decline", *Journal of Economic History*, 1981:2.

Lazonick, W (1981c): "Production Relations, Labor Productivity, and Choice of Technique: British and U.S. Cotton Spinning", *Journal of Economic History*, 1981:3.

Lazonick, W (1982): "Production, Productivity, and Development. Theoretical Implications of some Historical Research", Seminar paper, Harvard University June 1982.

Lazonick, W (1983): "Industrial Organization and Technological Change: The Decline of the British Cotton Industry", *Business History Review*, 57, 1983:2.

Lazonick, W (1984): "Rings and Mules in Britain: Reply", *Quarterly Journal of Economics*, 1984:2.

Lazonick, W (1986a): "The Cotton Industry", in Elbaum, B and Lazonick, W: *The Decline of the British Economy*, Oxford.

Lazonick, W (1986b): "Klasserna i det kapitalistiska företaget", *Häften för kritiska studier*, 1986:3.

Lazonick, W (1987): "Stubborn Mules: Some Comments", *Economic History Review*, 1987:1.

Lazonick, W and Mass, W (1984): "The Performance of the British Cotton Industry, 1870-1913", *Research in Economic History*, 9.

Lea, A J (1975): "Cotton Textiles and the Federal Child Labor Act of 1916", *Labor History*, 16, 1975:4.

Lee, C H (1972): *A Cotton Enterprise 1795-1840. A History of M'Connel and Kennedy, fine Cotton Spinners*, Manchester.

Levine, D: "Industrialization and the Proletarian Family in England", *Past and Present*, no 107, May 1985.

Liddington, J and Norris, J (1978): *One Hand Tied Behind Us. The Rise of the Women's Suffrage Movement*, London.

Littler, C R (1982): *The Development of the Labour Process in Capitalist Societies. A Comparative Study of the Transformation of Work Organisation in Britain, Japan and the U.S.A.*, Guildford.

Ludwig, K-H (1965): "Die Fabrikarbeit von Kindern im 19. Jahrhundert. Ein Problem der Technikgeschichte", *Vierteljahrschrift fur Social- und Wirtschaftsgeschichte*.

MacDonagh, O (1958): "The Nineteenth-Century Revolution in Government: A Reappraisal", *The Historical Journal*, 1958.

MacDonagh, O (1977): *Early Victorian Government 1830-1870*, Birkenhead.

Magnusson, L (1986): "Patriarkalism och social kontroll", *Arkiv för studier i arbetarrörelsens historia*, nr 33.

Magnusson, L (1987): *Arbetet vid en svensk verkstad: Munktells 1900-1920*, Lund.

Martin, B (1969): "Leonard Horner: A Portrait of an Inspector of Factories", *International Review of Social History*, 1969:3.

Marvel, H P (1977): "Factory Regulation: A Reinterpretation of Early English Experience", *Journal of Law and Economics*, vol 20.

Marwick, W H (1924): "The Cotton Industry and the Industrial Revolution in Scotland", *Scottish Historical Review*, vol 21.

Mason, J (1987a): "Cotton Spinning in the Industrial Revolution", in Fowler, A and Wyke, T (ed): *The Barefoot Aristocrats*, Otley.

Mason, J (1987b): "Mule Spinner Societies and the early Federations", in Fowler, A and Wyke, T (ed): *The Barefoot Aristocrats*, Otley.

Mason, J (1987c): "Spinners and Minders", in Fowler, A and Wyke, T (ed): *The Barefoot Aristocrats*, Otley.

Mass, W (1984): *Technological Change and Industrial Relations: The Diffusion of Automatic Weaving in the United States and Britain*, PhD Thesis, Boston College, U.S.A.

Mathias, P (1980): *The First Industrial Nation. An Economic History of Britain 1700-1914*, Frome.

McHugh, J and Ripley, B (1987): "The Spinners and the Rise of Labour", in Fowler, A and Wyke, T (ed): *The Barefoot Aristocrats*, Otley.

Medick, H (1974): "Anfänge und Voraussetzungen des Organisierten Kapitalismus in Grossbritannien 1873-1914", in Winkler, H A (ed): *Organisierter Kapitalismus. Voraussetzungen und Anfänge*, Göttingen.

Miles, C (1968): *Lancashire Textiles. A Case Study of Industrial Change*, Cambridge.

Mitchell, G M (1925): "The English and Scottish Cotton Industries. A Study in Interrelations", *Scottish Historical Review*, Vol 22.

Montgomery, D (1980): *Workers' Control in America. Studies in the History of Work, Technology, and Labor Struggles*, Cambridge.

Montgomery, D (1987): *The fall of the house of labor. The workplace, the state, and American labor activism, 1865-1925*, Cambridge.

Murray, N (1978): *The Scottish Handloom Weavers 1790-1850: A Social History*, Glasgow.

Mörner, M (1981): "Komparation: att vidga historiska perspektiv", *Scandia*, 47, 1981:2.

Nardinelli, C (1980): "Child Labor and the Factory Act", *Journal of Economic History*, 1980:4.

Nardinelli, C (1982): "Corporal Punishment and Children's Wages in Nineteenth Century Britain", *Explorations in Economic History*, 19, 1982:3.

Nardinelli, C (1985): "A Successful Prosecution of the Factory Acts: A Suggested Explanation", *Economic History Review*, vol 38, 1985:3.

Olsson, L (1974): "Barn- och ungdomsarbete i svensk industri 1860-1970", *Scandia*, 1974:2.

Olsson, L (1978): "Barnarbete i de svenska tobaksfabrikerna", *Scandia*, 1978:2.

Olsson, L (1980): *Då barn var lönsamma. Om arbetsdelning, barnarbete och teknologiska förändringar i några svenska industrier under 1800- och början av 1900-talet*, Borås.

Olsson, L (1986): *Gamla typer och nya produktionsförhållanden*, Lund.

Ormerod, A (1963): "The Prospects of the British Cotton Industry", *Yorkshire Bulletin of Economic and Social Research*, 15, 1963:1.

Parris, H (1960): "The Nineteenth-Century Revolution in Government: A Re-appraisal reappraised", *The Historical Journal*.

Peacock, A E (1984): "The Successful prosecution of the Factory Acts, 1833-55", *Economic History Review*, vol 37, 1984:2.

Peacock, A E (1985): "Factory Act Prosecutions: A Hidden Consensus?" *Economic History Review*, vol 38, 1985:3.

Pellew, J (1982): *The Home Office 1848-1914. From Clerks to Bureaucrats*, Guildford.

Penn, R (1983): "Trade Union Organization and Skill in the Cotton and Engineering Industries in Britain, 1850-1960", *Social History*, 8, 1983:1.

Penn, R (1985): Skilled Workers in the Class Structure. Cambridge 1985.

Pinchbeck, I (1981): *Women Workers and the Industrial Revolution*, Thetford.

Pinchbeck, I and Hewitt, M (1972-73): *Children in English Society*, London.

Pope, L (1971): *Millhands and Preachers. A Study of Gastonia*, Forge Village 1971.

Portelli, A (1985): "Oral Testimony, the Law, and the Making of History: the April 7 Murder Trial" *History Workshop Journal*, no 20, 1985:2.

Porter, J H (1967): "Industrial Peace in the Cotton Trade 1875-1913", *Yorkshire Bulletin of Economic and Social Research*, 19, 1967:1.

Price, R (1980): *Masters, Unions and Men. Work Control in Building and the Rise of Labour 1830-1914*, Cambridge.

Price, R (1983): "The labour process and labour history", *Social History*, 8, 1983:1.

Price, R (1984): "Conflict and co-operation: a reply to Patrick Joyce". *Social History*, 9, 1984:2.

Price, R (1986): *Labour in British Society. An Interpretative History*, Chatham.

Reid, D (1985): "Industrial Paternalism: Discourse and Practice in Nineteenth-Century French Mining and Metallurgy", *Comparative Studies in Society and History*, 27, 1985:4.

Reid, D (1986): "Putting Social Reform into Practice: Labor Inspectors in France, 1892-1914" *Journal of Social History*, 1986:3.

Roberts, E (1985): *A Woman's Place. An oral history of working-class women 1890-1940*, Worcester.

Robertson, A J (1970): "The Decline of the Scottish Cotton Industry 1860-1914", *Business History*, July 1970.

Rose, M B (1977): *The Gregs of Styal 1750-1914: - The Emergence and Development of a Family Business*, PhD thesis, University of Manchester.

Rose, M B (1986): *The Gregs of Quarry Bank Mill. The Rise and Decline of a Family Firm, 1750-1914*, Cambridge.

Rose, M B, Taylor, P and Winstanley, M J (1989): "The economic origins of paternalism: some objections", *Social History*, 14, 1989:1.

Rose, S O (1986): "Gender at Work: Sex, Class and Industrial Capitalism", *History Workshop Journal*, no 21, 1986:1.

Rueschmeyer, D (1986): *Power and the Division of Labour*, Worcester.

Russell, A (1987): "Local Elites and the Working-Class Response in the North-West, 1870-1895: Paternalism and Deference Reconsidered", *Northern History*, 23,.

Sabel, C and Zeitlin, J (1985): "Historical Alternatives to Mass Production", *Past and Present*, no 108, August 1985.

Sandberg, L G (1974): *Lancashire in Decline*, Columbus.

Sandberg, L G (1984): "The Remembrance of Things Past: Rings and Mules Revisited", *Quarterly Journal of Economics*, 1984:2.

Sanderson, M (1967): "Education and the Factory in Industrial Lancashire, 1780-1840", *Economic History Review*, 1967:2.

Sandin, B (1986): *Hemmet, gatan, fabriken eller skolan. Folkundervisning och barnuppfostran i svenska städer 1600-1850*, Lund.

Sandin, B (1987): "Om skolans nu svaga makt. Barnarbetslagstiftning och folkundervisning i Sverige under 1860- och 1870-talen" in *Över gränser. Festskrift till Birgitta Ode'n*, Lund.

Sandin, B (1988a): "Education, popular culture and the surveillance of the population in Stockholm between 1600 and the 1840s", *Continuity and Change*, 3, 1988:3.

Sandin, B (1988b): "Den karolinska ämbetsmannastaten, barnen och kulturen. Förhållandet mellan statsmakt och barn under 1600-talets denare hälft", in *Karolinska Förbundets Årsbok*, 1987.

Savage, M (1985): "Capitalist and Patriarchal Relations at Work: Preston Cotton Weaving, 1890-1940", in *The Lancaster Regionalism Group: Localities, Class and Gender*, London.

Saxonhouse, G (1974): "A Tale of Japanese Technological Diffusion in the Meiji Period", *Journal of Economic History*, 1974:1.

Saxonhouse, G and Wright, G (1984a): "Two Forms of Cheap Labor in Textile History", *Research in Economic History*, Supplement 3 1984.

Saxonhouse, G and Wright, G (1984b): "Rings and Mules Around the World: A Comparative Study in Technological Choice", *Research in Economic History*, Supplement 3 1984.

Saxonhouse, G and Wright, G (1984c): "New Evidence on the Stubborn English Mule and the Cotton Industry, 1878-1920", *Economic History Review*, 1984:4.

Saxonhouse, G and Wright, G (1987): "Stubborn Mules and Vertical Integration: A Disappearing Constraint?", *Economic History Review*, 1987:1.

Schmiechen, J A (1984): *Sweated Industries and Sweated Labour. The London Clothing Trades, 1860-1914*, Beckenham.

Seccombe, W (1986): "Patriarchy stabilized: the construction of the male breadwinner wage norm in nineteenth century Britain", *Social History*, 11, 1986:1.

Silver, H (1977): "Ideology and the Factory Child: Attitudes to Half-time Education", in McCann, P (ed): *Popular Education and Socialization in the Nineteenth Century*, Cambridge.

Silvia, P T (1975): "The Position of Workers in a Textile Community: Fall River in the Early 1880s", *Labor History*, 16, 1975:2.

Simon, B (1965): *Education and the Labour Movement, 1870-1920*, London.

Skocpol, T and Somers, M (1980): "The Uses of Comparative History in Macrosocial Inquiry", *Comparative Studies in Society and History*, 22, 1980:2.

Slaven, A (1975): *The Development of the West of Scotland 1750-1960*, Birkenhead.

Smelser, N (1959): *Social Change in the Industrial Revolution*, London.

Smith, R (1954): *A History of the Lancashire Cotton Industry between the years 1873 and 1896*, PhD Thesis, University of Birmingham.

Sund, B (1987): *Nattens vita slavar. Makt, politik och teknologi inom den svenska bagerinäringen 1896-1955*, Täby.

Svensson, T (1986): "Japansk företagsledning och svenska bruk - en felande länk?" *Arkiv för studier i arbetarrörelsens historia*, nr 33.

Taylor, A J (1949): "Concentration and Specialization in the Lancashire Cotton Industry 1825-1850", *Economic History Review*.

Thomas, M W (1948): *The Early Factory Legislation*, Leigh-on-Sea.

Thompson, E P (1980): *The Making of the English Working Class*, Aylesbury.

Thorpe, E (1969): *Industrial Relations and the Social Structure: A Case Study of Bolton Cotton Mule-spinners 1884-1910*, MSc Thesis, University of Salford.

Tilly, L A and Scott, J W (1975): "Women's Work and the Family in Nineteenth-Century Europe", *Comparative Studies in Society and History*, 17, 1975:1.

Tilly, L A and Scott, J W (1978): *Women, Work, and Family*, New York.

Treble, J H (1978): "The Market for Unskilled Male Labour in Glasgow, 1891-1914", in MacDougall, I (ed): *Essays in Scottish Labour History*, Edinburgh.

Treble, J H (1983): *Urban Poverty in Britain 1830-1914*, Cambridge.

Trodd, G (1978): *Political Change and the Working Class in Blackburn and Burnley, 1880-1914*, PhD Thesis, University of Lancaster.

Tsurumi, P (1984): "Female Textile Workers and the Failure of Early Trade Unionism in Japan", *History Workshop Journal*, no 18, 1984:2.

Tucker, B M: "The Family and Industrial Discipline in Ante-Bellum New England", *Labor History*, 21, 1980:1.

von Tunzelmann, G N (1978): *Steam Power and British Industrialization to 1860*, Bath.

Turner, H A (1962): *Trade Union Growth, Structure and Policy. A Comparative Study of the Cotton Unions*, London.

Unwin, G, Hulme, A and Taylor, G (1924): *Samuel Oldknow and the Arkwrights. The Industrial Revolution in Stockport and Marple*, Manchester.

Valverde, M (1988): "Giving the Female a Domestic Turn: The Social, Legal and Moral Regulation of Women's Work in the British Cotton Mills, 1820-1850", *Journal of Social History*, 21, 1988:4.

Walker, R W (1970): "The A.F.L. and Child Labor Legislation: An Exercise in Frustration", *Labor History*, 11, 1970:3.

Walvin, J (1982): *A Child's World. A Social History of English Childhood 1800-1914*, Bungay.

Ward, D C (1987): "Industrial Workers in the Mid-Nineteenth Century South: Family and Labor in the Graniteville (SC) Textile Mill, 1845-1880", *Labor History*, 1987:3.

Ward, J T (1962a): *The Factory Movement 1830-1855*, London.

Ward, J T (1962b): "The Factory Reform Movement in Scotland", *Scottish Historical Review*, 41.

Ward, J T (1971): "Owen as Factory Reformer", in Butt, J (ed): *Robert Owen Prince of Cotton Spinners*, Newton Abbot.

Ward, J T (1987): "Textile Trade Unionism in Nineteenth-Century Scotland", in Butt, J and Ponting, K (ed): *Scottish Textile History*, Aberdeen.

Ware, C F (1966): *The Early New England Cotton Manufacture*, New York.

White, J L (1978): *The Limits of Trade Union Militancy. The Lancashire Textile Workers, 1910-1914*, Westport, Connecticut.

White, J L (1982): "Lancashire Cotton Textiles", in Wrigley, C (ed): *A History of British Industrial Relations 1875-1914*, Witham.

Wikander, U (1988): *Kvinnors och mäns arbeten: Gustavsberg 1880-1980*, Lund.

Winberg, C (1989): *Fabriksfolket. Textilindustrin i Mark och arbetarrörelsens genombrott*, Göteborg.

Wood, S (1982): "Introduction", in Wood, S (ed): *The Degradation of Work? Skill, Deskilling and the Labour Process*, Tiptree.

Wright, G (1981): "Cheap Labor and Southern Textiles, 1880-1930", *Quarterly Journal of Economics*, 96, 1981:4.

Zeitlin, J (1987): "From Labour History to the History of Industrial Relations", *Economic History Review*, 1987:2.

Åmark, K (1986): *Facklig makt och fackligt medlemskap. De svenska fackförbundens medlemsutveckling 1890-1940*, Lund.

Österberg, E (1982): "Barnarbetet i Sverige", *Historisk Tidskrift*, 102, 1982:1.

# BIBLIOTHECA HISTORICA LUNDENSIS
## EDIDERUNT BIRGITTA ODÉN ET GÖRAN RYSTAD

1. *Birgitta Odén*, Rikets uppbörd och utgift. Statsfinanser och finansförvaltning under senare 1500-talet. 1955.
2. *Göran Rystad*, Johan Gyllenstierna, rådet och kungamakten. 1955.
3. *Kjell-Gunnar Lundholm*, Sten Sture den äldre och stormännen. 1956.
4. *Ola Lindqvist, Jakob Gyllenborg* och reduktionen. 1956.
5. *Åke Sällström*, Bologna och Norden intill Avignonpåvedömets tid. 1957.
6. *Jörgen Weibull*. Carl Johan och Norge 1810–1814. 1957.
7. *Lars-Arne Norborg*, Storföretaget Vadstena kloster. Studier i senmedeltida godspolitik och ekonomiförvaltning. 1958.
8. *Helle Stiegung*, Ludvig XV:s hemliga diplomati och Sverige 1752–1774. 1961.
9. *Sven Tägil*, Valdemar Atterdag och Europa. 1962.
10. *Ingvar Elmroth*, Nyrekryteringen till de högre ämbetena 1720–1809. En socialhistorisk studie. 1962.
11. *Kerstin Strömberg-Back*, Lagen-Rätten-Läran. Politisk och kyrklig idédebatt i Sverige under Johan III:s tid. 1963.
12. *Lars-Olof Larsson*, Det medeltida Värend. Studier i det småländska gränslandets historia fram till 1500-talets mitt. 1964.
13. *Olafia Einarsdóttir*, Studier i kronologisk metode i tidlig islandsk historieskrivning. 1964.
14. *Sten Körner*, The Battle of Hastings. England and Europe 1035–1066. 1964.
15. *Tore Nyberg*, Birgittinische Klostergründungen des Mittelalters. 1965.
16. *Carl-Axel Gemzell*, Raeder, Hitler und Skandinavien. Der Kampf für einen maritimen Operationsplan, 1965.
17. *Ulf Sjödell*, Kungamakt och högaristokrati. En studie i Sveriges inre historia under Karl XI. 1966.
18. *Alf Erlandsson*. Skånska generalguvernementet 1658–1693 och dess arkiv. Förvaltnings- och arkivhistoriska undersökningar. 1967.
19. *Anna Christina Meurling*, Den svenska domstolsförvaltningen i Livland 1634–1700. 1967.
20. *Arne Remgård*, Carl Gustaf Tessin och 1746–1747 års riksdag. 1968.
21. *Sven Anders Söderpalm*. Storföretagarna och det demokratiska genombrottet. Ett perspektiv på första världskrigets svenska historia. 1969.
22. *H. Bertil A. Petersson*, Anglo-Saxon Currency. King Edgar's Reform to the Norman Conquest. 1969.
23. *Lars Linge*, Gränshandeln i svensk politik under äldre Vasatid. 1969.
24. *Sverker Oredsson*, Järnvägarna och det allmänna. Svensk järnvägspolitik fram till 1890. 1969.
25. *Kerstin Malcus*, Maktpolitik och länsrättslig förvaltning. Den regalrättsliga doktrinen i Sverige under 1560-talet. 1971.
26. *Eva Österberg*, Gränsbygd under krig. Ekonomiska, demografiska och administrativa förhållanden i sydvästra Sverige under och efter nordiska sjuårskriget. 1971.
27. *Lars-Olof Larsson*, Kolonisation och befolkningsutveckling i det svenska agrarsamhället 1500–1640. 1972.
28. *Conny Blom*, Förbindelsedikten och de medeltida rimkrönikorna. Studier kring omarbetningen av Erikskrönikan och tillkomsten av Förbindelsedikten samt dessa krönikedelars plats i den medeltida rimkröniketraditionen. 1972.
29. *Göran Wensheim*, Studier kring freden i Nystad. 1973.

30. *Lars Lundgren*, Vattenförorening. Debatten i Sverige 1890–1921. 1974.
31. *Sveinbjörn Rafnsson*, Studier i Landnámabók. Kritiska bidrag till den isländska fristatstidens historia. 1974.
32. *Göte Paulsson*, Annales Suecici medii aevi. Svensk medeltidsannalistik kommenterad och utgiven. 1974.
33. *Lars H. Niléhn*, Nyhumanism och medborgarfostran. Åsikter om läroverkets målsättning 1820–1880. 1975.
34. *Agnes Wirén*, uppbrott från örtagård. Utvandring från Blekinge till och med år 1870. 1975.
35. *Roland Persson*, Rustningar i Sverige under det stora nordiska kriget. Studier rörande makten över krigsfinansieringen i det karolinska samhället 1700–1709. 1975.
36. *Erland Alexandersson*, Bondeståndet i riksdagen 1760–1772. 1975.
37. *Leokadia Postén*. De polska emigranternas agentverksamhet i Sverige 1862–1863. 1975.
38. *Ulf Sjödell*. Riksråd och kungliga råd. Rådskarriären 1602–1718. 1975.
39. *Birgitta Odén*, Lauritz Weibull och forskarsamhället. 1975.
40. *Sven G. Trulsson*, British and Swedish Policies and Strategies in the Baltic after the Peace of Tilsit in 1807. 1976.
41. *Eva Block*, Amerikabilden i svensk dagspress 1948–1968. 1976.
42. *Rune Ivarsson*, Jordförvärvslagen, socialdemokratin och bönderna. En studie över jordförvärvslagstiftningen i svensk politik 1945–1965, 1977.
43. *Eva Österberg*, Kolonisation och kriser. Bebyggelse, skattetryck, odling och agrarstruktur i västra Värmland ca 1300–1600. 1977.
44. *Bo Blomkvist*, International i miniatyr. Studier i skånsk arbetarrörelse före 1880 och dess internationella kontakter. 1979.
45. *Jan Brunius*, Bondebygd i förändring. Bebyggelse och befolkning i västra Närke ca 1300–1600. 1980.
46. *Anna-Brita Lövgren*, Handläggning och inflytande. Beredning, föredragning och kontrasignering under Karl XI:s envälde. 1980.
47. *Hans-Albin Larsson*. Partireformationen från bondeförbund till centerparti. 1980.
48. *Kjell Emanuelson*, Den svensknorska utrikesförvaltningen 1870–1905. Dess organisations- och verksamhetsförändring. 1980.
49. *Eva Queckfeldt*, "Vietnam". Tre svenska tidningars syn på Vietnamfrågan 1963–1968. 1981.
50. *Ingvar Elmroth*, För kung och fosterland. Studier i den svenska adelns demografi och offentliga funktioner 1600–1900. 1981.
51. *Käthe Bååth*, Öde sedan stora döden var. Bebyggelse och befolkning i Norra Vedbo under senmedeltid och 1500-tal. 1983.
52. *Imants Alksnis*, Den marxistiska publicistiken i Lettland, 1912–1914. En studie i effektiv propaganda. 1983.
53. *Christer Strahl*, Nationalism & socialism. Fosterlandet i den politiska idédebatten i Sverige 1890–1914.
54. *Lars Niléhn*, Peregrinatio Academica. Det svenska samhället och de utrikes studieresorna under 1600-talet.
55. *Anders Lindberg*, Småstat mot stormakt. Beslutssystemet vid tillkomsten av 1911 års svensk-tyska handels- och sjöfartraktat. 1983.
56. *Carl Gustaf Stenkula*, Gammal i Lund. Utvecklingstendenser inom kommunal, kyrklig och enskild åldringsvård i Lund, 1900–1918. 1983.
57. *Ingemar Norrlid*, Demokrati, skatterättvisa och ideologisk förändring. Den kommunala självstyrelsen och demokratins genombrott i Sverige. 1983.

58. *Bengt Nilson*, Handelspolitik under skärpt konkurrens. England och Sverige 1929–39. 1983.
59. *Göran V Johansson*, Kristen demokrati på svenska. Studier om KDS tillkomst och utveckling 1964–1982. 1985.
60. *Lars J. Larsson*, Sören Norby och östersjöpolitiken 1523–1525. 1986.
61. *Ingemar Ottosson*, Krig i fredens intresse eller neutralitet till varje pris. Sverige, NF och frågan om kollektiv säkerhet 1935–1936. 1986.
62. *Marie Nordström*, Pojkskola, flickskola, samskola. Samundervisningens utveckling i svenskt skolväsen, 1866-1962. 1987.
63. *Désirée Haraldsson*, Skydda vår natur! Svenska Naturskyddsföreningens framväxt och tidiga utveckling. 1987.
64. *Stefan Håkansson*, Konsulerna och exporten 1905-1921. Ett "government failure"? 1989.
65. *Yvonne M. Werner*, Svensk-tyska förbindelser kring sekelskiftet 1900. Politik och ekonomi vid tillkomsten av 1906 års svensk-tyska handels- och sjöfartstraktat. 1989.
66. *Per Bolin-Hort*, Work, Family and the State. Child Labour and the Organization of Production in the British Cotton Industry, 1780-1920. 1989.